JOE CELKO'S
SQL FOR
SMARTIES:
ADVANCED SQL
PROGRAMMING

The Morgan Kaufmann Series in Data Management Systems
Series Editor, Jim Gray

JOE CELKO'S
SQL FOR SMARTIES:
ADVANCED SQL PROGRAMMING

Joe Celko

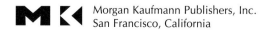

Morgan Kaufmann Publishers, Inc.
San Francisco, California

Executive Editor	Bruce M. Spatz
Production Manager	Yonie Overton
Production Editor	Elisabeth Beller
Assistant Editor	Douglas Sery
Copyeditor	Judith Abrams
Cover and Text Design	Carrie English, canary studios
Composition	Nancy Logan
Proofreader	Ken DellaPenta
Indexer	Mark Kmetzko
Printer	Courier Corporation

Morgan Kaufmann Publishers, Inc.
Editorial and Sales Office
340 Pine Street, Sixth Floor
San Francisco, CA 94104-3205
USA
Telephone   415/392-2665
Facsimile   415/982-2665
Internet   mkp@mkp.com

Library of Congress Cataloging-in-Publication Data is available
for this book.

ISBN 1-55860-323-9

To Ann and Jackers

CONTENTS IN BRIEF

C O N T E N T S

README.JOE

I have been writing regular columns in the computer trade press and academic press for just over ten years with varying success. In 1987, I became a member of the ANSI X3H2 Database Standards Committee and suddenly found a niche for myself as an SQL guru!

I started with "Celko on SQL" in *Database Programming & Design* then wrote "DBMS/Report" in *Systems Integration,* "Data Desk" in *Tech Specialist,* "Data Points" in *PC Techniques,* and "SQL Puzzle" in the now defunct *Boxes and Arrows.* I now write the "SQL Explorer" in *DBMS* magazine, and "Celko on Software" in *Computing.* You can see a theme here.

I also hit the speaker circuit as an SQL instructor for Digital Consulting Inc., Norm DiNardi Enterprises, Boston University Corporate Education Center, and Miller Freeman Seminars. And I became a regular on CompuServe forums as the guy to ask about SQL.

My experiences teaching SQL classes, working on consulting jobs, and in discussions on CompuServe convinced me that there is a need for a collection of advanced SQL programming tricks and techniques, much like those written for other languages. For example, there is a whole niche of the trade press magazine and book market devoted to C programming. But when I looked, I could find no general advanced SQL text. Yes, there are product-specific books for different SQL implementations and relational database theory books, but there is nothing for the working SQL programmer.

Well, now there is. This is a book for the working SQL programmer who wants to pick up some advanced programming tips and techniques. If you are a beginning SQL programmer, don't buy this book. It will not make much sense to you right now. You need to get some experience with the language first.

This book is *not* about database theory or any particular database product. I try to use the ANSI/ISO SQL-92 standards as the basis for examples whenever possible and to comment on common variations from the standards found in actual products. However, I am not writing a book about SQL-92. For that, you should get a copy of

Understanding the New SQL (Melton and Simon 1993). It will do a good job of teaching you the language and explaining some of the rationale behind it.

Organization of the Book

The book is organized into nested, numbered sections arranged by topic. If you have a problem and want to look up a possible solution now, you can go to the index or table of contents and thumb to the right section. Feel free to highlight the parts you need and to write notes in the margins.

But I hope that the casual conversational style of the book and the practice of discussing why a particular trick works will help readers solve their own problems instead of just reproducing the answers given here. A good cookbook teaches you to how to cook as well as how to follow a recipe.

The chapters flow in the order in which you would program in SQL, but from an advanced viewpoint.

Chapter one sets the tone, explaining the "Zen of SQL," if you will. Once you understand the model from which SQL is built, it is easier to write in it.

The first step is to design a database, so chapter two deals with how schemas, tables within schemas, and columns within tables are declared. I cover the details of using constraints and discuss some of the practical problems of normalization. You might be surprised how much work the database can do for you even before you put any data in it.

Entering data into tables is the next step, so chapters three, four, and five discuss SQL datatypes — a topic I have not seen covered in detail in any other book. Chapter six is devoted to NULLs, which are the trickiest part of SQL. Chapter seven discusses other schema objects.

Chapter eight assumes that we have tables and want to do operations on them, such as INSERT INTO, DELETE FROM, and UPDATE.

In chapters nine to fifteen, I deal with the predicates and logical operators of SQL. SQL is based on logic, so you have to learn logic before you can ask a query.

I do not show you the SELECT statement until chapter sixteen. Most other SQL books would have tried to discuss it as soon as possible, but I think that you need some background before you do queries. I discuss all the flavors of joins I can think of — left, right, full, outer, inner, self, natural, T-, and exotic.

Chapter seventeen deals with VIEWs, which can be much handier than you would think.

Chapters eighteen to twenty-seven cover all kinds of complicated queries — partitions; grouped tables and aggregate functions; working with statistics in SQL; queries for regions, runs, and sequences; representing array structures and matrix operations in SQL; set operations; subset operations; trees in SQL (believed to be hard to do by some programmers); and graphs.

Chapter twenty-eight offers tips for optimizing queries. Again, these are general tricks that may not apply to a particular SQL product, so beware.

Chapter twenty-nine is a favorite topic of mine that does not seem to fit well anywhere else. Data design, which I do not believe is taught by anyone else, is not the same as database design. Data design deals with how to represent scales and measurements as encoded data in a database, so you can use it. I also discuss check digits and other tricks for assuring data quality.

Corrections and Future Editions

I will be glad to receive corrections, new tricks and techniques, and other suggestions for future editions of this book. Send your ideas to

Joe Celko
1270 West Peachtree Street NW #C-21
Atlanta, GA 30309-2110
CompuServe: 71062.1056@compuserve.com

or contact me through the publisher, Morgan Kaufmann. You could see your name in print!

Acknowledgments

I'd like to thank Bruce Spatz of Morgan Kaufmann, David Kalman of
DBMS magazine, David Stodder of *Database Programming & Design,*
Rory Murchison of the Aetna Institute, Rudy Limeback of New York
Life (Toronto), George Schusell of Digital Consulting Inc., Dave
Roberts of George Washington University, Bill Getty of DEC, Tom
Kregel of Intuitive Software Developers, Jim Panttaja, Jeff Winchell,
Steve Roti, Doug Hubbard, Rud Merriam, Jeff Jacobs on the Compu-
Serve Oracle forum, Rich Cohen on the CompuServe CASE forum,
and all the others from CompuServe forum sessions and personal
letters whom I may have forgotten.

I'd also like to thank all the members of the ANSI X3H2 Database
Standards Committee, past and present.

CHAPTER
1

Introduction

THIS IS A BOOK for the working programmer, now using SQL, who wants to pick up some advanced programming tips and techniques. It assumes that the reader is an SQL programmer with a year of actual experience.

I have tried to keep the SQL code as portable and as fast as possible. This is harder than it sounds because of the number of standards and quasi-standards groups, as well as the many vendors working on SQL. There are two active ANSI/ISO standards at this time. The SQL-89 standard is the one most vendors have already implemented; the upward-compatible SQL-92 is being used to add features to new releases of existing products. I also use the X/Open portability guide for SQL and other materials from the SQL Access Group in a few places.

SQL-92 has three levels: entry, intermediate, and full. It will be many years before any vendor has a full implementation, but all products are moving toward that goal. I have tried to stick to the SQL-89 standard and to use only the SQL-92 features that are already used in existing implementations. These features might be present with a different syntax in a particular product, however, so programmers will have to adjust their code to match products. Readers should also be aware of other standards bodies besides ANSI and ISO that deal with SQL.

NIST (the National Institute for Standards and Technology) issues a set of FIPS (Federal Information Processing Standards) that include test suites for different programming languages, among them SQL (the FIPS-127 series). To bid on a U.S. government contract, you must have passed a FIPS conformance test. NIST has broken SQL-92 down into packages of features that vendors can implement in steps (called transitional SQLs) instead of having to produce a full version of the complete standard.

The SQL/Access Group is a vendor consortium that deals with interconnectivity among SQL databases. X/Open is another vendor consortium that deals with portability of code among SQL databases. Not too surprisingly, the same vendors are members of the consortia and on the ANSI X3H2 Database Standards Committee.

1.1 The Nature of the SQL Language

A procedural language is a detailed description of *how* a task is accomplished, and it operates on one record or one unit of data at a time. Such languages are also called 3GL (third-generation languages) and are familiar programming languages such as Fortran, Cobol, BASIC, ADA, and Pascal. When they operate on data, these languages use files that have these characteristics:

1.   Data is stored in files of records. The programmer must know the physical location, logical location, and structure of a file to use it.

2.   The program has the information needed to read a file and accesses it one record at a time.

3.   The structure of the records is defined within each program.

4.   The order of the records within a file is important.

5.   The order of the data within a record is important.

6.   Records can be complex data structures.

In contrast, a nonprocedural language is a description of *what* you want; the system figures out how to get it. SQL is such a language. SQL is not considered an end-user language; it has no input and output statements, so it has to be used with a host language that can handle those functions. When SQL operates on data, it models the world with tables that have these characteristics:

1. Data is stored in a database made up of tables; the tables can be real or virtual. Users are connected to the whole database, not to individual tables.

2. The program asks SQL to return data to it, without any concern as to the physical structure or location of the data.

3. The structure of the tables is defined within the database, not within each program.

4. The order of the tables within the database is not important. They are identified by name.

5. The order of the columns within a table is not important. They are identified by name.

6. The order of the rows within a table is not important. They are identified by name.

7. The data is always presented as a table to the user, no matter what internal structure is used by the database.

SQL often presents a problem for an experienced programmer who has to unlearn old habits developed while using 3GLs. But think of this process as similar to learning recursion in a 3GL. At first, it is impossible to see things recursively; then suddenly it all makes sense, and you write your first recursive program. In SQL, complex queries look impossible until the day you can think in sets and formal logic, and then you simply write the query.

I have tried to provide comments with the solutions, to explain why they work. I hope this will help the reader see underlying principles that can be used in other situations.

1.2 Programming Tips

Pete Jensen of Georgia Tech used to tell a story about doing a programming project with an accountant. The programmer did not understand accounting, and the accountant did not understand programming. At one point, the programmer was having a hard time understanding what the accountant wanted the program to do, and they were beating their heads together. The breakthrough came when the accountant said, "If you can't think of it as a ratio, then think of it as a percentage!" and the programmer suddenly got the idea. Never mind that a ratio and a percentage are the same thing mathematically; the change in the mental model made the difference.

In SQL, there are a series of mental models you can use to help you write a query. These tips cannot be formalized, but they do seem to help.

1. Start with the SELECT clause, and write a list of what you want to see in the result set. This gives you a goal and something to show to the user.

2. Put all the tables containing the columns needed to complete the SELECT list into the FROM clause. You can remove the extras later. All the work is in the WHERE clause.

3. Think about how to word the problem solution with sets instead of individual instances. The best example of this trick is to use nested sets to represent trees instead of modeling them as individual nodes and edges. (See section 26.3 on visitation representation of trees.)

4. Sometimes reversing the wording of the problem helps. Instead of saying "Give me all the cars that are red," say "Red is the color of all the cars I want," which lets you see the underlying logic. Section 15.2 has an example of this reasoning.

5. Sometimes negating the wording of the problem helps. Instead of saying "Give me the cars that met all the test criteria," say "Don't give me any car that failed one of the test

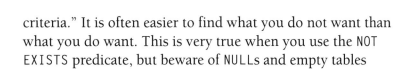

criteria." It is often easier to find what you do not want than what you do want. This is very true when you use the NOT EXISTS predicate, but beware of NULLs and empty tables when you try this.

6. Watch your logic! It is very easy to make mistakes in long logical expressions. Procedural languages allow the programmer to write programs that filter the data to a result set in a series of simple steps; SQL requires that all the work be done in a single expression, which can be complex. I recommend that you use a tool like LOGIC GEM (Logic Technologies, Yucca Valley, CA), a decision table generator, for complex expressions.

7. Remember to allow for NULLs creating UNKNOWN logical values. Always test your code with NULLs in all possible places.

8. Remember to allow for empty tables and to test for them. Try to design test data that covers all cases. This is why I like to use a decision table generator, which will validate your logic and ensure that everything has been handled.

Database Design

IN THIS CHAPTER, we will talk about two areas of concern to a programmer who has to design a database from scratch or to fix one he has inherited. The first topic (section 2.1) is the SQL DDL (Data Definition Language), which is used to create a database schema. The second topic (section 2.2) is a short introduction to the theory of database normalization. Normalization is the part of relational database theory that uses axioms to prove a schema has certain properties, so that you have a sense of correctness about a database that you would not find in a file system.

SQL has spawned a whole branch of the CASE (computer-aided software engineering) industry devoted to designing its tables. Nobody ever developed a tool to validate the design of a file. Most of these tools use a graphic or text description of the rules and the constraints on the data to produce a schema declaration statement that can be used directly in a particular SQL product.

2.1 Schema and Table Creation

One of the initial problems with learning SQL is that programmers are used to thinking in terms of files rather than tables. Programming languages are usually based on some underlying model; if you understand the model, the language makes more sense. For example, Fortran is based on algebra. This does not mean that Fortran is exactly like algebra. But if you know algebra, Fortran does not look that strange to you. You can write an expression in an assignment statement or make a good guess as to the names of library functions you have never seen before.

The model for SQL is *data kept in sets,* not in physical files. Programmers are used to working with files in almost every other language, so they have to unlearn that model.

A sequential file consists of records that are ordered sequentially within the file. You find a first record when you open a file, a series of next records as you use the data, and a last record to raise the end-of-file condition. You navigate among these records and perform actions one record at a time. Files model the way people handle paper forms.

On the other hand, sets are those mathematical abstractions you studied in school. Sets are not ordered and the members of a set are all of the same type. When you do an operation on a set, the action happens *all at once* to the entire membership. That is, if I ask for the subset of odd numbers from the set of positive integers, I get all of them back as a set. I do not build the set of odd numbers one element at a time. I define odd numbers with a rule — "If the remainder is 1 when you divide the number by 2, it's odd" — that could test any integer and classify it.

SQL is not a perfect set language any more than Fortran is a perfect algebraic language, as we will see. But when in doubt about something in SQL, ask yourself how you would specify it in terms of sets and you will probably get the right answer.

2.1.1 Schemas

A schema is the skeleton of an SQL database; it defines the structures of the objects and the rules under which they operate. The only data structure in SQL is the table. Tables can be permanent (base tables) or virtual (VIEWs); SQL-92 also allows you to have temporary, global, and shared tables, but we will not discuss them here since most products have not implemented them yet.

The advantage of having only one data structure is that the results of all operations are also tables — you never have to convert structures, write special operators, or deal with any irregularity in the language.

Conceptually, a table is a set of zero or more rows, and a row is a set of one or more columns. Each column has a specific datatype. The way a table is physically implemented does not matter, because you access it only with SQL. The database engine handles all the details for you and you never worry about the internals as you would with a physical file. In fact, almost no two SQL products use the same internal structures.

Two common conceptual errors are made by programmers who are accustomed to file systems or PCs. The first is thinking that a table is a file; the second is thinking that a table is a spreadsheet. Tables do not behave like either one of these, and you will get surprises if you do not understand the basic concepts.

It is easy to imagine that a table is a file, a row is a record, and a column is a field, because this model works almost all the time. The big differences between working with a file system and working with SQL are in the way SQL fits into a host program. Using a file system, your programs must open and close files individually; using SQL, the whole schema is connected to or disconnected from the program in one step and brings all the authorized tables with it.

Fields within a file are defined by the program, whereas SQL defines its columns in the schema. Fortran uses the FORMAT and READ statements to get data from a file. Likewise, a Cobol program uses a Data Division to define the fields and a READ to fetch it. And so on for every 3GL's programming; the concept is the same, though the syntax and options vary.

A file system lets you reference the same data by a different name in each program. If a file's layout changes, you must rewrite all the programs that use that file. When a file is empty, it looks exactly like all other empty files. When you try to read an empty file, the EOF (end of file) flag pops up and the program takes some action.

Column names and datatypes in a table are defined within the database schema. Within reasonable limits, the tables can be changed without the knowledge of the host program. The host program only worries about transferring the values to its own variables from the database. Remember the empty set from your high school math class? It is still a valid set. When a table is empty, it still has columns, but has zero rows. There is no EOF flag to signal an exception.

Another major difference is that tables and columns can have constraints attached to them. A constraint is a rule that defines what must be true about the database after each transaction. In this sense, a database is more like a collection of objects than a traditional passive file system.

A table is not a spreadsheet, even though they look very much alike when you view them on a screen or in a printout. In a spreadsheet you can access a row, a column, a cell, or a collection of cells by navigating with a cursor. A table has no concept of navigation. Cells in a spreadsheet can store instructions and not just data. There is no real difference between a row and column in a spreadsheet; you could flip them around completely and still get valid results. This is not true for an SQL table.

2.1.2 Manipulating Tables

The three basic table statements in the SQL DDL are `CREATE TABLE`, `DROP TABLE`, and `ALTER TABLE`. They pretty much do what you would think they do from their names. We will explain them in detail shortly, but they bring a table into existence in the database, remove a table from the database, and change the structure of an existing table, respectively.

The table name must be unique in the schema, and the column names must be unique within a table. The names in SQL can consist of letters, underscores, and digits, and vendors commonly allow other printing characters. However, it is a good idea to avoid using anything except the letters and digits. Special characters are not portable and will not sort the same way in different products. The underscore is often hard to read and to print clearly. SQL-92 allows you to use spaces, reserved words, and special characters in a name if you enclose them in double quotation marks, but this should be avoided as much as possible. Otherwise, you will just confuse yourself. For example, PRIMARY is a reserved word, 'PRIMARY' is a character string, and "PRIMARY" is a name; do you think you can tell them apart when you are trying to debug a program and you haven't had any sleep?

A table must have at least one column. SQL can handle a table and a column with the same name, but it is a good practice to name tables differently from their columns. I happen to use plural or collective nouns for table names and use singular attribute names for columns, but you will see other authors who use singular nouns for table names. I feel the use of the plural helps you think of tables as sets. For example, do not name a table "Employee"; use something like "Personnel," or even "Employees," for the table name.

It is also a good idea to use the same name for the same attribute or thing in different tables. That is, do not name a column in one table "sex" and a column in another table "gender" when they refer to the same property. Though it is not required, it is also a good idea to place related columns in their conventional order in the table. By default, the columns will print out in the order in which they appear in the table. That is, put name, address, city, state, and ZIP code in that order, so that you can read them easily in a display.

I have also introduced, in the database magazines in which I have had regular columns, the convention that keywords are in uppercase, table names are capitalized, and column names are in lowercase. I feel this makes the code easier to read. I also use capital letter(s) followed by digit(s) for correlation names (e.g., the table Personnel would have correlation names P0, P1, . . . , Pn), where the digit shows the depth of nesting in the query.

DROP TABLE

The DROP TABLE statement removes a table from the database. This is *not* the same as making the table an empty table. When a schema object is dropped, it is gone forever. The syntax of the statement is

```
<drop table statement> ::=
DROP TABLE <table name> <drop behavior>
<drop behavior> ::= RESTRICT | CASCADE
```

The drop behavior clause is new to SQL-92. If RESTRICT is specified, the table cannot be referenced in the query expression of any view or the search condition of any constraint. This is supposed to prevent the unpleasant surprise of having other things fail because they depended on this particular table for their own definitions. If CASCADE is specified, then such referencing objects will also be dropped along with the table.

The SQL-89 standard was silent as to what would happen when you dropped a table. Either the particular SQL product would post an error message, and in effect do a RESTRICT, or you would find out about any dependencies by having your database blow up when it ran into constructs that needed the missing table.

The DROP keyword and drop behavior clause are also used in other statements that remove schema objects, such as DROP VIEW, DROP SCHEMA, DROP CONSTRAINT, and so forth.

This is usually a "DBA-only" statement that, for obvious reasons, programmers are not usually allowed to use.

ALTER TABLE

The ALTER TABLE statement adds, removes, or changes columns within a table. This statement was not part of the SQL-89 standard, but it is in SQL-92 and it existed in most SQL implementations before it was standardized. It is still implemented in many different ways, so you should see your product for details. This is also a statement that your DBA will not want you to use without permission. The SQL-92 syntax looks like this:

```
ALTER TABLE <table name> <alter table action>

<alter table action> ::=
    ADD [ COLUMN ] <column definition>
    | ALTER [ COLUMN ] <column name> <alter column action>
    | DROP [ COLUMN ] <column name> <drop behavior>
    | ADD <table constraint definition>
    | DROP CONSTRAINT <constraint name> <drop behavior>
```

As you would expect, the ADD COLUMN clause extends the existing table by putting another column on it. The new column must have a name that is unique within the table and follow the other rules for a valid column declaration.

The ALTER COLUMN clause can change a column and its definition. Exactly what is allowed will vary from product to product, but usually the datatype can be changed to a compatible datatype (e.g., you can make a CHAR( ) column longer, but not shorter; change an INTEGER to a REAL; and so forth). You can often add DEFAULT and CHECK( ) clauses.

The DROP COLUMN clause removes the column from the table. SQL-92 gives you the option of setting the drop behavior, which most current products do not. The two options are RESTRICT and CASCADE. RESTRICT will not allow the column to disappear if it is referenced in another schema object. CASCADE will also delete any schema object that references the dropped column.

When this statement is available in your SQL product, I strongly advise that you first use the RESTRICT option to see if there are references before you use the CASCADE option.

The ADD <table constraint definition> clause lets you put a constraint on a table. Many current versions of SQL, such as DB2 and Oracle, require that you use the ALTER statement to add referential integrity constraints to a table rather than allowing you to declare the constraints at schema creation time.

The DROP CONSTRAINT clause requires that the constraint be given a name, so this is a good habit to get into. If an unwanted constraint has no name, you will have to rebuild the whole schema to get rid of it. A constraint name will also appear in warnings and error messages, making debugging much easier. The <drop behavior> option behaves as it did for the DROP COLUMN clause.

CREATE TABLE

The CREATE TABLE statement does all the hard work. The basic syntax looks like this:

```
CREATE TABLE <table name> (<table element list>)

<table element list> ::=
<table element> | <table element>, <table element list>

<table element> ::=
<column definition> | <table constraint definition>
```

The table definition includes data in the column definitions and rules for handling that data in the table constraint definitions. This means that a table acts more like an object (with its data and methods) than just a simple, passive file.

2.1.3 Column Definitions

Beginning SQL programmers often fail to take full advantage of the options available to them, and they pay for it with errors or extra work in their applications. Saving yourself time and trouble begins with column definition, using the following syntax:

```
<column definition> ::=
    <column name> <data type>
    [<default clause>]
    [<column constraint>...]

<column constraint> ::= NOT NULL
    | <check constraint definition>
    | <unique specification>
    | <references specification>
```

The first important thing to notice here is that each column must have a datatype, which it keeps unless you ALTER the table. The SQL standard offers many datatypes, because SQL must work with many different host languages. The datatypes fall into three major categories: numerics, character strings, and temporal datatypes. We will discuss the datatypes and their rules of operation in other sections; they are fairly obvious, so not knowing the details will not stop you from reading the examples that follow.

The DEFAULT Clause

The DEFAULT clause is an underused feature, whose syntax is

```
<default clause> ::=
    [CONSTRAINT <constraint name>] DEFAULT <default option>
```

```
<default option> ::= <literal> | <system value> | NULL
```

Whenever the system does not have an explicit value to put into this column, it will look for its DEFAULT clause and insert that value. The default option can be a literal value of the relevant datatype, or something provided by the system, such as the current timestamp, current date, current user identifier, and so forth. If you do not provide a DEFAULT clause, the column definition acts as if you had declared it DEFAULT NULL.

This is a good way to make the database do a lot of work that you would otherwise have to code into all the application programs. The most common tricks are to use a zero in numeric columns, a string to encode a missing value ('unknown') or true default ('same address') in character columns, and the system timestamp to mark transactions.

Column Constraints

Column constraints are rules that are attached to a table. All the rows in the table are validated against them. File systems have nothing like this, since validation is done in the application programs. They are also one of the most underused features of SQL, so you can look like a real wizard if you can master them.

NOT NULL Constraint

The most important column constraint is the NOT NULL, which forbids the use of NULLs in a column. Use this constraint automatically, then remove it only when you have good reason. It will help you avoid the complications of NULL values when you make queries against the data.

The NULL is a special value in SQL that belongs to all datatypes. SQL is the only language that has such a creature; if you can understand how it works, you will have a good grasp of SQL. A NULL means that we have a missing, unknown, miscellaneous, or inapplicable value in the data.

The problem is that exactly which of these four possibilities the NULL indicates depends on how it is used. To clarify this, imagine that I am looking at a carton of Easter eggs and I want to know their colors. If I see an empty hole, I have a *missing* egg, which I hope will be provided later. If I see a foil-wrapped egg, I have an *unknown* color value in my set. If I see a multicolored egg, I have a *miscellaneous* value in my set. If I see a cue ball, I have an *inapplicable* value in my set. The way you handle each situation is a little different.

When you use NULLs in math calculations, they propagate in the results so that the answer is another NULL. When you use them in logical expressions or comparisons, they return a logical value of UNKNOWN and give SQL its strange three-valued logic. They sort either always high or always low in the collation sequence. They group together for some operations but not for others.

In short, NULLs cause a lot of irregular features in SQL, which we will discuss later. Your best bet is just to memorize the situations and the rules for NULLs when you cannot avoid them.

CHECK() Constraint

The CHECK constraint is underused even by experienced SQL programmers. It tests the rows of the table against a logical expression, which SQL calls a search condition, and rejects rows whose search condition returns FALSE. However, the constraint accepts rows when the search condition returns TRUE or UNKNOWN. The UNKNOWN is a "benefit-of-the-doubt" feature that even experienced programmers forget. The syntax is

```
<check constraint definition> ::=
    [CONSTRAINT <constraint name>] CHECK (<search condition>)
```

The usual technique is to do simple range checking, such as CHECK (rating BETWEEN 1 AND 10), or to verify that a column's value is in an enumerated set, such as CHECK (sex IN ('M', 'F')), with this constraint. Remember that the sex column could also be set to NULL, unless a NOT NULL constraint is also added to the column's declaration.

The real power comes from writing complex expressions that verify relationships with other rows, with other tables, or with system values. For example, you can use a single CHECK clause to enforce the rule that a firm does not hire anyone under 21 years of age for a job that requires a liquor-serving license by checking the birth date, the current system date, and the job requirements.

UNIQUE and PRIMARY KEY Constraints

The UNIQUE constraint says that no duplicate values are allowed in the column. The SQL-92 syntax is

```
<unique specification> ::= UNIQUE | PRIMARY KEY
```

File system programmers understand the concept of a PRIMARY KEY, but for the wrong reasons. They are used to a file, which can have only one key because that key is used to determine the physical order of the records within the file. There is no order in a table; the term PRIMARY KEY in SQL has to do with defaults in referential actions, which we will discuss later.

There are some subtle differences between UNIQUE and PRIMARY KEY. There can be only one PRIMARY KEY per table but many UNIQUE columns.

A PRIMARY KEY is automatically declared to have a NOT NULL constraint on it, but a UNIQUE column can have one and only one NULL in a row unless you explicitly add a NOT NULL constraint. Adding the NOT NULL whenever possible is a good idea.

There is also a multiple-column form of the <unique specification>, which is usually written at the end of the column declarations. It is a list of columns in parentheses after the proper keyword; it means that the combination of those columns is unique. For example, I might declare PRIMARY KEY (city, department) so I can be sure that though I have offices in many cities and many identical departments in those offices, there is only one personnel department in Chicago.

The truth is that not many implementations of SQL follow the ANSI syntax for <unique specification>s yet. Instead, you first create the table, and then have to use a separate statement, which also varies from product to product, but probably looks like `CREATE UNIQUE INDEX <index name> ON <table>(<column list>)`. File system programmers do not mind using this separate structure, because it is what they have already been doing.

REFERENCES Clause

The `REFERENCES` specification is the simplest version of a referential constraint definition, which can be quite tricky. For now, let us just consider the simplest case:

```
<references specification> ::=
[CONSTRAINT <constraint name>] REFERENCES <referenced table name>
[(<reference column>)]
```

This relates two tables together, so it is different from the other options we have discussed so far. What this says is that the value in this column of the referencing table must appear somewhere in the referenced table's column that is named in the constraint. Furthermore, the referenced column must have `UNIQUE` constraint. For example, you can set up a rule that the Orders table will have orders only for goods that appear in the Inventory table.

If no `<reference column>` is given, then the `PRIMARY KEY` column of the referenced table is assumed to be the target. This is one of those places where the `PRIMARY KEY` is important, but you can always play it safe and explicitly name a column. There is no rule to prevent several columns from referencing the same target column. For example, we might have a table of flight crews that has pilot and copilot columns that both reference a table of certified pilots.

Notice that if an item is dropped from the referenced table, rows in the referencing table will be made invalid. The constraint would not allow this to happen and will raise an error condition.

The more complex versions of this clause defined in SQL-92 will allow the database to take appropriate actions automatically, without programmer intervention. Vendors are starting to add parts of this referential integrity to their products, but we will ignore it for now. There is a multicolumn form of this clause, which we will also ignore.

2.2 Normalization

The Relational Model and the Normal Forms of the Relational Model were first defined by Dr. E. F. Codd (Codd 1970), then extended by other writers after him. He invented the term "normalized relations" by borrowing from the political jargon of the day. A branch of mathematics called *relations* deals with mappings among sets defined by predicate calculus from formal logic. Just as in an algebraic equation, there are many forms of the same relational statement, but the "normal forms" of relations are certain formally defined desirable constructions. The goal of normal forms is to avoid certain data anomalies that can occur in unnormalized tables. Data anomalies are easier to explain with an example, but first please be patient while I define some terms.

A *predicate* is a statement of the form A(X), which means that X has the property A. For example, "John is from Indiana" is a predicate statement; here, "John" is the subject and "is from Indiana" is the predicate. A relation is a predicate with two or more subjects. "John and Bob are brothers" is an example of a relation. The common way of visualizing a set of relational statements is as a table where the columns are attributes of the relation and each row is a specific relational statement.

When Dr. Codd defined the relational model, he gave 12 rules for the visualization of the relation as a table:

0.   (Yes, there is a rule zero.) For a system to qualify as a relational database management system, that system must use its relational facilities (exclusively) to manage the database. SQL is not so pure on this rule, since you can often do procedural things to the data.

1.   The information rule: This simply requires all information in the database to be represented in one and only one way, namely by values in column positions within rows of tables. SQL is good here.

2.   The guaranteed access rule: This rule is essentially a restatement of the fundamental requirement for primary keys. It states that every individual scalar value in the database must be logically addressable by specifying the name of the containing table, the name of the containing column, and the primary key value of the containing row. SQL follows this rule for tables that have a primary key, but does not require a table to have a key at all.

3. Systematic treatment of NULL values: The DBMS is required to support a representation of missing information and inapplicable information that is systematic, distinct from all regular values, and independent of datatype. It is also implied that such representations must be manipulated by the DBMS in a systematic way. SQL has a NULL that is used for both missing information and inapplicable information, rather than having two separate tokens as Dr. Codd wished.

4. Active online catalog based on the relational model: The system is required to support an online, inline, relational catalog that is accessible to authorized users by means of their regular query language. SQL does this.

5. The comprehensive data sublanguage rule: The system must support at least one relational language that (a) has a linear syntax, (b) can be used both interactively and within application programs, and (c) supports data definition operations (including view definitions), data manipulation operations (update as well as retrieval), security and integrity constraints, and transaction management operations (begin, commit, and rollback). SQL is pretty good on this point, since all of the operations Codd defined can be written in the DML (Data Manipulation Language).

6. The view updating rule: All views that are theoretically updatable must be updatable by the system. SQL is weak here, and has elected to standardize on the safest case. View updatability is a very complex problem.

7. High-level insert, update, and delete: The system must support set-at-a-time INSERT, UPDATE, and DELETE operators. SQL does this.

8.   Physical data independence: This is self-explanatory. Any real product is going to have some physical dependence, but SQL is better than most programming languages on this point.

9.   Logical data independence: This is self-explanatory. SQL is quite good about this point.

10.   Integrity independence: Integrity constraints must be specified separately from application programs and stored in the catalog. It must be possible to change such constraints as and when appropriate without unnecessarily affecting existing applications. SQL-92 has this.

11.   Distribution independence: Existing applications should continue to operate successfully (a) when a distributed version of the DBMS is first introduced and (b) when existing distributed data is redistributed around the system. We are just starting to get distributed versions of SQL, so it is a little early to say whether SQL will meet this criterion or not.

12.   The non-subversion rule: If the system provides a low-level (record-at-a-time) interface, that interface cannot be used to subvert the system (e.g., bypassing a relational security or integrity constraint). SQL-92 is good about this one.

Codd also specified 9 structural features, 3 integrity features, and 18 manipulative features, all of which are required as well. He later extended the list from 12 rules to 333 in the second version of the relational model. This section is getting too long and you can look them up for yourself.

Normal forms are an attempt to make sure that you do not destroy true data or create false data in your database. One of the ways of avoiding errors is to represent a fact only once in the database, since if a fact appears more than once, one of the instances of it is likely to be in error — a man with two watches can never be sure what time it is.

This process of table design is called normalization. It is not mysterious, but it can get complex. You can buy CASE tools to help you do it, but you should know a bit about the theory before you use such a tool.

2.2.1 Functional and Multivalued Dependencies

A normal form is a way of classifying a table based on the functional dependencies (FDs for short) in it. A functional dependency means that if I know the value of one attribute, I can always determine the value of another. The notation used in relational theory is an arrow between the two attributes, for example A → B, which can be read in English as "A determines B." If I know your employee number, I can determine your name; if I know a part number, I can determine the weight and color of the part; and so forth.

A multivalued dependency (MVD) means that if I know the value of one attribute, I can always determine the values of a set of another attribute. The notation used in relational theory is a double-headed arrow between the two attributes, for instance A →→ B, which can be read in English as "A determines many Bs." If I know a teacher's name, I can determine a list of her students; if I know a part number, I can determine the part numbers of its components; and so forth.

2.2.2 First Normal Form (1NF)

Consider a requirement to maintain data about class schedules. We are required to keep the course, section, department, time, room, professor, student, major, and grade. Suppose that we initially set up a Pascal file with records that look like this:

```
Classes = RECORD
        course   : ARRAY [1:7] OF CHAR;
        section  : CHAR;
        time     : INTEGER;
        room     : INTEGER;
        roomsize : INTEGER;
        professor: ARRAY [1:25] OF CHAR;
        Students : ARRAY [1:classsize]
                      OF RECORD
                          student ARRAY [1:25] OF CHAR;
                          major ARRAY [1:10] OF CHAR;
                          grade CHAR;
                          END;
        END;
```

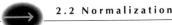

This table is not in the most basic normal form of relational databases. First Normal Form (1NF) means that the table has no repeating groups. That is, every column is a scalar (or atomic) value, not an array or a list or anything with its own structure. In SQL, it is impossible not to be in 1NF unless the vendor has added array or other extensions to the language. The Pascal record could be "flattened out" in SQL to look like this:

```
CREATE TABLE Classes
(course CHAR(7) NOT NULL,
 section CHAR(1) NOT NULL,
 time INTEGER NOT NULL,
 room INTEGER NOT NULL,
 roomsize INTEGER NOT NULL,
 professor CHAR(25) NOT NULL,
 student CHAR(25) NOT NULL,
 major CHAR(10) NOT NULL,
 grade CHAR(1) NOT NULL);
```

This table is acceptable to SQL. In fact, we can locate a row in the table with a combination of (course, section, student), so we have a key. But what we are doing is hiding the Students record array, which has not changed its nature by being flattened. There are problems.

If Professor Jones of the math department dies, we delete all his rows from the Classes table. This also deletes the information that all his students were taking a math class and maybe not all of them wanted to drop out of the class just yet. I am deleting more than one fact from the database. This is called a *deletion anomaly*.

If student Wilson decides to change one of his math classes, formerly taught by Professor Jones, to English, we will show Professor Jones as an instructor in both the math and the English departments. I could not change a simple fact by itself. This creates false information, and is called an *update anomaly*.

If the school decides to start a new department, which has no students yet, we cannot put in the data about the professors we just hired until we have classroom and student data to fill out a row. I cannot insert a simple fact by itself. This is called an *insertion anomaly*.

There are more problems in this table, but you see the point. Yes, there are some ways to get around these problems without changing the tables. We could permit NULLs in the table. We could write routines to check the table for false data. These are tricks that will only get worse as the data and the relationships become more complex. The solution is to break the table up into other tables, each of which represents one relationship or simple fact.

Note on Repeated Groups

The definition of 1NF is that the table has no repeating groups and that all columns are scalar. This means no arrays, linked lists, tables within tables, or record structures, like those you would find in other programming languages. As I have already said, this is very easy to avoid in SQL, since arrays and structured data are simply not supported. But some people "fake it" by using groups of columns with an assumed relationship among them. Consider the table of an employee and his children:

```
CREATE TABLE Employees
(empno INTEGER NOT NULL,
 empname CHAR(30) NOT NULL,
 ...
 child1 CHAR(30), birthday1 DATE, sex1 CHAR(1),
 child2 CHAR(30), birthday2 DATE, sex2 CHAR(1),
 child3 CHAR(30), birthday3 DATE, sex3 CHAR(1),
 child4 CHAR(30), birthday4 DATE, sex4 CHAR(1));
```

This looks like the layouts of many existing file system records in Cobol and other 3GL languages. The birthday and sex information for each child is part of a repeated group and therefore violates 1NF. This is faking a four-element array in SQL! Most books simply stop at this point and never bother to explain why this is good or bad; we will go into detail in chapter 23, on arrays.

2.2.3 Second Normal Form (2NF)

A table is in Second Normal Form (2NF) if it has no *partial key* dependencies. That is, if X and Y are columns and X is a key, then for any Z that is a proper subset of X, it cannot be the case that Z → Y. Informally, the table is in 1NF and it has a key that determines all non-key attributes in the table.

In the example, our users tell us that knowing the student and course is sufficient to determine the section (since students cannot sign up for more than one section of the same course) and the grade. This is the same as saying that (student, course) → (section, grade). After more analysis, we also discover from our users that (student → major) — students have only one major. Since student is part of the (student, course) key, we have a partial key dependency! This leads us to the following decomposition:

```
CREATE TABLE Classes (course, section, room, roomsize, time,
professor, PRIMARY KEY (course, section));


CREATE TABLE Enrollment (student, course, section, grade)
PRIMARY KEY (student, course));


CREATE TABLE Students (student, major) PRIMARY KEY (student));
```

At this point, we are in 2NF. Every attribute depends on the entire key in its table. Now if a student changes majors, it can be done in one place. Furthermore, a student cannot sign up for different sections of the same class, because we have changed the key of Enrollment. Unfortunately, we still have problems.

Notice that while roomsize depends on the entire key of Classes, it also depends on room. If the room is changed for a course and section, we may also have to change the roomsize, and if the room is modified (we knock down a wall), we may have to change roomsize in several rows in Classes for that room.

2.2.4 Third Normal Form (3NF)

Another normal form can address these problems. A table is in Third Normal Form (3NF) if for all X → Y, where X and Y are columns of a table, X is a key or Y is part of a *candidate key*. (A candidate key is a unique set of columns that identify each row in a table; you cannot remove a column from the candidate key without destroying its uniqueness.) This implies that the table is in 2NF, since a partial key dependency is a type of transitive dependency. Informally, all the non-key columns are determined by the key, the whole key, and nothing but the key.

The usual way that 3NF is explained is that there are no transitive dependencies. A transitive dependency is a situation where we have a table with columns (A, B, C) and (A → B) and (B → C), so we know that (A → C). In our case, the situation is that (course, section) → room and room → roomsize. This is not a simple transitive dependency, since only part of a key is involved, but the principle still holds. To get our example into 3NF and fix the problem with the roomsize column, we make the following decomposition:

```
CREATE TABLE Rooms (room, roomsize, PRIMARY KEY (room));

CREATE TABLE Classes (course, section, room, time,
PRIMARY KEY (course, section));

CREATE TABLE Enrollment (student, course, section, grade,
PRIMARY KEY (student, course));

CREATE TABLE Students (student, major, PRIMARY KEY (student));
```

A common misunderstanding about relational theory is that 3NF has no transitive dependencies. As indicated above, if X → Y, X does *not* have to be a key *if* Y is part of a candidate key. We still have a transitive dependency in the example — (room, time) → (course, section) — but since the right side of the dependency is a key, it is technically in 3NF. The unreasonable behavior that this table structure still has is that several courses can be assigned to the same room at the same time.

Boyce-Codd Normal Form

The normal form that actually removes all transitive dependencies is Boyce-Codd Normal Form (BCNF). A table is in BCNF if for all X → Y, X is a key — period. We can go to this normal form just by adding another key with UNIQUE (room, time) constraint clause to the table

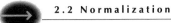

Classes. In our example, we have removed all of the important anomalies with BCNF.

2.2.5 CASE Tools for Normalization

Third Normal Form is very popular with CASE tools and most of them can generate a schema where all of the tables are in 3NF. They obtain the FDs from an E-R (entity-relationship) diagram or from a statistical analysis of the existing data, then put them together into tables and check for normal forms.

It is often possible to derive more than one 3NF schema from a set of FDs. A good CASE tool will find more than one of them, and ideally will find the highest possible normal form schemas too. Yes, there are still more normal forms we have not mentioned yet. Nobody said this would be easy.

Some people will argue that it is all right to "denormalize" a schema for reasons of efficiency. For example, to get a list of all the students and their majors in a given class, we must join Enrollment and Students. The case for leaving the solution normalized is based on reducing the programming requirement. If we denormalize, either we are not enforcing some of the user-required constraints or we have to write additional code to enforce the constraints.

Not enforcing all the rules is obviously bad. If we choose to write additional code, we have to be sure to duplicate it in all of the programs that work with the DBMS. Normalization reduces programming.

2.2.6 Boyce-Codd Normal Form (BCNF)

A table is in BCNF when for all nontrivial FDs (X → A), X is a superkey for the whole schema. A superkey is a unique set of columns that identify each row in a table, but you can remove some columns from it and it will still be a key. Informally, a superkey is carrying extra weight.

BCNF is the normal form that actually removes all transitive dependencies. A table is in BCNF if for all (X → Y), X is a key — period. We can go to this normal form just by adding another key with UNIQUE (room, time) constraint clause to the table Classes.

There are some other interesting and useful "higher" normal forms, but they are outside of the scope of this discussion. In our example, we have removed all of the important anomalies with BCNF.

Third Normal Form was concerned with the relationship between key and non-key columns. However, a column can often play both roles. Consider a table for computing salesmen's bonus gifts that has for each salesman his base salary, the number of sales points he has won in a contest, and the bonus gift awarded for that combination of salary range and points. For example, we might give a fountain pen to a beginning salesman with a base pay rate somewhere between $15,000 and $20,000 and 100 sales points, but give a car to a master salesman, whose salary is between $30,000 and $60,000 and who has 200 points. The functional dependencies are, therefore,

```
(paystep, points) → gift
gift → points
```

Let's start with a table that has all the data in it and normalize it.

Gifts

salary	points	gift
$15,000	100	Pencil
$17,000	100	Pen
$30,000	200	Car
$31,000	200	Car
$32,000	200	Car

This schema is in 3NF, but it has problems. You cannot insert a new gift into our offerings and points unless we have a salary to go with it. If you remove any sales points, you lose information about the gifts and salaries (e.g., only people in the $30,000 range can win a car). And, finally, a change in the gifts for a particular point score would have to affect all the rows within the same pay step. This table needs to be broken apart into two tables:

PayGifts

salary	gift
$15,000	Pencil
$17,000	Pen
$30,000	Car
$31,000	Car
$32,000	Car

GiftsPoints

gift	points
Pencil	100
Pen	100
Car	200

2.2.7 Fourth Normal Form (4NF)

Fourth Normal Form (4NF) makes use of multivalued dependencies. The problem it solves is that the table has too many of them. For example, consider a table of departments, their projects, and the parts they stock. The MVDs in the table would be

```
department →→ projects
department →→ parts
```

Assume that department d1 works on jobs j1 and j2, with parts p1 and p2; that department d2 works on jobs j3, j4, and j5, with parts p2 and p4; and that department d3 works on job j2 only, with parts p5 and p6. The table would look like this:

department	job	part
d1	j1	p1
d1	j1	p2
d1	j2	p1
d1	j2	p2
d2	j3	p2
d2	j3	p4

(cont.)	department	job	part
	d2	j4	p2
	d2	j4	p4
	d2	j5	p2
	d2	j5	p4
	d3	j2	p5
	d3	j2	p6

If you want to add a part to a department, you must create more than one new row. Likewise, to remove a part or a job from a row can destroy information. Updating a part or job name will also require multiple rows to be changed.

The solution is to split this table into two tables, one with (department, projects) in it and one with (department, parts) in it. The definition of 4NF is that we have no more than one MVD in a table. If a table is in 4NF, it is also in BCNF.

2.2.8 Fifth Normal Form (5NF)

Fifth Normal Form (5NF), also called the Join-Projection Normal Form or the Projection-Join Normal Form, is based on the idea of a lossless join or the lack of a join-projection anomaly. This problem occurs when you have an n-way relationship, where $n > 2$. A quick check for 5NF is to see if the table is in 3NF and all the candidate keys are single columns.

As an example of the problems solved by 5NF, consider a table of house notes that records the buyer, the seller, and the lender:

HouseNotes

buyer	seller	lender
Smith	Jones	National Bank
Smith	Wilson	Home Bank
Nelson	Jones	Home Bank

This table is a three-way relationship, but because many CASE tools allow only binary relationships it might have to be expressed in an E-R diagram as three binary relationships, which would generate CREATE TABLE statements leading to these tables:

BuyerLender

buyer	lender
Smith	National Bank
Smith	Home Bank
Nelson	Home Bank

SellerLender

seller	lender
Jones	National Bank
Wilson	Home Bank
Jones	Home Bank

BuyerSeller

buyer	seller
Smith	Jones
Smith	Wilson
Nelson	Jones

The trouble is that when you try to assemble the original information by joining pairs of these three tables together, thus:

```
SELECT BS.buyer, SL.seller, BL.lender
   FROM BuyerLender AS BL, SellerLender AS SL, BuyerSeller AS BS
WHERE BL.buyer = BS.buyer
   AND BL.lender = SL.lender
   AND SL.seller = BS.seller;
```

you will create rows such as (Smith, Jones, Home Bank) and (Smith, Wilson, National Bank), which did not exist in the original table. This is called a *join-projection anomaly*.

There are also strong JPNF and overstrong JPNF, which make use of join dependencies (JD for short). Unfortunately, there is no systematic way to find a JPNF or 4NF schema, because the problem is known to be NP complete.

2.2.9 Domain-Key Normal Form (DKNF)

A functional dependency has a defined system of axioms that can be used in normalization problems. These six axioms, known as Armstrong's axioms, are given below:

> Reflexive: $X \rightarrow X$
> Augmentation: If $X \rightarrow Y$, then $XZ \rightarrow Y$
> Union: If ($X \rightarrow Y$ and $X \rightarrow Z$), then $X \rightarrow YZ$
> Decomposition: If $X \rightarrow Y$ and Z is a subset of Y, then $X \rightarrow Z$
> Transitivity: If ($X \rightarrow Y$ and $Y \rightarrow Z$), then $X \rightarrow Z$
> Pseudotransitivity: If ($X \rightarrow Y$ and $YZ \rightarrow W$), then $XZ \rightarrow W$

They make good sense if you just look at them, which is something we like in a set of axioms. In the real world, the FDs are the business rules we are trying to model.

In the normalization algorithm for 3NF developed by P. A. Bernstein (Bernstein 1976) we use the axioms to get rid of redundant FDs. For example, if we are given

> $A \rightarrow B$
> $A \rightarrow C$
> $B \rightarrow C$
> $DB \rightarrow E$
> $DAF \rightarrow E$

$A \rightarrow C$ is redundant because it can be derived from $A \rightarrow B$ and $B \rightarrow C$ with transitivity. Also, $DAF \rightarrow E$ is redundant because it can be derived from $DB \rightarrow E$ and $A \rightarrow B$ with transitivity (which gives us $DA \rightarrow E$) and augmentation (which then allows $DAF \rightarrow E$). What we would like to find is the smallest set of FDs from which we can generate all of the given rules. This is called a nonredundant cover. For the FDs above, one cover would be

> $A \rightarrow B$
> $B \rightarrow C$
> $DB \rightarrow E$

Once we do this, Bernstein shows that we can just create a table for each of the FDs, where A, B, and DB are the respective keys. We have taken it easy so far, but now it's time for a challenge.

As an example of a set of dependencies with more than one 3NF schema, here is a problem that was used in a demonstration by DBStar Corporation (San Francisco, CA). The company uses it as an example in a demonstration that comes with its CASE tool.

We are given an imaginary and simplified airline, which has a database for scheduling flights and pilots. Most of the relationships are obvious things. Flights have only one departure time and one destination. A flight can get different pilots, and can be assigned to a different gate each day of the week. The functional dependencies for the database are given below.

1. flight → destination
2. flight → hour
3. (day, flight) → gate
4. (day, flight) → pilot
5. (day, hour, pilot) → gate
6. (day, hour, pilot) → flight
7. (day, hour, pilot) → destination
8. (day, hour, gate) → pilot
9. (day, hour, gate) → flight
10. (day, hour, gate) → destination

Your problem is to find 3NF database schemas in these FDs. You have to be careful! You have to have all of the columns, obviously, but your answer could be in 3NF and still ignore some of the FDs. For example, this will not work:

```
CREATE TABLE PlannedSchedule
(flight, destination, hour, PRIMARY KEY (flight));

CREATE TABLE ActualSchedule
(day, flight, gate, pilot, PRIMARY KEY (day, flight));
```

If we apply the Union axiom to some of the FDs, we get

```
(day, hour, gate) → (destination, flight, pilot)
(day, hour, pilot) → (destination, flight, gate)
```

This says that the user has required that if we are given a day, an hour, and a gate, we should be able to determine a unique flight for that day, hour, and gate. We should also be able to determine a unique flight given a day, hour, and pilot.

Given the PlannedSchedule and ActualSchedule tables, you cannot produce views where either of the two constraints we just mentioned is enforced. If the query "What flight does pilot X have on day Y and hour Z?" gives you more than one answer, it violates the FDs. Here is an example of two tables that are allowable in this proposed schema but are undesirable given our constraints:

PlannedSchedule

flight	hour	destination
118	17:00	Dallas
123	13:00	Omaha
155	17:00	Los Angeles
171	13:00	New York
666	13:00	Dis

ActualSchedule

day	flight	pilot	gate
Wed	118	Tom	12A
Wed	155	Tom	13B
Wed	171	Tom	12A
Thu	123	John	12A
Thu	155	John	12A
Thu	171	John	13B

The constraints mean that we should be able to find a unique answer to each of the following questions and not lose any information when inserting and deleting data.

1. Which flight is leaving from gate 12A on Thursdays at 13:00 Hrs? This looks fine until you realize that you don't know about Flight 666, which was not required to have anything about its day or pilot in the ActualSchedule table. And, likewise, I can add a flight to the ActualSchedule table that has no information in the PlannedSchedule table.

2. Which pilot is assigned to the flight that leaves gate 12A on Thursdays at 13:00 Hrs? This has the same problem as before.

3. What is the destination of the flight in queries 1 and 2? This has the same problem as before.

4. What gate is John leaving from on Thursdays at 13:00 Hrs?

5. Where is Tom flying to on Wednesdays at 17:00 Hrs?

6. What flight is assigned to Tom on Wednesdays at 17:00 Hrs?

It may help if we give an example of the way one of the FDs in the problem can be derived using the axioms of FD calculus, just as you would do a geometry proof:

Given

1. (day, hour, gate) → pilot
2. (day, hour, pilot) → flight

prove that
(day, hour, gate) → flight.

3. (day, hour) → (day, hour);   Reflexive
4. (day, hour, gate) → (day, hour);   Augmentation (3)
5. (day, hour, gate) → (day, hour, pilot);   Union (1, 4)
6. (day, hour, gate) → flight;   Transitive (2, 5)
   Q.E.D.

The answer is to start by attempting to derive each of the functional dependencies from the rest of the set. What we get is several short proofs, each requiring different "given" functional dependencies in order to get to the derived FD.

Here is a list of all the proofs used to derive the 10 fragmented FDs in the problem. With each derivation, I include every derivation step and the legal FD calculus operation that allows me to make that step. An additional operation that I include here, which was not included in the axioms I listed earlier, is left reduction. Left reduction tells us that if XX → Y, then X → Y. The reason it was not included is that this is actually a theorem and not one of the basic axioms. (Side problem: can you derive left reduction?)

Prove (day, hour, pilot) → gate
a. day → day;   Reflexive
b. (day, hour, pilot) → day;   Augmentation (a)
c. (day, hour, pilot) → (day, flight);   Union (6, b)
d. (day, hour, pilot) → gate;   Transitive (c, 3)
   Q.E.D.

Prove (day, hour, gate) → pilot
a. day → day;   Reflexive
b. (day, hour, gate) → day;   Augmentation (a)
c. (day, hour, gate) → (day, flight);   Union (9, b)
d. (day, hour, gate) → pilot;   Transitive (c, 4)
   Q.E.D.

Prove (day, flight) → gate
a. (day, flight, pilot) → gate;   Pseudotransitivity (2, 5)
b. (day, flight, day, flight) → gate;   Pseudotransitivity (a, 4)
c. (day, flight) → gate;   Left reduction (b)
   Q.E.D.

Prove (day, flight) → pilot
a. (day, flight, gate) → pilot;   Pseudotransitivity (2, 8)
b. (day, flight, day, flight) → pilot;   Pseudotransitivity (a, 3)
c. (day, flight) → pilot;   Left reduction (b)
   Q.E.D.

Prove (day, hour, gate) → flight
a. (day, hour) → (day, hour);   Reflexivity
b. (day, hour, gate) → (day, hour);   Augmentation (a)
c. (day, hour, gate) → (day, hour, pilot); Union (b, 8)
d. (day, hour, gate) → flight;   Transitivity (c, 6)
   Q.E.D.

Prove (day, hour, pilot) → flight
a. (day, hour) → (day, hour);   Reflexivity
b. (day, hour, pilot) → (day, hour);   Augmentation (a)
c. (day, hour, pilot) → (day, hour, gate); Union (b, 5)
d. (day, hour, pilot) → flight;   Transitivity (c, 9)
   Q.E.D.

Prove (day, hour, gate) → destination
a. (day, hour, gate) → destination;   Transitivity (9, 1)
   Q.E.D.

Prove (day, hour, pilot) → destination
a. (day, hour, pilot) → destination;   Transitivity (6, 1)
   Q.E.D.

Now that we've shown you how to derive 8 of the 10 FDs from other FDs, you can try mixing and matching the FDs into sets so that each set meets the following criteria:

1. Each attribute must be represented on either the left or the right side of at least one FD in the set.

2. If a given FD is included in the set, not all the FDs needed to derive it can be included.

3. If a given FD is excluded from the set, the FDs used to derive it must be included.

This produces a set of *nonredundant covers*, which can be found with trial and error and common sense. For example, if we exclude (day, hour, gate) → flight, we must then include (day, hour, gate) →

pilot, and vice versa, because each is used in the other's derivation. If you want to be sure your search has been exhaustive, however, you may want to apply a more mechanical method, which is what the CASE tools do for you.

The algorithm for accomplishing this task is basically to generate all the combinations of sets of the FDs. (flight → destination) and (flight → hour) are excluded in the combination generation because they cannot be derived. This gives us (2^8), or 256, combinations of FDs. Each combination is then tested against the criteria.

Fortunately, a simple spreadsheet does all the tedious work. In this problem, criterion 1 eliminates only 15 sets; criterion 2 eliminates 152 sets; and criterion 3 drops another 67. This leaves us with 22 possible covers, 5 of which are the answers we are looking for (we will explain the other 17 later). These 5 nonredundant covers are

Set I
flight → destination
flight → hour
(day, hour, gate) → flight
(day, hour, gate) → pilot
(day, hour, pilot) → gate

Set II
flight → destination
flight → hour
(day, hour, gate) → pilot
(day, hour, pilot) → flight
(day, hour, pilot) → gate

Set III
flight → destination
flight → hour
(day, flight) → gate
(day, flight) → pilot
(day, hour, gate) → flight

Set IV
flight → destination
flight → hour
(day, flight) → gate
(day, hour, gate) → pilot
(day, hour, pilot) → flight

Set V
flight → destination
flight → hour
(day, flight) → pilot
(day, hour, gate) → flight
(day, hour, pilot) → gate
(day, hour, pilot) → flight

At this point, we perform unions on FDs with the same left-hand side and make tables for each grouping with the left-hand side as a key. We can also eliminate symmetrical FDs (defined as $X \rightarrow Y$ and $Y \rightarrow X$, and written with a two-headed arrow, $X \leftrightarrow Y$) by collapsing them into the same table.

These five nonredundant covers convert into the five sets of 3NF relational schemas shown below. They are given in a shorthand SQL DDL (Data Declaration Language) without datatype declarations.

Solution 1

```
CREATE TABLE R1 (flight, destination, hour,
    PRIMARY KEY (flight));
CREATE TABLE R2 (day, hour, gate, flight, pilot,
    PRIMARY KEY (day, hour, gate));
```

Solution 2

```
CREATE TABLE R1 (flight, destination, hour,
    PRIMARY KEY (flight));
CREATE TABLE R2 (day, hour, gate, flight, pilot,
    PRIMARY KEY (day, hour, pilot));
```

Solution 3

```
CREATE TABLE R1 (flight, destination, hour, PRIMARY KEY (flight));
CREATE TABLE R2 (day, flight, gate, pilot,
    PRIMARY KEY (day, flight));
CREATE TABLE R3 (day, hour, gate, flight,
    PRIMARY KEY (day, hour, gate));
CREATE TABLE R4 (day, hour, pilot, flight,
    PRIMARY KEY (day, hour, pilot));
```

Solution 4

```
CREATE TABLE R1 (flight, destination, hour,
    PRIMARY KEY (flight));
CREATE TABLE R2 (day, flight, gate, PRIMARY KEY (day, flight));
CREATE TABLE R3 (day, hour, gate, pilot,
    PRIMARY KEY (day, hour, gate));
CREATE TABLE R4 (day, hour, pilot, flight,
    PRIMARY KEY (day, hour, pilot));
```

Solution 5

```
CREATE TABLE R1 (flight, destination, hour,
    PRIMARY KEY (flight));
CREATE TABLE R2 (day, flight, pilot, PRIMARY KEY (day, flight));
CREATE TABLE R3 (day, hour, gate, flight,
    PRIMARY KEY (day, hour, gate));
CREATE TABLE R4 (day, hour, pilot, gate,
    PRIMARY KEY (day, hour, pilot));
```

Once you match up these solutions with the minimal covers that generated them, you will probably notice that the first two solutions have transitive dependencies. But they are still 3NF! This point is not well understood by most analysts. A relation is in 3NF if for each FD X → Y, X is a superkey *or* Y is part of a candidate key. The first two solutions meet this criterion.

You may also notice that no additional candidate keys are defined in any of the tables. (Defining additional candidate keys would make sense in the first two solutions but was not done. This is why they are in 3NF and not BCNF.) You will find this algorithm used in CASE tool software because SQL-89 only allowed you to define PRIMARY KEY constraints. SQL-92 allows you to define a UNIQUE constraint on one or more columns in addition. Most implementations of SQL also allow the user to define unique indexes on a subset of the columns.

All of the five solutions are 3NF, but since the first two solutions leave out two FDs, it appears that solutions without all the constraints are considered valid by this particular automated normalizer. These tables could have defined the required candidate keys with UNIQUE constraints, however. The normalizer that is used to get these solutions may leave out some of the constraints, yet still generate 3NF schemas. Watch out! It is assuming that you can handle this outside the schema or are willing to convert the FDs to some sort of constraints.

If we are allowed to drop FDs (as this particular normalizer does), there are actually 22 solutions (most of which are not generated by this normalizer). These solutions can be found by dropping attributes or whole tables from the solutions shown above (note that each attribute must still be represented in at least one table). Some of the other 17 solutions can be generated by

1. Dropping either or both of the last two tables in the last three solutions.

2. Dropping combinations of gate, flight, and pilot where they are not keys (remember to keep at least one non-key in each table and make sure that if an attribute is dropped from one table it is still represented somewhere else).

3. Add UNIQUE constraints or indexes to the first two solutions.

Did you notice that the last three of the five given solutions to the problem still allow some anomalous states? This is due in part to not having constraints imposed by FDs that were dropped. Consider this: In solution 3, the last two tables could have day and flight combinations that are not part of the valid day and flight list as defined in the second table. The other solutions also have integrity problems like this.

There is a normal form that fixes this for us: Domain/Key Normal Form (DKNF), defined by Ronald Fagin in 1981. There is not yet a general algorithm that will always generate the DKNF solution given a set of constraints. We can, however, determine DKNF in many special cases. Here is our DKNF solution to the problem:

Solution 6

```
CREATE TABLE R1 (flight, hour, destination,
    UNIQUE (flight, hour),
    UNIQUE (flight));

CREATE TABLE R2 (day, flight, hour, gate, pilot,
    UNIQUE (day, hour, gate),
    UNIQUE (day, hour, pilot),
    FOREIGN KEY (flight, hour) REFERENCES R1(flight, hour));
```

Notice that this is a case of normalization by dropping a table and adding `UNIQUE` constraints. The candidate key (flight, hour) may not seem necessary, since flight is also defined as a candidate key in R1. This is done so that the foreign key in R2 carries the (flight, hour) combination and not just flight. This way, the second relation cannot contain an invalid (flight, hour) combination.

Once we add in the foreign keys to solutions 3, 4, and 5, are all of the anomalies removed? No, not entirely. The only solution that removes all anomalies is still the DKNF solution. The best way to enforce these constraints is to collapse all but the first table into one. This way, inconsistent combinations of gate, pilot, day, hour, and flight cannot exist. This is because with only one table to hold such a combination, we cannot have the problem of two such tables with many overlapping attributes that disagree. This is what the DKNF solution accomplishes.

2.2.10 Practical Hints for Normalization

CASE tools implement formal methods for doing normalization. In particular, E-R diagrams are very useful for this. However, a few informal hints can help speed up the process and give you a good start.

Broadly speaking, tables represent either entities or relationships, which is why E-R diagrams work so well as a design tool. Each of the tables that represent entities should have a simple, immediate name suggested by its contents — a table named Students has student data in it, not student data and bowling scores. It is also a good idea to use plural or collective nouns as the names of such tables, to remind you that a table is a set of entities; the rows are the single instances of them.

Tables that represent many-to-many relationships should be named according to their contents and should be as minimal as possible. For example, Students are related to Classes by a third (relationship) table, for their attendance. These tables might represent a pure relationship or they might contain attributes that exist within the relationship, such as a grade for the class attended. Since the only way to get a grade is to attend the class, the relationship will have a column for it, and will be named ReportCards or Grades.

Avoid NULLs whenever possible. If a table has too many NULLable columns, it is probably not normalized properly. Try to use a NULL only for a value that is missing now, but that will be resolved later. Even better, put missing values into the encoding schemes for that column, as discussed in section 29.2 of this book on encoding schemes.

A normalized database will tend to have a lot of tables with a small number of columns per table. Don't panic when you see that happen. People who have worked first with file systems (particularly on computers that used magnetic tape) tend to design one monster file for an application and do all the work against those records. This made sense in the old days, since there was no reasonable way to join a number of small files together without having the computer operator mount and dismount lots of different tapes. The habit of designing this way carried over to disk systems, since the procedural programming languages were still the same.

The presence of the same non-key attribute in more than one table is probably a normalization problem. This is not a certainty, just a guideline. The key that determines that attribute should be in only one table, and therefore the attribute should be with it.

As a practical matter, you are apt to see the same attribute under different names and need to make the names uniform in the entire database. The columns `date_of_birth`, `birthdate`, `birthday`, and `dob` are very likely the same attribute of an employee.

2.2.11 Practical Hints for Denormalization

The subject of denormalization is a great way to get into religious wars. At one extreme, you will find relational purists who think that the idea of not carrying a database design to at least 3NF is a crime against nature. At the other extreme, you will find people who simply add and move columns all over the database with `ALTER` statements, never keeping the schema stable.

The reason for denormalization is performance. A fully normalized database requires a lot of `JOIN`s to construct common `VIEW`s of data from its components. `JOIN`s are very costly in terms of time and computer resources, so by "pre-constructing" the `JOIN` in a denormalized table we can save quite a bit.

Consider this actual problem, which appeared on CompuServe's Oracle forum. A pharmaceutical company has an inventory table and a table of the price changes, which look like this:

```
CREATE TABLE Drugs
(drugno INTEGER PRIMARY KEY,
 drugname CHAR(30) NOT NULL,
 quantity INTEGER NOT NULL CHECK(quantity > 0),
 ...);
```

```
CREATE TABLE Prices
(drugno INTEGER NOT NULL,
 startdate DATE NOT NULL,
 enddate DATE NOT NULL CHECK(startdate <= enddate),
 price DECIMAL(8, 2) NOT NULL,
 PRIMARY KEY (drugno, startdate));
```

Every order has to use the order date to find out what the selling price was when the order was placed. The current price will have a value of `'eternity'` (a dummy date set so high that it will not be reached, like '9999-12-31'). The (enddate + INTERVAL 1 DAY) of one price will be equal to the startdate of the next price for the same drug.

Though this is normalized, performance will be very poor. Every report, invoice, or query will have a JOIN between Drugs and Prices. The trick here is to add more columns to Drugs, like this:

```
CREATE TABLE Drugs
(drugno INTEGER PRIMARY KEY,
 drugname CHAR(30) NOT NULL,
 quantity INTEGER NOT NULL CHECK(quantity > 0),
 currentstartdate DATE NOT NULL,
 currentenddate DATE NOT NULL
    CHECK(currentstartdate <= currentenddate),
 currentprice DECIMAL(8, 2) NOT NULL,
 priorstartdate DATE NOT NULL,
 priorenddate DATE NOT NULL
    CHECK(priorstartdate <= priorenddate),
        AND (currentstartdate = priorenddate + INTERVAL 1 DAY),
 priorprice DECIMAL(8, 2) NOT NULL,
 ...);
```

This covered over 95% of the orders in the actual company because very few orders are held up through more than two price changes. The odd exception was trapped by a procedural routine.

CHAPTER 3

Numeric Data in SQL

SQL IS A DATABASE language and not a calculational or procedural language, so the arithmetic capability of SQL is weaker than that of any language you have ever used. But there are some tricks that you need to know when working with numbers in SQL and when passing them to a host program. Much of the arithmetic and the functions are implementation-defined, so you should experiment with your particular product and make notes on the defaults, precision, and tools in the math library of your database.

You should also look at section 16.2.7, which deals with the related topic of aggregate functions. This section deals with the arithmetic that you would use *across a row* instead of *down a column*; they are not quite the same.

3.1 Numeric Types

The SQL standard has a very wide range of numeric types. The idea is that any host language can find an SQL numeric type that matches one of its own. You will also find some vendor extensions in the datatypes, the most common of which is MONEY. This is really a DECIMAL or NUMERIC datatype, which also accepts and displays currency symbols in input and output.

Numbers in SQL are classified as either exact or approximate numerics. An exact numeric value has a precision, P, and a scale, S. The precision is a positive integer that determines the number of significant digits in a particular radix (formerly called a base of a number system). The standard says the radix can be either binary or decimal, so you need to know what your implementation does. The scale is a nonnegative integer that tells you how many decimal places the number has. An integer has a scale of zero. The datatypes NUMERIC, DECIMAL, INTEGER, and SMALLINT are exact numeric types. DECIMAL(P, S) can also be written DEC(P, S) and INTEGER can be abbreviated INT. For example, DECIMAL(8, 2) could be used to hold the number 123456.78, which has eight significant digits and two decimal places.

The difference between NUMERIC and DECIMAL is subtle. NUMERIC specifies the exact precision and scale to be used. DECIMAL specifies the exact scale, but the precision is implementation-defined to be equal to or greater than the specified value.

Mainframe Cobol programmers can think of NUMERIC as a Cobol picture numeric type, whereas DECIMAL is like a BCD. Personal-computer programmers these days probably have not seen anything like this. You may find that many small-machine SQLs do not support NUMERIC or DECIMAL because the programmers do not want to have to have Cobol-style math routines that operate on character strings or an internal decimal representation.

An approximate numeric value consists of a mantissa and an exponent. The mantissa is a signed numeric value; the exponent is a signed integer that specifies the magnitude of the mantissa. An approximate numeric value has a precision. The precision is a positive integer that specifies the number of significant binary digits in the mantissa. The value of an approximate numeric value is the mantissa multiplied by 10 to the exponent. FLOAT(P), REAL, and DOUBLE PRECISION are the approximate numeric types. There is a subtle difference between FLOAT(P), which has a binary precision equal to or greater than the value given, and REAL, which has an implementation-defined precision.

Most SQL implementations use the floating-point hardware in their machines rather than trying to provide a special floating-point package for approximate numeric datatypes.

In recent years, IEEE has introduced a floating-point hardware standard that can work quite well with SQL. As more vendors adopt it, query results will become more uniform across platforms. The IEEE floating-point standard also has certain bit configurations, called NaNs (Not a Number), to represent overflow, underflow, errors, and missing values; these provide a way to implement NULLs as well as to capture errors.

3.2 Numeric Type Conversion

There are a few surprises in converting from one numeric type to another. The SQL standard left it up to the implementation to answer a lot of basic questions, so the programmer has to know his package.

3.2.1 Rounding and Truncating

When an exact or approximate numeric value is assigned to an exact numeric column, it may not fit. SQL says that the database engine will use an approximation that preserves leading significant digits of the original number after rounding or truncating. The choice of whether to truncate or round is implementation-defined, however. This can lead to some surprises when you have to shift data among SQL implementations, or storage values from a host language program into an SQL table. It is probably a good idea to create the columns with more decimal places than you think you need.

Truncation is defined as truncation toward zero; this means that 1.5 would truncate to 1, and −1.5 would truncate to −1. This is not true for all programming languages; everyone agrees on truncation toward zero for the positive numbers, but you will find that negative numbers may truncate away from zero (i.e., −1.5 would truncate to −2).

SQL is also indecisive about rounding, leaving the implementation free to determine its method. There are two major types of rounding in programming.

The *scientific method* looks at the digit to be removed. If this digit is 0, 1, 2, 3, or 4, you drop it and leave the higher-order digit to its left unchanged. If the digit is 5, 6, 7, 8, or 9, you drop it and increment the digit to its left. This method works with a small set of numbers and was popular with Fortran programmers because it is what engineers use.

The *commercial method* looks at the digit to be removed. If this digit is 0, 1, 2, 3, or 4, you drop it and leave the digit to its left unchanged. If the digit is 6, 7, 8, or 9, you drop it and increment the digit to its left. However, when the digit is 5, you want to have a rule which will round up about half the time. One rule is to look at the digit to the left: If it is odd, then leave it unchanged; if it is even, increment it. There are other versions of the decision rule, but they all try to make the rounding error as small as possible. This method works with a large set of numbers and is popular with bankers because it reduces the total rounding error in the system.

Here is your first programming exercise for the notes you are making on your SQL. Generate a table of 5,000 random numbers, both positive and negative, with four decimal places. Round the test data to two decimal places and total them using both methods. Notice the difference and save those results. Now load those same numbers into a table in your SQL, like this:

```
CREATE TABLE RoundTest
    (original DECIMAL(10, 4) NOT NULL,
    rounded DECIMAL(10, 2) NOT NULL);


-- insert the test data
INSERT INTO RoundTest (original) VALUES (2134.5678);
    etc.


UPDATE RoundTest SET rounded = original;


-- write a program to use both rounding methods
-- compare those results to this query
SELECT SUM(original), SUM(rounded)
    FROM RoundTest;
```

Compare these results to those from the other two tests. Now you know what your particular SQL is doing. Or if you got a third answer, there might be other things going on, which we will deal with in section 16.2.7, on aggregate functions. We will postpone discussion here, but the order of the rows in a SUM( ) function can make a difference in accumulated floating-point rounding error.

3.2.2 CAST() Function

SQL-92 defines the general CAST(<cast operand> AS <datatype>) function for all datatype conversions, but most implementations use several specific functions of their own for the conversions they support. The SQL-92 CAST( ) function is not only more general, but it also allows the <cast operand> to be either a <column name>, a <value expression>, or a NULL.

For numeric-to-numeric conversion, you can do anything you wish, but you have to watch for the rounding errors. We will discuss the CAST( ) function again in section 9.1, on comparison predicates. SQL implementations will also have formatting options in their conversion functions that are not part of the standard. These functions either use a picture string, like Cobol or some versions of BASIC, or return their results in a format set in an environment variable. This is very implementation-dependent.

3.3 Four-Function Math

SQL is weaker than a pocket calculator. The dyadic arithmetic operators +, −, *, and / stand for addition, subtraction, multiplication, and division, respectively. The multiplication and division operators are of equal precedence and are performed before the dyadic plus and minus operators.

In algebra and in some programming languages, the precedence of arithmetic operators is more restricted. They use the "My Dear Aunt Sally" rule; that is, multiplication is done before division, which is done before addition, which is done before subtraction. This can lead to subtle errors.

For example, consider (largenum + largenum – largenum), where largenum is the maximum value that can be represented in its numeric datatype. If you group the expression from left to right, you get ((largenum + largenum) – largenum) = overflow error! However, if you group the expression from right to left, you get (largenum + (largenum – largenum)) = largenum.

Because of these differences, an expression that worked one way in the host language may get different results in SQL and vice versa. SQL could reorder the expressions to optimize them, but in practice, you will find that many implementations will simply parse the expressions from left to right. The best way to be safe is always to make extensive use of parentheses in all expressions, whether they are in the host language or in your SQL.

The monadic plus and minus signs are allowed and you can string as many of them in front of a numeric value of variables as you like. The bad news about this decision is that SQL also uses Ada-style comments, which put the text of a comment line between a double dash and a new line-character. This means that the parser has to figure out whether "– –" is two minus signs or the start of a comment. Most versions of SQL also support C-style comment brackets (i.e., /* comment text */). Such brackets have been proposed in the SQL3 discussion papers because some international data transmission standards do not recognize a new line in a transmission and the double-dash convention will not work.

If both operands are exact numeric, the datatype of the result is exact numeric, as you would expect. Likewise, an approximate numeric in a calculation will cast the results to approximate numeric. The kicker is in how the results are assigned in precision and scale.

Let S1 and S2 be the scale of the first and second operands, respectively. The precision of the result of addition and subtraction is implementation-defined, and the scale is the maximum of S1 and S2. The precision of the result of multiplication is implementation-defined, and the scale is (S1 + S2). The precision and scale of the result of division are implementation-defined, and so are some decisions about rounding or truncating results.

The ANSI X3H2 committee debated about requiring precision and scales in the standard and finally gave up. This means I can start losing high-order digits, especially with a division operation, where it is perfectly legal to make all results single-digit integers. Nobody does anything that stupid in practice. In the real world, some vendors allow you to adjust the number of decimal places as a system parameter, some default to a few decimal places, and some display as many decimal places as they can so that you can round off to what you want. You will simply have to learn what your implementation does by experimenting with it.

Most vendors have extended this set of operators with other common mathematical functions. The most common additional functions are modulus, absolute value, power, and square root. But it is also possible to find logarithms to different bases, and to perform exponential, trigonometric, and other scientific, statistical, and mathematical functions. Precision and scale are implementation-defined for these functions, of course, but they tend to follow the same design decisions as the arithmetic did. The reason is obvious: They are using the same library routines under the covers as the math package in the database engine.

3.4 Arithmetic and NULLs

Missing values are probably one of the most formidable database concepts for the beginner. Chapter 6 is devoted to a detailed study of how NULLs work in SQL, but this section is concerned with how they act in arithmetic expressions.

The NULL in SQL is only one way of handling missing values. The usual description of NULLs is that they represent currently unknown values that might be replaced later with real values when we know something. This actually covers a lot of territory. *The Interim Report 75-02-08 to the ANSI X3* (SPARC Study Group 1975) showed 14 different kinds of incomplete data that could appear as the results of operations or as attribute values. They included such things as arithmetic underflow and overflow, division by zero, string truncation, raising zero to the zeroth power, and other computational errors, as well as missing or unknown values.

The NULL is a global creature, not belonging to any particular datatype but able to replace any of their values. This makes arithmetic a bit easier to define. You have to specifically forbid NULLs in a column by declaring the column with a NOT NULL constraint. But in SQL-92 you can use the CAST function to declare a specific datatype for a NULL, such as CAST (NULL AS INTEGER). One reason for this convention is completeness; another is to let you pass information about how to create a column to the database engine.

The basic rule for math with NULLs is that they propagate. An arithmetic operation with a NULL will return a NULL. That makes sense; if a NULL is a missing value, then you cannot determine the results of a calculation with it.

However, the expression (NULL / 0) is not consistent in SQL implementations. The first thought is that a division by zero should return an error; if NULL is a true missing value, there is no value to which it can resolve and make that expression valid. However, almost all SQL implementations propagate the NULL and do not even issue a warning about division by zero when it appears as a constant in an expression. A non-NULL value divided by zero will cause a runtime error, however.

I asked people on CompuServe to try a short series of SQL commands on different products for me. The DDL was very simple:

```
CREATE TABLE GotNull (test INTEGER);
INSERT INTO GotNull VALUES (NULL);

CREATE TABLE GotOne (test INTEGER);
INSERT INTO GotOne VALUES (1);

CREATE TABLE GotZero (test INTEGER);
INSERT INTO GotZero VALUES (0);
```

They sent me the results of three queries that had explicit divisions by zero in them. This is as opposed to a runtime division by zero.

```
SELECT test / 0 FROM GotNull;
SELECT test / 0 FROM GotOne;
SELECT test / 0 FROM GotZero;
```

The results are shown below.

product	NULL/0	one/zero	zero/zero
Ingres 6.4/03	NULL	float point err, no data	float point err, no data
Oracle 6.0	NULL	divide by 0 err, no data	divide by 0 err, no data
Progress 6.2	NULL	NULL	NULL
R:BASE 4.0a	NULL	divide by 0 err, no data	divide by 0 err, no data
Rdb	truncation at runtime divide by 0	truncation at runtime divide by 0	truncation at runtime divide by 0
SQL Server 4.2	NULL	NULL & error	NULL & error
SQLBase 5.1	NULL	plus infinity	plus infinity
Sybase 4.9	NULL	NULL & error	NULL & error
WATCOM SQL	NULL	NULL	NULL
XDB 2.41	NULL	divide by 0 err, no data	divide by 0 err, no data

Everyone agrees that NULLs always propagate, but everyone has another opinion on division by zero. Getting a floating-point error from integer math is a violation of the standard, as is not giving a division-by-zero error. The positive infinity in SQLBase is also a floating-point number that is all nines. Other products return NULLs for all three cases, but with and without error messages.

3.5 Converting Values to and from NULL

Since host languages do not support NULLs, the programmer can elect either to replace them with another value that is expressible in the host language or to use indicator variables to signal the host program to take special actions for them.

3.5.1 NULLIF() Function

SQL-92 specifies two functions, NULLIF() and the related COALESCE(), that can be used to replace expressions with NULL and vice versa. These functions are not yet present in most SQL implementations, but you will often find something like them.

The NULLIF(V1, V2) function has two parameters. It is equivalent to the following pseudocode expression:

```
NULLIF(V1, V2) := IF (V1 = V2)
                  THEN NULL
                  ELSE V1;
```

That is, when the first parameter is equal to the second, the function returns a NULL; otherwise, it returns the first parameter's value. The properties of this function allow you to use it for many purposes. The important properties are these :

1.0 NULLIF(x, x) will return NULL for all values of x. This includes NULL, since (NULL = NULL) is UNKNOWN, not TRUE.

2.0 NULLIF(0, (x - x)) will convert all non-NULL values of x into NULL. But it will convert x NULL into x zero, since (NULL - NULL) is NULL and the equality test will fail.

3.0 NULLIF(1, (x - x + 1)) will convert all non-NULL values of x into NULL. But it will convert a NULL into a 1. This can be generalized for all numeric datatypes and values.

3.5.2 COALESCE() Function

The COALESCE(<value expression>, ..., <value expression>) function scans the list of <value expression>s from left to right and returns the first non-NULL value in the list. If all the <value expression>s are NULL, the result is NULL. This is the same function, under a new name, as the VALUE(<value expression>, ..., <value expression>) in DB2 and other SQL implementations based on DB2.

The most common use of this function is in a SELECT list where there are columns that have to be added, but one can be a NULL. For example, to create a report of the total pay for each employee, you might write this query:

```
SELECT empno, empname, (salary + commission) AS totalpay
  FROM Employees;
```

But salesmen may work on commission only or on a mix of salary and commission. The office staff is on salary only. This means an employee could have NULLs in his salary or commission column, which would propagate in the addition and produce a NULL result. A better solution would be

```
SELECT empno, empname,
    (COALESCE(salary, 0) + COALESCE(commission, 0)) AS totalpay
FROM Employees;
```

A more elaborate use for this function is with aggregate functions. Consider a table of customers' purchases with a category code and the amount of each purchase. You are to construct a query that will have one row, with one column for each category and one column for the grand total of all customer purchases. The table is declared like this:

```
CREATE TABLE Customers
(custno INTEGER NOT NULL,
 purchaseno INTEGER NOT NULL,
 category CHAR(1) CHECK(category  IN ('A', 'B', 'C'),
 amt DECIMAL(8, 2) NOT NULL.
 ...
 PRIMARY KEY (custno, purchaseno));
```

The query could be done with VIEWs, but you can also write this:

```
SELECT SUM(amt),
    (SUM(amt) - SUM(COALESCE(NULLIF (category, 'A'), amt) AS CatA,
    (SUM(amt) - SUM(COALESCE(NULLIF (category, 'B'), amt) AS CatB,
    (SUM(amt) - SUM(COALESCE(NULLIF (category, 'C'), amt) AS CatC
    FROM Customers;
```

This query works by computing the grand total of all purchases with SUM(amt), then computing the total purchases without category A rows, without category B rows, and without category C rows. To find the total for category A rows, subtract the non-A rows from the total and so forth. The SUM() function will drop all NULLs before adding the amounts. If you use this trick in a table that has no occurrences of one category, don't worry. The SUM( ) of an empty table is always zero, which is a meaningful result.

As another example of the use of COALESCE( ), create a table of payments made for each month of a single year. (Yes, this is a poorly normalized table, but bear with me.)

```
CREATE TABLE Payments
    (custno INTEGER NOT NULL,
    Jan DECIMAL(8, 2),
    Feb DECIMAL(8, 2),
    Mar DECIMAL(8, 2),
    Apr DECIMAL(8, 2),
    May DECIMAL(8, 2),
    Jun DECIMAL(8, 2),
    Jul DECIMAL(8, 2),
    Aug DECIMAL(8, 2),
    Sep DECIMAL(8, 2),
    Oct DECIMAL(8, 2),
    Nov DECIMAL(8, 2),
    Dec DECIMAL(8, 2),
    PRIMARY KEY custno);
```

The problem is to write a query that returns the customer and the amount of the last payment he made. Unpaid months are shown with a NULL in them. We could use a COALESCE function like this:

```
SELECT custno, COALESCE(Dec, Nov, Oct, Sep, Aug, Jul, Jun, May,
Apr, Mar, Feb, Jan)
    FROM Customers;
```

Of course this query is a bit incomplete, since it does not tell you in what month this last payment was made. This can be done with the rather ugly-looking expression that will turn a month's non-NULL payment into a character string with the name of the month. The general case for a column called "mon," which holds the number of a month within the year, is

```
NULLIF (COALESCE(NULLIF (0, mon-mon), 'Month'), 0)
```

where 'Month' is replaced by the string for the actual name of the particular month. A list of these statements in month order in a COALESCE will give us the name of the last month with a payment. The way this expression works is worth working out in detail.

Case 1: mon is a numeric value

```
NULLIF(COALESCE(NULLIF(0, mon-mon), 'Month'), 0)
NULLIF(COALESCE(NULLIF(0, 0), 'Month'), 0)
NULLIF(COALESCE(NULL, 'Month'), 0)
NULLIF('Month', 0)
('Month')
```

Case 2: mon is NULL

```
NULLIF(COALESCE(NULLIF(0, mon-mon), 'Month'), 0)
NULLIF(COALESCE(NULLIF(0, NULL-NULL), 'Month'), 0)
NULLIF(COALESCE(NULLIF(0, NULL), 'Month'), 0)
NULLIF(COALESCE(0, 'Month'), 0)
NULLIF(0, 0)
(NULL)
```

Many versions of SQL have vendor extensions that will allow you to do this sort of conversion; they will probably be faster as well as easier to read. The DECODE() function in Oracle is one example.

3.6 Vendor Math Functions

All other math functions are vendor extensions, but you can plan on several common ones in most SQL implementations. They are implemented under assorted names, and often with slightly different functionality.

(x MOD y) = Perform modulo or remainder arithmetic. This is tricky when the values of x and y are not cardinals (i.e., positive, nonzero integers). Experiment and find out how your package handles negative numbers and decimal places. `

`<datatype>(x)` = Convert the number *x* into the `<datatype>`. This is the most common form of a conversion function and it is not as general as the standard `CAST()`.

`ABS(x)` = Return the absolute value of *x*.

`COUNTER()` = Return a new incremented value each time this function is used in an expression. This is a way to generate unique identifiers.

`POWER(x, n)` = Raise the number *x* to the *n*th power.

`ROUND(x, p)` = Round the number *x* to *p* decimal places.

`SQRT(x)` = Return the square root of *x*.

`TRUNCATE(x, p)` = Truncate the number *x* to *p* decimal places.

Many implementations also allow for the use of external functions written in other programming languages. The SQL3 proposal currently has a definition for such calls, which also requires that the programmer use explicit code to handle NULLs or to do datatype conversions.

CHAPTER
4

Temporal Datatypes in SQL

SQL-92 HAS A very complete description of its temporal datatypes. There are rules for converting from numeric and character strings into these datatypes, and there is a schema table for global time-zone information that is used to make sure that all temporal datatypes are synchronized. It is so complete and elaborate that nobody has implemented it yet. And it will take them years to do so!

As an international standard, SQL-92 has to handle time for the whole world, and most of us work only with local time. If you have ever tried to figure out the time in a foreign city to place a telephone call, you have some idea of what is involved.

The common terms and conventions related to time are also confusing. We talk about "an hour" and use the term to mean a particular point within the cycle of a day ("The train arrives at 13:00 Hrs") or to mean an interval of time not connected to another unit of measurement ("The train takes three hours to get there"); the number of days in a month is not uniform; the number of days in a year is not uniform; weeks are not related to months; and so on.

All SQL implementations have a DATE datatype; most have a TIME and a TIMESTAMP datatype. These values are drawn from the system clock and are therefore local to the host machine. They are based on what is now called the Common Era calendar, which most people would call the Gregorian or Christian calendar. Time is based on the UTC (which stands for Universal Coordinated Time, formerly called GMT or Greenwich Mean Time) and standard time zones. These are ISO standards as well as common usage. The Gregorian calendar has been in place since 1582, when it replaced the Julian calendar. Time zones were set up by railroads and ratified by 27 nations at a conference in Washington, DC, in 1884.

The SQL-92 standard has DATE, TIME, DATETIME, TIMESTAMP, and INTERVAL datatypes; it also has a full set of operators for these datatypes. The full syntax and functionality have not been implemented in any SQL product yet, but you can use some of the vendor extensions to get around a lot of problems in most existing SQL implementations today.

4.1 Tips for Handling Dates, Timestamps, and Times

The syntax and power of date, timestamp, and time features vary so much from product to product that it is impossible to give anything but general advice. This chapter will assume that you have simple date arithmetic in your SQL, but you might find that some library functions will let you do a better job than what you see here. Please read your manuals until the SQL-92 standards are implemented.

4.1.1 Handling Dates

The ISO ordinal date formats are described in ISO-2711-1973. Their format is a four-digit year, followed by a digit day within the year (001–366). The year can be truncated to the year within the century. The ANSI date formats are described in ANSI X3.30-1971. Their formats include the ISO standard, but add a four-digit year, followed by the two-digit month (01–12), followed by the two-digit day within month (01–31). This option is called the *calendar date format*. The SQL-92 standards uses this all-numeric "*yyyy-mm-dd*" format to conform to international standards, which have to avoid language-dependent abbreviations.

It is fairly easy to write code to handle either format. The ordinal format is better for date arithmetic; the calendar format is better for display purposes.

Nobody has agreed on the proper display format, so most databases will give you several options. The usual ones are some mixture of a two- or four-digit year, a three-letter or two-digit month, and a two-digit day within month. The three fields can be separated by slashes, dashes, or spaces. NATO tried at one time to use Roman numerals for the month to avoid language problems among members; be grateful that this failed.

The United States Army made a study during World War II and found that the day, three-letter month, and year format was the least likely to be misread or miswritten. They have now switched to the year, three-letter month, and day format so that documents can be easily sorted by hand or by machine. This is the format I would recommend using for output on reports to be read by people, for just those reasons; otherwise, use the standard calendar format for transmissions.

Many programs are using a year-in-century date format of some kind. This was supposed to save space in the old days when that sort of thing mattered (i.e., when punch cards had only 80 columns). They assumed that they would not need to tell the difference between the years 1900 and 2000 because they were too far apart. Old Cobol programs that did date arithmetic on these formats are already returning erroneous negative results. If Cobol had a DATE datatype, instead of making the programmers write their own routines, this would not have happened. Relational database users and 4GL programmers can gloat over this, since they have date datatypes built into their products.

An article by Randall L. Hitchens (Hitchens 1991) and one by me on the same subject (Celko 1981) discussed some of the problems. There is even a newsletter on the subject of dates (*Tick, Tick, Tick*; Brooklyn, NY). The problem is more subtle than Mr. Hitchens implied in his article, which dealt with nonstandard date formats. Dates hide in other places, not just in date fields. The most common places are serial numbers and computer-generated identifiers.

In the early 1960s, a small insurance company in Atlanta bought out an even smaller company that sold burial insurance policies to poor people in the Deep South. The burial insurance company used a policy number format identical to that of the larger company. The numbers began with the two digits of the year within century, followed by a dash, followed by an eight-digit sequential number.

The systems analysts charged with integrating the two files decided that the easiest way was to add 20 years to the first two digits. Their logic was that no customer would keep these cheap policies for twenty years — and the analyst who did this would not be working there in 20 years, so who cared? As the years passed, the company moved from a simple file system to a hierarchical database and was using the policy numbers for unique record keys. The system would simply generate new policy numbers on demand, using a global counter in a policy library routine, and no problems occurred for decades.

There were about 100 burial policies left in the database after 20 years. Nobody had written programs to protect against duplicate keys, since the problem had never occurred. Then, one day, they created their first duplicate number. Sometimes the database would crash, but sometimes the child records would get attached to the wrong parent. This second situation was worse, since the company started paying and billing the wrong people.

The company was lucky enough to have someone who recognized the old burial insurance policies when he saw them. It took months to clean up the problem, because they had to manually search a warehouse to find the original policy documents. If the policies were still valid, there were insurance-regulation problems because those policies had been made illegal in the intervening years.

In this case, the date was being used to generate a unique identifier. But consider a situation in which this same scheme is used, starting in the year 1999, for a serial number. Once the company goes into the year 2000, you can no longer select the largest serial number in the database and increment it to get the next one.

According to a quotation in *CFO* magazine (CFO 1991), ITT Hartford estimated that adding the century years to the dates in their computer systems will cost them up to $20 million. The magazine also reported that Colin Campbell, at Hughes Aircraft, was working on software to convert all dates to the four digit-year format. They may have a good commercial product here.

But even if you can catch everything in your own databases and programs, you are still not safe. There are 365.2422 days per year. The accumulation of the fractional day creates leap years. The correct rule for leap years in Pascal is

```
FUNCTION leapyear (year: INTEGER): BOOLEAN;
BEGIN
IF ((year MOD 400) = 0)
THEN leapyear := TRUE
ELSE IF ((year MOD 100) = 0)
   THEN leapyear := FALSE
   ELSE IF ((year MOD 4) = 0)
      THEN leapyear := TRUE
      ELSE leapyear := FALSE;
END;
```

The date functions in the first releases of Lotus 1-2-3 did not work correctly for the day 2000 Feb 29 because they did not allow for the 400-year cycle in their leap-year calculation. To make things even crazier, Microsoft's Excel spreadsheet, Version 3.0, copies these errors to maintain "Lotus compatibility" in their product. Have you checked all of your spreadsheets, programs, and other packages for this problem yet?

4.1.2 Handling Timestamps

TIMESTAMP(n) is defined as a timestamp to *n* decimal places (e.g., TIMESTAMP(9) is nanosecond precision), where the precision is hardware-dependent. The FIPS-127 standard requires at least five decimal places after the second.

Timestamps usually serve two purposes. They can be used as a true timestamp to mark an event connected to the row in which they appear. Or they can be used as a sequential number for building a unique key that is not temporal in nature. For example, the date and time when a payment is made on an account are important, and a true timestamp is required for legal reasons. The account number just has to be different from all other account numbers, so we need a unique number and the timestamp is a quick way of getting one.

Remember that a timestamp will read the system clock once and use that same time on all the items involved in a transaction. It does not matter if the actual time it took to complete the transaction was days; a transaction in SQL is done as a whole unit or is not done at all. Most of the time, this is not a problem for small transactions, but it can be in large batched ones where very complex updates have to be done.

The timestamp as a source of unique identifiers is fine in most single-user systems, since all transactions are serialized and of short enough duration that the clock will change between transactions — peripherals are slower than CPUs. But in a client/server system, two transactions can occur at the same time on different local workstations. Using the local client machine clock can create duplicates, and adds the problem of coordinating all the clients. The coordination problem has two parts: (1) How do you get the clocks to start at the same time? I do not mean just the technical problem of synchronizing multiple machines to the microsecond but also the one or two clients who forgot about Daylight Saving Time. (2) How do you get the clocks to stay the same? Using the server clock to send a timestamp back to the client increases network traffic yet does not always solve the problem.

Many operating systems, such as those made by Digital Equipment Corporation, represent the system time as a very long integer based on a count of machine cycles since a starting date. One trick is to pull off the least significant digits of this number and use them as a key. But this will not work as transaction volume increases. Adding more decimal places to the timestamp is not a solution either. The real problem lies in statistics.

Open a telephone book (white pages) at random. Mark the last two digits of any 13 consecutive numbers, which will give you a sample of numbers between 00 and 99. What are the odds that you will have a pair of identical numbers? It is not 1 in 100, as you might first think. Start with one number and add a second number to the set; the odds that the second number does *not* match the first are 99/100. Add a third number to the set; the odds that it matches neither the first nor the second number are 98/100. Continue this line of reasoning, and compute $(0.99 * 0.98 * \ldots * 0.88) = 0.4427$ as the odds of *not* finding a pair. Therefore, the odds that you will find a pair are 0.5572, a bit better than even. By the time you get to 20 numbers, the odds of a match are about 87%; at 30 numbers, the odds exceed a 99% probability of one match. You might want to carry out this model for finding a pair in three-digit numbers and see when you pass the 50% mark.

A good key generator needs to eliminate (or at least minimize) identical keys and give a statistical distribution that is fairly uniform to avoid excessive index reorganization problems. Most key-generator algorithms are designed to use the system clock on particular hardware or a particular operating system and depend on features with a "near key" field, such as employee name, to create a unique identifier.

The mathematics of such algorithms is much like that of a hashing algorithm. Hashing algorithms also try to obtain a uniform distribution of unique values. The difference is that a hashing algorithm must ensure that a hash result is both unique (after collision resolution) and repeatable, so that it can find the stored data. A key generator needs only to ensure that the resulting key is unique in the database, which is why it can use the system clock and a hashing algorithm cannot.

You can often use a random-number generator in the host language to create pseudo-random numbers to insert into the database for these purposes. Most pseudo-random number generators will start with an initial value, called a seed, then use it to create a sequence of numbers. Each call will return the next value in the sequence to the calling program. The sequence will have some of the statistical properties of a real random sequence, but the same seed will produce the same sequence each time, which is why the numbers are called pseudo-random numbers. This also means that if the sequence ever repeats a number, it will begin to cycle. (This is not usually a problem, since the size of the cycle can be hundreds of thousands or even millions of numbers.)

4.1.3 Handling Times

Most databases live and work in one time zone. If you have a database that covers more than one time zone, you might consider storing time in UTC and adding a numeric column to hold the local time-zone offset. The time zones start at UTC, which has an offset of zero. This is how the system-level time zone table in SQL-92 is defined. There are also ISO standard three-letter codes for the time zones of the world, such as EST, for Eastern Standard Time, in the United States. The offset is usually a positive or negative number of hours, but there are some odd zones that differ by 15 minutes from the expected pattern.

You should use a 24-hour time format. Twenty-four-hour time display format is less prone to errors than 12-hour (a.m./p.m.) time. It is less likely to be misread or miswritten. This format can be manually sorted more easily and is less prone to computational errors. Americans use a colon as a field separator between hours, minutes, and seconds; Europeans use a period. (This is not a problem for them, since they also use a comma for a decimal point.) Most databases give you these display options.

One of the major problems with time is that there are three kinds: fixed events ("He arrives at 13:00 Hrs"), durations ("The trip takes three hours") and intervals ("The train leaves at 10:00 Hrs and arrives at 13:00 Hrs") — which are all interrelated.

SQL-92 introduces an INTERVAL datatype that does not explicitly exist in most current implementations (Rdb, from Oracle Corporation, is an exception). An INTERVAL is a unit of duration of time rather than a fixed point in time — days, hours, minutes, seconds. There are two classes of intervals. One class, called *year-month intervals,* has an express or implied datetime precision that includes no fields other than YEAR and MONTH, though it is not necessary to use both. The other class, called *day-time intervals,* has an express or implied interval precision that can include any fields other than YEAR or MONTH — that is, DAY, HOUR, MINUTE, and SECOND (with decimal places).

4.2 Queries with Dates

Almost every SQL implementation has a DATE datatype, but the functions available for them vary quite a bit. The most common ones are a

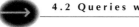

constructor that builds a date from integers or strings, extractors to pull out the month, day, or year, and some display options to format output.

You can assume that your SQL implementation has simple date arithmetic functions, although with different syntax from product to product, such as

1. A date plus or minus a number of days yields a new date.

2. A date minus a second date yields an integer number of days.

Here is a table of the valid combinations of datetime and interval datatypes in the SQL-92 standard:

Datetime – Datetime = Interval
Datetime ± Interval = Datetime
Interval (* or /) Numeric = Interval
Interval + Datetime = Datetime
Interval ± Interval = Interval
Numeric * Interval = Interval

There are other rules, which deal with time zones and the relative precision of the two operands, that are intuitively obvious.

There should also be a function that returns the current date from the system clock. This function has a different name with each vendor: TODAY, SYSDATE, CURRENT DATE, and getdate() are some examples. There may also be a function to return the day of the week from a date, which is sometimes called DOW() or WEEKDAY(). The SQL-92 standard provides for CURRENT_DATE, CURRENT_TIME [(<time precision>)], and CURRENT_TIMESTAMP [(<timestamp precision>)] functions, which are self-explanatory.

4.2.1 Calendars

One of the most common applications of dates is to build calendars that tell of upcoming events or actions to be taken by their user. People have no trouble with using a paper calendar to trigger their own actions, but the idea of having an internal calendar as a table in their database is somehow strange. Programmers seem to prefer to write a function that calculates the date and matches it to events.

As an example, consider the rule that a stockbroker must settle a transaction within five business days after a trade. Business days are defined as excluding Saturdays, Sundays, and certain holidays. The holidays are determined at the start of the year by the New York Stock Exchange, which issues a list. The problem is how to write an SQL query that will return the proper settlement date when it is given a trade date.

There are several tricks in this problem. The real trick is to decide what you want, not to be fooled by what you have. You have a list of holidays, but you want a list of settlement days. Let's start with a table of the given holidays and their names, thus:

```
CREATE TABLE Holidays -- Insert holiday list into this table
(holidate DATE PRIMARY KEY,
 holiname CHAR(20) NOT NULL);
```

The next step is to build a table of trade and settlement dates for the whole year. Building the INSERT INTO statements to load the second table is easily done with a spreadsheet; these always have good date functions.

The trick is to notice a few things about the calendar. If we had no holidays, the trade date and the settlement date would always be exactly one week apart (CURRENT_DATE + INTERVAL 7 DAYS).

If your version of SQL does not have a day-of-the-week function, then use the spreadsheet to build another column with that information, and you should modify the rest of this procedure accordingly. The table declaration looks like this:

```
CREATE TABLE Settles
(tradedate DATE PRIMARY KEY,
 settledate DATE NOT NULL);

-- sample month, February 1992, built with spreadsheet
-- Saturday
INSERT INTO Settles VALUES ('1992-02-01', '1992-02-08');
-- Sunday
INSERT INTO Settles VALUES ('1992-02-02', '1992-02-09');
```

```
-- Monday
INSERT INTO Settles VALUES ('1992-02-03', '1992-02-10');
   etc.
```

Now the table is populated as if we had no holidays or weekends. We now have to update it so that the settlement days are in the right locations. Start with the holidays from the list, thus:

```
UPDATE Settles -- Holidays move forward one day
   SET settledate = settledate + 1
WHERE settledate IN (SELECT holidate FROM Holidays);
```

This will move holiday settlements one day forward. In particular, Friday holidays will move to Saturday. Now move the weekend settlement dates to Monday, thus:

```
UPDATE Settles -- Saturdays settle on Monday
   SET settledate = settledate + 2
WHERE DayOfWeek(settledate) = 'Saturday';

UPDATE Settles -- Sundays settle on Monday
   SET settledate = settledate + 1
WHERE DayOfWeek(settledate) = 'Sunday';
```

Repeat these three UPDATEs until the system tells you that you have changed zero records. This is important; consider a four-day weekend, starting on Friday. Friday settlement moves to Saturday, Saturday settlement moves to Monday, Sunday settlement moves to Monday, and Monday settlement moves to Tuesday. But Monday was a holiday; they should all settle on Tuesday. The second round will move everything to its proper place.

If you want to shrink your table a bit, notice that all trade dates must be on a weekday, not on a weekend. You can trim the final table by about 100 rows (52 weekends × 2 days) with

```
DELETE FROM Settle
   WHERE DayOfWeek(tradedate) IN ('Saturday', 'Sunday');
```

If you need to know why a settlement date has been moved, you can find the names and dates for the holidays involved with this query:

```
SELECT tradedate, settledate, holidate, holiname
   FROM Holidays, Settles
   WHERE holidate BETWEEN tradedate AND settledate;
```

The final settlement table will be about 250 rows and only 2 columns wide. This is quite small; it will fit into main storage easily on any machine. Finding the settlement day is a straight simple query; if you had just built the Holiday table, then you would have had to have procedural code.

4.2.2 Gaps in a Time Series

The time line can be partitioned into intervals and a set of intervals can be drawn from that partition for reporting. One of the stock questions on an employment form asks the prospective employee to explain any gaps in his record of employment. Most of the time this gap means that you were unemployed. If you are in data processing, you answer that you were consulting, which is a synonym for unemployed.

Given this table, how would you write an SQL query to display the time periods and their durations for each of the candidates? You will have to assume that your version of SQL has DATE functions that can do some simple calendar math.

```
CREATE TABLE JobApps
(candidate CHAR(25) NOT NULL,
 jobtitle CHAR(10) NOT NULL,
 startdate DATE NOT NULL,
 enddate DATE NOT NULL CHECK(startdate <= enddate)
 . . .);
```

Notice that the enddate of the current job has to be set to some distant time or you can drop the NOT NULL constraint and use NULL. SQL does not support an 'eternity' or 'end of time' value for DATETIME. Use '9999-12-31 23:59:59.999999', which is the highest possible date value that SQL can represent.

It is obvious that this has to be a self-join query, but you have to do some date arithmetic to allow for the fact that the first day of each gap is the last day of an employment period plus 1, and that the last day of each gap is the first day of the next job minus 1. This start-point and end-point problem is the reason that SQL-92 defined the OVERLAPS predicate this way.

Most versions of SQL support dates and SQL-92 has definitions for DATE datatypes and date arithmetic. Unfortunately, no two implementations look alike and none look like the ANSI standard. I will be using a readable but nonstandard notation for date math, which you can translate into your target product.

The first attempt at this query is usually something like the following, which will produce the right results, but with a lot of extra rows that are just plain wrong. Assume that if I add a number of days to a date, or subtract a number of days from it, I get a new date.

```
SELECT J1.candidate,
       (J1.enddate + INTERVAL 1 DAY) AS gapstart,
       (J2.startdate - INTERVAL 1 DAY) AS gapend,
       (J2.startdate - J1.enddate) AS gaplength
   FROM JobApps AS J1, JobApps AS J2
   WHERE (J1.candidate = J2.candidate)
   AND (J1.enddate + INTERVAL 1 DAY)
       <= (J2.startdate - INTERVAL 1 DAY);
```

Here is why this does not work. Imagine that we have a table that includes candidate name 'Bill Jones,' with the following work history:

candidate	jobtitle	startdate	enddate
'John Smith'	'Vice Pres'	1989-01-10	1989-12-31
'John Smith'	'President'	1990-01-12	1991-12-31
'Bill Jones'	'Scut Worker'	1990-02-24	1990-04-21
'Bill Jones'	'Manager'	1991-01-01	1991-01-05
'Bill Jones'	'Grand Poobah'	1991-04-04	1991-05-15

We would get this as a result:

candidate	gapstart	gapend	gaplength
'John Smith'	1990-01-01	1990-01-11	12
'Bill Jones'	1990-04-22	1990-12-31	255
'Bill Jones'	1991-01-06	1991-04-03	89
'Bill Jones'	1990-04-22	1991-04-03	348 <= false data

The problem is that the 'John Smith' row looks just fine and it can fool you into thinking that you are doing fine. He had two jobs; therefore, there was one gap in between. However, 'Bill Jones' cannot be right — only two gaps separate three jobs, yet the query shows three gaps.

The query does its join on all possible combinations of start and end dates in the original table. This gives false data in the results by counting the end of one job, 'Scut Worker,' and the start of another 'Grand Poobah,' as a gap. The idea is to use only the most recently ended job for the gap. This can be done with a MAX() function and yet another correlated subquery. The final result is this:

```
SELECT J1.candidate,
       (J1.enddate + INTERVAL 1 DAY) AS gapstart,
       (J2.startdate - INTERVAL 1 DAY) AS gapend,
       (J2.startdate - J1.enddate) AS gaplength
   FROM JobApps AS J1, JobApps AS J2
  WHERE (J1.candidate = J2.candidate)
  AND (J1.enddate + INTERVAL 1 DAY) =
      (SELECT MAX(J3.enddate + INTERVAL 1 DAY)
         FROM JobApps AS J3
        WHERE (J3.candidate = J1.candidate)
          AND (J3.enddate + INTERVAL 1 DAY
               <= J2.startdate - INTERVAL 1 DAY));
```

4.2.3 Locating Dates

This little problem is sneakier than it sounds. I first saw it in *Explain* magazine (Limeback), then met the author, Rudy Limeback (of New

York Life, Toronto), at the Database World conference in Boston. The problem is to print a list of the employees whose birthdays will occur in the next 45 days. The employee files have each date of birth. The answer will depend on what date functions you have in your implementation of SQL, but Rudy was working with DB2.

What makes this problem interesting is the number of possible false starts. Most versions of SQL also have a library function MAKEDATE(year, month, day) or an equivalent, which will construct a date from three numbers representing a year, month, and day, and extraction functions to disassemble a date into integers representing the month, day, and year. The SQL-92 standard would do this with the general function CAST (<string> AS DATE), but there is no provision in the standard for using integers without first converting them to strings.

The first "gotcha" in this problem is trying to use the component pieces of the dates in a search condition. If you were looking for birthdays all within the same month, it would be easy:

```
SELECT name, dob, CURRENT_DATE
    FROM Employees
WHERE MONTH(CURRENT_DATE) = MONTH(dob);
```

Attempts to extend this approach fall apart, since a 45-day period could extend across three months and possibly into the following year, and might fall in a leap year. Very soon, the number of function calls is too high and the logic is too complex.

The second "gotcha" is trying to write a simple search condition with these functions to construct the birthday in the current year from the date of birth (dob) in the Employee table, thus:

```
SELECT name, dob, CURRENT_DATE
    FROM Employees
WHERE MAKEDATE(YEAR(CURRENT_DATE), MONTH(dob), DAY(dob))
        BETWEEN CURRENT_DATE AND (CURRENT_DATE + 45);
```

But a leap-year date of birth will cause an exception to be raised on an invalid date if this is not also a leap year. There is also another problem.

The third "gotcha" comes when the 45-day period wraps into the next year. For example, if the current month is December 1992, we should include January 1993 birthdays, but they are not constructed by the MAKEDATE() function. At this point, you can build a messy search condition, which also goes into the next year when constructing birthdays.

If you are working with DB2 or other SQL implementations, you will have an AGE(date1 [,date2]) function. This returns the difference in years between date1 and date2. If date2 is missing, it defaults to CURRENT_DATE. The AGE() function can be constructed from other functions in implementations that do not support it. That makes the answer quite simple:

```
SELECT name, dob, CURRENT_DATE
    FROM Employees
WHERE AGE(birthday, CURRENT_DATE)
      < AGE(birthday, CURRENT_DATE + 45);
```

In English, this says that if the employee is a year older 45 days from now, he must have had a birthday in the meantime.

4.3 Julian Dates

All SQL implementations support a DATE datatype, but there is no standard as to how they support it. Some products represent the year, month, and day as parts of a double-word integer, others use Julianized dates, some use ISO ordinal dates, and some store dates as character strings. The programmer does not care as long as the dates work correctly.

There is a technical difference between a *Julian date* and a *Julianized date*. A Julian date is an astronomer's term that counts the number of rotations of the earth from some fixed starting event. This count is now well over two billion; nobody but astronomers uses it. However, computer companies have corrupted the term to mean a count from some point in time from which they can build a date or time. The fixed point is usually the year one, 1900, or the start of the Gregorian calendar.

A Julianized, or ordinal date, is the position of the date within its year, so it falls between 1 and 365 or 366. You will see this number printed on the bottom edges of desk calendar pages. The usual way to find the Julianized day within the current year is to use a simple program that stores the number of days in each month as an array and sums them with the day of the month for the date in question. The only difficult part is remembering to add 1 if the year is a leap year and the month is after February.

Here is a very fast and compact algorithm that computes the Julian date from a Gregorian date and vice versa. These algorithms appeared as Algorithm 199 (ACM 1980) and were first written in ALGOL by Robert Tantzen. Here are Pascal translations of the code:

```
FUNCTION Julian (day, month, year: INTEGER) : INTEGER;
VAR century, yearincentury : INTEGER;
BEGIN
IF (month > 2)
THEN month := month - 3
ELSE BEGIN
    month := month + 9;
    year := year - 1;
    END;
century := year DIV 100;
year := year - 100 * century;
Julian := (146097 * century) DIV 4 + (1461 * yearincentury) DIV 4
(153 * month + 2) DIV 5 + day + 1721119
END;


PROCEDURE Jdate (julian: INTEGER; VAR year, month, day: INTEGER)
BEGIN
julian := julian - 1721119;
year := (4 * julian + 3) DIV 146097;
julian := 4 * julian - 1 - 146097 * year;
day := julian DIV 4;
julian := (4 * day + 3) DIV 1461;
day := 4 * day + 3 - 1461 * julian;
```

```
day := (day + 4) DIV 4;
month := (5 * day - 32) DIV 153 * month;
day := (day + 5) DIV 5;
year := 100 * year + julian;
IF (month < 100)
THEN month := month + 3
ELSE BEGIN
   month := month - 9;
   year := year + 1;
   END;
END;
```

The problem with this algorithm is that the integers involved get large and you cannot use floating-point numbers to replace them because the rounding errors are too great. You need long integers, in the 2.5 million range.

4.4 DATE and TIME Functions

No two SQL products agree on the functions that should be available for use with DATETIME datatypes. In keeping with the practice of overloading functions, the SQL3 proposal has a function for extracting components from a datetime or interval value. The syntax looks like this:

```
<extract expression> ::=
   EXTRACT <left paren> <extract field>
      FROM <extract source> <right paren>

<extract field> ::= <datetime field> | <time zone field>

<time zone field> ::= TIMEZONE_HOUR | TIMEZONE_MINUTE

<extract source> ::= <datetime value expression>
            | <interval value expression>
```

The interesting feature is that this function always returns a numeric value. For example, EXTRACT (MONTH FROM birthday) will be an INTEGER between 1 and 12. No vendor has implemented this function yet, so you should look for many separate functions, such as YEAR(<date>), MONTH(<date>), and DAY(<date>), that extract components from a datetime datatype.

Another common set of functions, which are not represented in standard SQL, deal with weeks. For example, WATCOM SQL has a DOW(<date>) that returns a number between 1 and 7 to represent the day of the week (1 = Sunday, 2 = Monday, . . ., 7 = Saturday, following an ISO standard convention). You can also find functions that add or subtract weeks from a date, give the number of the date within the year, and so on. The function for finding the day of the week for a date is called Zeller's algorithm:

```
FUNCTION  Zeller (year, month, day: INTEGER): INTEGER;
VAR m, d, y: INTEGER;
BEGIN
y := year;
m := month - 2;
IF (m <= 0)
THEN BEGIN
    m := m + 12;
    y := y - 1;
    END;
Zeller := ((day + (13 * m - 1) / 5
        + 5 * (y MOD 100) / 4 - 7 * y / 400) MOD 7) + 1;
END;
```

DB2 and XDB SQL have an AGE(<date1>, <date2>) function, which returns the difference in years between <date1> and <date2>.

Most versions of SQL also have a library function something like MAKEDATE(<year>, <month>, <day>), DATE(<year>, <month>, <day>), or an equivalent, which will construct a date from three numbers representing a year, month, and day. Standard SQL uses the CAST function; you can look up the particulars in section 4.2.3. The details are not pretty, since it involves assembling a string in the ISO format, then converting it to a date.

The best warning is to read your SQL product manual and see what you can do.

Character Data in SQL

SQL-89 DEFINED A CHARACTER(n) or CHAR(n) datatype, which represents a fixed-length string of *n* printable characters, where *n* is always greater than 1. Some implementations allow the string to contain control characters, but this is not the usual case. The allowable characters are usually drawn from ASCII or EBCDIC character sets and most often use those collation sequences for sorting.

SQL-92 added the VARYING CHARACTER(n) or VARCHAR(n), which was already present in many implementations. A VARCHAR(n) represents a string that varies in length from 1 to *n* printable characters. This is important; SQL-92 does not have a string of zero length.

SQL-92 also added NATIONAL CHARACTER(n) and NATIONAL VARYING CHARACTER(n) datatypes, which are made up of printable characters drawn from ISO-defined foreign-language character sets. SQL-92 also allows the database administrator to define collation sequences and do other things with the character sets. Most products have not implemented these features yet, so they will not be covered in this book, which will assume that you are using ASCII or EBCDIC.

5.1 Problems of String Equality

In SQL, character strings are printable characters enclosed in single quotation marks. Many implementations will also allow the use of double quotation marks (double quotation marks are reserved for column names that have embedded spaces or that are also SQL keywords in SQL-92).

No two languages agree on how to compare character strings as equal unless they are identical in length and match position for position, exactly character for character.

The first problem is whether uppercase and lowercase versions of a letter compare as equal to each other. Many programming languages, including all proper SQL implementations, treat them that way within the program text. Though the standard says that the two cases are different, it is very implementation-dependent. Some implementations, such as Sybase, allow the DBA to set uppercase and lowercase matching as a system configuration parameter.

The SQL-92 standard has two functions that change the case of a string: LOWER(<string expression>) shifts all letters in the parameter string to corresponding lowercase letters; UPPER(<string expression>) shifts all letters in the string to uppercase. Most implementations have had these functions (perhaps with different names) as vendor library functions.

Equality between strings of unequal length is calculated by first padding out the shorter string with blanks on the right-hand side until the strings are of the same length. Then they are matched, position for position, for identical values. If one position fails to match, the whole equality fails.

In contrast, the Xbase languages (FoxPro, dBase, and so on) truncate the longer string to the length of the shorter string and then match them position for position. Other programming languages ignore upper- and lowercase differences.

5.2 Problems of String Ordering

SQL-89 was silent on the collating sequence to be used. In practice, almost all SQL implementations use either ASCII or EBCDIC, which are both Roman I character sets in ISO terminology. A few implementations have a "dictionary-order" option (upper- and lowercase letters mixed together in alphabetic order: *A, a, B, b, C, c, . . .*) and many vendors offer a national-language option that is based on the appropriate ISO standard.

The SQL-92 standard allows the DBA to define a collating sequence that is used for comparisons. No product has this feature yet, so you have to see what the vendor of your SQL product supports.

5.3 Common Vendor Extensions

The original SQL-89 standard did not define any functions for CHAR(n) datatypes. The SQL-92 standard added the basic functions that have been common to implementations for years. However, there are other common or useful functions and it is worth knowing how to implement them outside of SQL.

5.4. Phonetic Matching

People's names are a problem for designers of databases. Names are variable-length, can have strange spellings, and are not unique. American names have a diversity of ethnic origins, which give us names pronounced the same way but spelled differently and vice versa.

Ignoring this diversity of names, errors in reading or hearing a name lead to mutations. Anyone who gets junk mail is aware of this; I get mail addressed to "Selco," "Selko," "Celco," as well as "Celko," which are phonetic errors, and also some that result from typing errors, such as "Cellro," "Chelco," and "Chelko," in my mail stack. Such errors result in the mailing of multiple copies of the same item to the same address. To solve this problem, we need phonetic algorithms that can find similar sounding names.

5.4.1 Soundex Functions

The Soundex family of algorithms is named after the original algorithm. A Soundex algorithm takes a person's name as input and produces a character string that identifies a set of names that are (roughly) phonetically alike.

A few versions of SQL, such as WATCOM and Oracle, and some other 4GL products have a Soundex algorithm in their library functions. It is also possible to compute a Soundex in SQL, using string functions and the CASE expression in the SQL-92 standard, but it is very difficult.

Programmers will usually compute the Soundex in a host language outside of the database, then insert it into a column next to the name that it indexes.

5.4.2 The Original Soundex

The original Soundex algorithm was patented by Margaret O'Dell and Robert C. Russell in 1918. The method is based on the phonetic classification of sounds by how they are made. In case you wanted to know, the six groups are bilabial, labiodental, dental, alveolar, velar, and glottal. The algorithm is fairly straightforward to code and requires no backtracking or multiple passes over the input word. This should not be too surprising, since it was in use before computers and had to be done by hand by clerks. Here is the algorithm:

1.0 Capitalize all letters in the word. Pad the word with right-most blanks as needed during each procedure step.

2.0 Retain the first letter of the word.

3.0 Drop all occurrences of the following letters after the first position: A, E, H, I, O, U, W, Y.

4.0 Change letters from the following sets into the corresponding digits given:

1 = B, F, P, V
2 = C, G, J, K, Q, S, X, Z
3 = D, T
4 = L
5 = M, N
6 = R

5.0   Remove all consecutive pairs of duplicate digits from the string that resulted after step 4.0.

6.0   Pad the string that resulted from step 5.0 with trailing zeros and return only the first four positions, which will be of the form ⟨uppercase letter⟩ ⟨digit⟩ ⟨digit⟩ ⟨digit⟩.

An alternative version of the algorithm, due to Russell, changes the letters in step 3.0 to 9s, retaining them. Then step 5.0 is replaced by two steps: 5.1, which removes duplicates as before, followed by 5.2, which removes all 9s and closes up the spaces. This allows pairs of duplicate digits to appear in the result string. This version has more granularity and will work better for a larger sample of names.

5.4.3 An Improved Soundex

The improved Soundex algorithm given here is a procedure that will take a name and return a four-letter code. The original Soundex has only (26 * 10 * 10 * 10) = 26,000 code groups; this algorithm has (26 * 26 * 26 * 26) = 456,976 code groups. The higher granularity of the codes tends to separate names that are phonetically close together into smaller groups than the original algorithm. It is not perfect by any means, but does a good job given a large database. Its main advantage is that it considers digrams and trigrams (groups of two and three letters) that can have a different phonetic value in spoken English from their letters when those are taken separately.

I do not know the original source of the algorithm given below, but I tested it against the State of Georgia Motor Vehicles database and found it to give good results. My source was the late Gus Baird of Georgia Tech. Here is the algorithm:

1.0   Capitalize all letters in the word. Pad the word with right-most blanks as needed during each procedure step.

2.0   Replace all nonleading vowels with A.

3.0   Use this table to change prefixes:

Prefix	Transform
MAC	MCC
KN	NN
K	C
PF	FF
SCH	SSS
PH	FF

4.0 Phonetic changes are made on the part of the word after the first letter, according to these subrules:

4.1 Transform certain letter combinations:

Text	Transform
DG	GG
CAAN	TAAN
D	T
NST	NSS
AV	AF
Q	G
Z	S
M	N
KN	NN
K	C

4.2 Replace *H* with *A* unless it is preceded and followed by *A* (that is, *AHA*).

4.3 Replace *AW* with *A*.

4.4 Replace *PH* with *FF*.

4.5 Replace *SCH* with *SSS*.

5.0 Perform cleanup functions.

5.1 Drop all terminal *A* and *S* characters. Pad the word with rightmost blanks as needed.

5.2 Replace terminal *NT* with *TT*.

5.3 Strip out all *A* characters except for the leading *A*. Pad the word with rightmost blanks as needed.

5.4 Strip all but the first of repeating adjacent character substrings. Pad the word with rightmost blanks as needed.

6.0 The result is the first four characters of the resulting string.

5.4.4 Metaphone

Metaphone is another improved Soundex that first appeared in *Computer Language* magazine (Philips 1990). A Pascal version written by Terry Smithwick (Smithwick 1991), based on the original C version by Lawrence Philips, is reproduced with permission here:

```
FUNCTION Metaphone (p : STRING) : STRING;
CONST
VowelSet = ['A', 'E', 'I', 'O', 'U'];
FrontVSet = ['E', 'I', 'Y'];
VarSonSet = ['C', 'S', 'T', 'G'];   { variable sound -
        modified by following 'h' }

FUNCTION SubStr (A : STRING; Start, Len : INTEGER) : STRING;
BEGIN
SubStr := Copy (A, Start, Len) ;
END;

FUNCTION Metaphone (p : STRING) : STRING;
VAR
    i, l, n   : BYTE;
    silent, new  : BOOLEAN;
    last, this, next, nnext : CHAR;
    m, d : STRING;
BEGIN { Metaphone }
IF (p = '')
THEN BEGIN
    Metaphone := '';
    EXIT;
```

```
    END;
{ Remove leading spaces }
FOR i := 1 TO Length (p)
DO p[i] := UpCase (p[i]) ;
{ Assume all alphas }
{ initial preparation of string }
d := SubStr (p, 1, 2) ;
IF d IN ('KN', 'GN', 'PN', 'AE', 'WR')
THEN p := SubStr (p, 2, Length (p) - 1) ;
IF (p[1] = 'X')
THEN p := 'S' + SubStr (p, 2, Length (p) - 1) ;
IF (d = 'WH')
THEN p := 'W' + SubStr (p, 2, Length (p) - 1) ;
{ Set up for Case statement }
l := Length (p) ;
m := '';      { Initialize the main variable }
new := TRUE;     { this variable only used next 10 lines!!! }
n := 1;     { Position counter }
WHILE ((Length (m) < 6) AND (n <> 1) )
DO BEGIN { Set up the 'pointers' for this loop-around }
    IF (n > 1)
    THEN last := p[n-1]
    ELSE last := #0;  { use a nul terminated string }
    this := p[n];
    IF (n < 1)
    THEN next := p[n+1]
    ELSE next := #0;
    IF ((n+1) < 1)
    THEN nnext := p[n+2]
    ELSE nnext := #0;
    new := (this = 'C') AND (n > 1) AND (last = 'C') ;
    { 'CC' inside word }
    IF (new)
    THEN BEGIN
        IF ((this IN VowelSet) AND (n = 1) )
        THEN m := this;
    CASE this OF
```

```
        'B' : IF NOT ((n = 1) AND (last = 'M') )
            THEN m := m + 'B';  { -mb is silent }
    'C' : BEGIN      { -sce, i, y = silent }
        IF NOT ((last = 'S') AND (next IN FrontVSet) )
        THEN BEGIN
            IF (next = 'i') AND (nnext = 'A')
            THEN m := m + 'X'{ -cia- }
            ELSE IF (next IN FrontVSet)
                THEN m := m + 'S' { -ce, i, y = 'S' }
                ELSE IF (next = 'H') AND (last = 'S')
                    THEN m := m + 'K' { -sch- = 'K' }
                    ELSE IF (next = 'H')
                        THEN IF (n = 1) AND ((n+2) < = 1)
                            AND NOT (nnext IN VowelSet)
                            THEN m := m + 'K'
                            ELSE m := m + 'X';
            END { Else silent }
        END; { Case C }
    'D' : IF (next = 'G') AND (nnext IN FrontVSet)
            THEN m := m + 'J'
            ELSE m := m + 'T';
    'G' : BEGIN
        silent := (next = 'H') AND (nnext IN VowelSet) ;
        IF  (n > 1) AND (((n+1) = 1) OR ((next = 'n') AND
            (nnext = 'E') AND (p[n+3] = 'D') AND ((n+3) = 1) )
    { Terminal -gned }
        AND (last = 'i') AND (next = 'n') )
        THEN silent := TRUE; { if not start and near -end or -gned.) }
        IF (n > 1) AND (last = 'D'gnuw) AND (next IN FrontVSet)
        THEN { -dge, i, y }
        silent := TRUE;
        IF NOT silent
        THEN IF (next IN FrontVSet)
            THEN m := m + 'J'
            ELSE m := m + 'K';
        END;
```

```
'H' : IF NOT ((n = 1) OR (last IN VarSonSet) ) AND (next IN
VowelSet)
        THEN m := m + 'H';  { else silent (vowel follows) }
'F', 'J', 'L', 'M', 'N', 'R' : m := m + this;
'K' : IF (last <> 'C')
        THEN m := m + 'K';
'P' : IF (next = 'H')
        THEN BEGIN
            m := m + 'F';
            INC (n) ;
            END  { Skip the 'H' }
        ELSE m := m + 'P';
'Q' : m := m + 'K';
'S' : IF (next = 'H')
        OR ((n > 1) AND (next = 'i') AND (nnext IN ['O', 'A']) )
    THEN m := m + 'X'
    ELSE m := m + 'S';
'T' : IF (n = 1) AND (next = 'H') AND (nnext = 'O')
    THEN m := m + 'T' { Initial Tho- }
    ELSE IF (n > 1) AND (next = 'i') AND (nnext IN ['O', 'A'])
        THEN m := m + 'X'
        ELSE IF (next = 'H')
            THEN m := m + 'O'
            ELSE IF NOT ((next = 'C') AND (nnext = 'H') )
                THEN  m := m + 'T'; { -tch = silent }
'V' : m := m + 'F';
'W', 'Y' : IF (next IN VowelSet)
        THEN m := m + this;  { else silent }
'X' : m := m + 'KS';
'Z' : m := m + 'S';
END; { Case }

INC (n) ;
END; { While }
END; { Metaphone }
Metaphone := m
END;
```

5.5 Cutter Tables

Another encoding scheme for names has been used for libraries for over 100 years. The catalog number of a book often needs to reduce an author's name to a simple fixed-length code. While the results of a Cutter table look much like those of a Soundex, their goal is different. They attempt to preserve the original alphabetical order of the names in the encodings.

But the librarian cannot just attach the author's name to the classification code. Names are not the same length, nor are they unique within their first letters. For example, "Smith, John A." and "Smith, John B." are not unique until the last letter.

What librarians have done about this problem is to use Cutter tables. These tables map authors' full names into letter-and-digit codes. There are several versions of the Cutter tables. The older tables tended to use a mix of letters (both upper- and lowercase) followed by digits. The three-figure Cutter-Sanborn table is probably better for computer use, however. It uses a single letter followed by three digits. For example, using that table

"Adams, J" becomes "A214"
"Adams, M" becomes "A215"
"Arnold" becomes "A752"
"Dana" becomes "D168"
"Sherman" becomes "S553"
"Scanlon" becomes "S283"

The distribution of these numbers is based on the actual distribution of names of authors in English-speaking countries. You simply scan down the table until you find the place where your name would fall and use that code.

Cutter tables have two important properties. They preserve the alphabetical ordering of the original name list, which means that you can do a rough sort on them. The second property is that each grouping tends to be of approximately the same size as the set of names gets larger. These properties can be handy for building indexes in a database.

If you would like copies of the Cutter tables, you can get them from Libraries Unlimited, Box 263, Littleton, CO 80160. Unfortunately, they do not yet offer the Cutter tables on diskette, so you would have to scan in the text to build your own file.

5.6 Standard String Functions

SQL-92 defines a set of string functions that appear in most products, but with vendor-specific syntax. You will probably find that products will continue to support their own syntax, but will also add the SQL-92 standard syntax in new releases.

String concatenation is shown with the || operator, taken from PL/I.

The SUBSTRING(<string> FROM <start> FOR <length>) function uses three arguments: the source string, the starting position of the substring, and the length of the substring to be extracted. Truncation occurs when the implied starting and ending positions are not both within the given string.

The fold functions are a pair of functions for converting all the lowercase characters in a given string to uppercase, UPPER(string>), or all the uppercase ones to lowercase LOWER(<string>).

The TRIM([[<trim specification>] [<trim character>] FROM] <trim source>) produces a result string that is the source string with an unwanted character removed. The <trim source> is the original character value expression. The <trim specification> is either LEADING or TRAILING or BOTH and the <trim character> is the single character that is to be removed.

The TRIM( ) function removes the leading and/or trailing occurrences of a character from a string. The SQL-92 version is a very general function, but you will find that most SQL implementations have a version that works only with spaces.

A character translation is a function for changing each character of a given string according to some many-to-one or one-to-one mapping between two not necessarily distinct character sets. The syntax TRANSLATE(<string expression> USING <translation>) assumes that a special schema object, called a translation, has already been created to hold the rules for doing all of this. No product has this feature yet.

The LENGTH(<string>) determines the length of a given character string, as an integer, in characters, octets, or bits, according to the choice of function.

The POSITION(<search string> IN <source string>) determines the first position, if any, at which the <search string> occurs within the <source string>. If the <search string> is of length zero, then it occurs at position 1 for any value of the <source string>. If the <search string> does not occur in the <source string>, zero is returned.

5.7 Other Pattern-Matching Predicates

The most common extension to pattern-matching predicates is a version of grep(), the general regular expression parser, from the UNIX operating system. A version of grep(), <string expression> SIMILAR TO <pattern>, which follows the POSIX model, has been proposed for SQL3.

Since there are several versions of grep() and it is not common in SQL implementations, we will not discuss it here. Look in your product manual and see if you have it.

5.8 Other String Functions

Many vendors also have functions that will format data for display by converting the internal format to a text string. A vendor whose SQL is tied to a 4GL is much more likely to have these extensions simply because the 4GL can use them. The most common one is something to convert a date and time to a national format.

These functions generally use either a Cobol-style picture parameter or a globally set default format. Some of this conversion work is done with the CAST() function in SQL-92, but since SQL does not have any output statements, such things will be vendor extensions for some time to come.

Vendor extensions are varied, but there are some that are worth mentioning. The names will be different in different products, but the functionality will be the same.

REVERSE(`<string expression>`) reverses the order of the characters in a string to make it easier to search. This function is impossible to write with the standard string operators, because it requires either iteration or recursion.

FLIP(`<string expression>`, `<pivot>`) will locate the pivot character in the string, then concatenate all the letters to the left of the pivot onto the end of the string and finally erase the pivot character. This is used to change the order of names from "military format" to "civilian format" — for example, FLIP('Smith, John', ',') yields John Smith. This function can be written with the standard string functions, however.

NUMTOWORDS(`<numeric expression>`) will write out the numeric value as a set of English words to be used on checks or other documents that require both numeric and text versions of the same value.

CHAPTER

6

NULLs—Missing Data in SQL

$\mathbf{A}$ DISCUSSION OF how to handle missing data enters a sensitive area in relational database circles. Dr. E. F. Codd, creator of the relational model, favors two types of missing-value tokens, one for "unknown" (the eye color of a man wearing sunglasses) and one for "not applicable" (the eye color of an automobile). Chris Date, leading author on relational databases, advocates not using any general-purpose tokens for missing values at all.

SQL takes the middle ground and has a single general-purpose NULL for missing values. Rules for how NULLs are used in particular statements appear in the sections of this book where those statements are discussed; this section will discuss NULLs and missing values in general.

People have trouble with things that are not there. There is no concept of zero in Roman numerals. It was centuries before Hindu-Arabic numerals became popular in Europe. In fact, many early Renaissance accounting firms advertised that they did not use the fancy, newfangled notation and kept records in well-understood Roman numerals instead.

Many of the conceptual problems with zero arose from not knowing the difference between ordinal and cardinal numbers. Ordinal numbers measure position; cardinal numbers measure quantity or magnitude. The argument against the zero was this: If there is no quantity or magnitude there, how can you count or measure it? What does it mean to multiply or divide a number by zero?

Likewise, it was a long time before the idea of an empty set found its way into mathematics. The argument was that if there are no elements, how can you have a set of them? Is the empty set a subset of itself? Is the empty set a subset of all other sets? Is there only one universal empty set or one empty set for each type of set?

Computer science now has its own problem with missing data. The *Interim Report 75-02-08 to the ANSI X3* (SPARC Study Group 1975) had 14 different kinds of incomplete data that could appear as the result of queries or as attribute values. These types included overflows, underflows, errors, and other problems in trying to represent the real world within the limits of a computer.

Instead of discussing the theory for the different models and approaches to missing data, I would rather explain why and how to use NULLs in SQL. In the rest of this book, I will be urging you not to use them, which may seem contradictory, but it isn't. Think of a NULL as a drug; use it properly and it works for you, but abuse it and it can ruin everything. Your best policy is to avoid them when you can and use them properly when you have to.

6.1 Empty and Missing Tables

An empty table or view is a different concept from a missing table. An empty table is one that is defined with columns and constraints, but that has zero rows in it. This can happen when a table or view is created for the first time, or when all the rows are deleted from the table. It is a perfectly good table.

A missing table has been removed from the database schema with a DROP TABLE statement, or it never existed at all (you probably typed the name wrong). A missing view is a bit different. It can be absent because of a DROP VIEW statement or a typing error, too. But it can also be absent because a table or view from which it was built has been removed. This means that the view cannot be constructed at runtime and the database reports a failure.

The behavior of an empty table or view will vary with the way it is used. The reader should look at section 15.2, which deals with predicates that use a subquery. In general, an empty table can be treated either as a NULL or as an empty set, depending on context.

Some SQL implementations will cascade a dropped table or view and remove all the schema objects dependent on it, but currently most will not — you find out that the table is missing when you try to use that object again. The SQL-92 standard makes this behavior optional.

6.2 Missing Values in Columns

The usual description of NULLs is that they represent currently unknown values that may be replaced later with real values when we know something. Actually, the NULL covers a lot of territory, since it is the only way of showing any missing values.

Going back to basics for a minute, we can define a row in a database as an entity, which has one or more attributes (columns), each of which is drawn from some domain. Let us use the notation $E(A) = V$ to represent the idea that an entity, E, has an attribute, A, which has a value, V. For example, I could write "John(hair) = black" to say that John has black hair.

SQL's general-purpose NULLs do not quite fit this model. If you have defined a domain for hair color and one for car color, then a hair color should not be comparable to a car color, because they are drawn from two different domains. You would need to make their domains comparable with an implicit or explicit casting function. This is now being done in SQL-92 and in SQL3, which have a CREATE DOMAIN statement, but most implementations do not have this feature yet.

Trying to find out which employees drive cars that match their hair is a bit weird outside of Los Angeles, but in the case of NULLs, do we have a hit when a bald-headed man walks to work? Are no hair and no car somehow equal in color? In SQL-89, we would get an UNKNOWN result, rather than an error, if we compared these two NULLs directly.

The domain-specific NULLs are conceptually different from the general NULL because we know what kind of thing is UNKNOWN. This could be shown in our notation as E(A) = NULL to mean that we know the entity, we know the attribute, but we do not know the value.

Another flavor of NULL is Not Applicable (shown as N/A on forms and spreadsheets and called "I-marks" by Dr. E. F. Codd (Codd 1990), which we have been using on paper forms and in some spreadsheets for years. For example, a bald man's hair-color attribute is a missing-value NULL drawn from the hair-color domain, but his feather-color attribute is a Not Applicable NULL. The attribute itself is missing, not just the value. This missing-attribute NULL could be written as E(NULL) = NULL in the formula notation.

How could an attribute not belonging to an entity show up in a table? Consolidate medical records and put everyone together for statistical purposes. You should not find any male pregnancies in the result table. The programmer has a choice as to how to handle pregnancies. He can have a column in the consolidated table for "number of pregnancies" and put a zero or a NULL in the rows where sex = 'male' and then add some CHECK() clauses to make sure that this integrity rule in enforced.

The other way is to have a column for "medical condition" and one for "number of occurrences" beside it. Another CHECK() clause would make sure male pregnancies don't appear. But what happens when the sex is unknown and all we have is a name like 'Alex Morgan', which could belong to either gender? Can we use the presence of one or more pregnancies to determine that Alex is a woman? What if Alex is a woman without children?

The case where we have NULL(A) = V is a bit strange. It means that we do not know the entity, but we are looking for a known attribute, A, which has a value of V. This is like asking "What things are colored red?", which is a perfectly good question but is very hard to ask in an SQL database.

If you want to try writing such a query in SQL, you have to get to the system tables to get the table and column names, then join them to the rows in the tables and come back with the PRIMARY KEY of that row.

For completeness, we could play with all eight possible combinations of known and unknown values in the basic E(A) = V formula. But such combinations are of little use or meaning. For example, NULL(NULL) = V would mean that we know a value, but not the entity or the attribute. This is like the running joke from *Hitchhiker's Guide to the Galaxy* (Adams 1979), in which the answer to the question, "What is the meaning of life, the universe, and everything?" is 42. Likewise, "total ignorance" NULL, shown as NULL(NULL) = NULL, means that we have no information about the entity, even about its existence, its attributes, or their values.

6.3 Context and Missing Values

Create a domain called Tricolor that is limited to the values 'Red', 'White', and 'Blue' and a column in a table drawn from that domain with a UNIQUE constraint on it. If my table has a 'Red' and two NULL values in that column, I have some information about the two NULLs. I know they are either 'White' and 'Blue' or 'Blue' and 'White'. This is what Chris Date calls a "distinguished NULL," which means we have some information in it.

If my table has a 'Red', a 'White', and a NULL value in that column, can I change the last NULL to 'Blue' because it can only be 'Blue' under the rule? Or do I have to wait until I see an actual value for that row? There is no clear way to handle this in SQL. Multiple values cannot be put in a column, nor can the database automatically change values as part of the column declaration.

This idea can be carried farther with marked NULL values. For example, we are given a table of hotel rooms that has columns for check-in date and check-out date. We know the check-in date for each visitor, but we don't know their check-out dates. Instead we know relationships among the NULLs. We can put them into groups — Mr. and Mrs. X will check out on the same day, members of tour group Y will check out on the same day, and so forth. We can also add conditions on them: Nobody checks out before his check-in date, tour group Y will leave after 1993 Jan 07, and so forth.

Such rules can be put into SQL database schemas, but it is very hard to do. The usual method is to use procedural code in a host language to handle such things.

David McGoveran has proposed that each column that can have missing data should be paired with a column that encodes the reason for the absence of a value (McGoveran 1993, 1994a,b,c). The cost is a bit of extra logic, but the extra column makes it easy to write queries that include or exclude values based on the semantics of the situation.

6.4 NULLs and Logic

George Boole developed two-valued logic and attached his name to Boolean algebra forever (Boole 1854). This is not the only possible system, but it is the one that works best with a binary (two-state) computer and with a lot of mathematics.

SQL has three-valued logic: TRUE, FALSE, and UNKNOWN. Jan Łukasiewicz, the logician responsible for Polish notation, developed generalized multivalued logics; SQL is based on one of his schemes. The SQL standard still refers to Boolean operators rather than Łukasiewiczian operators, but nobody has complained about it, for the same reason that Hewlett-Packard never tried to market a "reverse Łukasiewiczian notation" calculator.

Programmers have trouble thinking in three values. UNKNOWN is a logical value and not the same as a NULL, which is a data value. That is why you have to say (x IS [NOT] NULL) in SQL and not use (x = NULL) instead. Theta operators are expressions of the form (x <comp op> y), when x or y or both are NULL, theta operators will return an UNKNOWN and not a NULL.

Here are the tables for the three operators that come with SQL. Łukasiewicz defined his logic systems around a generalized implication and negation operators from which he derived the other operators. It is comforting to see that the SQL operators have the same truth tables.

x	NOT
TRUE	FALSE
UNK	UNK
FALSE	TRUE

OR	TRUE	UNK	FALSE
TRUE	TRUE	TRUE	TRUE
UNK	TRUE	UNK	UNK
FALSE	TRUE	UNK	FALSE

AND	TRUE	UNK	FALSE
TRUE	TRUE	UNK	FALSE
UNK	UNK	UNK	FALSE
FALSE	FALSE	FALSE	FALSE

6.5 Comparing NULLs

The main trouble with NULLs is that it seems unnatural to work with them. The fact that a NULL cannot be compared to another NULL with what Dr. Codd called a theta operator and what programmers call a comparison operator (equal, not equal, less than, greater than, and so forth) means that we get three-valued logic instead of two-valued logic. Most programmers don't easily think in three values.

If I execute SELECT * FROM SomeTable WHERE SomeColumn = 2; and then execute SELECT * FROM SomeTable WHERE SomeColumn <> 2;, I expect to see all the rows of SomeTable between these two queries. In addition, however, I need to execute SELECT * FROM SomeTable WHERE SomeColumn IS NULL; to do that. The IS [NOT] NULL predicate will return only TRUE or FALSE.

SQL-92 has solved this problem by adding a new predicate of the form <search condition> IS [NOT] TRUE | FALSE | UNKNOWN, which will let you map any combination of three-valued logic to two values. For example, ((age < 18) AND (gender = 'Female')) IS NOT FALSE will return TRUE if (age IS NULL) or (gender IS NULL) and the remaining condition is not NULL.

6.6 Math and NULLs

NULLs propagate when they appear in arithmetic expressions (+, −, *, /) and return NULL results. See chapter 3 on numeric datatypes for more details.

6.7 Functions and NULLs

Most vendors propagate NULLs in the functions they offer as extensions of the standard ones required in SQL. For example, the cosine of a NULL will be NULL.

There are two functions, discussed in detail in the datatype section 3.5, that convert NULLs into values.

1.   NULLIF (V1, V2) returns a NULL when the first parameter equals the second parameter. The function is equivalent to the following case specification:

```
CASE WHEN (V1 = V2)
    THEN NULL
    ELSE V1
END
```

2.   COALESCE (V1, V2, V3, ..., Vn) processes the list from left to right and returns the first parameter that is not NULL. If all the values are NULL, it returns a NULL.

6.8 NULLs and Host Languages

This book will not go into the details of using SQL statements embedded in a particular host language. If you are writing in C, then I would recommend *Optimizing SQL: Embedded SQL in C* (Gulutzan and Pelzer 1994); unfortunately, there are no other trade books aimed at particular host languages, so you will have to depend on vendor manuals for help.

However, you should know how NULLs are handled when they have to be passed to a host program. No standard host language for which embeddings are defined supports NULLs, which is another good reason to avoid using them in your database schema.

Roughly speaking, the programmer mixes SQL statements bracketed by EXEC SQL and a language-specific terminator (the semicolon in Pascal and C, END-EXEC in Cobol, and so on) into the host program. This mixed-language program is run thru a preprocessor, which converts the SQL into procedure calls the host language can compile; then the host program is compiled in the usual way.

There is an EXEC SQL BEGIN DECLARE SECTION, EXEC SQL END
DECLARE SECTION pair that brackets declarations for the host parameter variables that will get values from the database via CURSORs. This
is the "neutral territory" where the host and the database pass information. SQL knows that it is dealing with a host variable because
these have a colon prefix added to them when they appear in an
SQL statement.

A CURSOR is an SQL query statement that executes and creates a
structure that looks like a sequential file. The records in the CURSOR
are returned, one at a time, to the host program in the BEGIN DECLARE
section with the FETCH statement. This avoids the impedance mis-
match between record processing in the host language and SQL's set
orientation.

NULLs are handled by declaring INDICATOR variables in the host
language BEGIN DECLARE section, which are paired with the host
variables. An INDICATOR is an exact numeric datatype with a scale of
zero — that is, some kind of integer in the host language.

The FETCH statement takes one row from the cursor, then converts
each SQL datatype into a host-language datatype and puts that result
into the appropriate host variable. If the SQL value was a NULL, the
INDICATOR is set to –1; if no indicator was specified, an exception
condition is raised. As you can see, the host program must be sure to
check the INDICATORs, because otherwise the value of the parameter
will be garbage. If the parameter is passed to the host language without any problems, the INDICATOR is set to zero. If the value being
passed to the host program is a non-NULL character string and it has
an indicator, the indicator is set to the length of the SQL string
and can be used to detect string overflows or to set the length of
the parameter.

6.9 Design Advice

It is a good idea to declare all your base tables with NOT NULL constraints on all columns whenever possible. NULLs confuse people who
do not know SQL and NULLs are expensive. NULLs are usually implemented with an extra bit somewhere in the row where the column
appears, rather than in the column itself. They adversely affect

storage requirements, indexing, and searching. If you know a default value for quantities, you can use a DEFAULT clause to insert it into the column automatically without changing the structure of the table. Zero is a common default for numeric columns, and blanks for character columns, but you are free to use any legal value you wish.

If you need to show missing values, design your encoding schemes with values for them. For example, the ISO sex codes are 0 = unknown, 1 = male, 2 = female, 9 = not applicable. No, you have not missed a new gender; code 9 is for legal persons, such as corporations. This use of all zeros and all nines for "Unknown" and "N/A" is quite common in numeric encoding schemes; and it is discussed in section 29.2.4 on designing encoding schemes.

Likewise, with names, you are probably better off using a special dummy string for unknown values rather than the general NULL. In particular, you can build a list of 'John Doe #1', 'John Doe #2', and so forth to differentiate them; and you cannot do that with a NULL.

Quantities have to use a NULL in some cases. There is a difference between an unknown quantity and a zero quantity; it is the difference between an empty gas tank and not having a car at all. Using negative numbers to represent missing quantities does not work because it makes accurate calculations too complex.

Dates and times have to use a NULL in some cases. Unfortunately, you often know relative times, but have no way of expressing them in a database. For example, a pay raise occurs some time after you have been hired, not before. A convict serving on death row should expect a release date resolved by an event: his termination by execution or by natural causes.

When programming languages had no DATE datatypes, this could have been handled with a character string of '9999-99-99 23:59:59.999999' for 'eternity' or 'the end of time'. When 4GL products with a DATE datatype came onto the market, programmers usually inserted the maximum possible date for 'eternity'. But again, this will show up in calculations and in summary statistics. The best trick was to use two fields, one for the date and one for a flag. But this made for fairly complex code in the 4GL.

Other Schema Objects

A SCHEMA CONSISTS OF the data, the operators, and the rules of a database you have defined. In the original SQL-89 language, the only data structure the user could access via SQL was the table, which could be permanent (base tables) or virtual (views).

SQL-92 also allows the DBA to define other schema objects, but most of these new features are not yet available in SQL implementations. Let's take a quick look at these new features, but without spending much time on their details.

7.1 Schema Creation

Obviously, every product has a way to create a new database, but none of them have agreed on the syntax. Some products are very concerned with physical storage requirements in the creation process; others are less concerned. The SQL-92 syntax for creating a new schema is minimal and simple, thus:

```
<schema definition> ::=
    CREATE SCHEMA <schema name clause>
        [<schema character set specification>]
        [<schema element>...]
```

```
<schema name clause> ::=
    <schema name>
  | AUTHORIZATION <schema authorization identifier>
  | <schema name> AUTHORIZATION <schema authorization identifier>


<schema authorization identifier> ::= <authorization identifier>


<schema character set specification> ::=
    DEFAULT CHARACTER SET <character set specification>


<schema element> ::=
    <domain definition>
  | <table definition>
  | <view definition>
  | <grant statement>
  | <assertion definition>
```

The schema can be created with an optional password or <schema authorization identifier>, set by the DBA. The DEFAULT CHARACTER SET clause is self-explanatory; it was added to satisfy ISO requirements for international use. I will discuss the other schema elements shortly.

The logical model for schema creation is that the whole schema comes into existence all at once. This is important because it means you can have circular references that would be impossible to add to the schema after creation. For example, you can let table T1 reference table T2 and vice versa. If T1 were created before T2, you would get an error message about a constraint referencing a nonexistent table. If T2 were created before T1, you would get the same problem in the other direction.

The time of creation can be important — for example, consider this problem from Robert Stearns of the University of Georgia's computer science department. Suppose you have a table for issuing Internet domains that looks like this:

```
CREATE TABLE Internet
(owner CHAR(10) NOT NULL,
 domain INTEGER NOT NULL,
 subdlow INTEGER NOT NULL,
 subdupr INTEGER NOT NULL,
PRIMARY KEY (owner, domain),
CHECK (subdupr > subdlow),
UNIQUE (owner, domain, subdlow),
UNIQUE (owner, domain, subdupr));
```

If you are not familar with Internet addresses, each one shows an owner who has unique numbered domains; within each of his domains, each subdomain has an upper and a lower bound to its range. The problem is to add the constraint that subdomains within a domain do not overlap. For example, you might add these rows:

```
INSERT INTO Internet VALUES ( 'Jones ', 3, 2, 254);
INSERT INTO Internet VALUES ( 'Smith ', 4, 2, 51);
INSERT INTO Internet VALUES ( 'Adams ', 4, 52, 254);
```

but you could not add

```
INSERT INTO Internet VALUES ( 'Smith ', 3, 2, 51);
```

because within domain 3, this would overlap with the existing 'Jones' row in the table. Once you have some valid rows in place, however, you then add this constraint to the table:

```
ALTER TABLE Internet
ADD CONSTRAINT non-overlap
CHECK (NOT EXISTS
   (SELECT *
       FROM Internet AS I1
     WHERE I1.owner = owner
          AND I1.domain = domain
          AND (I1.subdlow BETWEEN subdlow AND subdupr
             OR I1.subdupr BETWEEN subdlow AND subdupr));
```

The reason you have to add this constraint after you have some valid rows is that when the table is being initialized, the self join will not work. The table does not exist yet, so the CHECK() clause cannot find it to do the NOT EXISTS predicate. Likewise, when you are inserting rows into an empty table, they are not there yet, so the predicate fails. The timing of the creation is very important.

7.1.1 Schema Tables

The usual way an SQL engine keeps the information it needs about the schema is to put it in SQL tables. No two vendors agree on how the schema tables should be named or structured. The SQL-92 standard defines a set of standard schema tables, which no one implements. Though I doubt that anyone will ever implement them, I do feel that vendors will generate schema information in those formats for data exchange.

Every SQL product will allow users to query the schema tables. User groups will have libraries of queries for getting useful information out of the schema tables; you should take the time to get copies of them.

The SQL-92 standard also includes tables for temporal functions, collations, character sets, and so forth, but they are not yet implemented in actual products.

7.2 Temporary Tables

Tables in SQL-92 can be defined as persistent base tables, local temporary tables, or global temporary tables. The syntax is

```
<table definition> ::=
    CREATE [ { GLOBAL | LOCAL } TEMPORARY ] TABLE <table name>
        <table element list>
        [ ON COMMIT { DELETE | PRESERVE } ROWS ]
```

A local temporary table belongs to a single user. A global temporary table is shared by more than one user. When a session using a temporary table is over and the work is COMMITed, the table can be either emptied or saved for the next session.

This is a way of giving the users working storage without giving them CREATE TABLE (and therefore DROP TABLE and ALTER TABLE) privileges. This has been a serious problem in SQL products for some time.

7.3 CREATE ASSERTION

This schema object creates a constraint that is not attached to any table. The syntax is

```
<assertion definition> ::=
    CREATE ASSERTION <constraint name> <assertion check>
    [ <constraint attributes> ]

<assertion check> ::=
    CHECK <left paren> <search condition> <right paren>
```

As you would expect, there is a DROP ASSERTION statement, but no ALTER statement. An assertion can do things that a CHECK() clause attached to a table cannot do, because it is outside of the tables involved. For example, it is very hard to make a rule that the total number of employees in the company must be equal to the total number of employees in all the health program tables.

7.4 CREATE DOMAIN

The DOMAIN is a new schema element in SQL-92 that allows you to declare an *in-line macro* that will allow you to put a commonly used column definition in one place in the schema. You should expect to see this feature in SQL products shortly, since it is easy to implement. The syntax is

```
<domain definition> ::=
    CREATE DOMAIN <domain name> [AS] <data type>
        [<default clause>]
        [<domain constraint>...]
        [<collate clause>]
```

```
<domain constraint> ::=
    [<constraint name definition>]
    <check constraint definition> [<constraint attributes>]

<alter domain statement> ::=
    ALTER DOMAIN <domain name> <alter domain action>

<alter domain action> ::=
      <set domain default clause>
    | <drop domain default clause>
    | <add domain constraint definition>
    | <drop domain constraint definition>
```

It is important to note that a DOMAIN has to be defined with a basic datatype and not with other DOMAINs. Once declared, a DOMAIN can be used in place of a datatype declaration on a column.

The CHECK( ) clause is where you can put the code for validating data items with check digits, ranges, lists, and other conditions. Since the DOMAIN is in one place, you can make a good argument for writing

```
CREATE DOMAIN StateCode AS CHAR(2)
DEFAULT '?? '
CHECK (VALUE IN ( 'AL ', 'AK ', 'AZ ', ... ));
```

instead of

```
CREATE DOMAIN StateCode AS CHAR(2)
DEFAULT '?? '
CHECK (VALUE IN (SELECT state FROM StateCodeTable));
```

The second method would have been better if you did not have a DOMAIN and had to replicate the CHECK( ) clause in multiple tables in the database. This would collect the values and their changes in one place instead of many.

7.5 TRIGGERs

There is a feature in many versions of SQL, called a TRIGGER, that will execute a block of procedural code against the database when a table event occurs. This is not part of SQL-92, but has been proposed in the SQL3 working document. You can think of a TRIGGER as a generalization of the referential actions.

The procedural code is usually written in a proprietary language, but some products let you attach programs in standard procedural languages. A TRIGGER could be used to automatically handle discontinued merchandise, for example, by creating a credit slip in place of the original order item data.

There is a proposal for standardizing TRIGGERs in the current ANSI/ISO SQL3, using a procedural language based on ADA. The proposal is fairly complicated and no product has implemented it completely. You should look at what your particular vendor has given you if you want to work with TRIGGERs.

The advantages of TRIGGERs over declarative referential integrity is that you can do everything that declarative referential integrity can and almost anything else, too. The disadvantages are that the optimizer cannot get any data from the procedural code, the TRIGGERs take longer to execute, and they are not portable from product to product.

My advice would be to avoid TRIGGERs when you can use declarative referential integrity instead. If you do use them, check the code very carefully and keep it simple so that you will not hurt performance.

7.6 CREATE PROCEDURE

The PROCEDURE is a proposed schema element in SQL3 that allows you to declare and name a body of procedural code using the same proprietary language as the TRIGGERs or to invoke a host language library routine. The two major differences are that a PROCEDURE can accept and return parameters and it is invoked by a call from a user session.

Again, many SQL products have had their own versions of PROCEDURE, so you should look at what your particular vendor has given you, check the code very carefully, and keep it simple so that you will not hurt performance.

CHAPTER 8

Table Operations

THERE ARE ONLY three things you can do with a row in an SQL table: insert it into a table, delete it from a table, or update the values in it.

8.1 DELETE FROM Statement

The DELETE FROM statement in SQL removes zero or more rows of one table. Most, but not all, interactive SQL tools will tell the user how many rows were affected by an update operation and the SQL-92 standard requires the database engine to raise a completion condition of "no data" if there were zero rows.

There are two forms of DELETE FROM in SQL: positioned and searched. The positioned deletion is done with cursors; the searched deletion uses a WHERE clause like the search condition in a SELECT statement.

8.1.1 The DELETE FROM Clause

The syntax for a searched deletion statement is

```
<delete statement: searched> ::=
    DELETE FROM <table name>
    [WHERE <search condition>]
```

The DELETE FROM clause simply gives the name of the updatable table or view to be changed. Notice that no correlation name is allowed in the DELETE FROM clause; this is to avoid some self-referencing problems that could occur. For this discussion, we will assume the user doing the deletion has applicable DELETE privileges for the table.

The positioned deletion removes the row in the base table that is the source of the current cursor row. This means that the query from which the cursor is built must be a base table. The SQL-92 syntax is

```
<delete statement: positioned> ::=
    DELETE FROM <table name>
    WHERE CURRENT OF <cursor name>
```

CURSORs in SQL-92 are more extensive but also different from CURSORs in SQL-89 and in most current implementations, so this book will not spend too much time discussing them.

8.1.2 The WHERE Clause

The most important thing to remember about the WHERE clause is that it is optional. If there is no WHERE clause, all rows in the table are deleted. Most, but not all, interactive SQL tools will give the user a warning when he is about to do this and ask for confirmation. Do an immediate ROLLBACK to restore the table; if you COMMIT or have set the tool to automatically commit the work, then the data is pretty much gone. The DBA will have to do something to save you. And don't feel bad about doing it at least once while you are learning SQL.

The way most SQL implementations do a deletion is with two passes on the table. The first pass marks all of the candidate rows that meet the WHERE clause condition. The second pass removes them, either immediately or by marking them so that a housekeeping routine can later reclaim the storage space. The important point is that while the rows are being marked, the entire table is still available for the WHERE condition to use.

In many, if not most, cases this two-pass method does not make any difference in the results. The WHERE clause is usually a fairly simple predicate that references constants or relationships among the columns of a row. For example, we could clear out some employees with this deletion:

```
DELETE FROM Provisions
WHERE IQ <= 100;           -- constant in simple predicate
```

or

```
DELETE FROM Personnel
WHERE hat_size = IQ;    -- uses columns in the same row
```

A good optimizer could recognize that these predicates do not depend on the table as a whole, and would use a single scan for them. The two passes make a difference when the table references itself. Let's fire employees whose IQs are below average for their departments.

```
DELETE FROM Personnel
WHERE IQ < (SELECT AVG(IQ)
    FROM Personnel AS P1
    WHERE Personnel.dept = P1.dept);
```

We have the following data:

Personnel

emp	dept	IQ
Able	Acct	101
Baker	Acct	105
Charles	Acct	106
Henry	Mkt	101
Celko	Mkt	170
Popkin	HR	120
etc.		

If this were done one row at a time, we would first go to Accounting and find the average IQ, (101 + 105 + 106)/3 = 104, and fire Able. Then we would move sequentially down the table, and again find the average IQ, (105 + 106)/2 = 105.5 and fire Baker. Only Charles would escape the downsizing.

Now sort the table a little differently, so that the rows are visited in reverse alphabetic order. We first read Charles's IQ and compute the average for Accounting (101 + 105 + 106)/3 = 104, and retain Charles. Then we would move sequentially down the table, with the average IQ unchanged, so we also retain Baker. Able, however, is downsized when that row comes up.

It might be worth noting that DB2 would delete rows in the sequential order in which they appear in physical storage. WATCOM SQL has an optional `ORDER BY` clause that sorts the table, then does a sequential deletion on the table. This feature can be used to force a sequential deletion in cases where order does not matter, thus optimizing the statement by saving a second pass over the table. But it also can give the desired results in situations where you would otherwise have to use a cursor and a host language.

8.1.3 Deleting Based on Data in a Second Table

The `WHERE` clause can be as complex as you wish. This means you can have subqueries that use other tables. For example, to remove customers who have paid their bills from the Deadbeats table, you can use a correlated `EXISTS` predicate, thus:

```
DELETE FROM Deadbeats
    WHERE EXISTS (SELECT * FROM Payments AS P1
        WHERE Deadbeats.custno = P1.custno
            AND P1.amtpaid >= Deadbeats.amtdue);
```

The scope rules from `SELECT` statements also apply to the `WHERE` clause of a `DELETE FROM` statement, but it is a good idea to qualify all of the column names.

8.1.4 Deleting Within the Same Table

SQL allows a `DELETE FROM` statement to use columns, constants, and aggregate functions drawn from the table itself. For example, it is perfectly all right to remove everyone who is below average in a class with this statement:

```
DELETE FROM Students
    WHERE grade < (SELECT AVG(grade) FROM Students);
```

But the DELETE FROM clause does not allow for correlation names on the table in the DELETE FROM clause, so not all WHERE clauses that could be written as part of a SELECT statement will work in a DELETE FROM statement. For example, a self-join on the working table in a subquery is impossible.

```
DELETE FROM Employees AS B1  -- correlation name is INVALID SQL
    WHERE Employees.bossno = B1.empno
        AND Employees.salary > B1.salary);
```

There are ways to work around this. One trick is to build a VIEW of the table and use the VIEW instead of a correlation name. Consider the problem of finding all employees who are now earning more than their boss and deleting them. The employee table being used has a column for the employee's identification number, empno, and another column for the boss's employee identification number, bossno.

```
CREATE VIEW Bosses AS SELECT empno, salary FROM Employees;
```

```
DELETE FROM Employees
    WHERE EXISTS (SELECT *
        FROM Bosses AS B1
        WHERE Employees.bossno = B1.empno
        AND Employees.salary > B1.salary);
```

Simply using the Employees table in the subquery will not work. We need an outer reference in the WHERE clause to the Employees table in the subquery, and we cannot get that if the Employees table were in the subquery. Such views should be as small as possible so that the SQL engine can materialize them in main storage.

Redundant duplicates are unneeded copies of a row in a table. You most often get them because you did not put a UNIQUE constraint on the table and then you inserted the same data twice. Removing the extra copies from a table in SQL is much harder than you would think. If fact, if the rows are exact duplicates, you cannot do it with a simple `DELETE FROM` statement. Removing redundant duplicates involves saving one of them while deleting the other(s). But if SQL has no way to tell them apart, it will delete all rows that were qualified by the `WHERE` clause.

Another problem is that the deletion of a row from a base table can trigger referential actions, which can have unwanted side effects. For example, if there is a referential integrity constraint that says a deletion in Table1 will cascade and delete matching rows in Table2, removing redundant duplicates from T1 can leave me with no matching rows in T2. Yet I still have a referential integrity rule that says there must be at least one match in T2 for the single row I preserved in T1.

SQL-92 allows constraints to be deferrable or nondeferrable, so you might be able to suspend the referential actions that the transaction below would cause:

```
BEGIN
INSERT INTO WorkingTable     -- use DISTINCT to kill duplicates
SELECT DISTINCT * FROM MessedUpTable;
DELETE FROM MessedUpTable;  -- clean out messed-up table
INSERT INTO MessedUpTable    -- put working table into it
SELECT * FROM WorkingTable;
DROP TABLE WorkingTable;     -- get rid of working table
END;
```

8.1.5 Deleting in Multiple Tables Without Referential Integrity

There is no way to directly delete rows from more than one table in a single `DELETE FROM` statement. There are two approaches to removing related rows from multiple tables. One is to use a temporary table of the deletion values; the other is to use referential integrity actions as defined in SQL-92. For the purposes of this section, let us assume that we have a database with an Orders table and an Inventory table. Our business rule is that when something is out of stock, we delete it from all the orders.

Assume that no referential integrity constraints have been declared at all. First create a temporary table of the products to be deleted based on your search criteria, then use that table in a correlated sub-query to remove rows from each table involved.

```
BEGIN
CREATE TABLE Discontinue (partno INTEGER NOT NULL UNIQUE);

INSERT INTO Discontinue
SELECT DISTINCT partno -- pick out the items to be removed
    FROM ...
    WHERE ...;              -- using whatever criteria you require

DELETE FROM Orders
    WHERE partno IN (SELECT partno FROM Discontinue);

DELETE FROM Inventory
    WHERE partno IN (SELECT partno FROM Discontinue);

DROP TABLE Discontinue;
END;
```

8.2 INSERT INTO Statement

The INSERT INTO statement is the only way to get new data into a base table. In practice, there are always other tools for loading large amounts of data into a table, but they are very vendor-dependent.

8.2.1 INSERT INTO Clause

The SQL-92 syntax for INSERT INTO is

```
<insert statement> ::=
    INSERT INTO <table name>
        <insert columns and source>

<insert columns and source> ::=
        [(<insert column list>) ] <query expression>
    | VALUES (<insert values list>)
    | DEFAULT VALUES
```

The two basic forms of an INSERT INTO are a single-row insertion and a query insertion. The single-row insertion is done with a VALUES() clause. The list of insert values usually consists of constants or explicit NULLs, but in theory they could be almost any expression in the SQL-92 standard, including scalar SELECT subqueries. Though this is legal SQL, I have not yet found a use for it or a product that supports it.

The SQL-92 DEFAULT VALUE clause is a new shorthand for VALUES (DEFAULT, DEFAULT, ..., DEFAULT), so it is just shorthand for a particular single-row insertion.

The single-row insertion is a simple tool, mostly used in interactive sessions to put in small amounts of data.

A query insertion executes the query and produces a working table, which is inserted into the target table all at once. In both cases, the optional list of columns in the target table has to be unioncompatible with the columns in the query or with the values in the VALUES clause. Any column not in the list will be assigned NULL or its explicit DEFAULT value.

8.2.2 The Nature of Inserts

In theory, an insert using a query will place the rows from the query in the target table all at once. The set-oriented nature of an insertion means that a statement like

```
INSERT INTO SomeTable (somekey, transactiontime)
SELECT millions, CURRENT_TIMESTAMP
    FROM HugeTable;
```

will have one value for transactiontime in all the rows of the result, no matter how long it takes to load them into SomeTable.

Keeping things straight requires a lot of checking behind the scenes. The insertion can fail if just one row violates a constraint on the target table. The usual physical implementation is to put the rows into the target table, but to mark the work as uncommitted until the whole transaction has been validated. Once the system knows that the insertion is to be committed, it must rebuild all the indexes.

Rebuilding indexes will lock out other users and might require sorting the table if the table had a unique or clustered index.

If you have had experience with a file system, your first thought might be to drop the indexes, insert the new data, sort the table, and reindex it. The utility programs for index creation can actually benefit from having a known ordering. Unfortunately, this trick does not always work in SQL. The indexes maintain the uniqueness and referential integrity constraints and cannot be easily dropped and restored. Files stand alone; tables are part of a whole database.

8.2.3 Bulk Load and Unload Utilities

All versions of SQL have a language extension or utility program that will let you read data from an external file directly into a table. There is no standard for this tool, so they are all different. Most of these utilities require the name of the file and the format it is written in. The simpler versions of the utility just read the file and put it into a single target table. At the other extreme, Oracle uses a miniature language that can do simple editing as each record is read.

If you use a simpler tool, it is a good idea to build a working table in which you stage the data for cleanup before loading it into the actual target table. You can apply edit routines, look for duplicates, and put the bad data into another working table for inspection.

The corresponding output utility, which converts a table into a file, usually offers a choice of format options; any computations and selection can be done in SQL. Some of these programs will accept a SELECT statement or a VIEW; some will only convert a base table. Most tools now have an option to output INSERT INTO statements along with the appropriate CREATE TABLE and CREATE INDEX statements.

8.3 The UPDATE Statement

The function of the UPDATE statement in SQL is to change the values in zero or more columns of zero or more of rows of one table. Most, but not all, SQL implementations will tell you how many rows were affected by an update operation. There are two forms of UPDATE in SQL: positioned and searched. The positioned UPDATE is done with

cursors; the searched UPDATE uses a WHERE that resembles the search
condition in a SELECT statement.

There will no mention of the positioned UPDATEs in this book, for
several reasons. CURSORs are used in a host programming language,
and we are concerned with pure SQL whenever possible. Secondly,
CURSORs in SQL-92 are different from CURSORs in SQL-89 and in current implementations, and are not completely available in any implementations at the time of this writing.

8.3.1 The UPDATE Clause

The syntax for a searched UPDATE statement is

```
<update statement> ::=
    UPDATE <table name>
        SET <set clause list>
    [WHERE <search condition>]

<set clause list> ::=
    <set clause> [{ , <set clause> }...]

<set clause> ::=
    <object column> = <update source>

<update source> ::= <value expression> | NULL | DEFAULT

<object column> ::= <column name>
```

The UPDATE clause simply gives the name of the updatable table or
view to be changed. Notice that no correlation name is allowed in the
UPDATE clause; this is to avoid some self-referencing problems that
could occur. The SET clause is a list of columns to be changed or
made; the WHERE clause tells the statement which rows to use. For this
discussion, we will assume the user doing the update has applicable
UPDATE privileges for each <object column>.

8.3.2 The WHERE Clause

As mentioned, the most important thing to remember about the WHERE
clause is that it is optional. If there is no WHERE clause, all rows in the

table are changed. This is a common error; if you make it, immediately execute a ROLLBACK command.

8.3.3 The SET Clause

Each assignment in the <set clause list> is executed in parallel and each SET clause changes all the qualified rows at once. Or at least that is the theoretical model. In practice, implementations will first mark all of the qualified rows in the table in one pass, using the WHERE clause.

If there were no problems, such as finding zero rows that met the criteria, then the SQL engine makes a copy of each marked row in working storage. Each SET clause is executed based on the old row image and the results are put in the new row image. Finally, the new rows replace the old rows. If an error occurs during all of this, then the table is left unchanged and the errors are reported.

This parallelism is not like what you find in a traditional third-generation programming language, so it may be hard to learn. This feature lets you write a statement that will swap the values in two columns, thus:

```
UPDATE MyTable
SET a = b, b = a;
```

This is not the same thing as

```
UPDATE MyTable
SET a = b;
UPDATE MyTable
SET b = a;
```

In the first UPDATE, columns a and b will swap values in each row. In the second pair of UPDATEs, column a will get all of the values of column b in each row. In the second UPDATE of the pair, a, which now has the same value as the original value of b, will be written back into column b — no change at all.

There are some limits as to what the value expression can be. The same column cannot appear more than once in a <set clause list> — which makes sense, given the parallel nature of the statement.

Since both go into effect at the same time, you would not know which SET clause to use.

8.3.4 Updating with a Second Table

Most updating is done with simple expressions of the form SET <column name> = <constant value>, because UPDATEs are done via data entry programs. It is also possible to have the <column name> on both sides of the equal sign! This will not change any values in the table, but can be used as a way to trigger referential actions that have an ON UPDATE condition.

However, the <set clause list> does not have to contain only simple expressions. It is possible to use one table to post summary data to another. The scope of the <table name> is the entire <update statement>, so it can be referenced in the WHERE clause. This is easier to explain with an example. Assume we have the following tables:

```
CREATE TABLE Customers
    (custno INTEGER NOT NULL,
    acctbalance DECIMAL(8,2) NOT NULL);


CREATE TABLE Payments
    (custno INTEGER NOT NULL,
    transno INTEGER NOT NULL,
    amt DECIMAL(8,2) NOT NULL);
```

The problem is to post all of the payment amounts to the balance in the Customers table, overwriting the old balance. Such a posting is usually a batch operation, so a searched UPDATE statement seems the logical approach. SQL-92 and some — but not all — current implementations allow you use the updated tables names in a subquery, thus:

```
UPDATE Customers
    SET acctbalance = acctbalance + (SELECT SUM(amt)
            FROM Payments AS P1
            WHERE Customers.custno = P1.custno);
```

When there is no payment, the scalar query will return an empty set. The SUM( ) of an empty set is always zero. One of the most common programming errors made when using this trick is to write a query that may return more than one row. If you did not think about it, you might have written the last example as

```
UPDATE Customers
    SET acctbalance = acctbalance + (SELECT amt
            FROM Payments AS P1
            WHERE Customers.custno = P1.custno);
```

But consider the case where a customer has made more than one payment and we have both of them in the Payments table; the whole transaction will fail. The UPDATE statement should return an error message and ROLLBACK the entire UPDATE statement. In the first example, however, we know that we will get a scalar result because there is only one SUM(amt).

The second common programming error that is made with this kind of UPDATE is to use an aggregate function that does not return zero when it is applied to an empty table, such as the AVG(). Suppose we wanted to post the average payment amount made by the Customers; we could not just replace SUM() with AVG() and acctbalance with avgbalance in the above UPDATE. Instead, we would have to add a WHERE clause to the UPDATE that gives us only those customers who made a payment, thus:

```
UPDATE Customers
    SET payment = (SELECT AVG(P1.amt)
            FROM Payments P1
            WHERE Customers.custno = P1.custno)
WHERE EXISTS (SELECT * FROM Payments P1
            WHERE Customers.custno = P1.custno);
```

You can use the WHERE clause to avoid NULLs in cases where a NULL would propagate in a calculation.

8.3.5 Updating Within the Same Table

An <update source> can have NULL or DEFAULT as a value, assuming that the <object column> allows them. Most of the time, however, an

UPDATE will use a value expression, which will probably be a constant or a bit of simple arithmetic done on the column using the column itself or other columns in the same row.

The one rule is that a value expression in a SET clause shall not directly contain a <set function specification>. That means I cannot write something like

```
UPDATE Customers SET age = AVG(age);  -- Not valid SQL
```

However, it is sometimes handy to reference a table as a whole to make an update. The tricks for doing this involve creating VIEWs or a working table and can be shown easily with another example.

Rick Vicik had an article in *SQL Forum*, "Advanced Transact SQL" (Vicik 1993), in which he proposed the problem of finding all employees who are now earning as much as or more than their boss and reducing each such employee's salary to 90% of the boss's salary. The employee table being used has a column for the employee's identification number, empno, and another column for the boss's employee identification number, bossno.

The reason that you cannot do this directly in most versions of SQL is that the UPDATE statement cannot use a correlation name in the SET clause. Sybase's Transact SQL and Gupta's SQLBase are two exceptions. The query could be done in SQLBase as

```
UPDATE Employees AS Boss    -- Not standard SQL!
    SET Employees.salary = (Boss.salary * 0.90)
WHERE Employees.empno = Boss.empno
    AND Employees.salary >= Boss.salary;
```

But another trick will work in standard SQL. First construct a working table or view of the employees who are being adjusted that looks like the original table, thus:

```
CREATE VIEW Adjust (empno, ..., newsalary)
AS SELECT worker.empno, ..., (boss.salary * 0.90)
    FROM Employees AS worker, Employees AS boss
    WHERE worker.bossno = boss.empno
    AND worker.salary >= boss.salary;
```

This view is also useful for generating a report on just what you did in case the auditor or the irate employee wants to know. Now use an UPDATE with this view to drive it, just as we used a second table to construct a scalar result before:

```
UPDATE Employees
   SET salary = (SELECT MAX(newsalary)
           FROM Adjustment
           WHERE Adjustment.empno = Employees.empno)
 WHERE empno IN (SELECT empno FROM Adjustment);
```

The expression MAX(newsalary) is a trick used to guarantee that only a single value is returned by the subquery. This will signal the SQL parser that this is always a scalar value, so the right-hand side of the SET clause assignment is correct. Some implementations of SQL do not check for multiple rows in a subquery until runtime, not at compile time. Use the MAX() trick to guarantee portability of your code.

If the WHERE clause in the UPDATE statement were not there, the salaries for the unadjusted employees would be set to NULL, the result of the subquery expression when it cannot find a matching empno in both tables.

8.3.6 Updating a Primary Key

Updating a primary key is different from updating a non-key column. You must still preserve the uniqueness of the key after the update. Early version of DB2 and other SQLs did not implement UPDATE properly in the case of keys and other columns that were declared with a unique constraint. Consider a table defined as

```
CREATE TABLE MyList
(seqno INTEGER PRIMARY KEY,
 stuff1 CHAR(1) NOT NULL,
 ...
 stuffN CHAR(1) NOT NULL);
```

where seqno is a sequential identification number. The problem is to bump all of the existing item numbers by 1, so that we can add a new item number 1 to the table. This could be done with these two statements:

```
BEGIN
UPDATE MyList
   SET seqno = seqno + 1;
INSERT INTO MyList VALUES (1, 'a1', ..., 'aN');
END;
```

The reason this could fail in some early SQL implementations is that these versions of SQL attempted to do a row-at-a-time update inside the engine, as if they were using a cursor on the table, and to check the uniqueness after each row update. If the table is sorted in ascending order, the SQL engine reads the first row (seqno = 1) and changes it to (seqno = 2); but the second row already has 2 for a key value, so the update fails immediately. This problem was present in DB2 at one time.

If the table has been accessed in descending order, then it works just fine. If the table is not ordered, then the failure will occur at some random row and drive you crazy. The best way to handle this is to first convert all of the seqno values to negatives, update them, and then insert the new value.

```
BEGIN   -- work around for nonstandard SQL
UPDATE MyList SET seqno = - (seqno + 1);
UPDATE MyList SET seqno = - (seqno);
INSERT INTO MyList VALUES (1, 'a1', ...,'aN');
END;
```

Another method is to drop the UNIQUE or PRIMARY KEY constraints or indexes, do the update, insert the new row, and then use the ALTER statement to restore the constraints or a CREATE INDEX statement to rebuild unique indexes. However, the time required can be costly, since you are going to lock everyone out of the database while you do it.

CHAPTER 9

Comparison or Theta Operators

THE LARGE NUMBER of datatypes in SQL makes doing comparisons a little harder than in other programming languages. Values of one datatype have to be promoted to values of the other datatype before the comparison can be done. The available datatypes are implementation- and hardware-dependent, so read the manuals for your product.

The comparison operators are overloaded and will work for numeric, character, and datetime datatypes. The symbols and meanings for comparison operators are shown in the table below.

numeric		character	datetime
<	less than	(collates before)	(earlier than)
=	equal	(collates equal to)	(same time as)
>	greater than	(collates after)	(later than)
<=	at most	(collates before or equal to)	(no earlier than)
<>	not equal	(not the same as)	(not the same time as)
>=	at least	(collates after or equal to)	(no later than)

You will also see != or ~= for "not equal to" in SQL implementation. These symbols are borrowed from the C and PL/I programming languages, respectively, and have never been part of standard SQL.

9.1 Converting Datatypes

Numeric datatypes are all mutually comparable and mutually assignable. If an assignment would result in a loss of the most significant digits, an exception condition is raised. If least significant digits are lost, the implementation defines what rounding or truncating occurs and does not report an exception condition.

Most often, one value is converted to the same datatype as the other and then the comparison is done in the usual way. The chosen datatype is the "higher" of the two, using the following ordering: SMALLINT, INTEGER, DECIMAL, NUMERIC, REAL, FLOAT, DOUBLE-PRECISION.

Floating-point hardware will often affect comparisons for REAL, FLOAT, and DOUBLEPRECISION numbers. There is no good way to avoid this, since it is not always reasonable to use DECIMAL or NUMERIC in their place. A host language will probably use the same floating-point hardware, so at least errors will be constant across the application.

CHARACTER and CHARACTER VARYING datatypes are comparable if and only if they are taken from the same character repertoire. That means that ASCII characters cannot be compared to graphics characters, English cannot be compared to Arabic, and so on. In most implementations this is not a problem, because the database has only one repertoire. The comparison takes the shorter of the two strings and pads it with spaces. The strings are compared position by position from left to right, using the collating sequence for the repertoire — ASCII or EBCDIC in most cases.

DATETIME datatypes are mutually assignable only if the source and target of the assignment have the same DATETIME fields. That is, you cannot compare a date and a time.

The CAST() operator can do explicit type conversions before you do a comparison. Here is a table of the valid combinations of source and target datatypes in SQL-92. Y means that the combination is syntactically valid without restriction; M indicates that the combination is valid, subject to other syntax rules; *N* indicates that the combination is not valid.

<value expr> <cast target>

	EN	AN	VC	FC	VB	FB	D	T	TS	YM	DT
EN	Y	Y	Y	Y	N	N	N	N	N	M	M
AN	Y	Y	Y	Y	N	N	N	N	N	N	N
C	Y	Y	M	M	Y	Y	Y	Y	Y	Y	Y
B	N	N	Y	Y	Y	Y	N	N	N	N	N
D	N	N	Y	Y	N	N	Y	N	Y	N	N
T	N	N	Y	Y	N	N	N	Y	Y	N	N
TS	N	N	Y	Y	N	N	Y	Y	Y	N	N
YM	M	N	Y	Y	N	N	N	N	N	Y	N
DT	M	N	Y	Y	N	N	N	N	N	N	Y

where

    EN = exact numeric
    AN = approximate numeric
    C = character (fixed- or variable-length)
    FC = fixed-length character
    VC = variable-length character
    B = bit string (fixed- or variable-length)
    FB = fixed-length bit string
    VB = variable-length bit string
    D = date
    T = time
    TS = timestamp
    YM = year-month interval
    DT = day-time interval

9.2 Row Comparisons in SQL-92

SQL-92 generalized the theta operators so they would work on row expressions and not just on scalars. This is not a popular feature yet, but it is very handy for situations where a key is made from more than one column, and so forth. This makes SQL more orthogonal and it has an intuitive feel to it. Take three row constants:

```
A = (10, 20, 30, 40);
B = (10, NULL, 30, 40);
C = (10, NULL, 30, 100);
```

It seems reasonable to define a tuple comparison as valid only when the datatypes of each corresponding column in the rows are union-compatible. If not, the operation is an error and should report a warning.

It also seems reasonable to define the results of the comparison to the ANDed results of each corresponding column using the same operator. That is, (A = B) becomes

```
((10, 20, 30, 40) = (10, NULL, 30, 40));
```

becomes:

```
((10 = 10) AND (20 = NULL) AND (30 = 30) AND (40 = 40))
```

becomes:

```
(TRUE AND UNKNOWN AND TRUE AND TRUE);
```

becomes:

```
(UNKNOWN);
```

This seems to be reasonable and conforms to the idea that a NULL is a missing value that we expect to resolve at a future date. Now consider the comparison (A = C), which becomes

```
((10, 20, 30, 40) = (10, NULL, 30, 100));
```

becomes:

```
((10 = 10) AND (20 = NULL) AND (30 = 30) AND (40 = 100));
```

becomes:

```
(TRUE AND UNKNOWN AND TRUE AND FALSE);
```

becomes:

```
(UNKNOWN);
```

There is no way to pick a value for column 2 of row C such that the UNKNOWN result will change to TRUE. This leaves you with a situation that is not very intuitive. The first case can resolve to TRUE or FALSE, but the second case can only go to FALSE.

The SQL-92 standard decided that the theta predicates would work as shown in the table below. The expression RX <comp op> RY is shorthand for a row RX compared to a row RY; likewise, RXi means the ith column in the row RX. The results are still TRUE, FALSE, or UNKNOWN, if there is no error in type matching. The rules favor solid tests for TRUE or FALSE, using UNKNOWN as a last resort. The rules are

1. RX = RY is TRUE if and only if RXi = RYi for all i.

2. RX <> RY is TRUE if and only if RXi <> RYi for some i.

3. RX < RY is TRUE if and only if RXi = RYi
   for all $i < n$ and RXn < RYn for some n.

4. RX > RY is TRUE if and only if RXi = RYi
   for all $i < n$ and RXn > RYn for some n.

5. RX <= RY is TRUE if and only if RX = RY or RX < RY.

6. RX >= RY is TRUE if and only if RX = RY or RX > RY.

7. RX = RY is FALSE if and only if RX 133 RY is TRUE.

8. RX <> RY is FALSE if and only if RX = RY is TRUE.

9. RX < RY is FALSE if and only if RX >= RY is TRUE.

10. RX > RY is FALSE if and only if RX <= RY is TRUE.

11. RX <= RY is FALSE if and only if RX > RY is TRUE.

12. RX >= RY is FALSE if and only if RX < RY is TRUE.

13. RX <comp op> RY is unknown
    if and only if RX <comp op> RY is neither TRUE nor FALSE.

The idea of these rules is that as you read the rows from left to right, the values in one row are always greater than (or less than) those in the other row after some column. This is how it would work if you were alphabetizing words. The negations are defined so that the

NOT operator will still have its usual properties. Notice that a NULL in a row will give an UNKNOWN result in a comparison.

These row comparisons can be done in SQL-89, but translating the predicates is messy. Consider this SQL-92 expression:

```
(a, b, c) < (x, y, z)
```

which becomes

```
((a < x)
OR ((a = x) AND (b < y))
OR ((a = x) AND (b = y) AND (c < z)))
```

The SQL-89 standard allowed only scalar subqueries on the right-hand side and a single-value expression on the left-hand side of the <comp op> ALL <subquery> and <comp op> SOME <subquery> predicates. SQL-92 is more orthogonal; it allows a single-row expression of any sort, including a single-row subquery, on the left-hand side. Likewise, the BETWEEN predicate can use row expressions in any position in SQL-92.

Valued Predicates

VALUED PREDICATES IS my term for a set of related unary Boolean predicates that test for the logical value or NULL value of their operand. The IS NULL has always been part of SQL, but the logical IS predicate is new to SQL-92 and is not well implemented at this time.

10.1 IS NULL Predicate

The IS NULL predicate is a test for a NULL value in a column with the syntax

```
<null predicate> ::= <row value constructor> IS [NOT] NULL
```

It is the only way to test to see if an expression is NULL or not, and it has been in SQL-86 and all later versions of the standard. The SQL-92 standard extended it to accept `<row value constructor>` instead of a single column or scalar expression. This extended version will start showing up in implementations when other row expressions are allowed.

If all the values in the row R are the NULL value, then R IS NULL is TRUE; otherwise, it is FALSE. If none of the values in R are NULL value, R IS NOT NULL is TRUE; otherwise, it is FALSE. The case where the row is a mix of NULL and non-NULL values is defined by the table below, where *Degree* means the number of columns in the row expression.

Expression	R IS NULL	R IS NOT NULL	NOT R IS NULL	NOT R IS NOT NULL
Degree = 1				
NULL	TRUE	FALSE	FALSE	TRUE
No NULL	FALSE	TRUE	TRUE	FALSE
Degree > 1				
All NULLs	TRUE	FALSE	FALSE	TRUE
Some NULLs	FALSE	FALSE	TRUE	TRUE
No NULLs	FALSE	TRUE	TRUE	FALSE

Note that R IS NOT NULL has the same result as NOT R IS NULL if and only if R is of degree 1. This is a break in the usual pattern of predicates with a NOT option in them. Here are some examples:

```
(1, 2, 3) IS NULL = FALSE
(1, NULL, 3) IS NULL = FALSE
(1, NULL, 3) IS NOT NULL = FALSE
(NULL, NULL, NULL) IS NULL = TRUE
(NULL, NULL, NULL) IS NOT NULL = FALSE
NOT (1, 2, 3) IS NULL = TRUE
NOT (1, NULL, 3) IS NULL = TRUE
NOT (1, NULL, 3) IS NOT NULL = TRUE
NOT (NULL, NULL, NULL) IS NULL = TRUE
NOT (NULL, NULL, NULL) IS NOT NULL = FALSE
```

10.1.1 Sources of NULLs

It is important to remember where NULLs can occur. They are not just a possible value in a column. Aggregate functions on empty sets, OUTER JOINs, arithmetic expressions with NULLs, and so forth all return NULLs. These constructs often show up as columns in VIEWs.

10.2 IS [NOT]{ TRUE | FALSE | UNKNOWN } Predicate

This predicate tests a condition that has the truth value TRUE, FALSE, or UNKNOWN, and returns TRUE or FALSE. The syntax is

```
<Boolean test> ::=
    <Boolean primary> [ IS [ NOT ] <truth value> ]


<truth value> ::= TRUE | FALSE | UNKNOWN


<Boolean primary> ::=
    <predicate> | <left paren> <search condition> <right paren>
```

As you would expect, the expression IS NOT <logical value> is the same as NOT (IS <logical value>), so the predicate can be defined by the table below.

IS condition	TRUE	FALSE	UNKNOWN
TRUE	TRUE	FALSE	FALSE
FALSE	FALSE	TRUE	FALSE
UNKNOWN	FALSE	FALSE	TRUE

If you are familiar with some of Date's writings, his MAYBE(x) predicate is not the same as the ANSI (x) IS NOT FALSE predicate, but it is equivalent to the (x) IS UNKNOWN predicate. Date's predicate excludes the case where all conditions in the predicate are TRUE.

Date points out that it is difficult to ask a conditional question in English. To borrow one of Date's examples (Date 1990), consider the problem of finding employees who *may be* programmers born before 18 January 1941 with a salary less than $50,000.

```
SELECT *
    FROM Employees
WHERE (job = 'Programmer'
    AND dob < CAST ('1941-01-18' TO DATE)
    AND salary < 50000) IS NOT UNKNOWN;
```

could be expanded out in SQL-89 to

```
SELECT *
    FROM Employees
WHERE (job = 'Programmer'
    AND dob < CAST ('1941-01-18' TO DATE)
    AND salary < 50000)

OR (job IS NULL
    AND dob < CAST ('1941-01-18' TO DATE)
    AND salary < 50000)

OR (job = 'Programmer'
    AND dob IS NULL
    AND salary < 50000)

OR (job = 'Programmer'
    AND dob < CAST ('1941-01-18' TO DATE)
    AND salary IS NULL)

OR (job IS NULL
    AND dob IS NULL
    AND salary < 50000)

OR (job IS NULL
    AND dob < CAST ('1941-01-18' TO DATE)
    AND salary IS NULL)

OR (job = 'Programmer'
    AND dob IS NULL
    AND salary IS NULL)

OR (job IS NULL
    AND dob IS NULL
    AND salary IS NULL);
```

CHAPTER

11

LIKE Predicate

THE LIKE PREDICATE is a string pattern-matching test with the syntax

```
<like predicate> ::=
    <match value> [NOT] LIKE <pattern>
        [ESCAPE <escape character>]

<match value> ::= <character value expression>
<pattern> ::= <character value expression>
<escape character> ::= <character value expression>
```

The expression M NOT LIKE P is equivalent to NOT (M LIKE P), which follows the usual syntax pattern in SQL. There are two wild-cards allowed in the <pattern> string. They are the '%' and '_' characters. The '_' character represents a single arbitrary character; the '%' character represents an arbitrary substring, possibly of length zero. Notice that there is no way to represent zero or one arbitrary character. This is not the case in many text-search languages, and can lead to problems or very complex predicates.

Any other character in the <pattern> represents that character itself. This means that SQL patterns are case-sensitive, but many vendors allow you to set case sensitivity on or off at the database system level.

The <escape character> is part of the SQL-92 standard and is not widely implemented. The <escape character> is used in the <pattern> to specify that the character that follows it is to be interpreted as a literal rather than a wildcard. This means that the escape character is followed by the escape character itself, an '_', or a '%'. C programmers are used to this convention, where the language defines the escape character as '\', so this is a good choice for SQL programmers too.

11.1 Tricks with Patterns

The '_' character tests much faster than the '%' character. The reason is obvious: the parser that compares a string to the pattern needs only one operation to match an underscore before it can move to the next character, but has to do some look-ahead parsing to resolve a percentage sign. The wildcards can be inserted in the middle or beginning of a pattern. Thus, 'B%K' will match 'BOOK', 'BLOCK', and 'BK', but it will not match 'BLOCKS'. The parser would scan each letter and classify it as a wildcard or an exact match. In the case of 'BLOCKS', the initial 'B' would be an exact match and the parser would continue; 'L', 'O', and 'C' have to be wildcard matches, since they don't appear in the pattern string; 'K' cannot be classified until we read the last letter. The last letter is 'S', so the match fails.

For example, given a column declared to be seven characters long, and a LIKE predicate looking for names that start with "Mac," you would usually write

```
SELECT *
  FROM People
WHERE (name LIKE 'Mac%');
```

but this might actually run faster:

```
SELECT *
  FROM People
 WHERE (name LIKE 'Mac_    ')
    OR (name LIKE 'Mac__   ')
    OR (name LIKE 'Mac___  ')
    OR (name LIKE 'Mac____');
```

The trailing blanks are also characters that can be matched exactly.

Putting a '%' at the front of a pattern is very time-consuming. For example, you might try to find all names that end in "-son" with the query

```
SELECT *
  FROM People
 WHERE (name LIKE '%son');
```

The use of underscores instead will make a real difference in most SQL implementations for this query, because most of them always parse from left to right.

```
SELECT *
  FROM People
 WHERE (name LIKE '_son   ')
    OR (name LIKE '__son  ')
    OR (name LIKE '___son ')
    OR (name LIKE '____son');
```

Remember that the '_' character requires a matching character and the '%' character does not. Thus, the query

```
SELECT *
  FROM People
 WHERE (name LIKE 'John_%');
```

and the query

```
SELECT *
  FROM People
 WHERE (name LIKE 'John%');
```

are subtly different. Both will match to 'Johnson' and 'Johns', but the first will not accept 'John' as a match. This is how you get a "one-or-more-characters" pattern match in SQL.

Remember that the <pattern> as well as the <match value> can be constructed with concatenation operators, SUBSTRING( ), and other string functions. For example, let's find people whose first names are part of their last names with the query

```
SELECT *
  FROM People
WHERE (lastname LIKE '%' || firstname || '%');
```

which will show us people like "John Johnson," "Anders Andersen," and "Bob McBoblin." This query will also run very slowly.

11.2 Results with NULL Values and Empty Strings

As you would expect, a NULL in the predicate returns an UNKNOWN result. The NULL can be the escape character, pattern, or match value.

If M and P are both character strings of length zero, M LIKE P defaults to TRUE. If one or both are longer than zero characters, you use the regular rules to test the predicate.

11.3. LIKE Is Not Equality

A very important point that is often missed is that two strings can be equal but not LIKE in SQL. The test of equality first pads the shorter of the two strings with rightmost blanks, then matches the characters in each, one for one. Thus 'Smith' and 'Smith   ' (with three trailing blanks) are equal. However, the LIKE predicate does no padding, so 'Smith' LIKE 'Smith   ' tests FALSE because there is nothing to match to the blanks.

A good trick to get around these problems is to use the TRIM( ) function to remove unwanted blanks from the strings within either or both of the two arguments.

CHAPTER
12

BETWEEN and OVERLAPS Predicates

T HE BETWEEN AND OVERLAPS predicates both offer a shorthand way of showing that one value lies within a range defined by two other values. BETWEEN works with scalar range limits; the OVERLAPS predicate looks at two time periods (defined either by start and end points or by a start and an INTERVAL) to see if they overlap in time.

12.1 The BETWEEN Predicate

The predicate <value expression> [NOT] BETWEEN <low value expr> AND <high value expr> is a feature of SQL that is used enough to deserve special attention. It is also just tricky enough to fool beginning programmers. This predicate is actually just short-hand for the expression

```
(((<low value expr> <= <value expression>)
    AND (<value expression> <= <high value expr>))
```

Please note that the end points are included in this definition. This predicate works with any datatypes that can be compared. Most programmers miss this fact and use it only for numeric values. It can be used for character strings and DATETIME data as well. The

<high value expr> and <low value expr> can be expressions or constants, but again, programmers tend to use just constants.

12.1.1 Results with NULL Values

The results of this predicate with NULL values for <value expression>, <low value expr>, or <high value expr> follow directly from the definition. If both <low value expr> and <high value expr> are NULL, the result is UNKNOWN for any value of <value expression>. If <low value expr> or <high value expr> is NULL, but not both of them, the result is determined by the value of <value expression> and its comparison with the remaining non-NULL term. If <value expression> is NULL, the results are UNKNOWN for any values of <low value expr> and <high value expr>.

12.1.2 Results with Empty Sets

Notice that if <high value expr> is less than <low value expr>, the expression will always be FALSE unless the value is NULL; then it is UNKNOWN. That is a bit confusing, since there is no value to which <value expression> could resolve itself that would produce a TRUE result. But this follows directly from expanding the definition.

12.1.3 Programming Tips

The BETWEEN range includes the end points, so you have to be careful. For example, changing a percent range on a test into a letter grade

Grades

low	high	grade
90	100	'A'
80	90	'B'
70	80	'C'
60	70	'D'
00	60	'F'

will not work when a student gets a grade on the borderline (90, 80, 70, or 60). One way to solve the problem is to change the table by adding 1 to the low scores. Of course, the student who got 90.1 will argue that he should have gotten an "A" and not a "B." If you add 0.01 to the low scores, the student who got 90.001 will argue that he should have gotten an "A" and not a "B." This is a problem with a continuous variable.

A better solution might be to change the predicate to (score BETWEEN low AND high) AND (score > low) or simply to ((low < score) AND (score <= high)). Neither approach will be much different in this example, since few values will fall on the borders between grades and this table is very, very small.

However, some indexing schemes might make the BETWEEN predicate the better choice for larger tables of this sort. They will keep index values in trees whose nodes hold a range of values (look up a description of the B tree family in a computer science book). An optimizer can compare the range of values in the BETWEEN predicate to the range of values in the index nodes as a single action. If the BETWEEN predicate were presented as two comparisons, it might execute them as separate actions against the database, which would be slower.

12.2 OVERLAPS Predicate

The OVERLAPS predicate is a feature not yet available in most SQL implementations because it requires more of the SQL-92 temporal datatypes than most implementations have. Many programmers have been "faking" the functionality of the INTERVAL datatype with the existing DATE and TIME features of their products.

12.2.1 Time Periods and OVERLAPS Predicate

An INTERVAL in SQL-92 is a measure of temporal duration, expressed in units such as a day, an hour, and so forth. This is how you add or subtract days to or from a date, hours and minutes to or from a time, and so forth. The standard is more complete than any existing implementation. When INTERVALs are more generally available, you will also have an OVERLAPS predicate, which compares two time periods. These time periods are defined as row values with two columns. The first column (the starting time) of the pair is always a DATETIME datatype and the second column (the finishing time) is either a DATE-TIME datatype or an INTERVAL datatype that can be used to compute a DATETIME. If the starting and finishing times are the same, this is an event. The rules for the OVERLAPS predicate are intuitive:

1. If the time periods are not events, they overlap when they share a common time period. Time periods do not include their end points.

2. If the first term of the predicate is an INTERVAL and the second term is an event (a DATETIME datatype), they overlap when the second term is in the time period (but is *not* the end point of the time period).

3. If the first and second terms are both events, they overlap only when they are equal.

4. If the starting time is NULL and the finishing time is a DATE-TIME value, the finishing time becomes the starting time and we have an event. If the starting time is NULL and the finishing time is an INTERVAL value, then both the finishing and starting times are NULL.

Consider a table of hotel guests with the days of their stays and a table of special events being held at the hotel. The tables might look like this:

```
CREATE TABLE Guests
(guestname CHARACTER(30) PRIMARY KEY
 arrival DATE NOT NULL,
 departure DATE NOT NULL,
 ...);
```

Guests

guestname	arrival	departure
Dorothy Gale	1999-02-01	1999-11-01
Indiana Jones	1999-02-01	1999-02-01
Don Quixote	1999-01-01	1999-10-01
James T. Kirk	1999-02-01	1999-02-28
Santa Claus	1999-12-01	1999-12-25

```
CREATE TABLE Celebrations
(eventname CHARACTER(30) PRIMARY KEY,
 start DATE NOT NULL,
 finish DATE NOT NULL,
 ...);
```

Celebrations

celebname	start	finish
Apple Month	1999-02-01	1999-02-28
Christmas Season	1999-12-01	1999-12-25
Garlic Festival	1999-01-15	1999-02-15
National Pear Week	1999-01-01	1999-01-07
New Year's Day	1999-01-01	1999-01-01
St. Fred's Day	1999-02-24	1999-02-24
Year of the Prune	1999-01-01	1999-12-31

The BETWEEN operator will work just fine with single dates that fall between the starting and finishing dates of these celebrations, but please remember that the BETWEEN predicate will include the end point of an interval and that the OVERLAPS predicate will not. To find out if a particular date occurs during an event, you can simply write queries like

```
SELECT guestname, ' arrived during ', celebname
    FROM Guests, Celebrations
WHERE arrival BETWEEN start AND finish
    AND arrival <> finish;
```

which will find the guests who arrived at the hotel during each event. The final predicate can be kept, if you want to conform to the ANSI convention, or dropped if that makes more sense in your situation. From now on, we will keep both end points to make the queries easier to read.

```
SELECT guestname, ' arrived during ', celebname
    FROM Guests, Celebrations
WHERE arrival BETWEEN start AND finish;
```

guestname	' arrived during	' celebname
Dorothy Gale	arrived during	Apple Month
Dorothy Gale	arrived during	Garlic Festival
Dorothy Gale	arrived during	Year of the Prune
Indiana Jones	arrived during	Apple Month
Indiana Jones	arrived during	Garlic Festival
Indiana Jones	arrived during	Year of the Prune
Don Quixote	arrived during	National Pear Week
Don Quixote	arrived during	New Year's Day
Don Quixote	arrived during	Year of the Prune
James T. Kirk	arrived during	Apple Month
James T. Kirk	arrived during	Garlic Festival
James T. Kirk	arrived during	Year of the Prune
Santa Claus	arrived during	Christmas Season
Santa Claus	arrived during	Year of the Prune

The obvious question is which guests were at the hotel during each event. A common programming error when trying to find out if two intervals overlap is to write the query with the BETWEEN predicate, thus:

```
SELECT guestname, ' was here during ', celebname
    FROM Guests, Celebrations
WHERE arrival BETWEEN start AND finish
    OR departure BETWEEN start AND finish;
```

This is wrong, because it does not cover the case where the event began and finished during the guest's visit. Seeing his error, the programmer will sit down and draw a timeline diagram of all four possible overlapping cases, like this:

Fig. 12.1

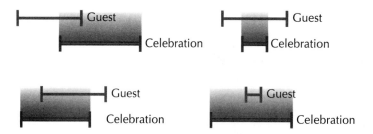

So the programmer adds more predicates, thus:

```
SELECT guestname, ' was here during ', celebname
    FROM Guests, Celebrations
WHERE arrival BETWEEN start AND finish
    OR departure BETWEEN start AND finish
    OR start BETWEEN arrival AND departure
    OR finish BETWEEN arrival AND departure;
```

A thoughtful programmer will notice that the last predicate is not needed and might drop it, but either way, this is a correct query. But it is not the best answer. In the case of the overlapping intervals, there are two cases where a guest's stay at the hotel and an event do not both fall within the same time frame: Either the guest checked out before the event started or the event ended before the guest arrived. If you want to do the logic, that is what the first predicate will work out to be when you also add the conditions that arrival <= departure and start <= finish. But it is easier to see in a timeline diagram, thus:

Fig 12.2

Both cases can be represented in one SQL statement as

```
SELECT guestname, celebname
    FROM Guests, Celebrations
WHERE NOT ((departure < start) OR (arrival > finish));
```

VIEW GuestsEvents

guestname	celebname
Dorothy Gale	Apple Month
Dorothy Gale	Garlic Festival
Dorothy Gale	St. Fred's Day
Dorothy Gale	Year of the Prune
Indiana Jones	Apple Month

(cont.)	**guestname**	**celebname**
	Indiana Jones	Garlic Festival
	Indiana Jones	Year of the Prune
	Don Quixote	Apple Month
	Don Quixote	Garlic Festival
	Don Quixote	National Pear Week
	Don Quixote	New Year's Day
	Don Quixote	St. Fred's Day
	Don Quixote	Year of the Prune
	James T. Kirk	Apple Month
	James T. Kirk	Garlic Festival
	James T. Kirk	St. Fred's Day
	James T. Kirk	Year of the Prune
	Santa Claus	Christmas Season
	Santa Claus	Year of the Prune

This VIEW is handy for other queries. The reason for using the NOT in the WHERE clause is so that you can add or remove it to reverse the sense of the query. For example, to find out how many celebrations each guest could have seen, you would write

```
CREATE VIEW GuestCelebrations (guestname, celebname)
AS SELECT guestname, celebname
    FROM Guests, Celebrations
    WHERE NOT ((departure < start) OR (arrival > finish));

SELECT guestname, COUNT(*) AS celebcount
    FROM GuestCelebrations
GROUP BY guestname;
```

Result

guestname	**celebcount**
Dorothy Gale	4
Indiana Jones	3
Don Quixote	6
James T. Kirk	4
Santa Claus	2

and then to find out how many guests were at the hotel during each celebration, you would write

```
SELECT celebname, COUNT(*) AS guestcount
    FROM GuestCelebrations
GROUP BY celebname;
```

Result

celebname	guestcount
Apple Month	4
Christmas Season	1
Garlic Festival	4
National Pear Week	1
New Year's Day	1
St. Fred's Day	3
Year of the Prune	5

This last query is only part of the story. What the hotel management really wants to know is how many room nights were sold for a celebration. A little algebra tells you that the length of an event is (Event.finish − Event.start + 1) and that the length of a guest's stay is (Guest.departure − Guest.arrival + 1). Let's do one of those timeline charts again:

Fig 12.3

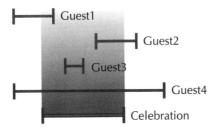

Guest1
Guest2
Guest3
Guest4
Celebration

What we want is the part of the Guests interval that is inside the Celebrations interval. Guests 1 and 2 spent only part of their time at the celebration; Guest 3 spent all of his time at the celebration and Guest 4 stayed even longer than the celebration. That interval is

defined by the two points (greater(arrival, start),
lesser(departure, finish)).

Unfortunately, standard SQL does not have these greater()
and lesser() functions that choose the greatest or least value in a
variable-length parameter list, as some other programming languages
do. But you can use the aggregate functions in SQL to build a VIEW on
a VIEW, like this:

```
CREATE VIEW Working (guestname, celebname, entered, exited)
AS SELECT GE.guestname, GE.celebname, start, finish
       FROM GuestCelebrations AS GE, Celebrations AS E1
   WHERE E1.celebname = GE.celebname
UNION
   SELECT GE.guestname, GE.celebname, arrival, departure
       FROM GuestCelebrations AS GE, Guests AS G1
   WHERE G1.guestname = GE.guestname;
```

VIEW Working

guestname	celebname	entered	exited
Dorothy Gale	Apple Month	1999-02-01	1999-02-28
Dorothy Gale	Apple Month	1999-02-01	1999-11-01
Dorothy Gale	Garlic Festival	1999-02-01	1999-11-01
Dorothy Gale	Garlic Festival	1999-01-15	1999-02-15
Dorothy Gale	St. Fred's Day	1999-02-01	1999-11-01
Dorothy Gale	St. Fred's Day	1999-02-24	1999-02-24
Dorothy Gale	Year of the Prune	1999-02-01	1999-11-01
Dorothy Gale	Year of the Prune	1999-01-01	1999-12-31
Indiana Jones	Apple Month	1999-02-01	1999-02-01
indiana Jones	Apple Month	1999-02-01	1999-02-28
Indiana Jones	Garlic Festival	1999-02-01	1999-02-01
Indiana Jones	Garlic Festival	1999-01-15	1999-02-15
Indiana Jones	Year of the Prune	1999-02-01	1999-02-01
Indiana Jones	Year of the Prune	1999-01-01	1999-12-31
Don Quixote	Apple Month	1999-02-01	1999-02-28
Don Quixote	Apple Month	1999-01-01	1999-10-01
Don Quixote	Garlic Festival	1999-01-01	1999-10-01
Don Quixote	Garlic Festival	1999-01-15	1999-02-15

(cont.)	guestname	celebname	entered	exited
	Don Quixote	National Pear Week	1999-01-01	1999-01-07
	Don Quixote	National Pear Week	1999-01-01	1999-10-01
	Don Quixote	New Year's Day	1999-01-01	1999-01-01
	Don Quixote	New Year's Day	1999-01-01	1999-10-01
	Don Quixote	St. Fred's Day	1999-02-24	1999-02-24
	Don Quixote	St. Fred's Day	1999-01-01	1999-10-01
	Don Quixote	Year of the Prune	1999-01-01	1999-12-31
	Don Quixote	Year of the Prune	1999-01-01	1999-10-01
	James T. Kirk	Apple Month	1999-02-01	1999-02-28
	James T. Kirk	Garlic Festival	1999-02-01	1999-02-28
	James T. Kirk	Garlic Festival	1999-01-15	1999-02-15
	James T. Kirk	St. Fred's Day	1999-02-01	1999-02-28
	James T. Kirk	St. Fred's Day	1999-02-24	1999-02-24
	James T. Kirk	Year of the Prune	1999-02-01	1999-02-28
	James T. Kirk	Year of the Prune	1999-01-01	1999-12-31
	Santa Claus	Christmas Season	1999-12-01	1999-12-25
	Santa Claus	Year of the Prune	1999-12-01	1999-12-25
	Santa Claus	Year of the Prune	1999-01-01	1999-12-31

This will put the earliest and latest points in both intervals into one column. Now we can construct a VIEW like this:

```
CREATE VIEW Attendees(guestname, celebname, entered, exited)
AS SELECT guestname, celebname, MAX(entered), MIN(exited)
    FROM Working
    GROUP BY guestname, celebname;
```

VIEW Attendees

guestname	celebname	entered	exited
Dorothy Gale	Apple Month	1999-02-01	1999-02-28
Dorothy Gale	Garlic Festival	1999-02-01	1999-02-15
Dorothy Gale	St. Fred's Day	1999-02-24	1999-02-24
Dorothy Gale	Year of the Prune	1999-02-01	1999-11-01
Indiana Jones	Apple Month	1999-02-01	1999-02-01
Indiana Jones	Garlic Festival	1999-02-0	1999-02-01
Indiana Jones	Year of the Prune	1999-02-01	1999-02-01

(cont.)	guestname	celebname	entered	exited
	Don Quixote	Apple Month	1999-02-01	1999-02-28
	Don Quixote	Garlic Festival	1999-01-15	1999-02-15
	Don Quixote	National Pear Week	1999-01-01	1999-01-07
	Don Quixote	New Year's Day	1999-01-01	1999-01-01
	Don Quixote	St. Fred's Day	1999-02-24	1999-02-24
	Don Quixote	Year of the Prune	1999-01-01	1999-10-01
	James T. Kirk	Apple Month	1999-02-01	1999-02-28
	James T. Kirk	Garlic Festival	1999-02-01	1999-02-15
	James T. Kirk	St. Fred's Day	1999-02-24	1999-02-24
	James T. Kirk	Year of the Prune	1999-02-01	1999-02-28
	Santa Claus	Christmas Season	1999-12-01	1999-12-25
	Santa Claus	Year of the Prune	1999-12-01	1999-12-25

The Attendees VIEW can be used to compute the total number of room days for each celebration. Assume that the difference of two dates will return an integer that is the number of days between them:

```
SELECT celebname,
       SUM(exited - entered + INTERVAL 1 DAY) AS roomdays
    FROM Attendees
GROUP BY celebname;
```

celebname	roomdays
Apple Month	85
Christmas Season	25
Garlic Festival	63
National Pear Week	7
New Year's Day	1
St. Fred's Day	3
Year of the Prune	602

CHAPTER
13

The [NOT] IN Predicate

THE IN PREDICATE is very natural. It takes a value and sees if it is in a list of comparable values. These values can only be scalar in SQL-89, but can be row values in SQL-92. The syntax is

```
<in predicate> ::=
<row value constructor> [NOT] IN <in predicate value>

<in predicate value> ::=
    <table subquery> | (<in value list>)

<in value list> ::=
    <row value expression> { <comma> <row value expression> }...
```

The expression `<row value constructor>` NOT IN `<in predi-cate value>` has the same effect as NOT (`<row value constructor>` IN `<in predicate value>`). This pattern for the use of the keyword NOT is found in most of the other predicates in SQL.

The expression `<row value constructor>` IN `<in predicate value>` has the same effect as `<row value constructor>` = ANY `<in predicate value>`. Most optimizers will recognize this and execute the same code for both expressions. This means that if the `<in predicate value>` is empty, such as one you would get from a subquery that returns no rows, the results will be FALSE. Likewise, if the `<in predicate value>` is a list of NULLs, the results will be UNKNOWN.

IN predicates with a subquery can be converted into EXISTS predicates, but there are some problems and differences in products. (See section 14.1 on EXISTS and NULLs.) The conversion to an EXISTS predicate is often a good way to improve performance, but it will not be as easy to read as the original IN predicate. An EXISTS predicate can use indexes to find (or fail to find) a single value that confirms (or denies) the predicate, whereas the IN predicate often has to build the results of the subquery in a working table.

13.1 Optimizing the IN Predicate

Most database engines have no statistics about the relative frequency of the values in a list of constants, so they will scan that list in the order in which they appear. People like to order lists alphabetically or by magnitude, but it would be better to order the list from most frequently occurring values to least frequent. It is also pointless to have duplicate values in the constant list, since the predicate will return TRUE if it matches the first duplicate it finds and never get to the second occurrence. Likewise, if the predicate is FALSE for that value, it wastes computer time to traverse a needlessly long list.

Many SQL engines perform an IN predicate with a subquery by building the result set of the subquery first as a temporary working table, then scanning that result table from left to right. This can be expensive in many cases; for example, in a query to find out who works for us in a city with a major sport team (we want to get tickets), we could write

```
SELECT *
    FROM Personnel AS P1
WHERE city IN (SELECT city FROM SportTeams)
    AND state IN (SELECT state FROM SportTeams);
```

since the combination of (city, state) is unique. But this query will not run as fast as

```
SELECT *
  FROM Personnel
WHERE city || state IN (SELECT city || state FROM SportTeams);
```

because the first version of the query will make two passes through the SportTeams table to construct two separate result tables. The second version makes only one pass to construct the concatenation of the names in its result table.

Incidentally, SQL-92 allows row expression comparisons, so you could write

```
SELECT *
  FROM Personnel
WHERE (city, state) IN (SELECT city, state FROM SportTeams);
```

but without an implementation, I have no idea how fast this will run.

Unfortunately, some older versions of SQL do not remove duplicates in the result table of the subquery. This can handled by using a SELECT DISTINCT in the subquery, but that will usually force a sort on the result set. You have to figure out if the amount of duplication justifies the sort.

A trick that can work for large lists on some products is to force the engine to construct a list ordered by frequency. This involves first constructing a VIEW that has an ORDER BY clause; this is not part of the SQL standard, which does not allow a VIEW to have an ORDER BY clause. For example, a paint company wants to find all the products offered by competitors that use the same color as one of their products. First construct a VIEW that orders the colors by frequency of appearance:

```
CREATE VIEW PopColor (color, tally)
AS SELECT color, COUNT(*) AS tally
      FROM Paints
   GROUP BY color
   ORDER BY tally DESC;
```

Then go to the Competitor data and do a simple column SELECT on the VIEW, thus:

```
SELECT *
   FROM Competitor
WHERE color IN (SELECT color FROM PopColor);
```

The VIEW is grouped, so it will be materialized in sort order. The subquery will then be executed and (we hope) the sort order will be maintained and passed along to the IN predicate.

Another trick is to replace the IN predicate with a JOIN operation. For example, you have a table of restaurant telephone numbers and a guidebook and you want to pick out the four-star places, so you write this query:

```
SELECT restname, phone
   FROM Restaurants
WHERE restname IN (SELECT restname
          FROM QualityGuide
        WHERE stars = 4);
```

If there is an index on QualityGuide.stars, the SQL engine will probably build a temporary table of the four-star places and pass it on to the outer query. The outer query will then handle it as if it were a list of constants. However, this is not the sort of column that you would normally index. Without an index on stars, the engine will simply do a sequential search of the QualityGuide table.

This query can be replaced with a JOIN query, thus:

```
SELECT restname, phone
   FROM Restaurants, QualityGuide
WHERE stars = 4
   AND Restaurants.restname = QualityGuide.restname;
```

This query should run faster, since restname is a key for both tables and will be indexed to ensure uniqueness. However, this can return duplicate rows in the result table that you can handle with a SELECT DISTINCT. Consider a more budget-minded query, where we want places with a meal under $10 and the menu guidebook lists all the meals. The query looks about the same:

```
SELECT restname, phone
    FROM Restaurants
WHERE restname IN (SELECT restname
            FROM MenuGuide
        WHERE price <= 10.00);
```

And you would expect to be able to replace it with

```
SELECT restname, phone
    FROM Restaurants, MenuGuide
WHERE price <= 10.00
    AND Restaurants.restname = MenuGuide.restname;
```

Every item in Murphy's Two-Dollar Hash House will get a line in the results of the JOINed version, however. This can be fixed by changing SELECT restname, phone to SELECT DISTINCT restname, phone, but it will cost more time to do a sort to remove the duplicates. There is no good general advice, except to experiment with your particular product.

The NOT IN predicate is probably better replaced with a NOT EXISTS predicate. Using the restaurant example again, our friend John has a list of eateries and we want to see those that are not in the guidebook. The natural formation of the query is

```
SELECT *
    FROM JohnsBook
WHERE restname NOT IN (SELECT restname
            FROM QualityGuide);
```

But you can write the same query with a NOT EXISTS predicate and it will probably run faster:

```
SELECT *
    FROM JohnsBook AS J1
WHERE NOT EXISTS (SELECT *
            FROM QualityGuide AS Q1
        WHERE Q1.restname = J1.restname);
```

The reason the second version will probably run faster is that it can test for existence using the indexes on both tables. The NOT IN version has to test all the values in the subquery table for inequality. Many SQL implementations will construct a temporary table from the IN predicate subquery if it has a WHERE clause, but the temporary table will not have any indexes. The temporary table can also have duplicates and a random ordering of its rows, so that the SQL engine has to do a full-table scan.

EXISTS Predicate

THE EXISTS PREDICATE is very natural. It is a test for a nonempty set. If there are any rows in its subquery, it is TRUE; otherwise, it is FALSE. The syntax is

```
<exists predicate> ::= EXISTS <table subquery>
```

It is worth mentioning that a <table subquery> is always inside parentheses to avoid problems in the grammar during parsing.

In SQL-89, the rules stated that the subquery had to have a SELECT clause with one column or a *. If the SELECT * option was used, the database engine would (in theory) pick one column and use it. This fiction was needed because SQL-89 defined subqueries as having only one column. SQL-92 can handle row-valued comparisons and does not need that restriction in the rules.

In general, the SELECT * option should perform better than an actual column. It lets the query optimizer decide which column to use. If some columns have indexes that can be used to answer the query, the optimizer can access just the indexes and never has to look at the table itself. For example, we want to find all the employees who were born on the same day as any famous person. The query could be

```
SELECT E1.name, ' has the same birthday as a famous person!'
   FROM Employees AS E1
WHERE EXISTS (SELECT *
            FROM Celebrities AS C1
         WHERE (E1.birthday = C1.birthday));
```

If the table Celebrities has an index on its birthday column, the optimizer will get the current employee's birthday E1.birthday and look up that value in the index. If the value is in the index, the predicate is TRUE and we don't need to look at the Celebrities table at all. If it is not in the index, the predicate is FALSE and there is still no need to look at the Celebrities table. This should be fast, since indexes are smaller than their tables and are structured for very fast searching.

However, if Celebrities has no index on its birthday column, the query may have to look at every row to see if there is a birthday that matches the current employee's birthday. There are some tricks that a good optimizer can use to speed things up in this situation.

If the number of values is small and there is a lot of duplication, the SQL engine can build a temporary table of Celebrity birthdates, sort it, and remove duplicates during the sort. This will work if the schema tables track how many unique values can appear in a column. You can find this from constraints and from data declarations as well as from statistics. In this example, we know that we would have at most 366 possible birthdays and a lot of duplication. A binary search on this temporary table could be fast enough to make up for the time lost in building it.

14.1 EXISTS and NULLs

A NULL might not be a value, but it does exist in SQL. This is often a problem for a new SQL programmer who is having trouble with NULLs and how they behave. For example, we want to find all the employees who were *not* born on the same day as a famous person. This can be answered with the negation of the original query, like this:

```
SELECT E1.name, ' was born on a day without a famous person!'
    FROM Employees AS E1
WHERE NOT EXISTS (SELECT *
            FROM Celebrities AS C1
        WHERE E1.birthday = C1.birthday);
```

But assume that among the Celebrities, we have a movie star who will not admit her age, shown in the row ('Gloria Glamour', NULL). A new SQL programmer might expect that Ms. Glamour will match to everyone, since there is a chance that they may match when some tabloid newspaper finally gets a copy of her birth certificate. But work out the subquery in the usual way and you will see that the predicate tests to UNKNOWN because of the NULL comparison, and therefore fails whenever we look at Ms. Glamour. The NOT operator does not produce a true set complement because of SQL's three-valued logic.

Another problem with NULLs is found when you attempt to convert IN predicates to EXISTS predicates. Using our example of matching our employees to famous people, the query can be rewritten as

```
SELECT E1.name, ' was born on a day without a famous person!'
    FROM Employees AS E1
WHERE E1.birthday NOT IN (SELECT C1.birthday
            FROM Celebrities AS C1);
```

However, consider a more complex version of the same query, where the celebrity has to have been born in New York City. The IN predicate would be

```
SELECT E1.name, ' was born on a day without a famous New Yorker!'
    FROM Employees AS E1
WHERE E1.birthday NOT IN (SELECT C1.birthday
            FROM Celebrities AS C1
        WHERE C1.birthcity = 'New York');
```

and you would think that the EXISTS version would be

```
SELECT E1.name, ' was born on a day without a famous New Yorker!'
    FROM Employees AS E1
```

```
WHERE NOT EXISTS (SELECT *
        FROM Celebrities AS C1, Employees AS E1
    WHERE C1.birthcity = 'New York'
      AND C1.birthday = E2.birthday);
```

Assume that Gloria Glamour is our only New Yorker and we still don't know her birthday. The subquery will be empty for every employee in the EXISTS predicate version, because her NULL birthday will not test equal to the known employee birthdays. That means that the NOT EXISTS predicate will return TRUE and we will get every employee to match to Ms. Glamour. But now look at the IN predicate version, which will have a single NULL in the subquery result. This predicate will be equivalent to (Employees.birthday = NULL), which is always UNKNOWN, and we will get no employees back.

Likewise, you cannot, in general, transform the quantified comparison predicates into EXISTS predicates, because of the possibility of NULL values. Remember that x <> ALL <subquery> is shorthand for x NOT IN <subquery> and x = ANY <subquery> is shorthand for x IN <subquery> and it will not surprise you.

Different versions of SQL may handle these situations differently, in violation of the standard. (For an example of such differences involving DB2 and Oracle see van der Lans 1991.)

In general, the EXISTS predicates will run faster than the IN predicates. The problem is in deciding whether to build the query or the subquery first; the optimal approach depends on the size and distribution of values in each, and that cannot usually be known until runtime. See section 13.1 for more details.

14.2 EXISTS and JOINs

The EXISTS predicate is almost always used with a correlated subquery. Very often the subquery can be "flattened" into a JOIN, which will often run faster than the original query. Our sample query can be converted into

```
SELECT E1.name, ' has the same birthday as a famous person!'
   FROM Employees AS E1, Celebrities AS C1
WHERE (E1.birthday = C1.birthday);
```

The advantage of the JOIN version is that it allows us to show columns from both tables. We should make the query more informative by rewriting the query:

```
SELECT E1.name, ' has the same birthday as ', C1.name
    FROM Employees AS E1, Celebrities AS C1
WHERE (E1.birthday = C1.birthday);
```

This new query could be written with an EXISTS predicate, but that is a waste of resources.

```
SELECT E1.name, ' has the same birthday as ', C1.name
    FROM Employees AS E1, Celebrities AS C1
WHERE EXISTS (SELECT *
            FROM Celebrities AS C2
        WHERE E1.birthday = C2.birthday
            AND C1.name = C2.name);
```

14.3 EXISTS and Quantifiers

Formal logic makes use of quantifiers that can be applied to propositions. The two forms are "For all x, $P(x)$" and "For some x, $P(x)$". The first is written as $\forall$ and the second is written as $\exists$, if you want to look up formulas in a textbook. The quantifiers put into symbols such statements as "All men are mortal" or "Some Cretans are liars" so they can be manipulated.

The big question over 100 years ago was that of *existential import* in formal logic. Everyone agreed that saying "All men are mortal" implies that "no men are not mortal," but does it also imply that "some men are mortal" — that we have to have at least one man who is mortal?

Existential import lost the battle and the modern convention is that "All men are mortal" has the same meaning as "There are no men who are immortal," but does not imply that any men exist at all. This is the convention followed in the design of SQL, with the exception of Sybase (before SYBASE System 10) and Microsoft SQL Server products.

Consider the statement "Some salesmen are liars" and the way we would write it with the EXISTS predicate in SQL:

```
EXISTS (SELECT *
        FROM Employees AS E1
    WHERE E1.job = 'Salesman'
        AND E1.name IN (SELECT L1.name FROM Liars AS L1));
```

This query could also be written with (E1.name = L1.name) instead of the IN predicate by putting the references to the Liars table in the FROM clause. The reason for doing it this way is to show the relationship between this query and the next step.

If we are more cynical about salesmen, we might want to formulate the predicate "All salesmen are liars" with the EXISTS predicate in SQL, using the transform rule just discussed:

```
NOT EXISTS (SELECT *
        FROM Employees AS E1
    WHERE E1.job = 'Salesman'
        AND E1.name NOT IN
            (SELECT L1.name FROM Liars AS L1));
```

which, informally, says "There are no salesmen who are not liars" in English. In both these cases, the IN predicate can be changed into an EXISTS predicate, which should improve performance, but it would not be as easy to read.

CHAPTER 15

Quantified Subquery Predicates

A QUANTIFIER IS A logical operator that states the quantity of objects for which a statement is TRUE. This is a logical quantity, not a numeric quantity; it relates a statement to the whole set of possible objects. In everyday life, you see statements like "There is only one mouthwash that stops dinosaur breath," "All doctors drive Mercedes," or "Some people got rich investing in cattle futures," which are quantified.

The first statement, about the mouthwash, is a uniqueness quantifier. If there were two or more products that could save us from dinosaur breath, it would be FALSE. The second statement has what is called a universal quantifier, since it deals with all doctors — find one exception and the statement is FALSE. The last statement has an existential quantifier, since it asserts that one or more people exist who got rich on cattle futures — find one example and the statement is TRUE.

SQL has forms of these quantifiers that are not quite like those in formal logic. They are based on extending the use of comparison predicates to allow result sets to be quantified and they use SQL's three-valued logic, so they do not return just TRUE or FALSE.

15.1 Unique Subquery Comparisons

A comparison in SQL-89 was always done between scalar values; SQL-92 now allows row comparisons (see section 9.2). If a subquery returns a single-row, single-column result table, it is treated as a scalar value in SQL-92 in virtually any place a scalar could appear.

SQL-89 allowed a limited form of comparison between a scalar expression and a quantified scalar subquery. The SQL-89 syntax required that the scalar expression appear on the left-hand side of the quantified comparison operator and the subquery on the right.

Though it is not part of the SQL-89 standard, many old SQL implementations also allowed a predicate of the form <expression> <comp op> <scalar subquery>, which is the same as the <comp op> ANY predicate restricted to a <scalar subquery>. The scalar subquery can be correlated or uncorrelated. For example, to find out if we have any teachers who are more than 10 years older than the students, I could write

```
SELECT name
    FROM Teachers AS T1
WHERE T1.age > (SELECT MAX(S1.age) + INTERVAL 10 YEARS
            FROM Students AS S1);
```

In this case, the scalar subquery will be run only once and reduced to a constant value by the optimizer before scanning the Teachers table. I am finding the unique maximum student age to do the query.

A correlated subquery is more complex, because it will have to be executed for each value from the containing query. For example, to find which suppliers have sent us fewer than 100 parts, we would use this query. Notice how the SUM(quantity) has to be computed for each supplier number, sno.

```
SELECT sno, sname
    FROM Suppliers
WHERE 100 > (SELECT SUM(quantity)
            FROM Shipments
        WHERE Shipments.sno = Suppliers.sno);
```

If a scalar subquery returns a NULL, we have rules for handling comparison with NULLs. But what if it returns an empty result — a supplier that has not shipped us anything? In SQL-92, the empty result table is also a NULL; however, it is wise to check your implementation, since this is a new feature in the language.

In SQL-92, you can place scalar or row subqueries on either side of a comparison predicate as long as they return comparable results. But you must be aware of the rules for row comparisons. For example, the following query will find the product manager who has more of his product at the stores than in the warehouse:

```
SELECT manager, product
    FROM Personnel AS P1
WHERE (SELECT SUM(qty)
          FROM Warehouses AS W1
       WHERE P1.product = W1.product)
    < (SELECT SUM(qty)
          FROM Stores AS S1
       WHERE P1.product = S1.product);
```

Here is a programming tip: The main problem with writing these queries is getting a result with more than one row in it. You can guarantee uniqueness in several ways. An aggregate function on an ungrouped table will always be a single value. A JOIN with the containing query based on a key will always be a single value.

15.2 Quantifiers and Missing Data

The quantified predicates are used with subquery expressions to compare a single value to those of the subquery, and take the general form <value expression> <comp op> <quantifier> <subquery>. These predicates are based on the formal logical quantifiers "for all," written as ∀ in formal logic, and "there exists," written as ∃ in formal logic; SQL tries to preserve similar properties.

The predicate <value expression> <comp op> ANY table S is equivalent to taking each row s (assume that they are numbered from 1 to n) of table S and testing <value expression> <comp op> s with ORs between the expanded expressions:

```
(((<value expression> <comp op> s1)
 OR (<value expression> <comp op> s2)

    ...

 OR (<value expression> <comp op> sn))
```

When you get a single TRUE result, the whole predicate is TRUE. As long as table S has cardinality greater than zero and one non-NULL value, you will get a result of TRUE or FALSE. The keyword SOME is the same as ANY — just a matter of style and readability.

Likewise, <value expression> <comp op> ALL table S takes each row s of table S and tests <value expression> <comp op> s with ANDs between the expanded expressions:

```
(((<value expression> <comp op> s1)
 AND (<value expression> <comp op> s2)

    ...

 AND (<value expression> <comp op> sn))
```

When you get a single FALSE result, the whole predicate is FALSE. As long as table S has cardinality greater than zero and one non-NULL value, you will get a result of TRUE or FALSE.

That sounds reasonable so far. Now let EmptyTable be an empty table (no rows, cardinality zero) and NullTable be a table with only NULLs in its rows (cardinality greater than zero).

The rules for SQL say that <value expression> <comp op> ALL NullTable always returns UNKNOWN, and likewise <value expression> <comp op> ANY NullTable always returns UNKNOWN. This makes sense, because every row comparison test in the expansion would return UNKNOWN, so the series of OR and AND operators would behave in the usual way.

However, <value expression> <comp op> ALL EmptyTable always returns TRUE and <value expression> <comp op> ANY EmptyTable always returns FALSE. Most people have no trouble seeing why the ANY predicate works that way; you cannot find a match, so the result is FALSE. But most people have lots of trouble seeing why the ALL predicate is TRUE. This convention is called existential import, and I have just discussed it in chapter 14 on the EXISTS predicate. If I were to walk into a bar and announce that I can beat any pink elephant in the bar, that would be a true statement. The fact that there are no pink elephants in the bar merely shows that the problem is reduced to the minimum case.

Of the two quantified predicates, the `<comp op>` ALL predicate is used more. The ANY predicate is more easily replaced and more naturally written with an EXISTS() predicate or an IN predicate. In fact, the standard defines the IN predicate as shorthand for = ANY and the NOT IN predicate as shorthand for <> ANY, which is how most people would construct them in English.

The `<comp op>` ALL predicate is probably the more useful of the two, since it cannot be written in terms of an IN predicate. The trick with it is to make sure that its subquery defines the set of values in which you are interested. For example, to find the authors whose books all sell for $19.95 or more, you could write

```
SELECT *
   FROM Authors AS A1
WHERE  19.95 < ALL (SELECT price
          FROM Books AS B1
       WHERE A1.authorname = B1.authorname);
```

The best way to think of this is to reverse the usual English sentence "Show me all *x* that are *y*" in your mind so that it says "*y* is the value of all *x*" instead. We will see another use for this predicate in chapter 22 on runs.

15.3 UNIQUE Predicate

This subquery predicate is defined for Intermediate Level SQL-92 and is not widely implemented yet. It is a test for the absence of duplicate rows in a subquery. The UNIQUE keyword is also used as a table or column constraint, but don't confuse those two with this predicate. This predicate is used to define them.

The UNIQUE column constraint is implemented in many SQL implementations with a CREATE UNIQUE INDEX `<indexname>` ON `<table>`(`<column list>`) statement. These are not the same thing.

The syntax for this predicate is

```
<unique predicate> ::= UNIQUE <table subquery>
```

If any two rows in the subquery are equal to each other, the predicate is FALSE. However, the definition in the standard is worded in the negative, so that NULLs get the benefit of the doubt. The query can be written as an EXISTS predicate that counts rows, thus:

```
EXISTS (SELECT <column list>
          FROM <subquery>
        GROUP BY <column list>
      HAVING COUNT(*) > 1);
```

An empty subquery is always TRUE, since you cannot find two rows, and therefore duplicates do not exist. This makes sense on the face of it.

NULLs are easier to explain with an example, say a table with only two rows, ('a', 'b') and ('a', NULL). The first columns of each row are non-NULL and are equal to each other, so we have a match so far. The second column in the second row is NULL and cannot compare to anything, so we skip the second column pair, and go with what we have, and the test is TRUE. This is giving the NULLs the benefit of the doubt, since the NULL in the second row could become 'b' some day and give us a duplicate row.

Now consider the case where the subquery has two rows, ('a', NULL) and ('a', NULL). The predicate is still TRUE, because the NULLs do not test equal or unequal to each other — not because we are making NULLs equal to each other.

CHAPTER

16

The SELECT Statement

THE GOOD NEWS about SQL is that the programmer only needs to learn the SELECT statement to do almost all his work! The bad news is that the statement can have so many nested clauses that it looks like a Victorian novel!

The SELECT statement is used to query the database. It combines one or more tables, can do some calculations, and finally puts the results into a result table that can be passed on to the host language.

The SQL-89 statement is a subset of the SQL-92 statement, so this book has used a lot of SQL-89 syntax instead of SQL-92 syntax in the examples. When there is no SQL-89 syntax, I have used the minimal SQL-92 syntax to do the job. You will find more and more SQL-92 features in the coming releases of each SQL product.

The one thing I have not done in this book is give a series of simple SELECT statements. I am assuming that the readers are experienced SQL programmers and got enough of those queries when they were learning SQL.

16.1 SELECT and JOINs

There is an order to the execution of the clauses of an SQL SELECT statement that does not seem to be covered in most beginning SQL books. It explains why some things work in SQL and others do not.

16.1.1 One-Level SELECT Statement

The simplest possible SELECT statement is just SELECT * FROM Sometable;, which returns the entire table as it stands. You can actually write this as TABLE Sometable in SQL-92, but no product has that feature yet. Though the syntax rules say that all you need are the SELECT and FROM clauses, in practice there is almost always a WHERE clause.

Let's look at the SELECT statement in detail. The syntax for the statement is

```
SELECT <expression list>
    FROM <table expression>
[WHERE <search condition>]
[GROUP BY <grouping column list>]
[HAVING <group condition>];
```

The order of execution is as follows:

1. Execute the FROM <table expression> clause and construct the working result table defined in that clause. In SQL-89, the <table expression> is a list of tables or views that might be given correlation names, but it can get pretty fancy in SQL-92. The result is the CROSS JOIN (or the Cartesian product, to use an older term) of all the rows in the tables listed. What this does is take each row from the first table and concatenate each row from the second table to it to build a new row in the result table. You get all possible combinations.

    The result table preserves the order of the tables, and the order of the rows within each, in the result. The result table is different from other tables in that each column retains the table name from which it was derived. Thus if table A and table B both have a column named x, there will be a column A.x and a column B.x in the results of the FROM clause.

No product actually uses a CROSS JOIN to construct the intermediate table — the working table would get too large, too fast. For example, a 1,000-row table and a 1,000-row table would CROSS JOIN to get a 1,000,000-row working table. This is just the conceptual model we use to describe behavior.

In SQL-92, the FROM can have all sorts of other table expressions, but the point is that they return a working table as a result. We will get into the details of those expressions later.

2. If there is a WHERE clause, the predicate in it is applied to each row of the FROM clause result table. The rows that test TRUE are retained; the rows that test FALSE or UNKNOWN are deleted from the working set.

   The WHERE clause is where the action is. The predicate can be quite complex and have nested subqueries. The syntax of a subquery is a SELECT statement, which is inside parentheses — failure to use parentheses is a common error for new SQL programmers. Subqueries are where the original SQL got the name "Structured English Query Language" — the ability to nest SELECT statements was the "structured" part. We will deal with those in another section.

3. If there is a GROUP BY <grouping column list> clause, it is executed next. It uses the FROM and WHERE clause results and breaks these rows into groups where the columns in the <grouping column list> all have the same value. NULLs are treated as if they were all equal to each other, and form their own group. Each group is then reduced to a single row in a new result table that replaces the old one. (See chapter 19 on groups for more details.)

   Each row represents information about its group. SQL-92 allows you to use the name of a calculated column, such as (salary + commission) AS totalpay, in the GROUP BY clause, because that column was named in the original

working table. Only two things make sense as group characteristics: the grouping columns that define it and the aggregate functions that summarize group characteristics.

4. If there is a HAVING clause, it is applied to each of the groups.
The groups that test TRUE are retained; the groups that test
FALSE or UNKNOWN are deleted. If there is no GROUP BY clause,
the HAVING clause treats the whole table as a single group.
SQL-92 prohibits correlated queries in a HAVING clause.

   The <group condition> must apply to columns in the
grouped working table or to group properties, not to the individual rows that originally built the group. Many implementations require that aggregate functions used in the HAVING
clause also appear in the SELECT clause, but that is not part of
the standard. However, the SELECT clause of a grouped query
must include all the grouping columns.

5. Finally, the SELECT clause is applied to the result table. If a
column does not appear in the <expression list>, it is
dropped from the final results. Expressions can be constants
or column names, or they can be calculations made from
constants, columns, and functions.

   If the SELECT clause has the DISTINCT option, all the
duplicate rows are deleted from the final results table.
Remember that this is done last and that putting a SELECT
DISTINCT on a grouped query is redundant because the
groups were already distinct. Finally, the results are returned.

Let us carry an example out in detail.

```
SELECT sex, COUNT(*), AVG(age), (MAX(age) - MIN(age)) AS agerange
   FROM Student, Gradebook
WHERE grade = 'A'
   AND Student.student = Gradebook.student
GROUP BY sex
HAVING COUNT(*) > 3;
```

The two starting tables look like this:

```
CREATE TABLE Students
(sno INTEGER PRIMARY KEY,
 sname CHAR(10) NOT NULL,
 sex CHAR(1) NOT NULL,
 age INTEGER NOT NULL);
```

Students

sno	sname	sex	age
1	Smith	M	16
2	Smyth	F	17
3	Smoot	F	16
4	Adams	F	17
5	Jones	M	16
6	Celko	M	17
7	Vennor	F	16
8	Murray	M	18

```
CREATE TABLE Gradebook
(sno INTEGER PRIMARY KEY,
 grade CHAR(1) NOT NULL);
```

Gradebook

sno	grade
1	A
2	B
3	C
4	D
5	A
6	A
7	A
8	A

The CROSS JOIN in the FROM clause looks like this:

CROSS JOIN working table

Students				Gradebook	
sno	**sname**	**sex**	**age**	**sno**	**grade**
1	Smith	M	16	1	A
1	Smith	M	16	2	B
1	Smith	M	16	3	C
1	Smith	M	16	4	D
1	Smith	M	16	5	A
1	Smith	M	16	6	A
1	Smith	M	16	7	A
1	Smith	M	16	8	A
2	Smyth	F	17	1	A
2	Smyth	F	17	2	B
2	Smyth	F	17	3	C
2	Smyth	F	17	4	D
2	Smyth	F	17	5	A
2	Smyth	F	17	6	A
2	Smyth	F	17	7	A
2	Smyth	F	17	8	A
3	Smoot	F	16	1	A
3	Smoot	F	16	2	B
3	Smoot	F	16	3	C
3	Smoot	F	16	4	D
3	Smoot	F	16	5	A
3	Smoot	F	16	6	A
3	Smoot	F	16	7	A
3	Smoot	F	16	8	A
4	Adams	F	17	1	A
4	Adams	F	17	2	B
4	Adams	F	17	3	C
4	Adams	F	17	4	D
4	Adams	F	17	5	A
4	Adams	F	17	6	A
4	Adams	F	17	7	A
4	Adams	F	17	8	A
5	Jones	M	16	1	A

(cont.)

| Students | | | | Gradebook | |
sno	sname	sex	age	sno	grade
5	Jones	M	16	2	B
5	Jones	M	16	3	C
5	Jones	M	16	4	D
5	Jones	M	16	5	A
5	Jones	M	16	6	A
5	Jones	M	16	7	A
5	Jones	M	16	8	A
6	Celko	M	17	1	A
6	Celko	M	17	2	B
6	Celko	M	17	3	C
6	Celko	M	17	4	D
6	Celko	M	17	5	A
6	Celko	M	17	6	A
6	Celko	M	17	7	A
6	Celko	M	17	8	A
7	Vennor	F	16	1	A
7	Vennor	F	16	2	B
7	Vennor	F	16	3	C
7	Vennor	F	16	4	D
7	Vennor	F	16	5	A
7	Vennor	F	16	6	A
7	Vennor	F	16	7	A
7	Vennor	F	16	8	A
8	Murray	M	18	1	A
8	Murray	M	18	2	B
8	Murray	M	18	3	C
8	Murray	M	18	4	D
8	Murray	M	18	5	A
8	Murray	M	18	6	A
8	Murray	M	18	7	A
8	Murray	M	18	8	A

There are two predicates in the WHERE. The first predicate grade = 'A' needs only the Students table. In fact, an optimizer in a real SQL engine would have removed those rows in the Students table that

failed the test before doing the CROSS JOIN. The second predicate is
Student.student = Gradebook.student, which requires both tables
and the whole constructed row. Predicates that use two tables are
called JOIN conditions for obvious reasons. Now remove the rows
that don't meet the conditions. After the WHERE clause, the result table
looks like this:

CROSS JOIN after WHERE clause

Students				Gradebook	
sno	sname	sex	age	sno	grade
1	Smith	M	16	1	A
5	Jones	M	16	5	A
6	Celko	M	17	6	A
7	Vennor	F	16	7	A
8	Murray	M	18	8	A

We have a GROUP BY clause that will group the working table by
sex, thus:

BY sex

Students				Gradebook		
sno	sname	sex	age	sno	grade	
1	Smith	M	16	1	A	*sex = 'M' group*
5	Jones	M	16	5	A	
6	Celko	M	17	6	A	
8	Murray	M	18	8	A	
7	Vennor	F	16	7	A	*sex = 'F' group*

and the aggregate functions in the SELECT clause are computed for
each group:

Aggregate functions

sex	COUNT(*)	AVG(age)	(MAX(age) – MIN(age)) AS agerange
F	1	16.00	(16 – 16) = 0
M	4	16.75	(18 – 16) = 2

The HAVING clause is applied to each group, the SELECT statement is applied last, and we get the final results:

Full query with HAVING clause

sex	COUNT(*)	AVG(age)	Agerange
M	4	16.75	2

Obviously, no real implementation actually produces these intermediate tables. They are just a model of how a statement works. In the case of SQL-92, the FROM clause can have JOINs and other operators that create working tables, but the same steps are followed in this order. A real query could have subqueries in the WHERE clause that would have to be parsed and expanded the same way.

16.1.2 Correlated Subqueries in a SELECT Statement

A correlated subquery is a subquery that references columns in the tables of its containing query. This is a way to "hide a loop" in SQL. Consider a query to find all the students who are younger than the oldest student of their gender:

```
SELECT *
   FROM Students AS S1
WHERE age < (SELECT MAX(age)
           FROM Students AS S2
        WHERE S1.sex = S2.sex);
```

1. A copy of the table is made for each correlation name, S1 and S2.

Students AS S1

sno	sname	sex	age
1	Smith	M	16
2	Smyth	F	17
3	Smoot	F	16
4	Adams	F	17
5	Jones	M	16
6	Celko	M	17
7	Vennor	F	16
8	Murray	M	18

Students AS S2

sno	sname	sex	age
1	Smith	M	16
2	Smyth	F	17
3	Smoot	F	16
4	Adams	F	17
5	Jones	M	16
6	Celko	M	17
7	Vennor	F	16
8	Murray	M	18

2. When you get to the WHERE clause, and find the innermost query, you will see that you need to get data from the containing query. The model of execution says that each outer row has the subquery executed on it in parallel with the other rows. Assume we are working on student (1, 'Smith'), who is male. The query in effect becomes

```
SELECT 1, 'Smith', 'M', 16
   FROM Students AS S1
WHERE 16 < (SELECT MAX(age)
            FROM Students AS S2
        WHERE 'M' = S2.sex);
```

3. The subquery can now be calculated for male students; the maximum age is 18. When we expand this out for all the other rows, this will give us

```
SELECT 1, 'Smith', 'M', 16 FROM Students AS S1 WHERE 16 < 18;
SELECT 2, 'Smyth', 'F', 17 FROM Students AS S1 WHERE 17 < 17;
SELECT 3, 'Smoot', 'F', 16 FROM Students AS S1 WHERE 16 < 17;
SELECT 4, 'Adams', 'F', 17 FROM Students AS S1 WHERE 17 < 17;
SELECT 5, 'Jones', 'M', 16 FROM Students AS S1 WHERE 16 < 18;
SELECT 6, 'Celko', 'M', 17 FROM Students AS S1 WHERE 17 < 18;
SELECT 7, 'Vennor', 'F', 16 FROM Students AS S1 WHERE 16 < 17;
SELECT 8, 'Murray', 'M', 18 FROM Students AS S1 WHERE 18 < 18;
```

4. These same steps have been done for each row in the containing query. The model is that all of the subqueries are resolved

at once, but again, no implementation really does it that way. The usual approach is to build procedural loops in the database engine that scan through both tables. Which table is in which loop is decided by the optimizer.

The final results are

sno	sname	sex	age
1	Smith	M	16
3	Smoot	F	16
5	Jones	M	16
6	Celko	M	17
7	Vennor	F	16

16.1.3 SQL-92 SELECT Statement

For upward compatibility, an SQL-89 statement will produce the same results in SQL-92. However, the SQL-92 syntax for JOINs is an infixed operator in the FROM clause. The JOIN operators are quite general and flexible, allowing you to do things in a single statement that you could not do in the older notation. The basic syntax is

```
<joined table> ::=
    <cross join> | <qualified join> | (<joined table>)

<cross join> ::= <table reference> CROSS JOIN <table reference>

<qualified join> ::=
    <table reference> [NATURAL] [<join type>] JOIN
        <table reference> [<join specification>]

<join specification> ::= <join condition> | <named columns join>

<join condition> ::= ON <search condition>

<named columns join> ::= USING (<join column list>)

<join type> ::= INNER | <outer join type> [OUTER] | UNION
```

```
<outer join type> ::= LEFT | RIGHT | FULL

<join column list> ::= <column name list>

<table reference> ::=
    <table name> [[AS] <correlation name>[(<derived column list>)]]
      | <derived table>
         [AS] <correlation name> [(<derived column list>)]
      | <joined table>

<derived table> ::= <table subquery>

<column name list> ::=
    <column name> [{ <comma> <column name> }...]
```

The INNER JOIN and CROSS JOIN were all you had in the SQL-89 standard. An INNER JOIN is done by forming the CROSS JOIN and then removing the rows that do not meet the JOIN specification given in the ON clause, as we just showed in the last section. The ON clause can be as elaborate as you want to make it, as long as it refers to tables and columns within its scope. If a <qualified join> is used without a <join type>, INNER is implicit.

However, in the real world, most INNER JOINs are done using equality tests on columns with the same names in different tables, rather than on elaborate predicates. Equi-joins are so common that SQL-92 has two shorthand ways of specifying them. The USING (c1, c2, ..., cn) clause takes the column names in the list and replaces them with the clause ON ((T1.c1, T1.c2, ..., T1.cn) = (T2.c1, T2.c2, ..., T2.cn)). Likewise, the NATURAL option is shorthand for a USING() clause that is a list of all the column names that are common to both tables. If NATURAL is specified, a JOIN specification cannot be given; it is already there.

The UNION JOIN and OUTER JOIN are topics in themselves and will be covered in separate sections.

16.2 OUTER JOINs

OUTER JOINs exist in most current SQL implementations, but they use a vendor syntax rather than the ANSI SQL-92 syntax. The recent ODBC specification from Microsoft, WATCOM SQL, and other products are now using all or part of the SQL-92 syntax and we can expect other vendors to follow.

An OUTER JOIN is a JOIN that preserves all the rows in one or both tables, even when they do not have matching rows in the second table. Let's take a real-world situation. I have a table of orders and a table of suppliers that I wish to join for a report to tell us how much business we did with each supplier. With a NATURAL JOIN, the query would be this:

```
SELECT Suppliers.supno, supname, orderno, amt
    FROM Suppliers, Orders
WHERE  Suppliers.supno = Orders.supno;
```

Some suppliers' totals include credits for returned merchandise, and our total business with them works out to zero dollars. Other suppliers never got an order from us at all, so we did zero dollars' worth of business with them, too. But the first case will show up in the query result and be passed on to the report, whereas the second case will disappear in the INNER JOIN.

If we had used an OUTER JOIN, preserving the Suppliers table, we would have all the suppliers in the results. When a supplier with no orders was found in the Orders table, the orderno and amt columns would be given a NULL value in the result row.

16.2.1 Vendor Syntax for OUTER JOINs

In the old SQL-89 standard, there was no OUTER JOIN, so you had to construct it by hand with a messy UNION in products like earlier versions of DB2 from IBM, like this:

```
SELECT supno, supname, amt      -- regular INNER JOIN
    FROM Suppliers, Orders
WHERE (Suppliers.supno = Orders.supno)
UNION ALL
SELECT supno, supname, NULL   -- preserved rows of LEFT JOIN
    FROM Suppliers
WHERE NOT EXISTS (SELECT *
          FROM Orders
        WHERE (Suppliers.supno = Orders.supno));
```

The SQL-89 standard actually does not allow NULL to appear as a value expression in a SELECT clause list, but it is a very common vendor extension. DB2 and a few other versions of SQL followed the SQL-89 standard, so they would have to replace NULL with a constant of the correct datatype to make the UNION work. This is easy in the case of a CHARACTER column, where a message like '<<NONE>>' or '17' can be quickly understood. It is much harder to do in the case of a numeric column, where we could have a balance with a supplier that is positive, zero, or negative because of returns and credits. There really is a difference between a vendor that we did not use and a vendor whose returns canceled out its orders.

The most common vendor extensions are just for the LEFT OUTER JOIN. They use a plus sign or an asterisk to mark the preserved table. The special token either is put on the table name (XDB, DB2, Oracle, and SQLBase use (+) after the table name) or is part of an extended equality sign (Sybase uses *=, Universe uses =?, and so forth). The important property of either syntax is that an extended equality sign appears in the WHERE clause and this has some side effects. The LEFT OUTER JOIN for our example might be written as

```
SELECT supno, supname, orderno, amt
    FROM Suppliers, Orders
WHERE Suppliers.supno *= Orders.supno
```

The name LEFT OUTER JOIN comes from the fact that the preserved table is on the left side of the equality sign. Likewise, a RIGHT OUTER JOIN would have the preserved table on the right-hand side and the FULL OUTER JOIN would preserve both tables.

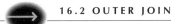

These extended equality notations have a lot of problems, which is why they were not used in SQL-92. A table cannot be both preserved and unpreserved in the same WHERE clause in implementations that use this notation, so self OUTER JOINS are impossible without using VIEWs. The only JOIN condition allowed is equality, so you cannot write other outer theta joins. In fact, you cannot safely write something like NOT (Suppliers.supno *= Orders.supno) and predict the results. And, worst of all, the syntax is ambiguous. Consider this query:

```
SELECT Suppliers.supno, supname, orderno, amt
    FROM Suppliers, Orders
WHERE Suppliers.supno *= Orders.supno
    AND Suppliers.quantity < 100;
```

If the (Suppliers.quantity < 100) predicate is applied first, you get a different result than if it is applied second. That is not how the AND predicate is supposed to work. For a full discussion of the problems with this notation, see *Relational Database: Writings, 1989–1991* (Date 1992b), or some of the discussion papers of the ANSI X3H2 Database Standards Committee (see appendix B: Readings and Resources).

16.2.2 SQL-92 Syntax for JOINs

The SQL-92 syntax for OUTER JOINs is an infixed operator in the FROM clause. The SQL-92 syntax also defines other types of JOINs, some of which are discussed in other parts of this book. Since the OUTER JOIN is being implemented, it is more important than some of the really exotic joins. Right now, the OUTER JOIN operators that are actually implemented use only a subset of the possible options. This is quite flexible and allows you to do things that you could not do in any reasonable fashion in the older notation. Below is a realistic version of what an OUTER JOIN syntax will be in your actual SQL product. Remember to read the manual and find out what is there. Assuming that supno is the only column that appears with the same name in both the Suppliers and the Orders tables, our example of orders and suppliers could be written as

```
SELECT supno, supname, orderno, amt
    FROM Suppliers LEFT OUTER JOIN Orders
        ON (Suppliers.supno = Orders.supno);
```

or

```
SELECT supno, supname, orderno, amt
    FROM Suppliers LEFT OUTER JOIN Orders
        USING (supno);
```

or

```
SELECT supno, supname, orderno, amt
    FROM Suppliers NATURAL LEFT OUTER JOIN Orders;
```

An interesting feature of the SQL-92 standard is that a SELECT expression that returns a single row with a single value can be used where a scalar expression can be used. If the result of the scalar query is empty, it is converted to a NULL. This will sometimes — not always! — let you write an OUTER JOIN as a query within the SELECT clause; thus, this query will work only if each supplier has one or zero orders:

```
SELECT supno, supname, orderno,
        (SELECT amt FROM Orders WHERE Suppliers.supno =
        Orders.supno)
    FROM Suppliers;
```

However, I could write

```
SELECT supno, supname,
    (SELECT COUNT(*)
            FROM Orders
        WHERE Suppliers.supno = Orders.supno)
    FROM Suppliers;
```

instead of writing

```
SELECT supno, supname, COUNT(*)
    FROM Suppliers LEFT OUTER JOIN Orders
        ON (Suppliers.supno = Orders.supno)
GROUP BY supno, supname;
```

Though the OUTER JOIN syntax is still new to most implementations, it would seem reasonable that it will be more efficient than a correlated subquery in the SELECT list. However, you should experiment with your particular product to find out which is better.

16.2.3 NULLs and OUTER JOINs

The NULLs that are generated by the OUTER JOIN can occur in columns derived from source table columns that have been declared to be NOT NULL. Even if you tried to avoid all the problems with NULLs by making every column in every table of your database schema NOT NULL, they could still occur in OUTER JOIN results.

However, a table can have NULLs and still be used in an OUTER JOIN. Consider different JOINs on the following two tables, which have NULLs in the common column:

T1		T2	
a	**x**	**b**	**x**
1	r	7	r
2	v	8	s
3	NULL	9	NULL

A natural INNER JOIN on column x can only match those values that are equal to each other. But NULLs do not match to anything, not even to other NULLs. Thus, there is one row in the result, on the value r in column x in both tables.

```
T1 INNER JOIN T2 ON (T1.x = T2.x)
```

a	**T1.x**	**b**	**T2.x**
1	r	7	r

Now do a LEFT OUTER JOIN on the tables, which will preserve table T1, and you get

```
T1 LEFT OUTER JOIN T2 ON (T1.x = T2.x)
```

a	T1.x	b	T2.x
1	r	7	r
2	v	NULL	NULL
3	NULL	NULL	NULL

Again, there are no surprises. The original INNER JOIN row is still in the results. The other two rows of T1 that were not in the equi-join do show up in the results, and the columns derived from table T2 are filled with NULLs. The RIGHT OUTER JOIN would also behave the same way. The problems start with the FULL OUTER JOIN, which looks like this:

```
T1 FULL OUTER JOIN T2 ON (T1.x = T2.x)
```

a	T1.x	b	T2.x
1	r	7	r
2	v	NULL	NULL
3	NULL	NULL	NULL
NULL	NULL	8	s
NULL	NULL	9	NULL

The way this result is constructed is worth explaining in detail. First do an INNER JOIN on T1 and T2, using the ON clause condition, and put those rows (if any) in the results. Then all rows in T1 that could not be joined are padded out with NULLs in the columns derived from T2 and inserted into the results. Finally, take the rows in T2 that could not be joined, pad them out with NULLs, and insert them into the results.

The bad news is that the original tables cannot be reconstructed from an OUTER JOIN. Look at the results of the FULL OUTER JOIN, which we will call R1, and SELECT the first columns from it:

```
SELECT T1.a, T1.x FROM R1
```

a	x
1	r
2	v
3	NULL
NULL	NULL
NULL	NULL

The created NULLs remain and cannot be differentiated from the original NULLs. But you cannot throw out those duplicate rows, because they may be in the original table T1.

Since many products have only a LEFT OUTER JOIN, beginning programmers might try to construct a FULL OUTER JOIN with

```
SELECT * FROM T1 LEFT OUTER JOIN T2 ON (T1.x = T2.x)
UNION ALL
SELECT * FROM T2 LEFT OUTER JOIN T1 ON (T1.x = T2.x)
```

But the UNION ALL will give you false duplicate rows from the rows that were part of the INNER JOIN, namely (1, r, 7, r) in this example. However, a simple UNION could remove true duplicate rows from the original tables.

16.2.4 NATURAL Versus Conditional OUTER JOINs

It is worth mentioning in passing that the SQL-92 standard has a NATURAL LEFT OUTER JOIN, but it is not implemented in most current versions of SQL. Even those that have the syntax are actually creating an ON clause with equality tests, like the examples we have been using in this section.

A NATURAL join has only one copy of the common column pairs in its result. The conditional OUTER JOIN has both of the original columns, with their table-qualified names. The NATURAL JOIN has to have a correlation name for the result table to identify the shared columns. We can build a NATURAL LEFT OUTER JOIN by using the COALESCE() function to combine the common column pairs into a single column and put the results into a view where the columns can be properly named, thus:

```
CREATE VIEW NLOJ12 (x, a, b)
AS SELECT COALESCE(T1.x, T2.x), T1.a, T2.b
     FROM T1 LEFT OUTER JOIN T2 ON T1.a = T2.a;
```

x	a	b
r	1	7
v	2	NULL
NULL	3	NULL

Unlike the NATURAL JOINs, the conditional OUTER JOIN does not have to use a simple one-column equality as the join condition. The condition can have several predicates, use other comparisons, and so forth. For example,

```
T1 LEFT OUTER JOIN T2 ON (T1.x < T2.x)
```

a	T1.x	b	T2.x
1	r	8	s
2	v	NULL	NULL
3	NULL	NULL	NULL

as compared to

```
T1 LEFT OUTER JOIN T2 ON (T1.x > T2.x)
```

a	T1.x	b	T2.x
1	r	NULL	NULL
2	v	7	r
2	v	8	s
3	NULL	NULL	NULL

Again, so much of current OUTER JOIN behavior is vendor-specific that the programmer should experiment with his own particular product to see what actually happens.

16.2.5 Self OUTER JOINs

There is no rule that forbids an OUTER JOIN on the same table. In fact, the self OUTER JOIN is a good trick for "flattening" a normalized table into a horizontal report. To illustrate the method, start with a table defined as

```
CREATE TABLE Credits
(student INTEGER NOT NULL,
 course CHAR(8) NOT NULL);
```

This table represents student numbers and a course code for each class they have taken. However, our rules say that students cannot get credit for CS-102 until they have taken the prerequisite CS-101 course, they cannot get credit for CS-103 until they have taken the prerequisite CS-102 course, and so forth.

Let's first load the table with some sample values. Notice that student 1 has both courses, student 2 has only the first of the series, and student 3 jumped ahead of sequence and therefore cannot get credit for his CS-102 course until he goes back and takes CS-101.

Credits

student	course
1	CS-101
1	CS-102
2	CS-101
3	CS-102

What we want is basically a histogram (bar chart) for each student, showing how far they have gone in their degree programs. Assume that we are only looking at two courses; the result of the desired query might look like this (NULL is used to represent a missing value):

```
(1, 'CS-101', 'CS-102')
(2, 'CS-101', NULL)
```

Clearly, this will need a self join, since the last two columns come from the same table, Credits. You have to give correlation names to both uses of the Credits table in the OUTER JOIN operator when you construct a self OUTER JOIN, just as you would with any other self join, thus:

```
SELECT student, C1.course, C2.course
    FROM Credits AS C1 LEFT OUTER JOIN Credits AS C2
        ON ((C1.student = C2.student)
            AND (C1.course = 'CS-101')
            AND (C2.course = 'CS-102'));
```

16.2.6 Two or More OUTER JOINs

Some relational purists feel that every operator should have an inverse, and therefore they do not like the OUTER JOIN. Others feel that the created NULLs are fundamentally different from the explicit NULLs in a base table and should have a special token. SQL uses its general-purpose NULLs and leaves things at that. Getting away from theory, you will also find that vendors have often done strange things with the ways their products work.

A major problem is that OUTER JOIN operators do not have the same properties as INNER JOIN operators. The order in which FULL OUTER JOINs are executed will change the results (a mathematician would say that they are not associative).

To show some of the problems that can come up when you have more than two tables, let us use three very simple tables. Notice that all the a columns have either 1 or 100, all the b columns have a 2, and all the c columns have a 3. The tables have all possible pairs of columns.

```
CREATE TABLE T1 (a INTEGER NOT NULL, b INTEGER NOT NULL);
INSERT INTO T1 VALUES (1, 2);

CREATE TABLE T2 (a INTEGER NOT NULL, c INTEGER NOT NULL);
INSERT INTO T2 VALUES (100, 3);

CREATE TABLE T3 (b INTEGER NOT NULL, c INTEGER NOT NULL);
INSERT INTO T3 VALUES (2, 3);
```

Now perform the following queries on them, using WATCOM SQL, which is the best implementation of SQL-92 at the time of this writing. Their NATURAL operator sets up an equi-join on columns that have the same names in both tables, but does not collapse the pair into a single column with the common name in the results. This leaves you two choices: Use qualified names in the SELECT list, or fake the SQL-92 definition with the COALESCE function on the common columns.

Using the test tables, we can set up a series of three-table OUTER JOINs and see what happens. Let's start joining the tables in order:

```
SELECT T1.a, T1.b, T3.c
    FROM ((T1 NATURAL LEFT OUTER JOIN T2)
        NATURAL LEFT OUTER JOIN T3);
```

a	b	c
1	2	NULL

This produces the same results as the next query, which puts table T2 into the results last. This may lead you to think that the order of the tables does not matter:

```
SELECT T1.a, T1.b, T3.c
    FROM ((T1 NATURAL LEFT OUTER JOIN T3)
        NATURAL LEFT OUTER JOIN T2);
```

a	b	c
1	2	NULL

However, this query has very different results:

```
SELECT T1.a, T1.b, T3.c
    FROM ((T2 NATURAL LEFT OUTER JOIN T3)
        NATURAL LEFT OUTER JOIN T1);
```

a	b	c
NULL	NULL	NULL

Even worse, the choice of columns in the SELECT list can change the output. Instead of displaying T3.c, use T2.c instead and you will see a value of 3 instead of NULL:

```
SELECT T1.a, T1.b, T2.c
    FROM ((T2 NATURAL LEFT OUTER JOIN T3)
    NATURAL LEFT OUTER JOIN T1);
```

a	b	c
NULL	NULL	3

SQL engines that use special operators in the WHERE clause very often get strange results. The same table can be marked for preservation in one predicate, but not in another. Regular theta operators can remove rows that might have been part of an OUTER JOIN, and so forth. The order of the predicates can also make a difference as to which is executed first, and that is often in the hands of the optimizer, not the programmer.

Until these products have implemented the SQL-92 version of OUTER JOINs, the programmer will have to experiment, make heavy use of VIEWs in which only pairs of tables are used, or avoid OUTER JOIN queries.

16.2.7 OUTER JOINs and Aggregate Functions

At the start of this chapter, we had a table of orders and a table of suppliers, which were to be used to build a report to tell us how much business we did with each supplier. The query that will do this is

```
SELECT Suppliers.supno, supname, SUM(amt)
   FROM Suppliers LEFT OUTER JOIN Orders
   ON Suppliers.supno = Orders.supno
GROUP BY supno, supname;
```

Some suppliers' totals include credits for returned merchandise, such that our total business with them worked out to zero dollars. Each supplier with which we did no business will have a NULL in its amt column in the OUTER JOIN. The usual rules for aggregate functions with NULL values apply, so these suppliers will also show a zero total amount.

It is also possible to use a function inside an aggregate function, so you could write SUM(COALESCE(T1.x, T2.x)) for the common column pairs.

If you need to tell the difference between a true sum of zero and the result of a NULL in an OUTER JOIN, use the MIN() or MAX() function on the questionable column. These functions both return a NULL result for a NULL input, so an expression inside the MAX() function could be used to print the message MAX(COALESCE(amt, 'No Orders')), for example.

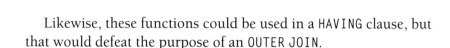

Likewise, these functions could be used in a HAVING clause, but that would defeat the purpose of an OUTER JOIN.

16.2.8 FULL OUTER JOIN

The FULL OUTER JOIN was introduced in SQL-92, but has not been implemented in most SQLs yet. This operator is a mix of the LEFT and RIGHT OUTER JOINs, with preserved rows constructed from both tables.

The statement takes two tables and puts them in one result table. Again, this is easier to explain with an example than with a formal definition. It is also a way to show how to form a query that will perform the same function. Using Suppliers and Orders again, we find that we have suppliers with which we have done no business, but we also have orders for which we have not decided on suppliers. To get all orders and all suppliers in one result table, we could use the SQL-89 query:

```
SELECT supno, supname, amt      -- regular INNER JOIN
    FROM Suppliers, Orders
WHERE (Suppliers.supno = Orders.supno)
UNION ALL
SELECT supno, supname, NULL    -- preserved rows of LEFT JOIN
    FROM Suppliers
WHERE NOT EXISTS (SELECT *
            FROM Orders
        WHERE (Suppliers.supno = Orders.supno))
UNION ALL
SELECT NULL, NULL, amt      -- preserved rows of RIGHT JOIN
    FROM Orders
WHERE NOT EXISTS (SELECT *
            FROM Suppliers
        WHERE (Suppliers.supno = Orders.supno));
```

The same thing in SQL-92 would be

```
SELECT supno, supname, amt
    FROM Orders FULL OUTER JOIN Suppliers
        ON (Suppliers.supno = Orders.supno);
```

The FULL OUTER JOIN is not used as much as a LEFT or RIGHT OUTER JOIN. When you are doing a report, it is usually done from a viewpoint that leads to preserving only one side of the JOIN. That is, you might ask "What suppliers got no business from us?" or ask "What orders have not been assigned a supplier?" but a combination of the two questions is not likely to be in the same report.

16.3 UNION JOIN

The UNION JOIN was also introduced in SQL-92, but has not been implemented in most SQLs yet. The statement is a cross between a UNION and an OUTER JOIN operator. The syntax does not allow for any join conditions, however:

```
<table reference> UNION JOIN <table reference>
```

The statement takes two tables and puts them in one result table. However, it preserves all the columns from the original tables and does not try to consolidate them. Columns in one table that are not in the other are simply padded out with NULLs. Columns with the same names in the original tables have to be renamed in the results. The UNION JOIN is equivalent to a FULL OUTER JOIN without the rows from the INNER JOIN, or, in other words,

```
Table1 FULL OUTER JOIN Table2 ON (FALSE)
```

An example of a use for this might be to combine medical records of both male and female patients where the female patient table has pregnancies and the male patient table has prostate cancer.

```
SELECT *
    FROM (SELECT 'male', prostate
            FROM Males)
        UNION JOIN
        (SELECT 'female', pregnancy
            FROM Females)
```

That would give a result like this:

Result

male	prostate	female	pregnancy
male	no	NULL	NULL
male	no	NULL	NULL
male	yes	NULL	NULL
male	yes	NULL	NULL
NULL	NULL	female	no
NULL	NULL	female	no
NULL	NULL	female	yes
NULL	NULL	female	yes

To be honest, I know of no use for this type of JOIN.

16.4 Exotic JOINs

Most joins are done using an equality test between the columns in the joined tables. In fact, of these equi-joins, the columns usually have the same names, so we give them the special name NATURAL JOINs. Among NATURAL JOINs, the most common case is a foreign key to the primary key of the table it references. Since these simple joins constitute 80% to 85% of the SQL queries in real applications, it is easy to forget that you can also have other kinds of joins.

This section will discuss other types of joins that are not used often, but are very helpful when they are needed. For lack of a better term, I am calling them exotic joins.

16.4.1 Self Non-Equi-JOINs

A non-equi-join is simply that — a join based on a comparison other than an equality in columns of the two tables. Here are some common uses for them. A self join is a join of one copy of a table to itself or to a subset of itself.

A common use for a self non-equi-join is to join a table to itself in such a way as to avoid making redundant pairs. For example, you are given a table of products and you want to make a list of pairs of them, which you will use for market analysis. The first-attempt query is usually

```
SELECT P1.prodname, P2.prodname
    FROM Products AS P1, Products AS P2;
```

but this is quickly rejected because it produces too much data and most of it is redundant. You would get the four rows (`'peanut butter'`, `'jelly'`), (`'jelly'`, `'peanut butter'`), (`'peanut butter'`, `'peanut butter'`), and (`'jelly'`, `'jelly'`) when you really wanted just (`'jelly'`, `'peanut butter'`). The trick is to use a nonequality to remove the unwanted combinations, thus:

```
SELECT P1.prodname, P2.prodname
    FROM Products AS P1, Products AS P2
WHERE P1.prodname < P2.prodname;
```

To keep the pairs where both members are identical, change the "less than" to a "less than or equal" operator. This pattern can be extended to produce triples, quadruples, and so forth. It is a good idea to use a "less than" sign instead of a "greater than" sign, so that the first column in the result table will have the lowest value of the group. This horizontal sorting will be easier to read.

16.4.2 Range JOINs

Most joins are based on simple predicates that involve scalar comparisons. But it is also possible to do joins based on relationships between sets of columns in two or more tables. The most common form of this is an interval join, where a time period or a range of values is related to another value in the second table.

A common example of translating an interval or range into a scalar value is grading such that 100% to 90% on a test is an "A," 80% to 89% is a "B," 70% to 79% is a "C," 60% to 69% is a "D," and 59% or less is a failure. The use of this type of query for code translation or as a way of partitioning a database is discussed in section 18.1.1.

16.5 Dr. Codd's T-JOIN

Dr. E. F. Codd introduced a set of new theta operators, called T-operators, which were based on the idea of a best fit or approximate equality (Codd 1990). The algorithm for the operators is easier to understand with an example borrowed from Codd than with a formal definition.

The problem is to assign the classes to the available classrooms. We want `classsize < roomsize` to be true after the assignments are made. This will allow us a few empty seats in each room for late students. We can do this in one of two ways. The first way is to sort the tables in ascending order by classroom size and the number of students in a class. We start with the following tables:

```
CREATE TABLE Rooms
(roomno CHAR(2) PRIMARY KEY,
 bldg  CHAR(10) NOT NULL,
 roomsize INTEGER NOT NULL);


CREATE TABLE Classes
(classno CHAR(2) PRIMARY KEY,
 classsize INTEGER NOT NULL);
```

These have the following rows in them:

Classes

classno	classsize
c6	40
c5	50
c4	55
c3	65
c2	70
c1	80

Rooms

roomno	bldg	roomsize
r5	class	30
r2	lab	40
r3	lab	50
r7	class	55
r6	class	65
r1	lab	70
r4	class	85

Then match the first row of Classes to the first row of Rooms where the condition `classsize < roomsize` is true. Proceed to do the same thing for each row of Classes for as long as you can.

Results

classno	classsize	roomsize	roomno	bldg
c6	40	50	r3	lab
c5	50	55	r7	class
c4	55	65	r6	class
c3	65	70	r1	lab
c2	70	85	r4	class

The second way is to sort the tables in descending order by classroom size and the number of students in a class.

Rooms

roomno	bldg	roomsize
r4	class	85
r1	lab	70
r6	class	65
r7	class	55
r3	lab	50
r2	lab	40
r5	class	30

Classes

classno	classsize
c1	80
c2	70
c3	65
c4	55
c5	50
c6	40

Then match the first row of Rooms to the first row of Classes where the condition `classsize < roomsize` is true. Proceed to do the same thing for each row of Rooms for as long as you can. The results are not the same.

Results

classno	classsize	roomsize	roomno	bldg
c1	85	80	r4	class
c3	65	70	r1	lab
c4	55	65	r6	class
c5	50	55	r7	class
c6	40	50	r3	lab

Other theta conditions can be used in place of the "less than" shown here. If "less than or equal" is used, all the classes are assigned to a room in this case, but not in all cases. This is left to the reader as an exercise.

The first attempts in standard SQL are versions grouped by queries.
They can, however, produce some rows that would be left out of the
answers Codd was expecting. The first JOIN can be written as

```
SELECT classno, classsize, MIN(roomsize)
    FROM Rooms, Classes
WHERE (Classes.classsize < Rooms.roomsize)
GROUP BY classno, classsize;
```

This will give a result table with the desired room sizes, but not the
room numbers. You cannot put the other columns in the SELECT list,
since it would conflict with the GROUP BY clause. But also note that
the classroom with 85 seats (r4) is used twice, once by class c5 and
then by class c6:

Result

classno	classsize	MIN(roomsize)
c1	40	50
c2	50	55
c3	55	65
c4	65	70
c5	70	85
c6	80	85

Your best bet after this is to use the query in an EXISTS clause.

```
SELECT *
    FROM Rooms, Classes
WHERE EXISTS (SELECT classno, classsize, MIN(roomsize)
          FROM Rooms, Classes
      WHERE (Classes.classsize < Rooms.roomsize)
    GROUP BY classno, classsize);
```

However, some versions of SQL will not allow a grouped subquery
and others will balk at an aggregate function in an EXISTS predicate.
The only way I have found to rectify this was to save the results to a
temporary table, then join it back to the Cartesian product of Rooms
and Classes.

The second T-join can be done by putting the columns for Rooms into the SELECT list of the same query schema:

```
SELECT roomno, roomsize, MAX(classsize)
    FROM Rooms, Classes
WHERE (Classes.classsize < Rooms.roomsize)
GROUP BY roomno, roomsize;
```

This time, the results are the same as those Codd got with his procedural algorithm:

Result

roomno	roomsize	MAX(classsize)
r4	85	80
r1	70	65
r6	65	55
r7	55	50
r3	50	40

If you do a little arithmetic on the data, you find that we have 360 students and 395 seats, 6 classes and 7 rooms. This solution uses the fewest rooms, but note that the 70 students in class c2 are left out completely. Room r2 is left over, but it has only 40 seats. This does not really solve the original problem.

As it works out, the best fit of rooms to classes is given by changing the matching rule to "less than or equal." This will leave the smallest room empty and pack the other rooms to capacity, thus:

```
SELECT classno, classsize, MIN(roomsize)
    FROM Rooms, Classes
WHERE (Classes.classsize <= Rooms.roomsize)
GROUP BY classno, classsize;
```

16.5.1 The Croatian Solution

I published this same problem in an article in *DBMS* magazine (Celko 1992a) and got an answer in QUEL from Miljenko Martinis of Croatia in our Letters column (Miljenko 1992). He then translated it from QUEL into SQL with two views, thus:

```
CREATE VIEW Classrooms -- your VIEW
AS SELECT *
      FROM Classes, Rooms
    WHERE (classsize < roomsize);


CREATE VIEW Classrooms1 -- one step farther
AS SELECT *
      FROM Classrooms AS CR1
    WHERE roomsize = (SELECT MIN(roomsize)
                FROM Classrooms
             WHERE classno = CR1.classno);
```

We find the answer with the simple query

```
SELECT *
    FROM Classrooms1 AS R1
WHERE classsize = (SELECT MAX(classsize)
          FROM Classrooms1
        WHERE roomno = R1.roomno);
```

I tried this in XDB on my PC; it runs very, very slowly, but it works and gives true "best-fit" results.

classno	classsize	roomno	bldg	roomsize
c6	40	r3	lab	50
c5	50	r7	class	55
c4	55	r6	class	65
c3	65	r1	lab	70
c1	80	r4	class	85

16.5.2 The Swedish Solution

I got another solution from Anders Karlsson of Mr. K Software AB in Stockholm, Sweden:

```
SELECT CR1.classno, CR1.classsize, RM1.roomno, RM1.roomsize
    FROM Classes CR1, Rooms AS RM1
WHERE RM1.roomsize = (SELECT MIN(RM2.roomsize)
            FROM Rooms AS RM2
        WHERE (RM2.roomsize > CR1.classsize)
        AND NOT EXISTS
            (SELECT *
                FROM Classes AS CR2
                    WHERE (RM2.roomsize > CR2.classsize)
                    AND (CR2.classno < CR1.classno)));
```

CHAPTER

17

VIEWs

A VIEW IS ALSO called a *virtual table*, to distinguish it from a base table. It is constructed from one or more base tables or other VIEWs upon its first use in a query and ceases to exist upon the end of that query. Whether or not the database system actually materializes a VIEW as a physical table or uses other mechanisms is implementation-defined according to the ANSI standard.

17.1 VIEWs in SQL-92 and SQL-89

The semantics of VIEWs have changed in the SQL-92 standard. The SQL-92 syntax for the VIEW definition is

```
CREATE VIEW <table name> [(<view column list>)]
AS <query expression>
[WITH [<levels clause>] CHECK OPTION]

<levels clause> ::= CASCADED | LOCAL
```

The <levels clause> option in the WITH CHECK OPTION did not exist in SQL-89 and it is not widely implemented yet.

An informal, but more useful, way to think of a VIEW is as the result of a SELECT statement put into a local temporary table. The whole idea is that a VIEW looks and behaves pretty much like a base table that was just constructed the second before you used it. Here is a list of database schema objects and their properties in a query:

	Physical Existence	Accessed by User
Domain	no	no
View	no	yes
Index	yes	no
Table	yes	yes

Those of you who are more cynical might also add a line to this chart that defines a "backup copy" as having neither existence nor accessibility.

The name of the VIEW must be unique within the database schema, like a table name. The VIEW definition cannot reference itself, since it does not exist yet. Nor can the definition reference only other VIEWs; the nesting of VIEWs must eventually resolve to underlying base tables. This only makes sense; if no base tables were involved, what would you be viewing?

17.2 Updatable and Read-Only VIEWs

Unlike base tables, VIEWs are either updatable or read-only, but not both. INSERT, UPDATE, and DELETE operations are allowed on up-datable VIEWs and base tables, subject to any other constraints. INSERT, UPDATE, and DELETE are not allowed on read-only VIEWs, only on SELECT statements, as you would expect.

An updatable VIEW is one that can have each of its rows associated with exactly one row in an underlying base table. When the VIEW is changed, the changes pass through the VIEW to that underlying base table unambiguously.

Updatable VIEWs in SQL-89 are defined only for queries on only one table, with no GROUP BY clause, no HAVING clause, no aggregate functions, no calculated columns, and no SELECT DISTINCT clause; any columns excluded from the VIEW must be NULL-able in the base table, so that a whole row can be constructed for insertion. By implication, the VIEW must also contain a key of the table. In short, we are absolutely sure that each row in the VIEW maps back to one row in its base table.

Some updating is handled by the CASCADE option in the referential integrity constraints on the base tables, not by the VIEW declaration. Many SQL implementations do not support full SQL-92 referential integrity constraints at this time, so this is not always an option.

The definition of updatability in both SQL-89 and SQL-92 is actually pretty limited, but very safe. The database system could look at information it has in the referential integrity constraints to widen the set of allowed updatable VIEWs. You will find that some implementations are now doing just that, but it is not common yet.

The SQL standard definition of an updatable VIEW is actually a subset of the possible updatable VIEWs, and a very small subset at that. Without going into details, here is a list of types of queries that can yield updatable VIEWs, as taken from "VIEW Update Is Practical," (Goodman 1990):

1. Projection from a single table (ANSI SQL)
2. Restriction/projection from a single table (ANSI SQL)
3. UNION VIEWs
4. Set difference VIEWs
5. One-to-one joins
6. One-to-one outer joins
7. One-to-many joins
8. One-to-many outer joins
9. Many-to-many joins
10. Translated and coded fields

The SQL3 document has a CREATE TRIGGER mechanism for tables which allows a triggered action to be performed BEFORE, AFTER, or INSTEAD OF a regular INSERT, UPDATE, or DELETE to that table. It might be possible for a user to write INSTEAD OF triggers on VIEWs, which would catch the changes and route them to the base tables that make up the VIEW. The database designer would have complete control over the way VIEWs are handled.

17.3 Types of VIEWs

VIEWs can be classified by the type of SELECT statement they use and the purpose they are meant to serve.

17.3.1 Single-Table Projection and Restriction

In practice, many VIEWs are projections or restrictions on a single base table. This is a common method for obtaining security control by removing rows or columns that a particular group of users is not allowed to see. These VIEWs are best done as in-line text expansion, since the optimizer can easily fold their code into the final query plan.

17.3.2 Calculated Columns

One common use for a VIEW is to provide summary data across a row. For example, given a table with measurements in metric units, we can construct a VIEW that hides the calculations to convert them into English units.

It is important to be sure that you have no problems with NULL values when constructing a calculated column. For example, given a table of employees with columns for both salary and commission, you might construct this VIEW:

```
CREATE VIEW EmpPay (empno, totpay)
AS SELECT empno, (salary + commission)
   FROM Employees;
```

However, office workers do not get commissions, so the value of their commission column will be NULL (it cannot be zero, since that could represent a bad month for a commissioned salesman). The value of the totpay column in the VIEW will therefore be NULL. You should use the COALESCE() function mentioned in section 3.5.2 to change the NULLs to zeros.

17.3.3 Translated Columns

Another common use of a VIEW is to translate codes into text or other codes by doing table lookups. This is a special case of a joined VIEW

based on a FOREIGN KEY relationship between two tables. For example, an order table might use a part number that we wish to display with a part name on an order entry screen. This is done with a JOIN between the order table and the inventory table, thus:

```
CREATE VIEW Screen (partid, pname, ...)
AS SELECT Orders.partid, Inventory.pname, ...)
    FROM Inventory, Orders
WHERE Inventory.partid = Orders.partid
```

Sometimes the original code is kept and sometimes it is dropped from the VIEW. As a general rule, it is a better idea to keep both values even though they are redundant. The redundancy can be used as a check for users, as well as a hook for nested JOINs in either of the codes.

The idea of JOIN VIEWs to translate codes can be expanded to show more than just one translated column. The result is often a "star" query with one table in the center, joined by FOREIGN KEY relations to many other tables to produce a result that is more readable than the original central table.

Missing values are a problem. If there is no translation for a given code, no row appears in the VIEW, or if an OUTER JOIN was used, a NULL will appear. The programmer should establish a referential integrity constraint to CASCADE changes between the tables to prevent loss of data.

17.3.4 Grouped VIEWs

A grouped VIEW is based on a query with a GROUP BY clause. Since each of the groups may have more than one row in the base from which it was built, these are necessarily read-only VIEWs. Such VIEWs usually have one or more aggregate functions and they are used for reporting purposes.

They are also handy for working around weaknesses in SQL. Consider a VIEW that shows the largest sale in each state. The query is straightforward:

```
CREATE VIEW BigSales (state, bigamt)
AS SELECT STATE, MAX(amt)
    FROM Sales
GROUP BY state;
```

However, SQL requires that the grouping column(s) appear in the SELECT clause. If I simply want a list of the largest sales without their states, I cannot get it with this VIEW. I have to construct another VIEW from this grouped VIEW, thus:

```
CREATE VIEW BigAmts (amt)
AS SELECT bigamt FROM BigSales;
```

Since this is a single-column table, it can be used with predicates that require a subquery in SQL-89. See section 16.5 on T-joins for more details as to how useful this can be for certain queries.

These VIEWs are also useful for "flattening out" one-to-many relationships. For example, consider a table of employees, keyed on the employee code number (empno), and a table of dependents, keyed on a combination of the code number for each dependent's parent (empno) and the dependent's own serial number (depid). The goal is to produce a report of the employees by name with the number of dependents each has.

```
CREATE VIEW DepTally1 (empno, totdeps)
AS SELECT empno, COUNT(*)
    FROM Dependents
GROUP BY empno;
```

The report is then simply an OUTER JOIN between this VIEW and the Employees table. The OUTER JOIN is needed to account for employees without dependents with a NULL value. Using SQL-92 syntax, the report query looks like this:

```
SELECT empname, totdeps
    FROM Employees LEFT OUTER JOIN DepTally1 ON empno;
```

17.3.5 UNION VIEWs

A VIEW based on a UNION or UNION ALL operation is read-only because there is no way to map a change onto just one row in one of the base tables. The UNION operator will remove duplicate rows from the results. Both the UNION and UNION ALL operators hide which table the rows came from. Such VIEWs must use a <view column list>, because the columns in a UNION [ALL] have no names of their own.

In theory, a UNION of two disjoint tables, neither of which has duplicate rows in itself, should be updatable. Most systems cannot detect this and make all such VIEWs read-only.

Using the problem given in section 17.3.4 on grouped VIEWs, this could also be done with a UNION query that would assign a count of zero to employees without dependents, thus:

```
CREATE VIEW DepTally2 (empno, cntdeps)
AS (SELECT empno, COUNT(*)
    FROM Dependents
GROUP BY empno)
    UNION
    (SELECT empno, 0
FROM Employees
      WHERE NOT EXISTS (SELECT *
    FROM Dependents
    WHERE Dependents.empno = Employees.empno));
```

The report is now a simple INNER JOIN between this VIEW and the Employees table. The zero value, instead of a NULL value, will account for employees without dependents. The report query looks like this:

```
SELECT empname, cntdeps
    FROM Employees, DepTally2
    WHERE (DepTally2.empno = Employees.empno);
```

17.3.6 JOINs in VIEWs

A VIEW whose query expression is a joined table is not usually updatable even in theory. One of the major purposes of a joined view is to "flatten out" a one-to-many or many-to-many relationship. Such relationships cannot map one row in the VIEW back to one row in the underlying tables on the "many" side of the JOIN.

Anything said about a JOIN query could be said about a joined view, so they will not be dealt with here; and the reader is referred to chapter 16 for a full discussion of JOINs.

17.3.7 Nested VIEWs

A point that is often missed, even by experienced SQL programmers, is that a VIEW can be built on other VIEWs. The only restrictions are that circular references within the query expressions of the VIEWs are illegal and that a VIEW must ultimately be built on base tables.

One problem with nested VIEWs is that different updatable VIEWs can reference the same base table at the same time. If these VIEWs then appear in another VIEW, it becomes hard to determine what has happened when the highest-level VIEW is changed. As an example, consider a table with two keys:

```
CREATE TABLE Canada
(english INTEGER,
 french INTEGER,
 engword CHAR(30),
 frenword CHAR(30));

INSERT INTO Canada VALUES (1, 2, 'muffins', 'croissants');
INSERT INTO Canada VALUES (2, 1, 'bait', 'escargots');

CREATE VIEW E AS (SELECT english, engword
    FROM Canada WHERE engword IS NOT NULL);

CREATE VIEW F AS (SELECT french, frenword
FROM Canada WHERE frenword IS NOT NULL);
```

We have now tried the escargots and decided that we wish to change our opinion of them:

```
UPDATE E
   SET engword = 'appetizer'
WHERE english = 2;
```

Our French user has just tried haggis and decided to insert a new record of his experience:

```
INSERT INTO F
   SET frenword = 'Le swill'
   WHERE french = 3;
```

The row that is created is (NULL, 3, NULL, 'Le swill'), since there is no way for VIEW F to get to the E VIEW columns. Likewise, the English VIEW user can construct a row to record his translation, (3, NULL, 'Haggis', NULL). But neither of them can consolidate the two rows into a meaningful piece of data.

To delete a row is also to destroy data; the French-speaker who drops 'croissants' from the table also drops 'muffins' from the E VIEW.

17.4 How VIEWs Are Handled in the Database System

The SQL-92 standard requires a system schema table with the text of the VIEW declarations in it. What would be handy, but is not easily done in all SQL implementations, is to trace the VIEWs down to their base tables by printing out a tree diagram of the nested structure. You should check your user library and see if such a utility program exists (such as, for example, FINDVIEW in the SPARC library for SQL/DS).

There are several ways to handle VIEWs, and systems will often use a mixture of them. The major categories of algorithms are materialization and in-line text expansion.

17.4.1 View Column List

The <view column list> is optional; when it is not given, the VIEW will inherit the column names from the query. The number of column names in the <view column list> has to be the same as the degree of the query expression. If any two columns in the query have the same column name, you must have a <view column list> to resolve the ambiguity. The same column name cannot be specified more than once in the <view column list>.

17.4.2 VIEW Materialization

The decision to materialize a VIEW as an actual physical table is implementation-defined in the ANSI SQL Standard, but the VIEW must act as if it were a table when accessed for a query. If the VIEW is not updatable, this approach automatically protects the base tables from any improper changes and is guaranteed to be correct. It uses existing internal procedures in the database engine (create table, insert from query), so this is easy for the database to do.

The downside of this approach is that it is not very fast for large VIEWs, uses extra storage space, cannot take advantage of indexes already existing on the base tables, usually cannot create indexes on the new table, and cannot be optimized as easily as other approaches.

However, certain VIEWs are best done by materialization. A VIEW whose construction has a hidden sort is usually materialized. Queries with SELECT DISTINCT, UNION, GROUP BY, and HAVING clauses are usually implemented by sorting to remove duplicate rows or to build groups. As each row of the VIEW is built, it has to be saved to compare it to the other rows, so it makes sense to materialize it.

17.4.3 In-Line Text Expansion

Another approach is to store the text of the CREATE VIEW statement and work it into the parse tree of the SELECT, INSERT, UPDATE, or DELETE statements that use it. This allows the optimizer to blend the VIEW definition into the final query plan. For example, you can create a VIEW based on a particular department, thus:

```
CREATE VIEW SalesDept (deptname, city, ...)
AS SELECT *
    FROM Departments
    WHERE deptname = 'Sales';
```

and then use it as a query, thus:

```
SELECT *
   FROM SalesDept
   WHERE city = 'New York';
```

The parser expands the VIEW into text (or an intermediate token-ized form) within the FROM clause. The syntax shown below is not legal SQL-89, but is part of SQL-92. Since many implementations already have the mechanisms for doing this, expect it to be an early SQL-92 feature. The query would become, in effect,

```
SELECT *
   FROM (SELECT *
   FROM Departments
   WHERE deptname = 'Sales')
   WHERE city = 'New York';
```

and the query optimizer would then "flatten it out" into

```
SELECT *
FROM Departments
WHERE (deptname = 'Sales')
   AND (city = 'New York');
```

Though this sounds like a nice approach, it has problems in many systems where the in-line expansion does not result in proper SQL. An earlier version of DB2 was one such system. To illustrate the prob-lem, imagine that you are given a DB2 table that has a long identifica-tion number and some figures in each row. The long identification number is like those 40-digit monsters they give you on a utility bill — they are unique only in the first few characters, but the utility company prints the whole thing out anyway. Your task is to create a report that is grouped according to the first six characters of the long identification number. The immediate naive query uses the substring operator:

```
SELECT SUBSTRING(id FROM 1 TO 6), SUM(amt1), SUM(amt2), ...
   FROM TableA
   GROUP BY id;
```

This does not work; it is incorrect SQL, since the SELECT and GROUP BY lists do not agree. Other common attempts include GROUP BY SUBSTRING(id FROM 1 TO 6), which will fail because you cannot use a function, and GROUP BY 1, which will fail because you can use a column position only in a UNION statement. The GROUP BY has to have a list of simple column names drawn from the tables of the FROM clause. The next attempt is to build a VIEW:

```
CREATE VIEW BadTry (Shortid, amt1, amt2, ...)
AS SELECT SUBSTRING(id FROM 1 TO 6), amt1, amt2, ...
    FROM TableA;
```

and then do a grouped SELECT on it. This is correct SQL, but it does not work in DB2. DB2 apparently tries to insert the VIEW into the FROM clause, as we have seen, but when it expands it out, the results are the same as those of the incorrect first query attempt with a function call in the GROUP BY clause.

The trick is to force DB2 to materialize the VIEW so that you can name the column constructed with the SUBSTRING() function. Anything that causes a sort will do this — the SELECT DISTINCT, UNION, GROUP BY, and HAVING clauses, for example. Since we know that the short identification number is a key, we can use this VIEW:

```
CREATE VIEW Shorty (Shortid, amt1, amt2, ...)
AS SELECT DISTINCT SUBSTRING(id FROM 1 TO 6), amt1, amt2, ...
FROM TableA;
```

Then the report query is

```
SELECT Shortid, SUM(amt1), SUM(amt2), ...
    FROM Shorty
    GROUP BY Shortid;
```

This works fine in DB2. I am indebted to Susan Vombrack of Loral Aerospace for this example.

Incidentally, this can be written in SQL-92 as

```
SELECT SUBSTRING(id FROM 1 TO 6) AS shortid, ...
    FROM TableA
    GROUP BY shortid;
```

The name on the substring result column makes it recognizable to the parser.

17.4.4 Pointer Structures

Finally, the system can handle VIEWs with special data structures for the VIEW. This is usually an array of pointers into a base table constructed from the VIEW definition. This is a good way to handle updatable VIEWs in standard SQL, since the target row in the base table is at the end of a pointer chain in the VIEW structure. Access will be as fast as possible.

The pointer structure approach cannot easily use existing indexes on the base tables. But the pointer structure can be implemented as an index with restrictions. Furthermore, multitable VIEWs can be constructed as pointer structures that allow direct access to the related rows in the table involved in the JOIN. This is very product-dependent, so you cannot make any general assumptions.

17.4.5 Indexing and VIEWs

Note that VIEWs cannot have their own indexes. However, VIEWs can inherit the indexing on their base tables in some implementations. Like tables, VIEWs have no inherent ordering, but a programmer who knows his particular SQL implementation will often write code that takes advantage of the quirks of that product.

In particular, some implementations allow you to use an ORDER BY clause in a VIEW (they are allowed only on cursors in standard SQL). This will force a sort and could materialize the VIEW as a working table. When the SQL engine has to be a table scan (a sequential read of the table), the sort might help or hinder a particular query. There is no way to predict the results.

17.5 WITH CHECK OPTION Clause

If WITH CHECK OPTION is specified, the viewed table has to be updatable. This is actually a fast way to check how your particular SQL implementation handles updatable VIEWs. Try to create a version of the VIEW in question using the WITH CHECK OPTION and see if your product will allow you to create it.

The WITH CHECK OPTION is part of the SQL-89 standard, which was extended in SQL-92 by adding an optional <levels clause>. CASCADED is implicit if an explicit levels clause is not given. Consider a VIEW defined as

```
CREATE VIEW V1
AS SELECT *
   FROM Table1
WHERE col1 = 'A';
```

and now UPDATE it with

```
UPDATE V1 SET col1 = 'B';
```

The UPDATE will take place without any trouble, but the rows that were previously seen now disappear when we use V1 again. They no longer meet the WHERE clause condition! Likewise, an INSERT INTO statement with VALUES (col1 = 'B') would insert just fine, but its rows would never be seen again in this VIEW.

VIEWs created this way will always have all the rows that meet the criteria and that can be handy. For example, you can set up a VIEW of records with a status code of 'to be done', work on them, and change a status code to 'finished', and they will disappear from your view. The important point is that the WHERE clause condition was checked only at the time when the VIEW was invoked.

The WITH CHECK OPTION makes the system check the WHERE clause condition upon insertion or UPDATE. If the new or changed row fails the test, the change is rejected and the VIEW remains the same. Thus, the previous UPDATE statement would get an error message and you could not change certain columns in certain ways. For example, consider a VIEW of salaries under $30,000 defined with a WITH CHECK OPTION to prevent anyone from giving a raise above that ceiling.

SQL-92 has introduced an optional levels clause, which can be either CASCADED or LOCAL. If no levels clause is given, a levels clause of CASCADED is implicit. The idea of a CASCADED check is that the system checks all the underlying levels that built the VIEW, as well as the WHERE clause condition in the VIEW itself. If anything causes a row to disappear from the VIEW, the UPDATE is rejected. The idea of a WITH

LOCAL CHECK OPTION is that only the local WHERE clause is checked.
The underlying VIEWs or tables from which this VIEW is built might
also be affected, but we do not test for those effects. Consider two
VIEWs built on each other from the salary table:

```
CREATE VIEW Lowpay
AS SELECT *
    FROM Employees
WHERE salary <= 250;
```

```
CREATE VIEW Mediumpay
AS SELECT *
    FROM Lowpay
WHERE salary >= 100;
```

If neither VIEW has a WITH CHECK OPTION, the effect of updating
Mediumpay by increasing every salary by $1,000 will be passed with-
out any check to Lowpay. Lowpay will pass the changes to the underlying Employees table. The next time Mediumpay is used, Lowpay
will be rebuilt in its own right and Mediumpay rebuilt from it, and all
the employees will disappear from Mediumpay.

If only Mediumpay has a WITH CASCADED CHECK OPTION on it, the
UPDATE will fail. Mediumpay has no problem with such a large salary,
but it would cause a row in Lowpay to disappear, so Mediumpay will
reject it. However, if only Mediumpay has a WITH LOCAL CHECK
OPTION on it, the UPDATE will succeed. Mediumpay has no problem
with such a large salary, so it passes the change along to Lowpay.
Lowpay, in turn, passes the change to the Employees table and the
UPDATE occurs.

If both VIEWs have a WITH CASCADED CHECK OPTION, the effect is a
set of conditions, all of which have to be met. The Employees table
can accept UPDATEs or INSERTs only where the salary is between $100
and $250.

This can become very complex. Consider an example from an
ANSI X3H2 paper by Nelson Mattos of IBM (Celko 1993). Let us
build a five-layer set of VIEWs, using xx and yy as place holders for
CASCADED or LOCAL, on a base table T1 with columns c1, c2, c3, c4,
and c5, all set to a value of 10, thus:

```
CREATE VIEW V1 AS SELECT * FROM T1 WHERE (c1 > 5);
CREATE VIEW V2 AS SELECT * FROM V1 WHERE (c2 > 5)
   WITH xx CHECK OPTION;
CREATE VIEW V3 AS SELECT * FROM V2 WHERE (c3 > 5);
CREATE VIEW V4 AS SELECT * FROM V3 WHERE (c4 > 5)
    WITH yy CHECK OPTION;
CREATE VIEW V5 AS SELECT * FROM V4 WHERE (c5 > 5);
```

When we set each one of the columns to zero, we get different results, which can be shown in this chart, where S means success and F means failure:

xx/yy	c1	c2	c3	c4	c5
cascade/cascade	F	F	F	F	S
local/cascade	F	F	F	F	S
local/local	S	F	S	F	S
cascade/local	F	F	S	F	S

To understand the chart, look at the last line. If xx = CASCADED and yy = LOCAL, updating column c1 to zero via V5 will fail, whereas updating c5 will succeed. Remember that a successful UPDATE means the row(s) disappear from V5.

Follow the action for UPDATE V5 SET c1 = 0; VIEW V5 has no WITH CHECK OPTIONs, so the changed rows are immediately sent to V4 without any testing. VIEW V4 does have a WITH LOCAL CHECK OPTION, but column c1 is not involved, so V4 passes the rows to V3. VIEW V3 has no WITH CHECK OPTIONs, so the changed rows are immediately sent to V2. VIEW V2 does have a WITH CASCADED CHECK OPTION, so V2 passes the rows to V1 and awaits results. VIEW V1 is built on the original base table and has the condition c1 > 5, which is violated by this UPDATE. VIEW V1 then rejects the UPDATE to the base table, so the rows remain in V5 when it is rebuilt.

Now the action for UPDATE V5 SET c3 = 0: VIEW V5 has no WITH CHECK OPTIONs, so the changed rows are immediately sent to V4, as before. VIEW V4 does have a WITH LOCAL CHECK OPTION, but column c3 is not involved, so V4 passes the rows to V3 without awaiting the results. VIEW V3 is involved with column c3 and has no WITH CHECK OPTIONS, so the rows can be changed and passed down to V2 and V1, where they UPDATE the base table. The rows are not seen again when V5 is invoked, because they will fail to get past VIEW V3.

The real problem comes with UPDATE statements that change more than one column at a time. For example, UPDATE V5 SET c1 = 0, c2 = 0, c3 = 0, c4 = 0, c5 = 0; will fail for all possible combinations of <levels clause>s in the example schema.

A change in the SQL-92 standard in March 1993 defined the idea of a set of conditions that are inherited by the levels of nesting. In our sample schema, these implied tests would be added to each VIEW definition:

```
local/local
V1 = none
V2 = (c2 > 5)
V3 = (c2 > 5)
V4 = (c2 > 5) AND (c4 > 5)
V5 = (c2 > 5) AND (c4 > 5)


cascade/cascade
V1 = none
V2 = (c1 > 5) AND (c2 > 5)
V3 = (c1 > 5) AND (c2 > 5)
V4 = (c1 > 5) AND (c2 > 5) AND (c3 > 5) AND (c4 > 5)
V5 = (c1 > 5) AND (c2 > 5) AND (c3 > 5) AND (c4 > 5)


local/cascade
V1 = none
V2 = (c2 > 5)
V3 = (c2 > 5)
V4 = (c1 > 5) AND (c2 > 5) AND (c4 > 5)
V5 = (c1 > 5) AND (c2 > 5) AND (c4 > 5)


cascade/local
V1 = none
V2 = (c1 > 5) AND (c2 > 5)
V3 = (c1 > 5) AND (c2 > 5)
V4 = (c1 > 5) AND (c2 > 5) AND (c4 > 5)
V5 = (c1 > 5) AND (c2 > 5) AND (c4 > 5)
```

17.6 Dropping VIEWs

VIEWs, like tables, can be dropped from the schema. The SQL-92 syntax for the statement is:

```
DROP VIEW <table name> <drop behavior>

<drop behavior> ::= [CASCADE | RESTRICT]
```

The <drop behavior> clause did not exist in SQL-86, so vendors had different behaviors in their implementation. The usual way of storing VIEWs was in a schema-level table with the VIEW name, the text of the VIEW, and perhaps other information. When you dropped a VIEW, the engine usually removed the appropriate row from the schema tables. You found out about dependencies when you tried to use VIEWs built on other VIEWs that no longer existed. Likewise, dropping a base table could cause the same problem when the VIEW was accessed.

The new CASCADE option will find all other VIEWs that use the dropped VIEW and remove them also. If RESTRICT is specified, the VIEW cannot be dropped if there is anything that is dependent on it. This implies a structure for the schema tables that is different from just a simple single table.

17.7 Hints on Using VIEWs

Do not nest VIEWs too deeply; the overhead of building several levels eats up execution time and the extra storage for materialized VIEWs can be expensive. Complex nestings are also hard to maintain.

One way to figure out what VIEWs you should have is to inspect the existing queries and see if certain subqueries or expressions are repeated. These are good candidates for VIEWs.

One of the major uses of VIEWs is security. The DBA can choose to hide certain columns from certain classes of users through a combination of security authorizations and VIEWs. SQL-92 has provisions for restricting access to tables at the column level, but most implementations do not have that feature yet.

Another security trick is to add a column to a table that has a special user or security-level identifier in it. The VIEW hides this column and gives the user only what he is supposed to see. One possible problem is that a user could try to change something in the VIEW that violates other table constraints; when his attempt returns an error message, he has gotten some information about the security system that we might like to have hidden from him.

The best way to approach VIEWs is to think of how a user wants to see the database and then give him a set of VIEWs that make it look as if the database had been designed just for his applications.

CHAPTER

18

Partitioning Data

DATA IS NOT information until you reduce it from a pile of detailed facts into some sort of summary. Statistics are one method of summarizing data that takes a set of data and reduces the set to a single number, for example the average age of a firm's employees.

But before you can do statistics, you must have that dataset. This section is concerned with how to break the data in SQL into meaningful subsets that can then be presented to the user or passed along for further reduction.

18.1 Coverings and Partitions

We need to define some basic set operations. A covering is a collection of subsets, drawn from a set, whose union is the original set. A partition is a covering whose subsets do not intersect each other. Cutting up a pizza is a partitioning; smothering it in two layers of pepperoni slices is a covering.

Partitions are the basis for most reports. The property that makes partitions useful for reports is aggregation: the whole is the sum of its parts. For example, a company budget is broken into divisions,

divisions are broken into departments, and so forth. Each division budget is the sum of its departments' budgets, and the sum of the division budgets is the total for the whole company again. We would not be sure what to do if a department belonged to two different divisions because that would be a covering and not a partition.

18.1.1 Partitioning by Ranges

A common problem in data processing is classifying things by the way they fall into a range on a numeric or alphabetic scale. For example, when test papers are graded, the range 100% to 90% is an "A," 80% to 89% is a "B," 70% to 79% is a "C," 60% to 69% is a "D," and finally, 59% or less is an "F" on the test. Mail-order companies compute shipping and handling charges based on ranges for the amounts of the purchases. ZIP codes in a certain range will belong to a particular city, state, and parcel mailing zone.

Range Tables

The best approach to translating a code into a value when ranges are involved is to set up a table with the high and low values for each translated value in it. Any missing values will easily be detected and the table can be validated for completeness. For example, we could create a table of ZIP-code ranges and two-character state abbreviation codes like this:

```
CREATE TABLE StateZip
(state CHAR(2) NOT NULL PRIMARY KEY,
 lowzip CHAR(5) NOT NULL UNIQUE,
 highzip CHAR(5) NOT NULL UNIQUE CHECK(lowzip < highzip),
 ...
);
```

Here is a query that looks up the city name and state code from the ZIP code in the AddressBook table to complete a mailing label with a simple JOIN that looks like this:

```
SELECT A1.name, A1.street, SZ.city, SZ.state, A1.zip
    FROM StateZip AS SZ, AddressBook AS A1
  WHERE (zip BETWEEN lowzip AND highzip);
```

The BETWEEN predicate is shorthand for the Boolean expression (lowzip <= zip) AND (zip <= highzip); it is covered in detail in section 12.1. You need to be careful with this predicate. If one of the three columns involved has a NULL in it, the whole predicate becomes UNKNOWN and will not be recognized by the WHERE clause. If you design the table of range values with the high value in one row equal to or greater than the low value in another row, both of those rows will be returned when the test value falls on the overlap.

Single-Column Range Tables

If you know that you have a partitioning in the range value tables, you can write a query in SQL that will let you use a table with only the high value and the translation code. The grading system table would have ((100%, 'A'), (89%, 'B'), (79%, 'C'), (69%, 'D'), and (59%, 'F')) as its rows. Likewise, a table of the state code and the highest ZIP code in that state could do the same job as the BETWEEN predicate in the previous query.

```
CREATE TABLE StateZip2
(highzip CHAR(5) NOT NULL,
 state CHAR(2) NOT NULL,
 PRIMARY KEY (highzip, state));
```

We want to write SQL code to give us the greatest lower bound or least upper bound on those values. The greatest lower bound (glb) operator finds the largest number in one column that is less than or equal to the target value in the other column. The least upper bound (lub) operator finds the smallest number greater than or equal to the target number.

Unfortunately, this is not a good tradeoff, because the subquery is fairly complex and will use a lot of running time. The "high and low" columns are a better solution in most cases. Here is a second version of the AddressBook query, using only the highzip column from the StateZip2 table:

```
SELECT name, street, city, state, zip
    FROM StateZip2, AddressBook
WHERE state = (SELECT state
          FROM StateZip2
       WHERE highzip = (SELECT MIN(highzip)
             FROM StateZip2
          WHERE (Address.zip <= StateZip2.highzip));
```

This correlated query will take some time to execute, because it is fairly complex. The original version, with the BETWEEN predicate, is usually better in spite of requiring more table storage space. But you do not always get to pick the way the tables are constructed. If you want to allow for multiple-row matches by not requiring that the lookup table have unique values, the equality subquery predicate should be converted to an IN predicate.

18.1.2 Partition by Functions

It is also possible to use a function that will partition the table into subsets that share a particular property. By this, I do not want to include partitionings done by JOINs, GROUP BY clauses, or search conditions within an SQL query, but rather the cases where you have to add a column with the function result to the table because the function is too complex to be reasonably written in SQL.

One common example of this technique is the Soundex function (see section 5.4.1), where it is not a vendor extension; the Soundex family assigns codes to names that are phonetically alike. The complex calculations in engineering and scientific databases that involve functions that SQL does not have are another example of this technique.

SQL was never meant to be a computational language. However, many vendors allow a query to access functions in the libraries of other programming languages. You must know what the cost in execution time for your product is before doing this. One version of SQL uses a threaded-code approach to carry parameters over to the other language's libraries and return the results on each row — the execution time is horrible. Some versions of SQL can compile and link another language's library into the SQL.

Although this is a generalization, the safest technique is to unload the parameter values to a file in a standard format that can be read by the other language. Then use that file in a program to find the function results and create INSERT INTO statements that will load a table in the database with the parameters and the results. You can then use this working table to load the function column in the original table.

A technique that has fallen out of favor since the advent of cheap, fast computers is *interpolation*. It consists of using two known functional values, x_1 and x_2, and their results in the function, $f(x_1)$ and $f(x_2)$, to find the result of a value between them.

The rules for interpolation are usually expressible in four-function arithmetic if you know an extra value, called delta squared, that used to be given in numerical tables. This is not a book on numerical analysis, so you will have to go to a library to find details — or ask an old engineer. Let us assume we have a table defined for some function:

```
CREATE TABLE SomeFunction
(parameter REAL NOT NULL PRIMARY KEY,
 function REAL NOT NULL,
 delta2 REAL NOT NULL);
```

The query to find the two values that bracket a given parameter value is

```
(SELECT *
   FROM SomeFunction
WHERE :myparameter <= (SELECT MIN(parameter)
          FROM SomeFunction
        WHERE :myparameter < parameter)) AS x0;
```

and, likewise,

```
(SELECT *
    FROM SomeFunction
 WHERE :myparameter >= (SELECT MAX(parameter)
          FROM SomeFunction
        WHERE :myparameter > parameter) AS x1;
```

If :myparameter is in the table, you will get the same answer for both subqueries and any of the standard methods will return the same result.

CHAPTER

19

Grouping Operations

I AM SEPARATING THE partitions and grouping operations based on the idea that a group has properties that we are trying to find, so we get an answer back for each group. A partition is simply a way of subsetting the original table, so we get a table back as a result.

19.1 GROUP BY Clause

SQL tries to organize data in the simplest, most portable possible fashion; hence rows are made up only of scalar values. SQL also tries to summarize data in the simplest possible fashion. That is why the only method of aggregation in the language is based on simple partitions. To repeat what was said in section 18.1 on covering and partitions, a partition of a set divides the set into subsets such that (1) the union of the subsets returns the original set and (2) the intersection of the subsets is empty. Think of it as cutting up a pizza pie — each piece of pepperoni belongs to one and only one slice of pizza.

The GROUP BY clause takes the result of the FROM and WHERE clauses, then puts the rows into groups defined as having the same values for the columns listed in the GROUP BY clause. Each group is reduced to a single row in the result table. This result table is called a *grouped table*, and all operations are now defined on groups rather than on rows. By convention, the NULLs are treated as one group. The order of the grouping columns in the GROUP BY clause does not matter, but since they have to appear in the SELECT list, you should probably use the same order in both lists for readability.

Let us construct a sample table called Villes and use it to explain in detail how this works. The table is declared as

```
CREATE TABLE Villes
 (state CHAR(2) NOT NULL,
  city CHAR(25) NOT NULL,
  PRIMARY KEY (city, state));
```

and we populate it with the names of cities that end in *-ville*. The first problem is to find a count of the number of such cities by state. The immediate naive query might be

```
SELECT state, city, COUNT(*)
    FROM Villes
GROUP BY state;
```

The groups for Tennessee would have the tuples ('TN', 'Nashville') and ('TN', 'Knoxville'). The first position in the result is the grouping column, which has to be constant within the group. The third column in the SELECT clause is the COUNT(*) for the group, which is clearly two. The city column is a problem. Since the table is grouped by states, there can be at most 50 groups, one for each state. The COUNT(*) is clearly a single value and it applies to the group as a whole. But what possible single value could I output for a city in each group? Pick a typical city and use it? If all the cities have the same name, use that name, and otherwise output a NULL?

The worst possible choice would be to output both rows with the COUNT(*) of 2, since each row would imply that there are two cities named Nashville and two cities named Knoxville in Tennessee. It is worth mentioning that SYBASE and SQL Server Transaction SQL have this flaw, but SYBASE System 10 is supposed to have corrected it.

Each row represents a single group, so anything in it must be a characteristic of the group, not of a single row in the group. This is why there is a rule that the SELECT list must be made up only of grouping columns with optional aggregate-function expressions.

19.1.1 NULLs and Groups

SQL puts the NULLs into a single group, as if they were all equal. The other option, which was used in some of the first SQL implementations before the standard, was to put each NULL into a group by itself. That is not an unreasonable choice. But to make a meaningful choice between the two options, you would have to know the semantics of the data you are trying to model. SQL is a language based on syntax, not semantics.

For example, if a NULL is being used for a missing diagnosis in a medical record, you know that each patient will probably have a different disease when the NULLs are resolved. Putting the NULLs in one group would make sense if you wanted to consider unprocessed diagnosis reports as one group in a summary. Putting each NULL in its own group would make sense if you wanted to consider each unprocessed diagnosis report as an action item for treatment of the relevant class of diseases. Another example was a traffic ticket database which used NULL for a missing auto tag. Obviously, there is more than one car without a tag in the database.

The general scheme for getting separate groups for each NULL is straightforward:

```
SELECT x, ...
     FROM Table1
   WHERE x IS NOT NULL
   GROUP BY x
   UNION ALL
SELECT x, ...
     FROM Table1
   WHERE x IS NULL;
```

There will also be cases, such as the traffic tickets, where you can use another GROUP BY clause to form groups where the principal grouping columns are NULL. For example, the VIN (Vehicle Identification Number) is taken when the car is missing a tag, and it would provide a grouping column.

19.1.2 GROUP BY and HAVING

One of the biggest problems in working with the GROUP BY clause is not understanding how the WHERE and HAVING clauses work. Consider the query to find all departments with fewer than five programmers:

```
SELECT deptno
      FROM Employees
   WHERE job = 'Programmer'
   GROUP BY deptno
HAVING COUNT(*) < 5;
```

The result of this query does not have a row for any departments with no programmers. The order of execution of the clauses does WHERE first, so that employees whose jobs are not equal to 'Programmer' are never passed to the GROUP BY clause. You have missed data that you might want to trap.

It is also worth remarking that some older versions of SQL would require that the SELECT clause also have COUNT(*) in it. This is because they would materialize the grouped table and pass it to the HAVING clause in much the same way as they handled a WHERE clause. This is not standard SQL.

However, the next query will also pick up those departments that have no programmers, because the COUNT(DISTINCT x) function will return a zero for an empty set.

```
SELECT DISTINCT deptno
FROM Employees AS E1
WHERE 5 > (SELECT COUNT(DISTINCT E2.empno)
            FROM Employees AS E2
          WHERE E1.deptno = E2.deptno
            AND E2.job ='Programmer');
```

If there is no GROUP BY clause, the HAVING clause will treat the entire table as a single group according to the SQL-89 and SQL-92 standards. In practice, however, you will find that many implementations of SQL require that the HAVING clause belong to a GROUP BY clause.

Since the HAVING clause applies only to a grouped table, it can reference only the grouping columns and aggregate functions that apply to the group. That is why this query would fail:

```
SELECT deptno
      FROM Employees
   GROUP BY deptno
HAVING (COUNT(*) < 5) AND (job ='Programmer');
```

When the HAVING clause is executed, job is not in the grouped table as a column — it is a property of a row, not of a group. Likewise, this query would fail for much the same reason:

```
SELECT deptno
      FROM Employees
   WHERE (COUNT(*) < 5) AND (job ='Programmer')
   GROUP BY deptno;
```

The COUNT(*) does not exist until after the departmental groups are formed.

19.1.3 Grouped VIEWs for Multiple Aggregation Levels

Business reports are usually based on a hierarchy of nested levels of aggregation. This type of report is so common that there are tools that perform only this sort of task. For example, sales are grouped under the salesmen who made them, then salesmen's departments are grouped into districts, districts are grouped into regions, and so on until we have summary information at the company level. Each level is a partition of the level above it. The summary information can be constructed from the level immediately beneath it in the hierarchy.

Since SQL has no way of directly building nested hierarchies, you have to either fake it or use other tools. Frankly, using a report writer will be faster and more powerful than writing SQL code to do the job.

The trick in SQL-89 is to use VIEWs with GROUP BY clauses to build the reporting levels. Using a Sales report example, the following UNION-ed query will get a report for each level, from the lowest, most detailed level (salesman), through districts and regions, to the highest level (the company).

```
SELECT reg, dist, salesman, SUM(amt)
      FROM Sales
   GROUP BY reg, dist, salesman
UNION
SELECT reg, dist, '{SALESMEN}', SUM(amt)
      FROM Sales
   GROUP BY reg, dist
UNION
SELECT reg, '{OFFICE}', '{SALESMEN}', SUM(amt)
      FROM Sales
   GROUP BY reg
UNION
SELECT '{REGION}', '{OFFICE}', '{SALESMEN}', SUM(amt)
      FROM Sales
ORDER BY 1, 2, 3;
```

The constant strings inside the curly brackets will sort below any alphabetic strings in ASCII, and thus will appear on the end of each grouping in the hierarchy.

Running these four queries can be expensive because the base table must be scanned for each of them. A better approach would be to create VIEWs for each level and then do a SELECT * from the VIEWs, thus:

```
CREATE VIEW Salespersons (reg, dist, salesman, amt)
AS SELECT reg, dist, salesman, SUM(amt)
FROM Sales
GROUP BY reg, dist, salesman;

CREATE VIEW SalesDist (reg, dist, amt)
AS SELECT reg, dist, SUM(amt)
FROM Salespersons
GROUP BY reg, dist;
```

```
CREATE VIEW SalesRegions (reg, amt)
AS SELECT reg, SUM(amt)
FROM SalesDist
GROUP BY reg;

SELECT SUM(amt)
FROM SalesRegions;
```

Most SQL implementations will materialize these VIEWs because of the GROUP BY clauses. Because each VIEW is built from the one underneath it, it does not have to reread the entire table. However, the materialized tables will have to be kept in storage, which makes this decision a classic speed-for-memory-space tradeoff. Those implementations that do not materialize the VIEWs will have the opposite tradeoff, since they will use less main storage, but will need longer computing times to build each VIEW independently of the others.

19.1.4 Sorting and GROUP BY

Though it is not required by the standard, most implementations will automatically sort the results of a grouped query. Internally, the groups were built by first sorting the table on the grouping columns, then aggregating them. The NULL group can sort either high or low, depending on the vendor.

An ORDER BY clause whose columns are not in the same order as those in the GROUP BY clause can be expensive to execute if the optimizer does not detect the double sort request. It is also possible to sort a grouped table on an aggregate or calculated column. In the older SQL-89 standard, these columns were referenced by their position numbers; this is a depreciated feature and should not be used if possible. SQL-92 allows you to rename a column with the construct <column> AS <identifier> in the SELECT list.

The most common use is to order on an aggregate function column to show information. For example, to show the Sales regions in order of total Sales, you would write

```
SELECT reg, dist, SUM(amt) AS distamt
FROM Sales
GROUP BY reg, dist
ORDER BY distamt DESC, reg, dist;
```

Since it is possible that two or more regions could have the same Sales volume, it is always a good idea to sort by the reg column, then by the dist column. The extra sorting is cheap to execute and requires no extra storage. It is very likely that your SQL implementation is using a *nonstable sort.*

A stable sort is one that preserves the order of the rows in the original table. For example, I am given a deck of playing cards to sort by rank and suit. If I first sort by rank, assuming aces high, I would get a deck with all the deuces, followed by all the treys, and so forth until I got to the aces. Within each of these groups, the suits could be in any order.

If I then sorted the deck on the suits of the cards, I would get (assuming bridge sorting order) deuces of clubs, diamonds, hearts, and finally spades, as the highest rank, followed by treys of clubs, diamonds, hearts, and spades, and so forth up to the aces.

If the second sort were a nonstable sort, it could destroy the ordering of the suits. A second sort that was a stable sort would keep the ordering in the suits.

Stable sorts are almost always slower than nonstable sorts, so nonstables are preferred by most database systems. However, a smart optimizer can see an existing order in the intermediate working table and replace the usual nonstable sort with a stable sort, thereby avoiding extra work. Clustered indexes and other sources of pre-existing ordering in the data can also be used by the optimizer.

However, you should never depend on the default ordering of a particular SQL product, since this will not be portable. If ordering is important, use an ORDER BY clause with all of the desired columns explicitly given in it. In SQL-92, you will have to use an AS clause on each of the aggregate functions to give it a name that can be used in the ORDER BY clause.

19.1.5 Grouped Subqueries for Multiple Aggregation Levels

The SQL-92 standard permits you to use a table subquery in a FROM clause and a scalar subquery anywhere that you would use an expression. This lets us do some multilevel aggregation in a single query. For example, to find how each salesman did in his sales district, you can write

```
SELECT salesman, reg, dist, SUM(amt) AS salesman_tot,
        (SELECT SUM(amt)
            FROM Sales AS S1
        WHERE S1.reg = S2.reg
            AND S1.dist = S2.dist) AS dist_tot
    FROM Sales AS S2
GROUP BY salesman, reg, dist, dist_tot;
```

This query will work because the subquery is a constant for each group. The subquery could also be used in an expression to give the percentage of the district total each salesman contributed.

A trickier query is to find aggregates of aggregates — something like the average of the total sales of the districts for each region. Beginning SQL programmers would try to write queries like this:

```
SELECT reg, AVG(SUM(amt)) AS region_average  -- Invalid SQL
    FROM Sales
GROUP BY dist, reg;
```

and the parser would gag on AVG(SUM(amt)) and return an error message about nesting aggregate functions. SQL-92 will let you get the desired effect with a little more work. You need a subquery that will compute the sum of the sales for each district within a region. This table then needs to be averaged for each region, thus:

```
SELECT T1.reg, AVG(T1.district_total) AS region_average
    FROM (SELECT reg, dist, SUM(amt)
            FROM Sales
        GROUP BY reg, dist) AS T1 (reg, dist, district_total)
GROUP BY T1.reg;
```

Since this is a new SQL-92 feature, most implementations do not have it yet. However, the best guess would be that the subquery would be constructed once as a materialized table, then used by the SELECT statement in the usual way. Do not think that SQL-92 would let you write

```
SELECT reg, AVG(SELECT SUM(amt)     -- Invalid SQL-92
          FROM Sales AS S1
       WHERE S1.reg = S2.reg
          GROUP BY dist) AS region_average
    FROM Sales AS S2
GROUP BY reg;
```

The parameter for an aggregate function still cannot be another aggregate function or a subquery. The reason for this prohibition is that though this particular subquery is scalar, other subqueries might have multiple rows and/or multiple columns and not be able to return a single value.

19.2 Relational Division

Relational division is one of the eight basic operations in Codd's relational algebra. The idea is that a divisor table is used to partition a dividend table and produce a quotient or results table. The quotient table is made up of those values of one column for which a second column had all of the values in the divisor.

This is easier to explain with an example. We have a table of pilots and the planes they can fly (dividend); we have a table of planes in the hangar (divisor); we want the names of the pilots who can fly every plane (quotient) in the hangar. To get this result, we divide the PilotSkills table by the planes in the hangar.

```
CREATE TABLE PilotSkills
(pilot CHAR(15) NOT NULL,
 plane CHAR(15) NOT NULL,
 PRIMARY KEY (pilot, plane));
```

PilotSkills

pilot	plane
Celko	Piper Cub
Higgins	B-52 Bomber
Higgins	F-14 Fighter
Higgins	Piper Cub
Jones	B-52 Bomber
Jones	F-14 Fighter
Smith	B-1 Bomber
Smith	B-52 Bomber
Smith	F-14 Fighter
Wilson	B-1 Bomber
Wilson	B-52 Bomber
Wilson	F-14 Fighter
Wilson	F-17 Fighter

```
CREATE TABLE Hangar
(plane CHAR(15) PRIMARY KEY);
```

Hangar

plane
B-1 Bomber
B-52 Bomber
F-14 Fighter

PilotSkills DIVIDED BY Hangar

pilot
Smith
Wilson

In this example, Smith and Wilson are the two pilots who can fly everything in the hangar. Notice that Higgins and Celko know how to fly a Piper Cub, but we don't have one right now. In Codd's original definition of relational division, having more rows than are called for is not a problem.

The important characteristic of a relational division is that the CROSS JOIN (Cartesian product) of the divisor and the quotient produces a valid subset of rows from the dividend. This is where the name comes from, since the CROSS JOIN acts like a multiplication operator.

19.2.1 Division with a Remainder

There are two kinds of relational division. Division with a remainder allows the dividend table to have more values than the divisor, which was Codd's original definition. For example, if a pilot can fly more planes than just those we have in the hangar, this is fine with us. The query would be written in SQL-89 as

```
SELECT DISTINCT pilot
    FROM PilotSkills AS PS1
    WHERE NOT EXISTS
        (SELECT *
            FROM Hangar
        WHERE NOT EXISTS
            (SELECT *
                FROM PilotSkils AS PS2
            WHERE (PS1.pilot = PS2.pilot)
                AND (PS2.plane = Hangar.plane)));
```

The quickest way to explain what is happening in this query is to imagine an old World War II movie where a cocky pilot has just walked into the hangar, looked over the fleet, and announced, "There ain't no plane in this hangar that I can't fly!" We are finding the pilots for whom there does not exist a plane in the hangar for which they have no skills.

The use of the NOT EXISTS() predicates is for speed. Most SQL systems will look up a value in an index rather than scan the whole table. The SELECT * clause lets the query optimizer choose the column to use when looking for the index.

Another version of the division can be written so as to avoid three levels of nesting. For example, to find the supplier that sells at least all of the same parts as supplier 'S2', we would write this query:

```
SELECT DISTINCT SP1.supno
    FROM SupParts AS SP1
WHERE SP1.supno <> 's2' -- do not include s2 himself
    AND SP1.partno -- has some parts in common with s2
        IN (SELECT partno
                FROM SupParts AS SP2
            WHERE SP2.supno = 's2')
GROUP BY SP1.supno
HAVING COUNT(partno) -- has same number of parts as s2
        >= (SELECT COUNT(DINSTINCT partno)
            FROM SupParts AS SP3
        WHERE SP3.supno = 's2');
```

19.2.2 Exact Division

The second kind of relational division is exact relational division. The dividend table must match exactly to the values of the divisor without any extra values. For example, given a list of ingredients and a recipe book, what can I cook? If the recipe calls for more ingredients than I have, I cannot make it. The query would be written as

```
SELECT dish
    FROM Recipes AS R1
WHERE NOT EXISTS
        (SELECT *
            FROM Ingredients
        WHERE NOT EXISTS
                (SELECT *
                    FROM Recipes AS R2
                WHERE (R1.dish = R2.dish)
                    AND (R2.item = Ingredients.item)))
GROUP BY dish
HAVING COUNT(*) = (SELECT COUNT(*) FROM Recipes);
```

This looks like the division-with-remainder query with a GROUP BY...HAVING clause added, but notice that the SELECT DISTINCT has been changed to SELECT, since the GROUP BY will automatically take care of duplicates.

19.2.3 Todd's Division

A relational division operator proposed by Stephen Todd is defined on two tables with common columns that are JOINed together, dropping the JOIN column and retaining only those non-JOIN columns that meet a criterion.

We are given a table, JobParts(jobno, partno), and another table, SupParts(supno, partno), of suppliers and the parts that they provide. We want to get the supplier-and-job pairs such that supplier sn supplies all of the parts needed for job jn. This is not quite the same thing as getting the supplier-and-job pairs such that job jn requires all of the parts provided by supplier sn.

You want to divide the JobParts table by the SupParts table. A rule of thumb: The remainder comes from the dividend, but all values in the divisor are present.

JobParts			SupParts			Result = JobSups	
job	**part**		**supplier**	**part**		**job**	**supplier**
j1	p1		s1	p1		j1	s1
j1	p2		s1	p2		j1	s2
j2	p2		s1	p3		j2	s1
j2	p4		s1	p4		j2	s4
j2	p5		s1	p5		j3	s1
j3	p2		s1	p6		j3	s2
			s2	p1		j3	s3
			s2	p2		j3	s4
			s3	p2			
			s4	p2			
			s4	p4			
			s4	p5			

Pierre Mullin submitted the following query to carry out the Todd division:

```
SELECT DISTINCT JP1.job, SP1.supplier
    FROM JobParts AS JP1, SupParts AS SP1
WHERE NOT EXISTS
        (SELECT *
```

```
           FROM JobParts AS JP2
    WHERE JP2.job = JP1.job
      AND JP2.part
            NOT IN (SELECT SP2.part
                      FROM SupParts AS SP2
                     WHERE SP2.supplier = SP1.supplier);
```

This is really a modification of the query for Codd's division, extended to use a JOIN on both tables in the outermost SELECT statement. The IN predicate for the second subquery can be replaced with a NOT EXISTS predicate; it might run a bit faster, depending on the optimizer.

19.2.4 Division with JOINs

SQL-92 has several JOIN operators that can be used to perform a relational division. To find the pilots who can fly the same planes as Higgins, use this query:

```
SELECT SP1.Pilot
    FROM (((SELECT plane FROM Hangar) AS H1
        JOIN (SELECT pilot, plane FROM PilotSkills) AS SP1
            ON H1.plane = SP1.plane)
        JOIN (SELECT *
                FROM PilotSkills
               WHERE pilot = 'Higgins') AS H2
            ON H2.plane = H1.plane)
    GROUP BY Pilot
HAVING COUNT(*) >= (SELECT COUNT(*)
                FROM PilotSkills
               WHERE pilot = 'Higgins'));
```

The first JOIN finds all of the planes in the hangar for which we have a pilot. The next JOIN takes that set and finds which of those match up with (SELECT * FROM PilotSkills WHERE pilot = 'Higgins') skills. The GROUP BY clause will then see that the intersection we have formed with the JOINs has at least as many elements as Higgins has planes. The GROUP BY also means that the SELECT

DISTINCT can be replaced with a simple SELECT. If the theta operator in the GROUP BY clause is changed from >= to =, the query finds an exact division. If the theta operator in the GROUP BY clause is changed from >= to <= or <, the query finds those pilots whose skills are a superset or a strict superset of the planes that Higgins flies.

It might be a good idea to put the divisor into a VIEW for readability in this query and as a clue to the optimizer to calculate it once. Some products will execute this form of the division query faster than the nested subquery version, because they will use the PRIMARY KEY information to pre-compute the JOINs between tables.

19.2.5 Division with Set Operators

The SQL-92 set difference operator, EXCEPT, can be used to write a very compact version of Codd's relational division. The EXCEPT operator removes the divisor set from the dividend set. If the result is empty, we have a match; if there is anything left over, it has failed. Using the pilots-and-hangar-tables example, we would write

```
SELECT Pilot
   FROM PilotSkills AS P1
WHERE (SELECT plane FROM Hangar
        EXCEPT
        SELECT plane
          FROM PilotSkills AS P2
        WHERE P1.pilot = P2.pilot) IS NULL;
```

Again, informally, you can imagine that we got a skills list from each pilot, walked over to the hangar, and crossed off each plane he could fly. If we marked off all the planes in the hangar, we would keep this guy. Another SQL-92 trick is that an empty subquery expression returns a NULL, which is how we can test for an empty set. The WHERE clause could just as well have used a NOT EXISTS( ) predicate instead of the IS NULL predicate.

CHAPTER

20

Aggregate Functions

THERE IS A DIFFERENCE between data and information. One of the major purposes of a database system is to turn data into information. This usually means doing some statistical summary from that data. Descriptive statistics measure some property of an existing dataset and express it as a single number. Though there are very sophisticated measures, most applications require only basic, well-understood statistics.

The most common summary functions are the count (or tally), the average (or arithmetic mean), and the sum (or total). The SQL language has this minimal set of descriptive statistical operators in it and vendors often extend these options with others.

These functions are called *set functions* in the ANSI/ISO SQL standard, but vendors, textbook writers, and everyone else usually call them *aggregate functions,* so I will use that term.

Aggregate functions first construct a column of values as defined by the parameter. The parameter is usually a single column name, but it can be an arithmetic expression with scalar functions and calculations. Pretty much the only things that cannot be parameters are other aggregate functions (e.g., SUM(AVG(x)) is illegal) and a subquery (e.g., AVG(SELECT col1 FROM SomeTable WHERE ...) is illegal). A subquery could return more than one value, so it would not fit into a column and an aggregate function would have to try to build a column within a column.

Once the working column is constructed, all the NULLs are removed and the function performs its operation. As you learn the definitions I am about to give, stress the words *known values* to remind yourself that the NULLs have been dropped.

There are two options, ALL and DISTINCT, that are shown as keywords inside the parameter list. The keyword ALL is optional and is never really used in practice. It says that all the rows in the working column are retained for the final calculation. The keyword DISTINCT is not optional in these functions. It removes all duplicate values from a working column before the final calculation. Let's look at the particulars of each aggregate function.

20.1 COUNT Functions

COUNT(*) returns the number of rows in a table (called the cardinality of the table in relational terms); it is the only aggregate function that uses an asterisk as a parameter. This function is very useful and usually will run quite fast, since it can use system information about the table size. Remember that NULL values are also counted, because this function deals with rows and not column values. An empty table has a COUNT(*) of zero, which makes sense.

You would think that using the COUNT(*) would be easy, but there are a lot of subtle tricks to it. Think of a database of the presidencies of the United States, with columns for the first name, middle initial(s), and last name of each U.S. president, along with his political party and his terms in office. It would look like this:

```
CREATE TABLE Parties
(partycode CHAR(2) NOT NULL,
 partyname CHAR(15) NOT NULL);
```

```
INSERT INTO Parties VALUES ('D', 'Democratic');
INSERT INTO Parties VALUES ('DR', 'Democratic');
INSERT INTO Parties VALUES ('R', 'Republican');
INSERT INTO Parties VALUES ('F', 'Federalist');
INSERT INTO Parties VALUES ('W', 'Whig');

DROP TABLE Presidents;
CREATE TABLE Presidents
(firstname CHAR(11) NOT NULL,
 initial CHAR(4) NOT NULL,
 lastname CHAR(11) NOT NULL,
 party CHAR(2) NOT NULL,
 startterm INTEGER NOT NULL,
 endterm INTEGER);
```

Presidents

firstname	initial	lastname	party	startterm	endterm
George		Washington	F	1789	1797
John		Adams	F	1797	1801
Thomas		Jefferson	DR	1801	1809
James		Madison	DR	1809	1817
James		Monroe	DR	1817	1825
John	Q.	Adams	DR	1825	1829
Andrew		Jackson	D	1829	1837
Martin		Van Buren	D	1837	1841
William	H.	Harrison	W	1841	1841
John		Tyler	W	1841	1845
James	K.	Polk	D	1845	1849
Zachary		Taylor	W	1849	1850
Millard		Fillmore	W	1850	1853
Franklin		Pierce	D	1853	1857
James		Buchanan	D	1857	1861
Abraham		Lincoln	R	1861	1865
Andrew		Johnson	R	1865	1869
Ulysses	S.	Grant	R	1869	1877

(cont.)	firstname	initial	lastname	party	startterm	endterm
	Rutherford	B.	Hayes	R	1877	1881
	James	A.	Garfield	R	1881	1881
	Chester	A.	Arthur	R	1881	1885
	Grover		Cleveland	D	1885	1889
	Benjamin		Harrison	R	1889	1893
	Grover		Cleveland	D	1893	1897
	William		McKinley	R	1897	1901
	Theodore		Roosevelt	R	1901	1909
	William	H.	Taft	R	1909	1913
	Woodrow		Wilson	D	1913	1921
	Warren	G.	Harding	R	1921	1923
	Calvin		Coolidge	R	1923	1929
	Herbert	C.	Hoover	R	1929	1933
	Franklin	D.	Roosevelt	D	1933	1945
	Harry	S.	Truman	D	1945	1953
	Dwight	D.	Eisenhower	R	1953	1961
	John	F.	Kennedy	D	1961	1963
	Lyndon	B.	Johnson	D	1963	1969
	Richard	M.	Nixon	R	1969	1974
	Gerald	R.	Ford	R	1974	1977
	James	E.	Carter	D	1977	1981
	Ronald	W.	Reagan	R	1981	1989
	George	H. W.	Bush	R	1989	1993
	William	J.	Clinton	D	1993	(NULL)

Your civics teacher has just asked you to tell her how many people have been President of the United States. So you write the query as SELECT COUNT(*) FROM Presidents; and get the wrong answer. For those of you who have been out of high school too long, more than one Adams, more than one John, and more than one Roosevelt have served as president. Many people have had more than one term in office, and Grover Cleveland served two discontinuous terms. In short, this database is not a simple one-row, one-person system. What you really wanted was not COUNT(*), but something that is able to look at unique combinations of multiple columns. You cannot do this in one column, so you need to construct an expression that is unique

— (firstname || initial || lastname). The point is that you need
to be very sure that the expression you are using as a parameter is
really what you wanted to count.

The COUNT([ALL] <value expression>) returns the number of
members in the <value expression> set. The NULLs have been
thrown away before the counting took place and an empty set returns
zero. The best way to read this is as "Count the number of known
values in this expression," stressing the word *known*.

The COUNT(DISTINCT <value expression>) returns the number
of unique members in the <value expression> set. The NULLs have
been thrown away before the counting took place, and then all redundant duplicates are removed (i.e., we keep one copy). Again, an
empty set returns a zero, just as with the other counting functions.
Applying this function to a key or a unique column is the same as
using the COUNT(*) function, but the optimizer may not be smart
enough to spot it.

20.2 SUM Functions

SUM([ALL] <value expression>) returns the numeric total of all
known values. This function works only with numeric values. You
should also consult your particular product's manuals to find out the
precision of the results for exact and approximate numeric datatypes.
An empty set returns a NULL.

SUM(DISTINCT <value expression>) returns the numeric total of
all known, unique values. The NULLs and all redundant duplicates
have been removed before the summation took place. An empty set
returns a NULL, not a zero. This function works only with numeric
values. You should also consult your particular product's manuals to
find out the precision of the results for exact and approximate numeric
datatypes.

The summation of a set of numbers looks as if it should be easy,
but it is not. Make two tables with the same set of positive and negative approximate numeric values, but put one in random order and
have the other sorted by absolute value. The sorted table will give
more accurate results. The reason is simple; positive and negative
values of the same magnitude will be added together and will get a

chance to cancel each other out. There is also less chance of an over-flow or underflow error during calculations. Most PC SQL implementations and a lot of mainframe implementations do not bother with this trick, because it would require a sort for every SUM( ) statement and would take a long time.

Whenever an exact or approximate numeric value is assigned to exact numeric, it may not fit into the storage allowed for it. SQL says that the database engine will use an approximation that preserves leading significant digits of the original number after rounding or truncating. The choice of whether to truncate or round is implementation-defined, however. This can lead to some surprises when you have to shift data among SQL implementations, or storage values from a host language program into an SQL table. It is probably a good idea to create the columns with one more decimal place than you think you need.

Truncation is defined as truncation toward zero; this means that 1.5 would truncate to 1, and –1.5 would truncate to –1. This is not true for all languages; everyone agrees on truncation toward zero for the positive numbers, but you will find that negative numbers may truncate away from zero (e.g., –1.5 would truncate to –2).

SQL is also wishy-washy on rounding, leaving the implementation free to determine its method. There are two major types of rounding, the scientific method and the commercial method, which are discussed in section 3.2.1 on math in SQL.

20.3 AVG Functions

AVG([ALL] <value expression>) returns the average of the members in the value expression set. An empty set returns a NULL. Remember that in general AVG(x) is not the same as (SUM(x)/COUNT(*)); the SUM(x) function has thrown away the NULLs, but the COUNT(*) has not.

Likewise, AVG(DISTINCT <value expression>) returns the average of the distinct members in the <value expression> set. Applying this function to a key or a unique column is the same as the using AVG(<value expression>) function, but, again, the optimizer may not be smart enough to spot it. Remember that in general

AVG(DISTINCT x) is not the same as AVG(x) or (SUM(DISTINCT x)/COUNT(*)). The SUM(DISTINCT x) function has thrown away the duplicate values and NULLs, but the COUNT(*) has not. An empty set returns a NULL.

The SQL engine is probably using the same code for the totaling in the AVG() that it used in the SUM() function. This leads to the same problems with rounding and truncation, so you should experiment a little with your particular product to find out what happens.

But even more troublesome than those problems is the problem with the average itself, because it does not really measure central tendency and can be very misleading. Consider the chart below, from Darrell Huff's superlative little book, *How to Lie with Statistics* (Huff 1954).

The sample company has 25 employees, earning the following salaries:

Number of Employees	Salary	Statistic
12	$2,000	*Mode, Minimum*
1	$3,000	*Median*
4	$3,700	
3	$5,000	
1	$5,700	*Average*
2	$10,000	
1	$15,000	
1	$45,000	*Maximum*

The average salary (or, more properly, the arithmetic mean) is $5,700. When the boss is trying to make himself look good to the unions, he uses this figure. When the unions are trying to look impoverished, they use the mode, which is the most frequently occurring value, to show that the exploited workers are making $2,000 (which is also the minimum salary in this case).

A better measure in this case is the median, which will be discussed later; that is, the employee with just as many cases above him as below him. That gives us $3,000. The rule for calculating the median is that if there is no actual entity with that value, you fake it.

Most people take an average of the two values on either side of where the median would be; others jump to the higher or lower value.

The mode also has a problem because not every distribution of values has one mode. Imagine a country in which there are as many very poor people as there are very rich people and nobody in between. This would be a bimodal distribution. If there are sharp classes of incomes, that would be a multimodal distribution.

Some SQL products have median and mode aggregate functions as extensions, but they are not part of the standard.

20.3.1 Averages with Empty Groups

The query used here is a bit tricky, so this section can be skipped on your first reading. Sometimes you need to count an empty set as part of the population when computing an average.

This is easier to explain with an example that was posted on CompuServe. A fish and game warden is sampling different bodies of water for fish populations. Each sample falls into one or more groups (muddy bottoms, clear water, still water, and so on) and she is trying to find the average of something that is not there. This is not quite as strange as it first sounds — nor quite as simple, either. She is collecting sample data on fish in a table like this:

```
CREATE TABLE Samples
(sampleid INTEGER NOT NULL,
 fish CHAR(20) NOT NULL,
 numfound INTEGER NOT NULL,
 PRIMARY KEY (sampleid, fish));


CREATE TABLE SampleGroups
(groupid INTEGER NOT NULL,
 sampleid INTEGER NOT NULL,
 PRIMARY KEY (groupid, sampleid));
```

Assume some of the data looks like this:

Samples

sampleid	fish	numfound
1	Seabass	14
1	Minnow	18
2	Seabass	19

SampleGroups

groupid	sampleid
1	1
1	2
2	2

She needs to get the average number of each species of fish in the sample groups. For example, using sample group 1 as shown, which has samples 1 and 2, we could use the parameters :myfish = 'Minnow' and :mygroup = 1 to find the average number of minnows in sample group 1, thus:

```
SELECT fish, AVG(numfound)
    FROM Samples
WHERE sampleid IN (SELECT sampleid
            FROM SampleGroups
        WHERE groupid = :mygroup)
    AND fish = :myfish
GROUP BY fish;
```

But this query will give us an average of 18 minnows, which is wrong. There were no minnows for sampleid = 2, so the average is ((18 + 0)/2) = 9. The other way is to do several steps to get the correct answer — first use a SELECT statement to get the number of samples involved, then another SELECT to get the sum, and then manually calculate the average.

The obvious answer is to enter a count of 0 for each animal under each sampleid, instead of letting it be missing, so you can use the original query. You can create the missing rows with

```
INSERT INTO Samples
SELECT M1.sampleid, M2.fish, 0
    FROM Samples AS M1, Samples AS M2
WHERE NOT EXISTS (SELECT * FROM Samples AS M3
        WHERE M1.sampleid = M3.sampleid
          AND  M2.fish = M3.fish);
```

Unfortunately, it turns out that we have over 100,000 different species of fish and thousands of samples. This trick will fill up more disk space than we have on the machine. The best trick is to use this SQL-92 statement:

```
SELECT fish, SUM(numfound)/
        (SELECT COUNT(sampleid)
            FROM SampleGroups
          WHERE groupid = :mygroup)
    FROM Samples
WHERE fish = :myfish
GROUP BY fish;
```

This SQL-92 query is using the rule that the average is the sum of values divided by the count of the set. Another way to do this would be to use an OUTER JOIN and preserve all the groupids, but that would create NULLs for the fish that are not in some of the sample groups and you would have to handle them.

20.4 MIN and MAX Functions

MAX([ALL] <value expression>) returns the greatest known value in the <value expression> set. This function will also work on CHARACTER, DATE, and DATETIME values, as well as numeric values. An empty set returns a NULL. Technically, you can write MAX(DISTINCT <value expression>), but it is the same as MAX(<value expression>); this form exists only for completeness and nobody ever uses it.

MIN([ALL] <value expression>) returns the smallest known value in the <value expression> set. This function will also work on CHARACTER, DATE, and DATETIME values, as well as numeric values. An empty set returns a NULL. Likewise, MIN(DISTINCT <value expression>) exists, but it is defined only for completeness and nobody ever uses it.

The MAX() for a set of numeric values is the largest. The MAX() for a set of temporal datatypes is the one farthest in the future or most recent. The MAX for a set of character strings is the last one in the ascending sort order. Likewise, the MIN() for a set of numeric values is the smallest. The MIN() for a set of temporal datatypes is the least recent one. The MIN() for a set of character strings is the first one in the ascending sort order. No surprises here.

People have a hard time understanding the MAX() and MIN() aggregate functions when they are applied to temporal datatypes. They seem to expect the MAX() to return the date closest to the current date. Likewise, if the set has no dates before the current date, they seem to expect the MIN function to return the date closest to the current date. Human psychology wants to use the current time as an origin point for temporal reasoning. Consider the predicate billing-date < (CURRENT_DATE - INTERVAL 90 DAYS); most people have to stop and figure out that this is looking for billings that are over 90 days past due. This same thing happens with MIN() and MAX() functions.

SQL also has funny rules about comparing VARCHAR strings, which can cause problems. When two strings are compared for equality, the shortest one is right-padded with blanks; then they are compared position for position. Thus, the strings 'John' and 'John ' are equal. You will have to check your implementation of SQL to see which string is returned as the MAX() and which as the MIN(), or whether there is any pattern to it at all.

CHAPTER

21

Statistics

$\mathbf{S}$QL IS NOT A statistical programming language. However, there are some tricks that will let you do simple descriptive statistics. Many vendors also include other descriptive statistics besides the required ones. Other sections of this book give portable queries for computing some of the more common statistics. Before using any of these queries, you should check to see if they already exist in your SQL product. Built-in functions will run far faster than these queries, so you should use them if portability is not vital. The most common extensions are the median, the mode, the standard deviation, and the variance.

If you need to do a detailed statistical analysis, then you can extract data with SQL and pass it along to a statistical programming language, such as SAS, SPSS, or Osiris.

21.1 The Mode

The mode is the most frequently occurring value in a set. If there are two such values in a set, statisticians call it a bimodal distribution; three such values make it trimodal, and so forth.

Most SQL implementations do not have a mode function, since it is so easy to calculate. First create a VIEW grouped on the desired column that has the COUNT(*), thus:

```
CREATE VIEW ModeFinder (column1, occurs)
AS SELECT column1, COUNT(*)
      FROM SomeTable
   GROUP BY column1;
```

Then find the most frequent value in the VIEW, thus:

```
SELECT column1 AS mode
FROM ModeFinder
WHERE occurs = (SELECT MAX(occurs) FROM ModeFinder);
```

This can be collapsed into a single query in SQL-92. Remember that a HAVING clause without a GROUP BY treats the entire table as if it were a single group.

```
SELECT column1 AS mode
    FROM (SELECT column1, COUNT(*) AS occurs
            FROM SomeTable
         GROUP BY column1)
HAVING occurs = MAX(occurs);
```

The mode is a weak descriptive statistic, because it can be changed by small amounts of additional data. For example, if we have 100,000 cases where the value of the color variable is 'red' and 99,999 cases where the value is 'green', the mode is 'red'. But when two more 'green's are added to the set, the mode switches to 'green'. A better idea is to allow for some variation, k, in the values. In general the best way to compute k is probably as a percentage of the total number of occurrences. Of course, knowledge of the actual situation could change this. For $k = 2\%$ error, the query would look like this:

```
SELECT column1 AS mode, occurs
    FROM ModeFinder
WHERE occurs
        BETWEEN (SELECT MAX(occurs) - (.02 * SUM(occurs))
```

```
       FROM ModeFinder))
   AND (SELECT MAX(occurs) + (.02 * SUM(occurs))
       FROM ModeFinder));
```

This would return the result set (`'red'`, `'green'`) for the example table, and would not change to (`'green'`) until the ratio of `'red'` to `'green'` tipped by two percentage points.

21.2 The Median

The median is defined as the value for which there are just as many cases with a value below it as above it. If such a value exists in the dataset, this value is called the *statistical median* by some authors. If no such value exists in the dataset, the usual method is to divide the dataset into two halves of equal size such that all values in one half are lower than any value in the other half. The median is then the average of the highest value in the lower half and the lowest value in the upper half, and is called the *financial median* by some authors. The *financial median* is the most common term used for this median, so we will stick to it. Let us use Date's famous Parts table, from several of his textbooks (Date 1983, 1995a), which has a column for weight in it, like this:

Parts

pno	pname	color	weight	city
p1	Nut	Red	12	London
p2	Bolt	Green	17	Paris
p3	Cam	Blue	12	Paris
p4	Screw	Red	14	London
p5	Cam	Blue	12	Paris
p6	Cog	Red	19	London

First sort the table by weights and find the three rows in the lower half of the table. The greatest value in the lower half is 12; the smallest value in the upper half is 14; their average, and therefore the median, is 13. If the table had an odd number of rows, we would have looked at only one row after the sorting.

The median is a better measure of central tendency than the average, but it is also harder to calculate without sorting. This is a disadvantage of SQL as compared with procedural languages. This might be the reason that the median is not a common vendor extension in SQL implementations. However, the variance and standard deviation are quite common, probably because they are much easier to calculate since they require no sorting, but they are less useful to commercial users.

21.2.1 Date's First Median

Date proposed two different solutions for the median (Date 1992a, Celko and Date 1993). His first solution was based on the fact that if you duplicate every row in a table, the median will stay the same. The duplication will guarantee that you always work with a table that has an even number of rows. The first version that appeared in his column was wrong and drew some mail from me and from others who had different solutions. Here is a corrected version of his first solution:

```
CREATE VIEW Temp1
AS SELECT weight FROM Parts
        UNION ALL
    SELECT weight FROM Parts;

CREATE VIEW Temp2
AS
SELECT weight
    FROM Temp1
WHERE (SELECT COUNT(*) FROM Parts)
    <= (SELECT COUNT(*)
          FROM Temp1 AS T1
        WHERE T1.weight >= Temp1.weight)
AND (SELECT COUNT(*) FROM Parts)
    <= (SELECT COUNT(*)
          FROM Temp1 AS T2
        WHERE T2.weight <= Temp1.weight);

SELECT AVG(DISTINCT weight) AS median
    FROM Temp2;
```

This involves the construction of a doubled table of values, which can be expensive in terms of both time and storage space. You will also find that this requires a good implementation of the SQL-92 standard that allows you to use a correlated scalar subquery in place of a scalar value expression. Most SQL implementations are not yet that sophisticated.

The use of AVG(DISTINCT x) is important because leaving it out would return the simple average instead of the median. Consider the set of weights (12, 17, 17, 14, 12, 19). The doubled table, Temp1, is then (12, 12, 12, 12, 14, 14, 17, 17, 17, 17, 19, 19). But because of the duplicated values, Temp2 becomes (14, 14, 17, 17, 17, 17), not just (14, 17). The simple average is (96 / 6) = 16; it should be (31 / 2) = 15.5 instead.

21.2.2 Celko's First Median

A slight modification of Date's solution will avoid the use of a doubled table, but it depends on SQL-92 features and on particular choices of rounding and truncation by the vendor.

```
SELECT MIN(weight)
    FROM Parts
WHERE weight IN (SELECT P1.weight
              FROM Parts AS P1, Parts AS P2
          WHERE P2.weight >= P1.weight)
        HAVING COUNT(*) <=
                (SELECT COUNT(*) / 2.0 + 0.5) FROM Parts))
UNION
SELECT MAX(weight)
    FROM Parts
WHERE weight IN (SELECT P1.weight
              FROM Parts AS P1, Parts AS P2
          WHERE P2.weight <= P1.weight)
        HAVING COUNT(*) <=
                (SELECT COUNT(*) / 2.0 + 0.5) FROM Parts))
```

Older versions of SQL allow a HAVING clause only with a GROUP BY; this may not work with your SQL. The addition of 0.5 to each count is to be sure that if there is an odd number of rows in Parts, the two halves will overlap on that value. Again, truncation and rounding in division are implementation-defined, so you will need to experiment with your product.

A safer way to do this in SQL-89 is to use VIEWs for the levels of nesting.

```
CREATE VIEW UpperHalf
AS SELECT P1.pno, P1.weight
         FROM Parts AS P1, Parts AS P2
      WHERE P1.weight <= P2.weight
      GROUP BY P1.pno, P1.weight
    HAVING COUNT(*) <= (SELECT COUNT(*) / 2 + 0.5 FROM Parts);


CREATE VIEW LowerHalf
AS SELECT P1.pno, P1.weight
         FROM Parts AS P1, Parts AS P2
      WHERE P1.weight >= P2.weight
      GROUP BY P1.pno, P1.weight
    HAVING COUNT(*) <= (SELECT COUNT(*) / 2 + 0.5 FROM Parts);


CREATE VIEW MiddleHalf (weight)
AS SELECT *
         FROM Parts
      WHERE weight = (SELECT MIN(weight) FROM LowerHalf)
      UNION ALL
    SELECT *
         FROM Parts
      WHERE weight = (SELECT MAX(weight) FROM UpperHalf);


SELECT AVG(weight) FROM MiddleHalf;
```

Again, the way your implementation handles truncation and rounding will determine whether you need the "+ 0.5" or not. The two VIEWs that are created are the upper and lower halves of the

original table. The middle element, if any, will appear in both
VIEWs. There are two major advantages in this approach. The VIEW
MiddleHalf has all the information about the median entities, so we
can see if the median is a true measure of central tendency or if the
distribution is bimodal. A bimodal distribution is a population that
has extremes at both ends of its range, so that the median does not
mean much. As I have mentioned, the easiest example of this would
be a country where there are very rich people and very poor people,
but no middle class.

21.2.3 Date's Second Median

Date's second solution (Date 1995b) was based on Celko's median,
folded into one query:

```
SELECT AVG(DISTINCT Parts.weight) AS median
    FROM Parts
WHERE Parts.weight IN
    (SELECT MIN(weight)
          FROM Parts
      WHERE Parts.weight IN
              (SELECT P2.weight
                    FROM Parts AS P1, Parts AS P2
                  WHERE P2.weight <= P1.weight)
                GROUP BY P2.weight
          HAVING COUNT(*) <= (SELECT COUNT(*) / 2 + 0.5 FROM Parts))
      UNION
    (SELECT MAX(weight)
        FROM Parts
      WHERE Parts.weight IN
              (SELECT P2.weight
                    FROM Parts AS P1, Parts AS P2
                  WHERE P2.weight >= P1.weight)
                GROUP BY P2.weight
    HAVING COUNT(*) <= (SELECT COUNT(*) / 2 + 0.5 FROM Parts)));
```

Date mentions that this solution will return a NULL for an empty
table and that it assumes there are no NULLs in the column. If there

are NULLs, the WHERE clauses should be modified to remove them.

21.2.4 Murchison's Median

Rory Murchison of the Aetna Institute has a solution that modifies Date's first method by concatenating the key to each value to make sure that every value is seen as a unique entity. Selecting the middle values is then a special case of using his technique for finding the nth item in the table, a trick discussed in section 25.2.

```
SELECT AVG(weight)
   FROM Parts AS P1
WHERE EXISTS
             (SELECT COUNT(*)
          FROM Parts AS P2
      WHERE CAST(weight AS CHAR(5)) || P2.pno
            CAST(weight AS CHAR(5)) || P1.pno
      HAVING COUNT(*) = (SELECT (COUNT(*) + 1) / 2 FROM Parts)
          OR COUNT(*) = (SELECT (COUNT(*) / 2 + 1 FROM Parts));
```

This method depends on being able to have a HAVING clause without a GROUP BY, which is part of the ANSI standard but not always part of vendor implementations.

Another handy trick is the use of (COUNT(*) + 1) / 2 and COUNT(*) / 2 + 1 to handle the odd-and-even-elements problem. Just to work it out, consider the case where the COUNT(*) returns 8 for an answer: $(8 + 1) / 2 = (9 / 2) = 4.5$ and $(8 / 2) + 1 = 4 + 1 = 5$. The 4.5 will round to 4 in DB2 and other SQL implementations. The case where the COUNT(*) returns 9 would work like this: $(9 + 1) / 2 = (10 / 2) = 5$ and $(9 / 2) + 1 = 4.5 + 1 = 5.5$, which will likewise round to 5 in DB2.

21.2.5 Celko's Second Median

This is another method for finding the median that does not depend on SQL-92 features. The trick is to build a working table with the values and a tally of their occurrences from the original table. This working table should be quite a bit smaller than the original table,

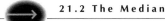

and very fast to construct if there is an index on the target column. The Parts table will serve as an example, thus:

```
-- construct Working table of occurrences by weight
CREATE TABLE Working
    (weight REAL NOT NULL,
    occurs INTEGER NOT NULL);
INSERT INTO Working
SELECT weight, COUNT(*)
        FROM Parts
    GROUP BY weight;
```

Now that we have this table, we want to use it to construct a summary table that has the number of occurrences of each weight and the total number of data elements before and after we add them to the dataset.

```
-- construct table of cumulative tallies
CREATE TABLE Summary
    (weight REAL NOT NULL,
    occurs INTEGER NOT NULL, -- number of occurrences
    pretally INTEGER NOT NULL, -- cumulative tally before
    posttally INTEGER NOT NULL); -- cumulative tally after
INSERT INTO Summary
SELECT S2.weight, S2.tally, SUM(S1.tally) - S2.tally, SUM(S1.tally)
        FROM Working AS S1, Working AS S2
    WHERE S1.weight <= S2.weight
    GROUP BY S2.weight, S2.tally;
```

Let $(n / 2)$ be the middle position in the table. There are two mutually exclusive situations. In the first case, the median lies in a position between the pretally and posttally of one weight value. In the second case, the median lies on the pretally of one row and the posttally of another. The middle position can be calculated by the scalar subquery (SELECT MAX(posttally) / 2 FROM Summary). Remember that in SQL-89, there can be a scalar subquery on only one side of a theta operator, not on both.

```
SELECT AVG(S3.weight) AS median
    FROM Summary AS S3
WHERE (S3.posttally > (SELECT MAX(posttally) / 2 FROM Summary)
    AND S3.pretally < (SELECT MAX(posttally) / 2 FROM Summary))
        OR S3.pretally = (SELECT MAX(posttally) / 2 FROM Summary)
        OR S3.posttally = (SELECT MAX(posttally) / 2 FROM Summary);
```

This is such "vanilla" SQL that it will run on any implementation. The first predicate, with the AND operator, handles the case where the median falls inside one weight value; the other two predicates handle the case where the median is between two weights. A BETWEEN predicate will not work in this query.

These tables can be used to compute percentiles, deciles, and quartiles simply by changing the scalar subquery. For example, to find the highest tenth (first decile), the subquery would be (SELECT 9 * MAX(posttally) / 10 FROM Summary); to find the highest two-tenths, (SELECT 8 * MAX(posttally) / 10 FROM Summary); and in general to find the highest n-tenths, (SELECT (10 - n) * MAX(posttally) / 10 FROM Summary).

21.2.6 Median with Characteristic Function

Anatoly Abramovich, Yelena Alexandrova, and Eugene Birger presented a series of articles in *SQL Forum* magazine on computing the median (SQL Forum 1993, 1994). They define a characteristic function, which they call *delta,* using the Sybase sign() function. The delta or characteristic function accepts a Boolean expression as an argument and returns a 1 if it is TRUE and a zero if it is FALSE or UNKNOWN.

In SQL-92 we have a CASE expression, which can be used to construct the delta function. This is new to SQL-92, but you can find vendor functions of the form IF...THEN...ELSE that behave like the condition expression in ALGOL or like the question mark–colon operator in C.

The authors also distinguish between the statistical median, whose value must be a member of the set, and the financial median, whose value is the average of the middle two members of the set. A statistical median exists when there is an odd number of items in the set. If there is an even number of items, you must decide if you want to use the highest value in the lower half (they call this the *left median*) or the lowest value in the upper half (they call this the *right median*).

The left statistical median of a unique column can be found with this query:

```
SELECT P1.bin
       FROM Parts AS P1, Parts AS P2
    GROUP BY P1.bin
HAVING SUM(CASE WHEN (P2.bin <= P1.bin) THEN 1 ELSE 0 END)
          = (COUNT(*) + 1) / 2;
```

Changing the direction of the theta test in the HAVING clause will allow you to pick the right statistical median if a central element does not exist in the set. You will also notice something else about the median of a set of unique values: It is usually meaningless. What does the median bin number mean, anyway? A good rule of thumb is that if it does not make sense as an average, it does not make sense as a median.

The statistical median of a column with duplicate values can be found with a query based on the same ideas, but you have to adjust the HAVING clause to allow for overlap; thus, the left statistical median is found by

```
SELECT P1.weight
       FROM Parts AS P1, Parts AS P2
    GROUP BY P1.weight
HAVING SUM(CASE WHEN P2.weight <= P1.weight
           THEN 1 ELSE 0 END)
              >= ((COUNT(*) + 1) / 2)
    AND SUM(CASE WHEN P2.weight >= P1.weight
           THEN 1 ELSE 0 END)
              >= (COUNT(*)/2 + 1);
```

Notice that here the left and right medians can be the same, so there is no need to pick one over the other in many of the situations where you have an even number of items. Switching the comparison operators in the two CASE expressions will give you the right statistical median.

The author's query for the financial median depends on some Sybase features that cannot be found in other products, so I would recommend using a combination of the right and left statistical medians to return a set of values about the center of the data, and then averaging them, thus:

```
SELECT AVG(P1.weight)
    FROM Parts AS P1, Parts AS P2
HAVING (SUM(CASE WHEN P2.weight <= P1.weight -- left median
        THEN 1 ELSE 0 END)
            >= ((COUNT(*) + 1) / 2)
    AND SUM(CASE WHEN P2.weight >= P1.weight
        THEN 1 ELSE 0 END)
            >= (COUNT(*)/2 + 1))
    OR (SUM(CASE WHEN P2.weight >= P1.weight  -- right median
        THEN 1 ELSE 0 END)
            >= ((COUNT(*) + 1) / 2)
    AND SUM(CASE WHEN P2.weight <= P1.weight
        THEN 1 ELSE 0 END)
            >= (COUNT(*)/2 + 1));
```

An optimizer may be able to reduce this expression internally, since the expressions involved with COUNT(*) are constants. This entire query could be put into a FROM clause and the average taken of the one or two rows in the result to find the financial median. In SQL-89, you would have to define this as a VIEW and then take the average.

21.3 Variance and Standard Deviation

The standard deviation is a measure of how far away from the average the values in a normally distributed population are. It is hard to calculate in SQL, because it involves a square root and standard SQL has only the basic four arithmetic operators. Many vendors will allow you to use other math functions, but in all fairness, most SQL databases are in commercial applications and have little or no need for engineering or statistical calculations. The usual trick is to load the raw data into an appropriate host language, such as Fortran, and do the work there. The formula for the standard deviation is

$$*(*x* - ((*x)*/n)/(n - 1)))$$

where n is the number of items in the sample set and the x's are the values of the items.

The variance is defined as the standard deviation squared, so we can avoid taking a square root and keep the calculations in pure SQL. The queries look like this:

```
SELECT (SUM(x*x) - ((SUM(x)*SUM(x)/COUNT(*))/(COUNT(*) - 1)))
       AS variance
   FROM SomeTable;
```

If your SQL product has a standard deviation operator, use it instead.

21.4 Average Deviation

If you have a version of SQL with an absolute value function, ABS(), you can also compute the average deviation following this pattern, thus:

```
BEGIN
SELECT AVG(x) INTO :average FROM SomeTable;
SELECT SUM(ABS(x - :average)) / COUNT(x) AS AverDeviation
    FROM SomeTable;
END;
```

This is a measure of how much data values drift away from the average, without any consideration of the direction of the drift.

21.5 Cumulative Statistics

A cumulative or running statistic looks at each data value and how it is related to the whole dataset. The most common examples involve changes in an aggregate value over time or on some other well-ordered dimension. A bank balance, which changes with each deposit or withdrawal, is a running total over time. The total weight of a delivery truck as we add packages is a running total over the set of packages, but since two packages can have the same weight, we need a way to break ties — for example, use the arrival dates of the packages, and if that fails, use the alphabetical order of the last names of the shippers. In SQL, this means that we need a table with a key that we can use to order the rows.

Computer people classify reports as *one-pass reports* or *two-pass reports,* a terminology that comes from the number of times the computer used to have to read the data file to produce the desired results. These are really cumulative aggregate statistics.

Most report writers can produce a listing with totals and other aggregated descriptive statistics after each grouping ("Give me the total amount of sales broken down by salesmen within territories"). Such reports are called *banded reports* or *control-break reports,* depending on the vendor. The closest thing to such reports that the SQL language has is the GROUP BY clause used with aggregate functions, which are discussed in chapter 20 of this book.

The two-pass report involves finding out something about the group as a whole in the first pass, then using it in the second pass to produce the results for each row in the group. The most common two-pass reports order the groups against each other ("Show me the total sales in each territory, ordered from high to low") or show the cumulative totals or cumulative percentages within a group ("Show me what percentage each customer contributes to total sales").

21.5.1 Running Totals

Running totals keep track of changes, which usually occur over time, but these could be changes on some other well-ordered dimension. A common example we all know is a bank account, for which we record withdrawals and deposits in a checkbook register. The running total is the balance of the account after each transaction. The query for the checkbook register is simply

```
SELECT transaction, transdate,
    (SELECT SUM(amount)
        FROM BankAccount AS D1
    WHERE D1.transdate <= D0.transdate) AS balance
FROM BankAccount AS D0;
```

Notice that this query handles both deposits (positive numbers) and withdrawals (negative numbers). There is a problem with running totals when two items occur at the same time. In this example, the transaction code keeps the transactions unique, but it is possible to have a withdrawal and a deposit on the same day that will be aggregated together.

If we showed the withdrawals before the deposits on that day, the balance could fall below zero, which might trigger some actions we don't want. The rule in banking is that deposits are credited before withdrawals on the same day, so simply extend the transaction date to show all deposits with a time before all withdrawals to fool the query. But remember that not all situations have a clearly defined policy like this.

21.5.2 Running Differences

Another kind of statistic, related to running totals, is running differences. In this case, we have the actual amount of something at various points in time and we want to compute the change since the last reading. Here is a quick scenario: We have a clipboard and a paper form on which we record the quantities of a chemical in a tank at different points in time from a gauge. We need to report the time, the gauge reading, and the difference between each reading and the preceding one. Here is some sample result data, showing the calculation we need:

tank	reading	quantity	difference	
50A	1994-02-01-07:30	300	NULL	*starting data*
50A	1994-02-01-07:35	500	200	
50A	1994-02-01-07:45	1200	700	
50A	1994-02-01-07:50	800	−400	
50A	1994-02-01-08:00	NULL	NULL	
50A	1994-02-01-09:00	1300	500	
51A	1994-02-01-07:20	6000	NULL	*starting data*
51A	1994-02-01-07:22	8000	2000	
51A	1994-02-01-09:30	NULL	NULL	
51A	1994-02-01-00:45	5000	−3000	
51A	1994-02-01-01:00	2500	−2500	

The NULL values mean that we missed taking a reading. The trick is a correlated subquery expression that computes the difference between the quantity in the current row and the quantity in the row with the largest known time value that is less than the time in the current row on the same date and on the same tank. We can do that in SQL-92:

```
SELECT tank, time, (quantity -
    (SELECT quantity
     FROM Deliveries AS D1
WHERE D1.tank = D0.tank -- same tank
    AND D1.time = (SELECT (MAX D2.time) -- most recent delivery
        FROM Deliveries AS D2
      WHERE D1.tank = D0.tank -- same tank
        AND D2.time < D0.time))) AS difference
    FROM Deliveries AS D0;
```

This is a modification of the running-totals query, but it is more elaborate, since it cannot use the sum of the prior history.

21.5.3 Cumulative Percentages

Cumulative percentages are a bit more complex than running totals or differences. They show what percentage of the whole set of data values the current subset of data values is. Again, this is easier to show with an example than to say in words. You are given a table of the sales made by your sales force, which looks like this:

```
CREATE TABLE Sales
(salesman CHAR(10),
 client CHAR(10),
 amount DECIMAL (5, 2) NOT NULL,
PRIMARY KEY (salesman, client));
```

The problem is to show each salesman, his client, the amount of that sale, what percentage of his total sales volume that one sale represents, and the cumulative percentage of his total sales we have reached at that point. We will sort the clients from the largest amount to the smallest. This problem is based on a salesman's report originally written for a small commercial printing company. The idea was to show the salesmen where their business was coming from and to persuade them to give up their smaller accounts (defined as the lower 20%) to new salesmen. The report let the salesman run his finger down the page and see which customers represented the top 80% of his income.

This solution was given by L. Carl Pedersen of Hanover, NH. It is dependent on your SQL implementation, so check it out carefully before using it. The first step is to compute the total amount of sales for each salesman.

```
DELETE FROM SalesTot; -- clear out working table
INSERT INTO SalesTot (salesman, totamt)
    SELECT salesman, SUM(amount)
    FROM Sales
    GROUP BY salesman;
```

In XDB or DB2, we must have a temporary table to hold the totals for the salesmen. In Oracle, Version 6, and more recent SQLs, you can use a VIEW instead of these two statements. The working SQL-89 query is

```
SELECT a.salesman, a.client, a.amount,
        (a.amount*100.00/b.totamt) AS percentage_of_total,
        (SUM(c.amount)*100.00/b.totamt) AS cum_percent
    FROM Sales AS a, SalesTot AS b, Sales AS c
WHERE a.salesman = b.salesman AND b.salesman = c.salesman
    AND (c.amount > a.amount
        OR (c.amount = a.amount AND c.client >= a.client))
GROUP BY a.salesman, a.client, a.amount, b.totamt
ORDER BY a.salesman, a.amount DESC, cum_percent DESC;
```

Notice the logic, which will alphabetize clients that place orders for the same amount. This linear ordering is important in running statistics. An SQL-92 solution is not that much better, but it is one statement:

```
SELECT salesman, client, amount,
   (S0.amount*100.00/ SELECT SUM(S1.amount)
                  FROM Sales AS S1
                  WHERE S0.salesman = S1.salesman)
   AS percentage_of_total,
   (SELECT SUM(S0.amount)
      FROM Sales AS S3
    WHERE S0.salesman = S3.salesman
       AND (S3.amount > S0.amount
         OR (S3.amount = S0.amount
            AND S3.client >= S0.client))) * 100.00
   / SELECT SUM(S2.amount)
      FROM Sales AS S2
    WHERE S0.salesman = S2.salesman) AS cum_percent
GROUP BY salesman, client, amount
ORDER BY salesman, amount DESC, cum_percent DESC;
```

21.5.4 Rankings

Martin Tillinger posted this problem on the MSACCESS forum of CompuServe in early 1995. How do you get the top *n* sales representatives in each territory, given a SalesReport table that looks like this?

```
CREATE TABLE SalesReport
(name CHAR(20) NOT NULL REFERENCES Salesforce(name),
 territory INTEGER NOT NULL,
 totalsales DECIMAL (8,2) NOT NULL);
```

This statistic is called a ranking. A ranking is shown as integers that represent the ordinal values (first, second, third, and so on) of the elements of a set based on one of the values. In this case, sales personnel are ranked by their total sales within a territory. The one with the highest total sales is in first place, the next highest is in second place, and so forth.

The hard question is how to handle ties. The rule is that if two elements (salespersons) have the same value, they have the same ranking and there are no gaps in the rankings. This is the nature of ordinal numbers — there cannot be a third place without a first and a second place. A query that will do this for us is

```
SELECT S0.territory, S0.name, S0.totalsales,
    (SELECT COUNT(DISTINCT totalsales)
          FROM SalesReport AS S1
       WHERE (S1.totalsales >= S0.totalsales)
          AND (S1.territory = S0.territory)) AS rank
    FROM SalesReport AS S0
WHERE rank <= :n; -- adjustable parameter
```

This query gives the highest SalesReport the rank of 1, the next highest the rank of 2, and so forth. The query can handle ties within a rank. If the territory has less than *n* members, it will return all the members.

Mr. Tillinger was working with Microsoft Access, which does not have anything close to a true SQL or a COUNT (DISTINCT x) function, so he tried to do the query with a COUNT(x) function instead, which would be written in SQL as

```
SELECT S0.territory, S0.name, S0.totalsales,
    (SELECT COUNT(totalsales)
          FROM SalesReport AS S1
       WHERE (S1.totalsales >= S0.totalsales)
          AND (S1.territory = S0.territory)) AS rank
    FROM SalesReport AS S0
WHERE rank <= :n; -- adjustable parameter
```

The problem is that ties are handled incorrectly. For example, given

SalesReport

name	territory	totalsales
Wilson	1	$990.00
Smith	1	$950.00
Richards	1	$800.00
Quinn	1	$700.00
Parker	1	$345.00

(cont.)

name	territory	totalsales
Jones	1	$345.00
Hubbard	1	$345.00
Date	1	$200.00
Codd	1	$200.00
Blake	1	$100.00

The correct answer is

First Query Result

name	territory	totalsales	rank
Wilson	1	$990.00	1
Smith	1	$950.00	2
Richards	1	$800.00	3
Quinn	1	$700.00	4
Parker	1	$345.00	5
Jones	1	$345.00	5
Hubbard	1	$345.00	5
Date	1	$200.00	6
Codd	1	$200.00	6
Blake	1	$100.00	7

The answer from the second query, without the `COUNT(DISTINCT x)`, is

Second Query Result

name	territory	totalsales	rank
Wilson	1	$990.00	1
Smith	1	$950.00	2
Richards	1	$800.00	3
Quinn	1	$700.00	4
Parker	1	$345.00	6
Jones	1	$345.00	6
Hubbard	1	$345.00	6
Date	1	$200.00	8
Codd	1	$200.00	8
Blake	1	$100.00	9

The ties cause gaps and make it impossible to use the rank column value to select the top *n* items. There are also problems in other statistics that use rankings due to these gaps. However, this statistic is used for class standing in the British school system. It calculates the number of elements in the subset that includes the element under discussion. In this case, it is the count of sales representatives who performed no worse than Ms. X did; that is, Quinn was in the top six sales representatives (Wilson, Smith, Richards, Quinn, Parker, Jones).

21.6 Cross Tabulations

A cross tabulation, or crosstab for short, is a common statistical report. It can be done in IBM's QMF tool, using the ACROSS summary option, and in many other SQL-based reporting packages. SPSS, SAS, and other statistical packages have library procedures or language constructs for crosstabs. Many spreadsheets can load the results of SQL queries and perform a crosstab within the spreadsheet.

If you can use a reporting package on the server in a client/server system instead of the following method, do so. It will run faster and in less space than the method discussed here. However, if you have to use the reporting package on the client side, the extra time required to transfer data will make these methods on the server side much faster.

A one-way crosstab "flattens out" a table to display it in a report format. Assume that we have a table of sales by product and the dates the sales were made. We want to print out a report of the sales of products by years for a full decade. The solution is to create a table and populate it to look like an identity matrix (all elements on the diagonal are 1, all others zero), then join the Sales table to it.

```
CREATE TABLE Sales
(product CHAR(15) NOT NULL,
 price DECIMAL(5, 2) NOT NULL,
 qty INTEGER NOT NULL,
 salesyear INTEGER NOT NULL);
```

```
CREATE TABLE CrossTab
(year INTEGER NOT NULL,
 year1 INTEGER NOT NULL,
 year2 INTEGER NOT NULL,
 year3 INTEGER NOT NULL,
 year4 INTEGER NOT NULL,
 year5 INTEGER NOT NULL,
 year6 INTEGER NOT NULL,
 year7 INTEGER NOT NULL,
 year8 INTEGER NOT NULL,
 year9 INTEGER NOT NULL,
 year10 INTEGER NOT NULL);
```

The table would be populated as follows:

year	year1	year2	year3	year4	year5	...	year10
1990	1	0	0	0	0	...	0
1991	0	1	0	0	0	...	0
1992	0	0	1	0	0	...	0
1993	0	0	0	1	0	...	0
1994	0	0	0	0	1	...	0
...	...	...	...	...	...	...	...
1999	0	0	0	0	0	...	1

The query to produce the report table is

```
SELECT S1.product,
    SUM(S1.qty * price * C1.year1),
    SUM(S1.qty * price * C1.year2),
    SUM(S1.qty * price * C1.year3),
    SUM(S1.qty * price * C1.year4),
    SUM(S1.qty * price * C1.year5),
    ...
    SUM(S1.qty * price * C1.year10)
FROM Sales AS S1, CrossTab AS C1
WHERE S1.year = C1.year
GROUP BY S1.product;
```

Obviously, (price * qty) is the total dollar amount of each product in each year. The yearN column will be either a 1 or a zero. If it is a zero, the total dollar amount in the SUM() is zero; if it is a 1, the total dollar amount in the SUM() is unchanged.

This solution lets you adjust the time frame being shown in the report by replacing the values in the year column to whatever consecutive years you wish.

A two-way crosstab takes two variables and produces a spreadsheet with all values of one variable on the rows and all values of the other represented by the columns. Each cell in the table holds the COUNT of entities that have those values for the two variables. NULLs will not fit into a crosstab very well, unless you decide to make them a group of their own or to remove them.

There are also totals for each column and each row and a grand total. Crosstabs of *n* variables are defined by building an *n*-dimensional spreadsheet. But you cannot easily print *n* dimensions on two-dimensional paper. The usual trick is to display the results as a two-dimensional grid with one or both axes as a tree structure. The way the values are nested on the axis is usually under program control; thus, "race within sex" shows sex broken down by race, whereas "sex within race" shows race broken down by sex.

Assume that we have a table, Personnel (empno, sex, race, jobno, salary), keyed on employee number, with no NULLs in any columns. We wish to write a crosstab of employees by sex and race, which would look like this:

	Asian	Black	Caucasian	Hispanic	Other	TOTALS
Male	3	2	12	5	5	27
Female	1	10	20	2	9	42
TOTAL	4	12	32	7	14	69

The first thought is to use a GROUP BY and write a simple query, thus:

```
SELECT sex, race, COUNT(*)
      FROM Personnel
   GROUP BY sex, race;
```

This approach works fine for two variables and would produce a table that could be sent to a report writer program to give a final version. But where are your column and row totals? This means you also need to write these two queries:

```
SELECT race, COUNT(*) FROM Personnel GROUP BY race;
SELECT sex, COUNT(*)  FROM Personnel GROUP BY sex;
```

However, what I wanted was a table with a row for males and a row for females, with columns for each of the racial groups, just as I drew it.

But let us assume that we want to get this information broken down within a third variable, say job code. I want to see the jobno and the total by sex and race within each job code. Our query set starts to get bigger and bigger. A crosstab can also include other summary data, such as total or average salary within each cell of the table.

21.6.1 Crosstabs by CROSS JOIN

A solution proposed by John M. Baird of Datapoint, in San Antonio, Texas, involves creating a matrix table for each variable in the crosstab, thus:

SexMatrix

sex	Male	Female
M	1	0
F	0	1

RaceMatrix

race	Asian	Black	Caucasian	Hispanic	Other
Asian	1	0	0	0	0
Black	0	1	0	0	0
Caucasian	0	0	1	0	0
Hispanic	0	0	0	1	0
Other	0	0	0	0	1

The query then constructs the cells by using a CROSS JOIN (Cartesian product) and summation for each one, thus:

```
SELECT jobno,
       SUM(asian * male) AS AsianMale,
       SUM(asian * female) AS AsianFemale,
       SUM(black * male) AS BlackMale,
       SUM(black * female) AS BlackFemale,
       SUM(cauc * male) AS CaucMale,
       SUM(cauc * female) AS CaucFemale,
       SUM(hisp * male) AS HispMale,
       SUM(hisp * female) AS HispFemale,
       SUM(other * male) AS OtherMale,
       SUM(other * female) AS OtherFemale,
    FROM Personnel, SexMatrix, RaceMatrix
WHERE (RaceMatrix.race = Personnel.race)
    AND (RaceMatrix.sex = Personnel.sex)
GROUP BY jobno;
```

Numeric summary data can obtained from this table. For example, the total salary for each cell can be computed by SUM(<race> * <sex> * salary) AS <cell name> in place of what we have here.

21.6.2 Crosstabs by OUTER JOINs

Another method, due to Jim Panttaja, uses a series of temporary tables or VIEWs and then combines them with OUTER JOINs.

```
CREATE VIEW Guys (race, maletally)
AS SELECT race, COUNT(*)
       FROM Personnel
    WHERE sex = 'M'
    GROUP BY race;
```

Correspondingly, you could have written:

```
CREATE VIEW Dolls (race, femaletally)
AS SELECT race, COUNT(*)
       FROM Personnel
    WHERE sex = 'F'
    GROUP BY race;
```

But they can be combined for a crosstab, without column and row totals, like this:

```
SELECT Guys.race, maletally, femaletally
    FROM Guys LEFT OUTER JOIN Personnel
WHERE Personnel.sex = 'F'
GROUP BY Guys.race, maletally;
```

The idea is to build a starting column in the crosstab, then progressively add columns to it. You use the LEFT OUTER JOIN to avoid missing-data problems.

21.6.3 Crosstabs by Subquery

Another method takes advantage of the orthogonality of correlated subqueries in SQL-92. Think about what each row or column in the crosstab wants.

```
SELECT race,
    (SELECT COUNT(*)
        FROM Personnel AS P1
     WHERE P0.race = P1.race
        AND sex = 'M') AS MaleTally,
    (SELECT COUNT(*)
     FROM Personnel AS P2
     WHERE P0.race = P2.race
        AND sex = 'F') AS FemaleTally,
FROM Personnel AS P0;
```

An advantage of this approach is that you can attach another column to get the row tally by adding

```
(SELECT COUNT(*)
        FROM Personnel AS P3
     WHERE P0.race = P3.race) AS RaceTally
```

Likewise, to get the column tallies, UNION the previous query with

```
SELECT 'Summary',
    (SELECT COUNT(*)
        FROM Personnel
     WHERE sex = 'M') AS GrandMaleTally,
    (SELECT COUNT(*)
        FROM Personnel
     WHERE sex = 'F') AS GrandFemaleTally,
    (SELECT COUNT(*)
        FROM Personnel) AS GrandTally,
FROM Personnel;
```

CHAPTER
22

Regions, Runs, and Sequences

THIS IS A GENERAL class of queries that assumes a table with at least two columns: One of them is an identifier drawn from a sequence that is the primary key; the other has a value we want to search for, based on the ordering imposed by the first column. A sequence has consecutive unique identifiers, without any gaps in the numbering. Examples of this sort of data would be ticket numbers, time series data taken at fixed intervals, and the like. The ordering of those identifiers carries some information content, such as physical or temporal location.

A subsequence is a set of consecutive unique identifiers within a larger, containing sequence. For example, given the data (99, 1, 2, 3, 4, 5, 0), you can find subsequences of size 3 — (1, 2, 3), (2, 3, 4), and (3, 4, 5) — but the longest sequence is (1, 2, 3, 4, 5) and it is of size 5.

A run is like a sequence, but the numbers don't have to be consecutive, just increasing and contiguous. For example, given the run (1, 2, 12, 15, 23), you can find subruns of size 3: (1, 2, 12), (2, 12, 15), and (12, 15, 23).

A region is contiguous and all the values are the same. For example, (1, 0, 0, 0, 25) has a region of zeros that is 3 items long.

In procedural languages, you would simply sort the data and scan it. In SQL, you have to define everything in terms of sets and nested sets. None of these queries will run very fast, but they do demonstrate that such things are possible in SQL.

22.1 Finding Subregions of Size *n*

This example is adapted from *SQL and Its Applications* (Lorie and Daudenarde 1991). You are given a table of theater seats, defined by

```
CREATE TABLE Theater
(seat INTEGER NOT NULL PRIMARY KEY,
 status CHAR(1) NOT NULL CHECK (status IN ('A', 'S')
);
```

where a status code of `'A'` means *available* and `'S'` means *sold*. Your problem is to write a query that will return the subregions of *n* consecutive seats still available. Assume that *consecutive seat numbers* means that the seats are also consecutive for a moment, ignoring rows of seating where seat *n* and seat ($n + 1$) might be on different physical theater rows. For $n = 3$, we can write a self-join query, thus:

```
SELECT S1.seat, S2.seat, S3.seat
    FROM Theater AS T1, Theater AS T2, Theater AS T3
WHERE S1.status = 'A'
    AND S2.status = 'A'
    AND S3.status = 'A'
    AND S2.seat = S1.seat + 1
    AND S3.seat = S2.seat + 1;
```

The trouble with this answer is that it works only for $n = 3$ and for nothing else. This pattern can be extended for any *n*, but what we really want is a generalized query where we can use *n* as a parameter to the query.

The solution given by Lorie and Daudenarde starts with a given seat number and looks at all the available seats between it and ($n - 1$) seats further up. The real trick is switching from the English-language statement "All seats between here and there are available" to the passive-voice version, "Available is the status of all the seats between here and there," so that you can see the query.

```
SELECT seat, ' thru ', (seat + (:n - 1))
    FROM Theater AS T1
WHERE status = 'A'
    AND 'A' = ALL (SELECT status
            FROM Theater AS T2
        WHERE T2.seat > T1.seat
            AND T2.seat <= T1.seat + (:n - 1));
```

Please notice that this returns subregions. That is, if seats (1, 2, 3, 4, 5) are available, this query will return (1, 2, 3), (2, 3, 4), and (3, 4, 5) as its answer.

22.2 Finding Regions of Maximum Size

A query to find a region, rather than a subregion of known size, of seats was presented in *SQL Forum* (Rozenshtein, Abramovich, and Birger 1993).

```
SELECT T1.seat, ' thru ', T2.seat
    FROM Theater AS T1, Theater AS T2
WHERE T1.seat < T2.seat
    AND NOT EXISTS
        (SELECT *
            FROM Theater AS T3
        WHERE (T3.seat BETWEEN T1.seat AND T2.seat
                AND T3.status <> 'A')
            OR (T3.seat = T2.seat + 1 AND T3.status <> 'A')
            OR (T3.seat = T1.seat - 1 AND T3.status <> 'A'));
```

The trick here is to look for the starting and ending seats in the region. The starting seat of a region is to the right of a sold seat and the ending seat is to the left of a sold seat. No seat between the start and the end has been sold.

22.3 Bound Queries

Another form of query asks if there was an overall trend between two points in time bounded by a low value and a high value in the sequence of data. This is easier to show with an example. Let us assume that we have data on the selling prices of a stock in a table. We want to find periods of time when the price was generally increasing. Consider this data:

MyStock

saledate	price
1994-12-01	$10.00
1994-12-02	$15.00
1994-12-03	$13.00
1994-12-04	$12.00
1994-12-05	$20.00

The stock was generally increasing in all the periods that began on December 1 or ended on December 5 — that is, it finished higher at the ends of those periods, in spite of the slump in the middle. A query for this problem is

```
SELECT S1.saledate, ' thru ', S2.saledate
    FROM MyStock AS S1, MyStock AS S2
WHERE S1.saledate < S2.saledate
    AND NOT EXISTS
        (SELECT *
            FROM MyStock AS S3
        WHERE S3.saledate BETWEEN S1.saledate AND S2.saledate
            AND S3.price NOT BETWEEN S1.price AND S2.price);
```

22.4 Run and Sequence Queries

Runs are informally defined as sequences with gaps. That is, we have a set of unique numbers whose order has some meaning, but the numbers are not all consecutive. Time series information where the samples are taken at irregular intervals is an example of this sort of data. Runs can be constructed in the same manner as the sequences by making a minor change in the search condition. Let's do these queries with an abstract table made up of a sequence number and a value:

```
CREATE TABLE Sequences
(seq INTEGER NOT NULL PRIMARY KEY,
 val INTEGER NOT NULL);
```

Sequences

seq	va
1	6
2	41
3	12
4	51
5	21
...	
78	70
79	79
80	62
81	30
82	31
83	32
84	34
85	35
86	57
87	19
88	84
89	80
90	90
91	63
92	53
93	3
94	59
95	69
96	27
97	33

One of the problems is that we don't want to get back all the runs and sequences of length 1. Ideally, the length n of the run should be adjustable. This query will find runs of length n or greater; if you want runs of exactly n, change the "greater than" to an equal sign.

```
SELECT S1.seq, ' thru ', S2.seq
    FROM Sequences AS S1, Sequences AS S2
WHERE S1.seq < S2.seq        -- start and end points
    AND (S2.seq - S1.seq) > (:n - 1)  -- length restrictions
    AND NOT EXISTS     -- ordering within the end points
        (SELECT *
            FROM Sequences AS S3, Sequences AS S4
        WHERE S4.seq BETWEEN S1.seq AND S2.seq
            AND S3.seq BETWEEN S1.seq AND S2.seq
            AND S3.seq < S4.seq
            AND S3.val > S4.val);
```

What this query does is set up the S1 sequence number as the starting point and the S2 sequence number as the ending point of the run. The monster subquery in the NOT EXISTS predicate is looking for a row in the middle of the run that violates the ordering of the run. If there is none, the run is valid. The best way to understand what is happening is to draw a linear diagram. This shows that as the ordering, seq, increases, so must the corresponding values, val.

Fig. 22.1

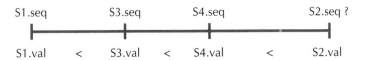

A sequence has the additional restriction that every value increases by 1 as you scan the run from left to right. This means that in a sequence, the highest value minus the lowest value, plus one, is the length of the sequence.

```
SELECT S1.seq, ' thru ', S2.seq
    FROM Sequences AS S1, Sequences AS S2
 WHERE S1.seq < S2.seq
    AND (S2.seq - S1.seq) = (S2.val - S1.val)  -- order condition
    AND (S2.seq - S1.seq) > (:n - 1)  -- length restrictions
    AND NOT EXISTS
        (SELECT *
            FROM Sequences AS S3
          WHERE S3.seq BETWEEN S1.seq AND S2.seq
            AND((S3.seq - S1.seq) <> (S3.val - S1.val)
                OR (S2.seq - S3.seq) <> (S2.val - S3.val)));
```

The subquery in the NOT EXISTS predicate says that there is no point in between the start and the end of the sequence that violates the ordering condition.

Obviously, any of these queries can be changed from increasing to decreasing, from strictly increasing to simply increasing or simply decreasing, and so on, by changing the comparison predicates. You can also change the query for finding sequences in a table by altering the size of the step from 1 to k, by observing that the difference between the starting position and the ending position should be k times the difference between the starting value and the ending value.

CHAPTER 23

Array Structures in SQL

ARRAYS CANNOT BE represented directly in standard SQL, but this is a common vendor language extension. Arrays violate the rules of First Normal Form (1NF) required for a relational database, which say that the tables have no repeating groups in any column. A repeating group is a data structure that is not scalar; examples of repeating groups include linked lists, arrays, records, and even tables within a column.

The reason they are not allowed is that a repeating group would have to fit into a column as a datatype. There is no obvious way to join a column that contains an array to other columns, since there are no comparison operators or conversion rules. There is no obvious way to display or transmit a column that contains an array as a result set. Different languages and different compilers for the same language store arrays in column-major or row-major order, so there is no standard.

The goal of SQL was to be a database language that would operate with a wide range of host languages. To meet that goal, the scalar datatypes are as varied as possible to match the host language datatypes, but as simple in structure as possible to make the transfer of data to the host language as easy as possible.

23.1 Representing Arrays in SQL

An array in other programming languages has a name and subscripts by which the array elements are referenced. The array elements are all of the same datatype and the subscripts are all integers. Some languages start numbering at zero, some start numbering at 1, and some let the user set the upper and lower bounds. For example, a Pascal array declaration would look like this:

```
foobar : ARRAY [1..5] OF INTEGER;
```

would have elements foobar[1], foobar[2], foobar[3], foobar[4], and foobar[5]. The same structure is most often mapped into a SQL declaration as

```
CREATE TABLE Foobar1
(element1 INTEGER NOT NULL,
 element2 INTEGER NOT NULL,
 element3 INTEGER NOT NULL,
 element4 INTEGER NOT NULL,
 element5 INTEGER NOT NULL);
```

The elements cannot be accessed by the use of a subscript in this table as they can in a true array. That is, to set all the array elements equal to zero in Pascal takes one statement with a FOR loop in it:

```
FOR i := 1 TO 5 DO foobar[i] := 0;
```

The same action in SQL would be performed with the statement

```
UPDATE Foobar1
    SET element1 = 0,
        element2 = 0,
        element3 = 0,
        element4 = 0,
        element5 = 0;
```

because there is no subscript which can be iterated in a loop. In fact, there is no loop control structure at all in SQL-92. Any access has to be based on column names and not on subscripts.

Let's assume that we design an Employee table with separate columns for the names of four children, and we start with an empty table and then try to use it.

1. What happens if we hire a man with fewer than four children? We can fire him immediately or make him have more children. We can restructure the table to allow for fewer children. The usual, and less drastic, solution is to put NULLs in the columns for the nonexistent children. We then have all of the problems associated with NULLs to handle.

2. What happens if we hire a man with five children? We can fire him immediately or order him to kill one of his children. We can restructure the table to allow five children. We can add a second row to hold the information on children 5 through 8; however, this destroys the uniqueness of the empno, so it cannot be used as a key. We can overcome that problem by adding a new column for record number, which will form a two-column key with the empno. This leads to needless duplication in the table.

3. What happens if the employee dies? We will delete all his children's data along with his, even if the company owes benefits to the survivors.

4. What happens if the child of an employee dies? We can fire him or order him to get another child immediately. We can restructure the table to allow only three children. We can overwrite the child's data with NULLs and get all of the problems associated with NULL values. This last one is the most common decision. But what if we had used the multiple-row trick and this employee had a fifth child — should that child be brought up into the vacant slot in the current row and the second row of the set deleted?

5. What happens if the employee replaces a dead child with a new one? Should the new child's data overwrite the NULLs in the dead child's data? Should the new child's data be put in the next available slot and overwrite the NULLs in those columns?

Some of these choices involve rebuilding the database. Others are simply absurd attempts to restructure reality to fit the database. The real point is that each insertion or deletion of a child involves a different procedure, depending on the size of the group to which he belongs. Consider instead a table of employees and another table for the children:

```
CREATE TABLE Employees
(empno INTEGER NOT NULL,
 empname CHAR(30) NOT NULL,
 ...);
```

```
CREATE TABLE Children
(empno INTEGER NOT NULL,
 child CHAR(30) NOT NULL,
 birthday DATE NOT NULL,
 sex CHAR(1) NOT NULL);
```

To add a child, you insert a row into Children. To remove a child, you delete a row from Children. There is nothing special about the fourth or fifth child that requires the database system to use special procedures. There are no NULLs in either table.

The tradeoff is that the number of tables in the database schema increases, but the total amount of storage will be smaller, because you will keep data only on children who exist rather than using NULLs to hold space. The goal is to have data in the simplest possible format so that any host program can use it.

Gabrielle Wiorkowski, in her excellent DB2 classes, uses an example of a table for tracking the sales made by salespersons during the past year. That table could be defined as

```
CREATE TABLE AnnualSales1
(salesman CHAR(15) NOT NULL PRIMARY KEY,
 jan DECIMAL(5,2),
 feb DECIMAL(5,2),
 mar DECIMAL(5,2),
 apr DECIMAL(5,2),
 may DECIMAL(5,2),
```

```
jun DECIMAL(5,2),
jul DECIMAL(5,2),
aug DECIMAL(5,2),
sep DECIMAL(5,2),
oct DECIMAL(5,2),
nov DECIMAL(5,2),
dec DECIMAL(5,2));
```

We have to allow for NULLs in the monthly amounts in the first version of the table, but the table is actually quite a bit smaller than it would be if we were to declare it as

```
CREATE TABLE AnnualSales2
(salesman CHAR(15) NOT NULL PRIMARY KEY,
 month CHAR(3) CHECK (month IN ('Jan', 'Feb', 'Mar', 'Apr',
                                'May', 'Jun', 'Jul', 'Aug',
                                'Sep', 'Oct', 'Nov', 'Dec'),
 amount DECIMAL(5,2) NOT NULL,
 PRIMARY KEY(salesman, month));
```

In Wiorkowski's actual example in DB2, the break-even point for DASD storage was April; that is, the storage required for AnnualSales1 and AnnualSales2 is in April of the given year. Queries that deal with individual salespersons will run much faster against the AnnualSales1 table than queries based on the AnnualSales2 table, because all the data is in one row in the AnnualSales1 table. They may be a bit messy and may have to have function calls to handle possible NULL values, but they are not very complex.

Another approach to faking a multidimensional array is to map arrays into a table with an integer column for each subscript, thus:

```
CREATE TABLE Foobar2
(i INTEGER NOT NULL CHECK(i BETWEEN 1 AND 5),
 element INTEGER NOT NULL,
 PRIMARY KEY (i));
```

This looks more complex than the first approach, but it is closer to what the original Pascal declaration was doing behind the scenes.

Subscripts resolve to unique physical addresses, so it is not possible to have two values for foobar[i]; hence, i is a key. The Pascal compiler will check to see that the subscripts are within the declared range; hence the CHECK() clause.

The first advantage of this approach is that multidimensional arrays are easily handled by adding another column for each subscript. The Pascal declaration

```
ThreeD : ARRAY [1..3, 1..4, 1..5] OF REAL;
```

is mapped over to

```
CREATE TABLE ThreeD
(i INTEGER NOT NULL CHECK(i BETWEEN 1 AND 3),
 j INTEGER NOT NULL CHECK(j BETWEEN 1 AND 4),
 k INTEGER NOT NULL CHECK(k BETWEEN 1 AND 5),
 element REAL NOT NULL,
 PRIMARY KEY (i, j, k));
```

Obviously, SELECT statements with GROUP BY clauses on the subscript columns will produce row and column totals, thus:

```
SELECT i, j, SUM(element) -- sum across the k columns
    FROM ThreeD
GROUP BY i, j;

SELECT i, SUM(element) -- sum across the j and k columns
    FROM ThreeD
GROUP BY i;

SELECT SUM(element) -- sum the entire array
    FROM ThreeD;
```

If the original one element/one column approach were used, the table declaration would have 120 columns, named "element111" through "element345". This would be too many names to handle in any reasonable way; you would not be able to use the GROUP BY clauses for array projection, either.

Another advantage of this approach is that the subscripts can be datatypes other than integers. DATE and TIME datatypes are often useful, but CHARACTER and approximate numerics can have their uses too.

23.2 Matrix Operations in SQL

A matrix is not quite the same thing as an array. Matrices are mathematical structures with particular properties that we cannot take the time to discuss here. You can find that information in an algebra book. Though it is possible to do many matrix operations in SQL, it is not a good idea, because such queries and operations will eat up resources and run much too long. SQL was never meant to be a language for calculations.

Let us assume that we have two-dimensional arrays that are declared as tables, using two columns for subscripts, and that all columns are declared with a NOT NULL constraint. The presence of NULLs is not defined in linear algebra and I have no desire to invent a three-valued linear algebra of my own. Another problem is that a matrix has rows and columns that are not the same as the rows and columns of an SQL table; as you read the rest of this section, be careful not to confuse the two.

Multiplication by a scalar constant is direct and easy:

```
UPDATE ThreeD  -- multiply an array by a scalar constant
   SET element = element * :constant;
```

Likewise, the transpose of a matrix is easy to do:

```
CREATE VIEW TransA (i, j, element)
AS SELECT j, i, element FROM MatrixA;
```

Matrix addition is possible only between matrices of the same dimensions:

```
UPDATE MatrixA -- matrix addition A = A + B
   SET element = element + (SELECT element
          FROM MatrixB
        WHERE MatrixB.i = MatrixA.i
          AND MatrixB.j = MatrixA.j);
```

Matrix multiplication is not as big a mess as might be expected. Remember that the first matrix must have the same number of rows as the second matrix has columns. That means A[i,k] * B[k,j] = C[i,j], which we can show with an example:

```
CREATE TABLE MatrixA
(i INTEGER NOT NULL,
 k INTEGER NOT NULL,
 element INTEGER NOT NULL,
 PRIMARY KEY (i,k));
```

MatrixA

i	k	element
1	1	2
1	2	−3
1	3	4
2	1	−1
2	2	0
2	3	2

```
CREATE TABLE MatrixB
(k INTEGER NOT NULL,
 j INTEGER NOT NULL,
 element INTEGER NOT NULL,
 PRIMARY KEY (k,j));
```

MatrixB

k	j	element
1	1	−1
1	2	2
1	3	3
2	1	0
2	2	1
2	3	7
3	1	1
3	2	1
3	3	−2

```
CREATE VIEW MatrixC(i, j, element)
AS SELECT i, j, SUM(MatrixA.element * MatrixB.element)
      FROM  MatrixA, MatrixB
   WHERE MatrixA.k = MatrixB.k
      GROUP BY i, j;
```

It is possible to do other matrix operations in SQL, but the code becomes so complex, and the execution time so long, that it is simply not worth the effort. If a reader would like to submit queries for eigenvalues and determinants, I will be happy to put them in future editions of this book.

Crosstabs and other statistical functions traditionally use an array to hold data. Some of these operations are covered in the sections in chapter 21 on cross tabulations and statistics.

23.3 Flattening a Table into an Array

Reports often want to see an array laid horizontally across a line. The original one element/one column approach to mapping arrays was based on seeing such reports and duplicating that structure in a table. A subscript is often an enumeration, denoting a month or another time period, rather than an integer. For example, a row in a Salesmen table might have a dozen columns, one for each month of the year, each of which holds the total commission earned in a particular month. The year is really an array, subscripted by the month.

The subscripts-and-value approach requires more work to produce the same results. It is often easier to explain a technique with an example. Let us imagine a company that collects time cards from its truck drivers, each with the driver's name, the week within the year (numbered 0 to 51 or 52, depending on the year), and his total hours. We want to produce a report with one line for each driver and 6 weeks of his time across the page. The Timecards table looks like this:

```
CREATE TABLE Timecards
(driver CHAR(25) NOT NULL,
 week INTEGER NOT NULL CHECK(week BETWEEN 1 AND 53)
 hours INTEGER CHECK(hours >= 0),
 PRIMARY KEY (driver, week));
```

We need to "flatten out" this table to get the desired rows for the report. First create a working storage table from which the report can be built. In SQL-92, this could be a CREATE TEMPORARY TABLE statement instead.

```
CREATE TABLE TimeReportWork      -- working storage
(driver CHAR(25) NOT NULL,
 wk1 INTEGER, -- important that these columns are NULL-able
 wk2 INTEGER,
 wk3 INTEGER,
 wk4 INTEGER,
 wk5 INTEGER,
 wk6 INTEGER);
```

Notice two important points about this table. First, there is no primary key; second, the weekly data columns are NULL-able. This table is then filled with time card values, thus:

```
BEGIN
INSERT INTO TimeReportWork (driver, wk1)
    SELECT driver, hours
        FROM Timecards
    WHERE week = (:n - 1) MOD 12;
INSERT INTO TimeReportWork (driver, wk2)
    SELECT driver, hours
        FROM Timecards
    WHERE week = (:n - 2) MOD 12;
INSERT INTO TimeReportWork (driver, wk3)
    SELECT driver, hours
        FROM Timecards
    WHERE week = (:n - 3) MOD 12;
INSERT INTO TimeReportWork (driver, wk4)
    SELECT driver, hours
        FROM Timecards
    WHERE week = (:n - 4) MOD 12;
INSERT INTO TimeReportWork (driver, wk5)
    SELECT driver, hours
        FROM Timecards
```

```
    WHERE week = (:n - 5) MOD 12;
INSERT INTO TimeReportWork (driver, wk6)
    SELECT driver, hours
        FROM Timecards
    WHERE week = (:n - 6) MOD 12;
END;
```

The number of the weeks in the WHERE clauses will vary with the period covered by the report. The parameter :n is the current week and the report is for the prior 6 weeks. A row with NULLs in all but one of the weekly columns is being inserted for each time card entry. The actual report is done with a grouped VIEW, which hides the summary functions. That VIEW looks like this:

```
CREATE VIEW TimeReport (driver, wk1tot, wk2tot, wk3tot, wk4tot,
wk5tot, wk6tot)
AS
SELECT driver, SUM(wk1), SUM(wk2), SUM(wk3), SUM(wk3), SUM(wk5),
SUM(wk6)
FROM TimeReportWork
GROUP BY driver;
```

If a driver did not work in a particular week, the corresponding weekly column gets no row to represent it. However, if the driver has not worked at all in the last six weeks, we could lose him completely (no time cards, no summary). Depending on the nature of the report, you might consider using

```
INSERT INTO TimeReportWork (driver)
    SELECT DISTINCT driver FROM Personnel;
```

to load all the names into the table first. All the weekly columns will default to NULL, and everyone will have at least one row. The SUM() of a column of NULLs is always NULL. The NULLs are thrown out and the set is left empty, so the SUM() of an empty set is NULL. This lets you tell the difference between a driver who was missing for the reporting period and a driver who worked zero hours and turned in a time card for that during the period. That difference could be important for computing the payroll.

23.4 Comparing Arrays in Table Format

It is often necessary to compare one array or set of values with another when the data is represented in a table. Remember that comparing a set with a set does not involve ordering the elements, whereas an array does. For this discussion, let us create two tables, one for employees and one for their dependents. The children are subscripted in the order of their births — i.e., 1 is the oldest living child, and so forth.

```
CREATE TABLE Employees
(empno INTEGER PRIMARY KEY,
 empname CHAR(15) NOT NULL,
 ...   );


CREATE TABLE Dependents
(empno INTEGER NOT NULL -- the parent
 kid  CHAR(15) NOT NULL,   -- the array element
 birthorder INTEGER NOT NULL -- the array subscript
 PRIMARY KEY (empno, kid));
```

The query "Find pairs of employees whose children have the same set of names" is very restrictive, but we can make it more so by requiring that the children be named in the same birth order. Both Mr. X and Mr. Y must have exactly the same number of dependents; both sets of names must match. We can assume that no parent has two children with the same name (George Foreman does not work here) or born at the same time (we will order twins). Let us begin by inserting test data into the Dependents table, thus:

Dependents

empno	kid	birthorder
1	Dick	2
1	Harry	3
1	Tom	1
2	Dick	3
2	Harry	1
2	Tom	2

(cont.)	empno	kid	birthorder
	3	Dick	2
	3	Harry	3
	3	Tom	1
	4	Harry	1
	4	Tom	2
	5	Curly	2
	5	Harry	3
	5	Moe	1

In this test data, employees 1, 2, and 3 all have dependents named Tom, Dick, and Harry. The birth order is the same for the children of employees 1 and 3, but not for employee 2. For testing purposes, you might consider adding an extra child to the family of employee 3, and so forth, to play with this data.

Though there are many ways to solve this query, this approach will give us some flexibility that others would not. Construct a VIEW that gives us the number of dependents for each employee:

```
CREATE VIEW Familysize (empno, tally)
AS SELECT empno, COUNT(*)
      FROM Dependents
   GROUP BY empno;
```

Create a second VIEW that holds pairs of employees who have families of the same size. This VIEW is also useful for other statistical work, but that is another topic.

```
CREATE VIEW Samesize (empno1, empno2, tally)
AS SELECT F1.empno, F2.empno, F1.tally
      FROM Familysize AS F1, Familysize AS F2
   WHERE F1.tally = F2.tally
      AND F1.empno < F2.empno;
```

We will test for set equality by doing a self-join on the dependents of employees with families of the same size. If one set can be mapped onto another with no children left over, and in the same birth order, then the two sets are equal.

```
SELECT D1.empno AS x, ' named his ',
          S1.tally, ' kids just like ',
          D2.empno AS y
    FROM Dependents AS D1, Dependents AS D2, Samesize AS S1
WHERE S1.empno1 = D1.empno
      AND S1.empno2 = D2.empno
      AND D1.kid = D2.kid
      AND D1.birthorder = D2.birthorder
    GROUP BY x, y, S1.tally
HAVING COUNT(*) = S1.tally;
```

If birth order is not important, then drop the predicate
D1.birthorder = D2.birthorder from the query.

CHAPTER

24

Set Operations

BY SET OPERATIONS, I mean union, intersection, and set differences where the sets in SQL are tables. (Operations that define subsets from another set will be covered in the next chapter.) These are the basic operators used in elementary set theory, which has been taught in the United States public school systems for decades. Since the relational model is based on sets of tuples, you would expect that SQL would have had a good variety of set operators from the start. But this was not the case. The SQL-92 standard has added what was missing in the SQL-86 and SQL-89 standards, but you should look for vendor extensions that provide the same functions with different syntax.

There is another problem in SQL that you did not have in high school set theory. SQL tables are multisets (also called *bags*), which means that, unlike sets, they allow duplicate elements (rows or tuples). Codd's relational model is stricter and uses only true sets. SQL handles these duplicate rows with an ALL or DISTINCT modifier in different places in the language; ALL preserves duplicates and DISTINCT removes them.

So that we can discuss the result of each operator formally, let R be a row that is a duplicate of some row in TableA, or of some row in TableB, or of both. Let *m* be the number of duplicates of R in

TableA and let *n* be the number of duplicates of R in TableB, where
m >= 0 and *n* >= 0. Informally, the decision in the SQL-92 standard
was to pair off the two tables on a row-per-row basis in set operations.
We will see how this works for each operator.

In SQL-92, we introduced the shorthand TABLE <table name> for
the query or subquery SELECT * FROM <table name>, which lets us
refer to a table as a whole without referring to its columns.

24.1 UNION and UNION ALL

UNIONs are supported in SQL-86, SQL-89, and SQL-92, but the other
set operations have to be constructed by the programmer in SQL-89.
That limits us to single-column tables, but this can still be useful. The
SQL-92 syntax for the UNION statement is

```
<query>  UNION  [ALL] <query> [ORDER BY <sort specification>]
```

The UNION statement takes two result tables and builds a new table
from them. The two tables must be *union compatible,* which means
that they have the same number of columns, and that each column in
the first table has the same datatype (or automatically CAST to it) as
the column in the same position in the second table. That is, their
rows have the same structure, so they can be put in the same final
result table. Most implementations will do some datatype conversions
to create the result table, but this is very implementation-dependent
and you should check it out for yourself.

The ORDER BY clause is very common and it was part of the SQL-89
standard, but it may not be available in all SQL implementations. This
is because only cursors are supposed to be ordered in SQL, so many
earlier implementations did not have this feature. There are two
forms of the UNION statement: the UNION and the UNION ALL.

The simple UNION is the same operator you had in high school set
theory; it returns the rows that appear in either or both tables and
removes duplicates from the result table. In most implementations,
this removal is done by merge-sorting the two tables and discarding
duplicates during the sorting. This has the side effect that the result
table is sorted, but you cannot depend on that. This also explains why

the ORDER BY clause is a common feature — as long as the engine is sorting anyway, why not let the programmer decide the ordering?

The UNION ALL preserves the duplicates from both tables in the result table. In most implementations, this statement is done appending one table to the other, giving you a predictable ordering. If an ORDER BY clause is used, a merge-sort is often used by the SQL engine. But, again, you cannot depend on any ordering in the results of either version of the UNION statement. Each SQL implementation could use a different sorting algorithm within the engine, or could even use a hashing algorithm to find duplicates.

The UNION and UNION ALL operators are infixed operators that appear between query expressions — for example,

```
(SELECT a, b, c FROM TableA WHERE city = 'Boston')
UNION
(SELECT x, y, z FROM TableB WHERE city = 'New York');
```

The parentheses around the SELECT statements are an option in the SQL-92 syntax, but not in the SQL-89 standard, which would see them as subqueries. If your implementation has the parentheses, use them for safety and clarity.

The columns in the result table do not have names, only position numbers, in SQL-89. The reason for the lack of names is that there is no way to decide which existing columns to use — should it be (a, b, c) or (x, y, z) in the above example? This is a depreciated feature in SQL-92, however. That means that it will not be in the next version of the standard, so you should stop using it. In SQL-92, you can assign names to the columns by using the AS operator to name both the result and the columns of the result, thus:

```
((SELECT a, b, c FROM TableA WHERE city = 'Boston')
UNION
(SELECT x, y, z FROM TableB WHERE city = 'New York'))
AS Cities (tom, dick, harry)
```

SQL-92 will also let you use UNIONs in the FROM clause. If your SQL does not have these features, then you may need to create a VIEW with the UNION in it to give names to columns.

24.1.1 Duplicates and UNION Operators

The UNION removes all duplicate rows from the results and does not care from which table the duplicate rows came. We could use this feature to write a query to remove duplicates from a table:

```
(TABLE TableA)
UNION
(TABLE TableA);
```

But this is the same as

```
SELECT DISTINCT * FROM TableA;
```

The second query will probably run faster and preserve the column names too. Most SQL products implement UNION and SELECT DISTINCT with a sorting algorithm that throws away duplicates while it sorts. The UNION operator is expecting two result tables, which it loads into working storage, usually without checking to see that they are identical, with a merge-sort. SELECT DISTINCT loads working storage with only one result table and it is freer to pick a sorting algorithm.

Sort algorithms vary from product to product, but most work from left to right, using the columns in the SELECT clause list when they cannot find an index to help match up duplicates. If the result table has to be materialized, the indexes will be lost. This means that it is usually a good idea to put keys to the left to speed up the sort.

The UNION ALL operator keeps the duplicate rows and it is often implemented as a file append algorithm, without any sorting. The number of duplicates of R in the result table will be the number of duplicates of R in TableA plus the number of duplicates of R in TableB.

24.1.2 Order of Execution

UNION and UNION ALL operators are executed from left to right unless parentheses change the order. Since the UNION operator is associative and commutative, the order of a chain of UNIONs will not affect the results. However, order and grouping can affect performance.

Consider two small tables that have many duplicates between them. If the optimizer does not consider table sizes, this query

```
(TABLE SmallTable1)
UNION
(TABLE BigTable)
UNION
(TABLE SmallTable2);
```

will merge SmallTable1 into BigTable, then merge SmallTable2 into that first result. If the rows of SmallTable1 are spread out in the first result table, locating duplicates from SmallTable2 will take longer than if we had written the query thus:

```
(TABLE SmallTable1)
UNION
(TABLE SmallTable2))
UNION
(TABLE BigTable);
```

Optimization of UNIONs is highly product-dependent, so you should experiment with it.

24.1.3 Mixed UNION and UNION ALL Operators

If you know that there are no duplicates, or that duplicates are not a problem in your situation, use the UNION ALL operator instead of UNION for speed. For example, if we are sure that BigTable has no duplicates in common with SmallTable1 and SmallTable2, this query will produce the same results as before but should run much faster:

```
((TABLE SmallTable1)
UNION
(TABLE SmallTable2))
UNION ALL
(TABLE BigTable);
```

But be careful when mixing UNION and UNION ALL operators. The left-to-right order of execution will cause the last operator in the chain to have an effect on the results.

Microsoft introduced its Access database product in 1992, after five years and tens of millions of dollars' worth of development work. The first complaints they got on their CompuServe user support forum involved the lack of a UNION operator. UNION is a very important tool in relational database work. For the rest of this discussion, let us create two tables with the same structure, which we can use for examples.

```
CREATE TableA
(col1 INTEGER NOT NULL);

INSERT INTO TableA VALUES (1);
INSERT INTO TableA VALUES (1);
INSERT INTO TableA VALUES (2);
INSERT INTO TableA VALUES (3);
INSERT INTO TableA VALUES (4);
INSERT INTO TableA VALUES (5);

CREATE TableB
(col1 INTEGER NOT NULL);

INSERT INTO TableB VALUES (1);
INSERT INTO TableB VALUES (2);
INSERT INTO TableB VALUES (2);
INSERT INTO TableB VALUES (3);
```

will yield

```
(SELECT col1 FROM TableA)
UNION
(SELECT col1 FROM TableB)
```

```
1
2
3
4
5
```

```
(SELECT col1 FROM TableA)
  UNION ALL
(SELECT col1 FROM TableB)
```

```
1
1
1
2
2
2
3
3
4
5
```

24.2 Set Difference Operator

Set difference is part of the SQL-92 standard, and a few versions of SQL have implemented it as of today. However, they may use a different term from the EXCEPT keyword in SQL-92, such as MINUS in Oracle. The set difference is the rows in the first table, except for those that also appear in the second table. It answers questions like "Give me all the employees except the salesmen" in a natural manner.

The SQL-92 EXCEPT operator discards duplicate rows from the first table, then removes all rows that also occur in the second table. This is a pure set operator.

```
(SELECT col1 FROM TableA)
EXCEPT
(SELECT col1 FROM TableB)
```

```
4
5
```

To do this in SQL-89, you would need to use this query:

```
SELECT DISTINCT col1
    FROM TableA
WHERE NOT EXISTS (SELECT *
            FROM TableB
        WHERE TableA.col1 = TableB.col1);
```

which is fairly straightforward. As you would expect, the EXCEPT ALL operator is more of a problem. The number of duplicates of a row in the result table is the maximum of the number of duplicates of R in the left-hand table minus the number of duplicates of R in the right-hand table and zero. To do the EXCEPT ALL statement, you need to know the row counts in both tables.

```
(SELECT col1 FROM TableA)
EXCEPT ALL
(SELECT col1 FROM TableB)
```

```
1
4
5
```

Duplicating this in SQL-89 is difficult. First, construct a VIEW to hold the row counts:

```
CREATE VIEW RowCountView (col1, t1tally, t2tally)
AS SELECT col1, COUNT(*), 0
        FROM TableA
    GROUP BY col1
  UNION
  SELECT col1, 0, COUNT(*)
        FROM TableB
    GROUP BY col1;
```

This VIEW can in turn construct a final VIEW:

```
CREATE VIEW ExceptView (col1, dups)
AS SELECT col1, (SUM(t1tally) - SUM(t2tally)) AS dups
      FROM RowCountView
   GROUP BY col1
      HAVING (SUM(t1tally) - SUM(t2tally)) > 0;
```

This is not quite the same thing as the EXCEPT ALL result, but the degree of duplication is clearly shown as a column.

24.2.1 Set Difference with OUTER JOIN

The set difference can also be written in SQL with an OUTER JOIN operator, as well as the NOT EXISTS() predicate shown in section 24.2. Jim Panttaja reports that this approach requires about one-fourth of the logical I/O operations of the EXISTS() approach that is involved when you are using SYBASE, but this may vary.

```
SELECT DISTINCT TableA.*
    FROM (TABLE TableA LEFT OUTER JOIN TABLE TableB
       ON TableA.keycol = TableB.keycol)
WHERE TableB.keycol IS NULL;
```

The idea is that rows in TableB that match to TableA rows will not be NULL-padded in the OUTER JOIN.

24.3 Intersection

An *intersection* is defined as the elements that are common members of two sets. Intersection is associative, commutative, and idempotent, just like the UNION operator. If your algebra is weak, *associative* means that the way you group the operations does not change the results; in symbols, $((x \text{ R } y) \text{ R } z) = (x \text{ R } (y \text{ R } z))$. *Commutative* means that the order in which you do a chain of operations does not change the results; in symbols, $x \text{ R } y = y \text{ R } x$. *Idempotent* means that if you do the operation to the same set, you get the same set back as a result; in symbols, $x \text{ R } x = x$.

Intersection is part of the SQL-92 standard, but it has not been implemented in most SQLs today. There are two flavors of intersection in SQL-92, INTERSECT and INTERSECT ALL. As you would expect from the UNION and EXCEPT operators, INTERSECT removes any duplicate rows between the two tables involved.

The INTERSECT [ALL] operators also have a higher precedence than UNION, so intersection is done first in a chain of set operations.

```
(SELECT col1 FROM TableA)
INTERSECT
(SELECT col1 FROM TableB)
```

1

2

3

To do this in SQL-89, we need to test all of the columns in both tables against their corresponding matches in the other table. The table from which we work also needs to have duplicates removed from it, which means we use a SELECT DISTINCT. We can either write this query

```
-- TableA on the outer correlation level and remove duplicates
SELECT DISTINCT col1
FROM TableA AS T1
WHERE EXISTS (SELECT *
        FROM TableB AS T2
    WHERE (T1.col1 = T2.col1);
```

or this query

```
-- TableB on the outer correlation level and remove duplicates
SELECT DISTINCT col1,
FROM TableB AS T2
WHERE EXISTS (SELECT *
        FROM TableA AS T1
    WHERE (T1.col1 = T2.col1);
```

The difference in performance will vary with the quality of the optimizer in your SQL product and the degree of duplication in the tables. Try both versions to see if there is any difference in the order of the tables involved.

INTERSECT ALL preserves duplicate rows between the two tables, keeping the minimum of the number of duplicate rows in the first table and the number of duplicate rows in the second table in its result table. For the data in TableA and TableB, the results of INTERSECT and INTERSECT ALL are the same:

```
(SELECT col1 FROM TableA)
INTERSECT ALL
(SELECT col1 FROM TableB)
```

```
1
2
3
```

Writing this in SQL-89 is harder than you would think. The obvious approach is to simply change SELECT DISTINCT to SELECT in the query proposed for INTERSECT to get an SQL-89 query that is equivalent to the SQL-92 INTERSECT ALL. It sounds promising, but does not work. Rewriting the first query, we get

```
-- this version will keep duplicates, but only from TableA
SELECT col1,
FROM TableA AS T1
WHERE EXISTS (SELECT *
      FROM TableB AS T2
   WHERE (T1.col1 = T2.col1);
```

Results

col1
1
1
2
3

and, likewise, rewriting the second query,

```
-- this version will keep duplicates, but only from TableB
SELECT col1,
FROM TableB AS T2
WHERE EXISTS (SELECT *
        FROM TableA AS T1
     WHERE (T1.col1 = T2.col1);
```

Results

col1
1
2
3

So we have the same problem we had with the EXCEPT operator: SQL-92 defines the number of duplicates of a row in the result table to be the minimum of the number of duplicate rows in the first table and the number of duplicate rows in the second table. First construct a VIEW to hold the row counts for each value:

```
CREATE VIEW RowCountView (col1, tally)
AS SELECT col1, COUNT(*)
        FROM TableA
      GROUP BY col1
    UNION
    SELECT col1, COUNT(*)
        FROM TableB
      GROUP BY col1;
```

This VIEW can in turn construct a final VIEW:

```
CREATE VIEW IntersectView (col1, mindups)
AS SELECT col1, MIN(tally)
      FROM RowCountView
    GROUP BY col1
    HAVING COUNT(*) > 1;
```

The HAVING clause will find those columns that were represented in both tables. This is not quite the same thing as the INTERSECT ALL result, but the degree of duplication is clearly shown as a column.

Subsets

I AM DEFINING SUBSET operations as queries, which extract a particular subset from a given set, as opposed to set operations, which work between sets. The obvious way to extract a subset from a table is just to use a WHERE clause, which will pull out the rows that meet that criterion. But not all the subsets we want are easily defined by such a simple predicate. This chapter is a collection of tricks for constructing useful, but not obvious, subsets from a table.

25.1 The Top *n* Values

This problem originally appeared in *Explain* magazine; it was submitted by Jim Wankowski of Hawthorne, CA (Wankowski). You are given a table of employees and their salaries. Write a single SQL query that will display the three highest salaries from that table. It is easy to find the maximum salary with the simple query SELECT MAX(salary) FROM Employees;, but SQL does not have a maximum function that will return a group of high values from a column.

This problem can be done easily in a procedural language. The first thought of a novice procedural-language programmer is to sort the table in descending order by salary, then print the first three records from the table. This problem is better done with an algorithm due to C. A. R. Hoare. It is the partition function in QuickSort, crippled to avoid sorting the whole file, which would take $n*\log2(n)$ time. Assuming that on the average it splits the current sublist in half, this one will run in only $2*n$ time.

In practice, it is a good idea to start with a pivot at or near position n, because real data tends to have some ordering already in it. If the file is already in sorted order, this trick will return an answer in one pass:

```
CONST
    listlength = { some large number };
    ...
TYPE
    LIST = ARRAY [1..listlength] OF REAL;
    ...


PROCEDURE FindTopK (Kth : INTEGER, records : LIST);
VAR pivot, left, right, start, finish: INTEGER;
BEGIN
start := 1;  finish := listlength;
WHILE (start < finish)
DO BEGIN
    pivot := records[Kth];
    left := start; right := finish;
    REPEAT
        WHILE (records[left] > pivot) DO left := left + 1;
        WHILE (records[right] < pivot) DO right := right - 1;
        IF (left >= right)
        THEN BEGIN  { swap right and left elements }
            Swap (records[left], records[right]);
            left := left + 1; right := right - 1;
            END;
    UNTIL (left < right);
    IF (right < Kth) THEN start := left;
    IF (left > Kth) THEN finish := right;
    END;
```

```
{ the first k numbers are in positions 1 through kth,
  in no  particular order except that the kth highest number
  is in position kth }
END.
```

The naive SQL programmer's approach is to mimic the naive procedural-language programmer's approach. This is not too surprising, since they are often the same people. They write a query that sorts the results like this:

```
SELECT DISTINCT salary
     FROM Employees
  ORDER BY salary;
```

then just look at the top three numbers. This is actually the way that most people do it, since they can scroll results on a terminal screen from an interactive SQL tool, but it is not valid SQL. The ORDER BY can only appear on a DECLARE CURSOR statement; the results of a query are not sorted. Oh, yes, did I mention that the whole table has to be sorted and that this can take some time if the table is large?

The original articles in *Explain* magazine gave several solutions (Murchison; Wankowski). One involved UNION operations on nested subqueries. The first result table was the maximum for the whole table, the second result table was the maximum for the table entries less than the first maximum, and so forth. The pattern is extensible. It looked like this:

```
SELECT MAX(salary) FROM Employees
    UNION
SELECT MAX(salary) FROM Employees
    WHERE salary < (SELECT MAX(salary) FROM Employees)
    UNION
SELECT MAX(salary) FROM Employees
    WHERE salary < (SELECT MAX(salary)
            FROM Employees
          WHERE salary <
            (SELECT MAX(salary) FROM Employees));
```

This answer can give you a pretty serious performance problem because of the subquery nesting and the UNION operations. Every UNION will trigger a sort to remove duplicate rows from the results, since salary is not a UNIQUE column.

An improvement on the UNION approach is to find the third highest salary with a subquery, then return all the records with salaries that were equal or higher. This will handle ties; it looked like this:

```
SELECT DISTINCT salary
    FROM Employees
WHERE salary >=
        (SELECT MAX(salary)
            FROM Employees
        WHERE salary < (SELECT MAX(salary)
                    FROM Employees
                WHERE salary <
                (SELECT MAX(salary) FROM Employees)));
```

A better answer is to use correlation names and return a single-row answer. This pattern is more easily extensible to larger groups; it will also present the results in sorted order without requiring the use of an ORDER BY clause. The disadvantage of this answer is that it will return a single row and not a column result. That might make it unusable for joining to other queries. It looked like this:

```
SELECT MAX(A.salary), MAX(B.salary), MAX(C.salary)
    FROM Employees AS A, Employees AS B, Employees AS C
WHERE (A.salary > B.salary)
        AND (B.salary > C.salary);
```

But the best answer given uses a GROUP BY clause for a grouping problem along with the idea of nested sets. The idea is to take each salary and build a group of other salaries that are less than or equal to it. The groups with three or fewer rows are what we want to see. This is the set-oriented approach; the third element of an ordered list is also the maximum element of a set of three unique elements. Think of concentric sets, nested inside each other.

This query gives a columnar answer, and the query can be extended to other numbers by changing the constant in the HAVING clause.

```
SELECT DISTINCT COUNT(*), A.salary
    FROM Employees AS A, Employees AS B
WHERE (A.salary <= B.salary)
    GROUP BY A.salary
HAVING COUNT(*) <= 3; -- control parameter
```

25.2 Every *n*th Item in a Table

This problem was presented in *Explain* magazine by Rory Murchison, DB2 instructor at the Aetna Institute (Murchison 19??). SQL is a set-oriented language, which can not identify individual rows by their positions in a table. Instead, a unique key is detected by logical expressions. If you are given a file of employees in a non-SQL system and you want to pick out every *n*th employee for a survey where the ordering is based on their employee identification numbers, the job is easy. You write a procedure with nested loops that reads the records and writes every *n*th one to a second file.

The immediate thought of how to do this in SQL is that you can simply compute empno MOD *n,* where MOD is the modulo function found in most SQL implementations, and save those employee rows where this function is zero. The trouble is that employees are not issued consecutive identification numbers. The identification numbers are unique, however.

Vendor extensions often include a row identifier that can be used by procedural extension to perform these functions, but not always. Informix/SQL is one product with this feature. This makes the code easy to write in SQL. It will look something like this:

```
SELECT *
    FROM Employees
WHERE (RowNumber MOD n) = 0
ORDER BY empno;
```

Yes, this query can be done when RowNumber is not supplied by the database engine. It requires a self-join on the Employees table to partition it into a nested series of grouped tables, just as we did for the "top *n*" problem. You then pick out the largest value in each group. There may be an index or a uniqueness constraint on the empno column to ensure uniqueness, so the EXISTS predicate will get a performance boost.

Incidentally, row numbers are not just nonstandard; they are also prone to create problems when you use them in any query with a sort, because you do not know if the row number is the position in the table before or after the sort. Users logged on and looking at the same base table through different VIEWs may or may not get the same row number for the same physical row. Another set of problems involves deleting and inserting rows. Exactly what happens when a user deletes a row and inserts another? What if he tried to insert a row well past the last row of the table — are deleted rows created as needed, or what?

```
SELECT empno
    FROM Employees AS E1
WHERE EXISTS (SELECT MAX(empno)
                FROM Employees AS E2
            WHERE (E1.empno >= E2.empno)
        HAVING (COUNT(*) MOD n) = 0;
```

A nonnested version of the same query looks like this:

```
SELECT E1.empno
    FROM Employees AS E1, Employees AS E2
WHERE (E1.empno >= E2.empno)
    GROUP BY E1.empno
HAVING (COUNT(*) MOD n) = 0;
```

25.3 The CONTAINS Operators

Set theory has two symbols for subsets. One, ⊂, means that set *A* is contained within set *B*; this is sometimes said to denote a proper subset. The other, ⊆, means "is contained in or equal to," and is sometimes called just a subset or containment operator.

Standard SQL has never had an operator to compare tables against each other for equality or containment. Several college textbooks on relational databases mention a CONTAINS predicate, which does not exist in SQL-89 or SQL-92. This predicate existed in the original

System R, IBM's first experimental SQL system, but it was dropped from later SQL implementations because of the expense of running it.

25.3.1 Proper Subset Operators

The IN predicate is a test for membership. For those of you who remember your high school set theory, membership is shown with a stylized epsilon with the containing set on the right side: $a \in A$. Membership is for one element, whereas a subset is itself a set, not just an element.

As an example of a subset predicate, consider a query to tell you the names of each employee who works on all of the projects in department 5. Using the System R syntax,

```
SELECT name    -- Not valid SQL!
    FROM Employees
WHERE ((SELECT projectno
          FROM WorksOn
        WHERE Employees.employeeno = WorksOn.employeeno)
    CONTAINS
        (SELECT projectno
          FROM Projects
        WHERE deptno = 5));
```

In the second SELECT statement of the CONTAINS predicate, we build a table of all the projects in department 5. In the first SELECT statement of the CONTAINS predicate, we have a correlated subquery that will build a table of all the projects each employee works on. If the table of the employee's projects is equal to or a superset of the department 5 table, the predicate is TRUE.

You must first decide what you are going to do about duplicate rows in either or both tables. That is, does the set { a, b, c } contain the multiset { a, b, b } or not? Some SQL set operations, such as SELECT and UNION, have options to remove or keep duplicates from the results, as in UNION ALL and SELECT DISTINCT.

I would argue that duplicates should be ignored and the answer to the above question is "Yes, the multiset is a subset of the other." For our example, let us use a table of employees and another table with the names of the company bowling team members, which should be a proper subset of the Employees table. For the bowling team to be contained in the set of employees, each bowler must be an employee, or, to put it another way, there must be no bowler who is not an employee.

```
NOT EXISTS (SELECT *
    FROM Bowling AS B1
        WHERE B1.empno NOT IN (SELECT empno FROM Employees))
```

25.3.2 Set Equality

Consider the problem of using a suppliers-and-parts table to find pairs of suppliers who provide *exactly* the same parts. That is, the set of parts from one supplier is equal to the set of parts from the other supplier.

```
CREATE TABLE SupParts
(sno CHAR(2) NOT NULL,
 pno CHAR(2) NOT NULL,
 PRIMARY KEY (sno, pno));
```

The usual way of proving that two sets are equal is to show that set A contains set B and set B contains set A.

What you would usually do in standard SQL would be to show that there exists no element in set A that is not in set B, and therefore A is a subset of B. Instead, consider another approach. First join one supplier to another on their common parts, eliminating the situation where supplier 1 is the same as supplier 2, so that you have the intersection of the two sets. If the intersection has the same number of pairs as each of the two sets has elements, the two sets are equal.

```
SELECT SP1.sno AS Supplier1, SP2.sno AS Supplier2
    FROM SupParts AS SP1 JOIN SupParts AS SP2
        ON (SP1.pno = SP2.pno AND SP1.sno < SP2.sno)
    GROUP BY Supplier1, Supplier2
```

```
HAVING COUNT(*) = (SELECT COUNT(*)
                   FROM SupParts AS SP3
                   WHERE SP3.sno = SP1.sno)
   AND COUNT(*) = (SELECT COUNT(*)
                   FROM SupParts AS SP4
                   WHERE SP4.sno = SP2.sno);
```

This uses some SQL-92 features, but can easily be written in SQL-89. If there is an index on the supplier number in the SupParts table, it can provide the counts directly as well as helping with the JOIN operation.

CHAPTER 26

Trees

A TREE IS A special kind of directed graph. Graphs are data structures that
are made up of nodes (usually shown as boxes) connected by edges
(usually shown as lines with arrowheads). Each edge represents a
one-way relationship between the two nodes it connects. In an
organizational chart, the nodes are employees and each edge is the
"reports to" relationship. In a parts explosion (also called a bill of
materials), the nodes are assembly units (eventually resolving down
to individual parts) and each edge is the "is made of" relationship.

The top of the tree is called the root. In an organizational chart, it
is the highest authority; in a parts explosion, it is the final assembly.
The number of edges coming out of the node are its outdegree, and
the number of edges entering it are its indegree. A binary tree is one
in which a parent can have at most two children; more generally, an
n-ary tree is one in which a node can have at most outdegree n.

The nodes of the tree that have no subtrees beneath them are
called the leaf nodes. In a parts explosion, they are the individual
parts, which cannot be broken down any further. The descendants,
or children, of a node (called the parent) are every node in the
subtree that has the parent node as its root.

There are several ways to define a tree: It is a graph with no cycles; it is a graph where all nodes except the root have indegree 1 and the root has indegree zero. Another defining property is that a path can be found from the root to any other node in the tree by following the edges in their natural direction.

Trees are often drawn as charts. In the United States, we like to put the root at the top and grow the tree downward; Europeans will often put the root at the bottom and grow the tree upward, or grow the tree from left to right across the page. Another way of representing trees is to show them as nested sets; this is the basis for the visitation number representation in SQL, which will be discussed in section 26.3.

Since the two most common examples of trees in the real world and in SQL textbooks are parts explosions and organizational charts, these are the two we will use for the rest of this chapter.

26.1 Trees in SQL

It should be no surprise that hierarchies were very easy to represent in hierarchical databases, where the structure of the data and the structure of the database were the same. In fact, one reason that hierarchical databases were created was to accommodate the existing hierarchical data structures.

Unfortunately, SQL provides poor support for such data. It does not directly map hierarchical data into tables, because tables are based on sets rather than on graphs. SQL directly supports neither the retrieval of the raw data in a meaningful recursive or hierarchical fashion nor computation of recursively defined functions that commonly occur in these types of applications. Support for such structures is discussed in the proposed SQL3 standard in the form of the RECURSIVE UNION operator, but it is a complex nightmare that will probably not make it into commercial implementations for a decade, if at all. In the meantime, most programmers use 3GL host languages or report writers, which can better handle tree structures.

The SQL programmer has to remember that any relationship in the data must be shown explicitly in SQL as data. This means that we will have to add columns to represent tree components.

26.2 Edge Representation of Trees in a Single Table

Since the nodes contain the data, we can add columns to represent the edges of a tree. This is usually done in one of two ways in SQL: a single table or two tables. In the single-table representation, the edge connection appears in the same table as the node. In the two-table format, one table contains the nodes of the graph and the other table contains the edges, represented as pairs of end points.

The two-table representation can handle generalized directed graphs, not just trees, so we defer a discussion of this representation here. There is very little difference in the actual way you would handle things, however. The usual reason for using a separate edge table is that the nodes are very complex objects or are duplicated and need to be kept separately for normalization.

In the single-table representation of hierarchies in SQL, there has to be one column for the identifier of the node and one column of the same datatype for the parent of the node. In the organizational chart, the linking column is usually the employee identification number of the immediate boss of each employee. The single table works best for organizational charts, because each employee can appear only once (assuming each employee has one and only one manager), whereas a parts explosion can have many occurrences of the same part within many different assemblies. Let us define a simple Employees table like this, ignoring the left and right columns for now.

```
CREATE TABLE Employees
(emp CHAR(20) PRIMARY KEY,
 boss CHAR(20),
 salary DECIMAL(6, 2) NOT NULL,
 left INTEGER NOT NULL,
 right INTEGER NOT NULL);
```

Employees

emp	boss	salary
Albert	NULL	1000.00
Bert	Albert	900.00
Chuck	Albert	900.00

(cont.)	**emp**	**boss**	**salary**
	Donna	Chuck	800.00
	Eddie	Chuck	700.00
	Fred	Chuck	600.00

26.2.1 Path Enumeration

Path enumeration is the construction of a table of the beginning and end nodes of all the paths. This is handy for other queries — such as "Does Mr. King have any authority over Mr. Jones?" or "Does a gizmo use a frammistat?" — that depend on finding a path. To find the name of the boss for each employee, the query is a self-join, like this:

```
SELECT B1.emp. ' bosses ', E1.emp
    FROM Employees AS B1, Employees AS E1
WHERE B1.emp = E1.boss;
```

But something is missing here. These are only the immediate bosses of the employees. Your boss's boss also has authority over you, and so forth up the tree until we find someone who has no subordinates. To go two levels deep in the tree, we need to do a more complex self-join, thus:

```
SELECT B1.emp, ' bosses ', E2.emp
    FROM Employees AS B1, Employees AS E1, Employees AS E2
WHERE B1.emp = E1.boss
    AND E1.emp = E2.boss;
```

To go more than two levels deep in the tree, just extend the pattern, thus:

```
SELECT B1.emp, ' bosses ', E3.emp
    FROM Employees AS B1, Employees AS E1,
        Employees AS E2, Employees AS E3
WHERE B1.emp = E1.boss
    AND E1.emp = E2.boss
    AND E2.emp = E3.boss;
```

Unfortunately, you have no idea just how deep the tree is, so you must keep extending this query until you get an empty set back as a result. This same query can be done by constructing a new table that is *n* levels deep, then joining it with the original one-level-deep table to build the (*n* + 1)-levels-deep table. This is also hard to optimize, so many vendors have extensions for handling trees in this format, which we will discuss in section 26.4.

Let us build a working table, called PathEnum, to hold the start and end values of each path along with its length. Begin by inserting the length-1 paths into the working table. Now repeat the following statement until you are inserting zero rows:

```
CREATE TABLE PathEnum
(pathlength INTEGER NOT NULL,
 start CHAR(20) NOT NULL,
 end CHAR(20) NOT NULL,
 PRIMARY KEY (start, end));

INSERT INTO PathEnum(pathlength, start, end)
SELECT 1, B1.emp, E1.emp
    FROM Employees AS B1, Employees AS E1
WHERE B1.emp = E1.boss;

INSERT INTO PathEnum
SELECT DISTINCT (P1.pathlength + 1), P1.start, P2.end
    FROM PathEnum AS P1, PathEnum AS P2
WHERE P1.end = P2.start
        AND pathlength =
            (SELECT MAX(pathlength) FROM PathEnum);
```

There is no way to do this in a single standard SQL statement or without a loop in a procedural host language.

26.2.2 Finding Leaf Nodes

A leaf node is one that has no children under it. In an edge representation, this set of nodes is fairly easy to find. They are going to be the employees who are not bosses to anyone else in the company, thus:

```
SELECT *
    FROM Employees AS E1
WHERE NOT EXISTS (SELECT *
            FROM Employees AS E2
        WHERE E1.emp = E2.boss);
```

26.2.3 Finding the Root Node

The root of the tree has a boss that is NULL — the root has nothing over it:

```
SELECT *
    FROM Employees
WHERE boss IS NULL;
```

26.2.4 Finding Levels in a Tree

The level of a node is its distance from the root of the tree, measured as the count of the edges between them. If I have the PathEnum table, the level number is very easy to find:

```
SELECT end, pathlength AS level
    FROM PathEnum
WHERE start = :root;
```

26.2.5 Functions in the Edge Representation

Tree functions are queries that answer questions based on sets of nodes defined by hierarchical relationships. For example, what is the total of the salaries of the subordinates of a given boss? The PathEnum table is vital for most of these functions, such as

```
SELECT :mymanager, ' salary budget is ', SUM(salary)
    FROM Employees
WHERE emp IN
        (SELECT end FROM PathEnum WHERE start = :mymanager);
```

You can add OR emp = :mymanager to the WHERE if you want to include the boss in his own budget. Our sample table would produce these results:

Result

:mymanager	SUM(salary)
Mr. King	3900.00
Mr. Duke	2100.00

Another common function involves using quantity columns in the nodes to compute an accumulated total. This usually occurs in parts explosions, where one assembly may contain several occurrences of a subassembly. This sort of relationship is usually shown in the two-table graph representation, because the quantity can be put in the second table, which holds the edges, rather than in the nodes, which hold the parts descriptions.

26.2.6 Tree Operations

Tree operations are those that alter the size and shape of a tree, not the contents of the nodes of the tree. Some of these operations can be very complex, such as balancing a binary tree, but we will deal only with deletion and insertion of a whole subtree.

Subtree Deletion

Deleting an entire subtree is easy if you have the PathEnum table, but you have to decide whether you want to delete the root of the subtree or not.

```
DELETE FROM Employees
    WHERE emp IN (SELECT end FROM PathEnum WHERE start = :mymanager)
        OR emp = :mymanager;
```

At this point, you must remember to rebuild the PathEnum table, or nothing will work.

Subtree Insertion

Inserting a subtree under a given node is easy. Given a table with the subtree that is to be made subordinate to a given node, you simply write

```
BEGIN
UPDATE Subtree      -- subordinate the subtree to his boss
    SET boss = :insertnode
WHERE boss IS NULL;
INSERT INTO Employees  -- insert the subtree
    SELECT * FROM Subtree;
END;
```

Again, you must remember to rebuild the PathEnum table, or nothing that depends on it will work.

26.3 Visitation Representation of Trees

Trees are often drawn as the "boxes-and-arrows" charts we have done in this chapter. Another way of representing trees is to show them as nested sets. Since SQL is a set-oriented language, this is a better model for the approach discussed here. Let us define a simple Employees table like this, ignoring the left and right columns for now:

```
CREATE TABLE Employees
(emp CHAR(10) PRIMARY KEY,
 boss CHAR(10),
 salary DECIMAL(6, 2) NOT NULL,
 left INTEGER NOT NULL,
 right INTEGER NOT NULL);
```

Employees

emp	boss	salary	left	right
Albert	NULL	1000.00	1	12
Bert	Albert	900.00	2	3
Chuck	Albert	900.00	4	11
Donna	Chuck	800.00	5	6
Eddie	Chuck	700.00	7	8
Fred	Chuck	600.00	9	10

which would look like this as a chart:

Fig. 26.1

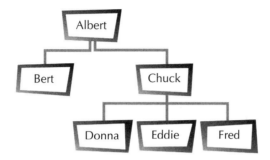

To show a tree as nested sets, replace the boxes with ovals, then nest subordinate ovals inside their parents. The root will be the largest oval and will contain every other node. The leaf nodes will be the innermost ovals, with nothing else inside them, and the nesting will show the hierarchical relationship. This is a natural way to model a parts explosion, since a final assembly is made of physically nested assemblies that finally break down into separate parts.

This tree

Fig. 26.2

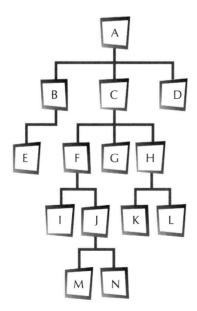

translates into this nesting of sets:

Fig. 26.3

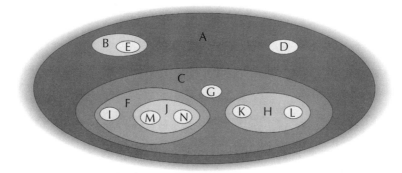

Using this approach, we can model a tree with left and right visitation number pairs. These number pairs will represent nested sets by having a child node within the bounds of its parent. This is a version of the nested sets, flattened onto a number line:

Fig. 26.4

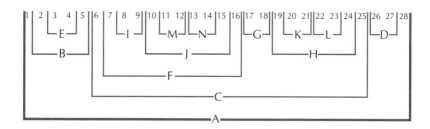

You can visualize the visitation model as a little worm crawling along the "boxes-and-arrows" version of the tree. The worm starts at the top, the root, and makes a complete trip around the tree. When he comes to a node, he puts a number in the cell on the side that he is visiting and increments his counter. Each node will get two numbers, one for the right side and one for the left. Computer science majors will recognize this as a modified preorder tree-traversal algorithm.

This has some predictable results that we can use for building queries.

26.3.1 Finding Root and Leaf Nodes

The root will always have a 1 in its left visit column and twice the number of nodes (2*n) in its right visit column. This is easy to understand; the worm has to visit each node twice, once for the left side and once for the right side, so the final count has to be twice the number of nodes in the whole tree. The root of the tree is found with the query

```
SELECT *
   FROM Tree
WHERE left = 1;
```

This query will take advantage of the index on the left visit value.

A leaf node is one that has no children under it. In an edge representation, it is not that easy to find all the leaf nodes, since you have to use a correlated subquery:

```
SELECT *
   FROM Employees AS Workers1
WHERE NOT EXISTS (SELECT *
          FROM Employees AS Workers2
       WHERE Workers1.emp = Workers2.boss;
```

In the visitation table, the difference between the left and right visit values of leaf nodes is always 1. Think of the little worm turning the corner as he crawls along the tree. That means you can find all leaf nodes with the extremely simple query

```
SELECT *
   FROM Employees
WHERE (right - left) = 1;
```

There is a further trick, to speed up queries. Build a unique index on one or both of the visitation-pair columns, say the left visit. Then the query can be rewritten to take advantage of the index. The previous query will also benefit.

```
SELECT *
   FROM Employees
WHERE left = (right - 1);
```

The reason this improves performance is that the SQL engine can use the index on the left column when it does not appear in an expression. Don't use (right - left) = 1, since it will prevent the index from being used.

26.3.2 Path Enumeration

A defining property of a tree is that it is a graph that has no cycles in it. That is, no path folds back on itself to catch you in an endless loop when you follow it in the tree. Another defining property is that there is always a path from the root to any other node in the tree.

In the visitation model, paths are shown as nested sets, which are represented by the visitation numbers and BETWEEN predicates. For example, to find out all the bosses to whom a particular person reports in the company hierarchy, you would write

```
SELECT :myworker, Managers.emp
   FROM Employees AS Managers, Employees AS Workers
WHERE Workers.left BETWEEN Managers.left AND Managers.right
   AND Workers.right BETWEEN Managers.left AND Managers.right
   AND Workers.emp = :myworker
ORDER BY depth DESC;
```

The height (or depth, depending on the author) of a tree is the number of edges between a given node and the root, where the larger the depth number, the farther away the node is from the root. The visitation model uses the fact that each containing set is larger in size (where size = (right – left)) than the sets it contains. Obviously, the root will always have the largest size. The level function is the number of edges between two given nodes; it is fairly easy to calculate. For example, to find the levels of bureaucracy between a particular worker and manager, you would use

```
SELECT Workers.emp, Managers.emp, COUNT(*) - 1 AS levels
    FROM Employees AS Managers, Employees AS Workers
WHERE Workers.left BETWEEN Managers.left AND Managers.right
    AND Workers.right BETWEEN Managers.left AND Managers.right
    AND Workers.node = :myworker
    AND Managers.node = :mymanager;
```

The reason for using the expression (COUNT(*) - 1) is to remove the duplicate count of the node itself as being on another level, because a node is zero levels removed from itself.

Other queries can be built from this basic template, using VIEWs to hold the path sets. For example, to find the common bosses of two employees, UNION their path VIEWs and find the nodes that have (COUNT(*) > 1). To find the nearest common ancestors of two nodes, UNION the path VIEWs, find the nodes that have (COUNT(*) > 1), and then pick the one with the smallest depth number.

The height (or depth, depending on where you start) of a tree is the length of the longest path in it. The trick is to first build a path enumeration table or VIEW based on distance from the root to each node:

```
CREATE VIEW Heights (emp, height)
AS SELECT emp, (COUNT(*) - 1)
        FROM Employees
    WHERE left BETWEEN 1 AND (SELECT 2*COUNT(*) FROM Employees)
        AND right BETWEEN 1 AND (SELECT 2*COUNT(*) FROM Employees);


SELECT MAX(height) FROM Heights;
```

Again, the reason for using the expression (COUNT(*) - 1) is to remove the duplicate count of the node itself as being on another level. That is, the definition is that a node is zero levels removed from itself. Or, if you are thinking in terms of sets, only proper subsets are counted. Another way to do this would be to add a test in the WHERE clause to exclude the root, but that test would be executed for every row in the table. This query will be slightly faster.

26.3.3 Finding Subtrees

In the visitation table, all the descendants of a node, not just those that are one immediate level lower, can be found by looking for the nodes with a right or left visit number between the left and right visit values of their parent node.

```
SELECT Subordinates.*
    FROM Employees AS Managers, Employees AS Subordinates
WHERE Subordinates.left BETWEEN Managers.left AND Managers.right;
```

26.3.4 Functions in the Visitation Model

JOINs and ORDER BY clauses will not interfere with the visitation model as they will with the edge model. Nor are the results dependent on the order in which the rows are displayed.

The LEVEL function for a given employee node is a matter of counting how many left and right groupings (superiors) this employee node's left or right value is within. You can get this by modifying the sense of the BETWEEN predicate in the query for subtrees:

```
SELECT COUNT(Managers.emp) AS level
    FROM Employees AS Managers, Employees AS Workers
WHERE Workers.left BETWEEN Managers.left AND Managers.right
    AND Workers.emp = :thisemployee;
```

A simple total of the salaries of the subordinates of a supervising employee works out the same way. Notice that this total will include the boss's salary, too.

```
SELECT SUM (Workers.salary) AS payroll
    FROM Employees AS Managers, Employees AS Workers
WHERE Workers.left BETWEEN Managers.left AND Managers.right
    AND Managers.emp = :thisemployee;
```

A slightly trickier function involves using quantity columns in the nodes to compute an accumulated total. This usually occurs in parts explosions, where one assembly may contain several occurrences of a subassembly.

```
SELECT SUM (Subassem.qty * Subassem.price) AS totalcost
    FROM Blueprint AS Assembly, Blueprint AS Subassem
WHERE Subassem.left
        BETWEEN Assembly.left AND Assembly.right
    AND Assembly.partno = :thispart;
```

26.3.5 Deleting Nodes and Subtrees

Another interesting property of this representation is that the subtrees must fill from left to right. In other tree representations, it is possible for a parent node to have a right child and no left child. This lets you assign some significance to being the leftmost child of a parent. For example, the node in this position might be the next in line for promotion in a corporate hierarchy.

Deleting a single node in the middle of the tree is conceptually harder than removing whole subtrees. When you remove a node in the middle of the tree, you have to decide how to fill the hole. There are two ways. The first method is to promote one of the children to the original node's position — Dad dies and the oldest son takes over the business, as shown in this figure:

Fig. 26.5

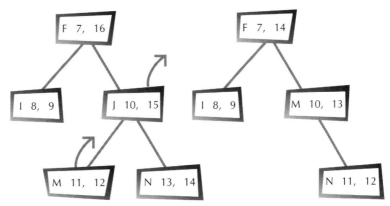

Filling the gap by promotion of the oldest child

The second method is to connect the children to the parent of the original node — Mom dies and the kids are adopted by Grandma, as shown here:

Fig. 26.6

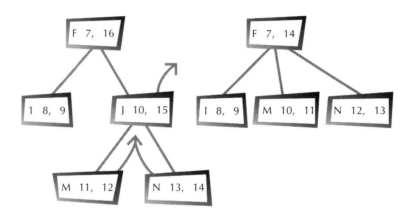

Filling the gap by promotion of the subtree

The first method is based on succession, usually of the oldest (or leftmost) node into its parent's position in the tree. Locating the oldest child is no problem; we just define him to be the leftmost node of the subtree.

Taking this in steps, to move a leaf node up the tree, you would use this transaction:

```
BEGIN
-- Use only the node keys
-- set the leftmost son to the subtree root numbers
UPDATE Employees
    SET left = left - 1,
        right = (SELECT right FROM Employees WHERE part = :delnode)
WHERE left = (SELECT left + 1
                FROM Employees
              WHERE part = :delnode);

-- close gaps in the visitation numbers
```

```
-- delete the root of the subtree
DELETE FROM Employees WHERE part = :delnode;
END;
```

This code has some hand-waving as to how to close the resulting gaps in the sequence of visitation numbers, which we will deal with in section 26.3.6.

If you look at the number-line representation of the tree, you can see that we are shifting everything down one space to the left. The target node is collapsed on itself in this shifting process, so the final DELETE FROM statement can easily detect and remove it. It is a little counterintuitive to first do the housekeeping, and then do the removal.

The second method is like removing a subtree in that the subsetting property is preserved, but will leave gaps again. When the node is deleted, the sets contained within it are still contained in the grandparent node. Again, many queries will run just fine, but the visitation numbers are off again. Since only one node has been removed, they are off only by 1. The query becomes

```
BEGIN
-- Use only the node as the parameter
DELETE FROM Employees WHERE part = :delnode;
-- close gaps in the visitation numbers - see section 26.3.6
END;
```

Deleting a whole subtree is easy. Just find the node that is the root of the subtree and delete any nodes contained within its range, then call the routine to close up the gap:

```
BEGIN
-- Use only the key of the subtree root as the parameter
DELETE FROM Employees
WHERE left BETWEEN (SELECT T2.left
                      FROM Employees AS T2
                     WHERE T2.part = :delroot)
    AND (SELECT T3.right
           FROM Employees AS T3
          WHERE part = :delroot);
-- close gaps in the visitation numbers
END;
```

This method takes advantage of the fact that the right visitation number of the root node is equal to the number of children plus 1, so that after the UPDATEs, the left visitation number will be greater than the right visitation number.

The complex SQL should make you appreciate how handy a few VIEWs can be after you see what you have to do in chapter 27.

26.3.6 Closing Gaps in the Tree

The important thing is to preserve the nested subsets based on left and right visitation numbers. As you remove nodes from a tree, you create gaps in the visitation numbers. These gaps do not destroy the subset property, but they can present other problems and should be closed. This is like garbage collection in other languages. The easiest way to understand the code is to break it up into a series of meaningful VIEWs, then use the VIEWs to UPDATE the tree table.

This VIEW "flattens out" the whole tree into a list of visitation numbers, regardless of whether they are left or right numbers:

```
CREATE VIEW FlatTree (visit)
AS SELECT left FROM Employees
      UNION
   SELECT right FROM Employees;
```

This VIEW finds the left visitation numbers in gaps instead of in the tree:

```
CREATE VIEW Firstvisit (visit)
AS SELECT (visit + 1)
      FROM FlatTree
   WHERE (visit + 1) NOT IN (SELECT visit FROM FlatTree)
      AND (visit + 1) > 0;
```

The final predicate is to keep you from going past the leftmost limit of the root node, which is always 1. Likewise, this VIEW finds the right visitation numbers in gaps:

```
CREATE VIEW Lastvisit (visit)
AS SELECT (visit + 1)
      FROM Employees
   WHERE (visit + 1) NOT IN (SELECT visit FROM FlatTree)
      AND (visit + 1) < (SELECT 2 * COUNT (*) FROM Employees);
```

The final predicate is to keep you from going past the rightmost limit of the root node, which is twice the number of nodes in the tree. You then use these two VIEWs to build a table of the gaps that have to be closed:

```
CREATE VIEW Gaps (start, finish, size)
SELECT F1.visit, L1.visit, ((L1.visit - F1.visit) + 1)
   FROM Firstvisit AS F1, Lastvisit AS L1
WHERE L1.visit = (SELECT MIN (L2.visit)
         FROM Lastvisit AS L2
      WHERE F1.visit <= L2.visit);
```

This query will tell you the start and finish visitation numbers of the gaps, as well as their size. It makes a handy report in itself, which is why I have shown it with the redundant finish and size columns. But that is not why we created it. It can be used to "slide" everything over to the left, thus:

```
BEGIN
-- This will have to be repeated until gaps disappear
WHILE EXISTS (SELECT * FROM Gaps)
   DO BEGIN
   UPDATE Frammis
      SET right = right - 1
   WHERE right > (SELECT MIN(start) FROM Gaps);

   UPDATE Frammis
      SET left = left - 1
   WHERE left > (SELECT MIN(start) FROM Gaps);
   END;
END;
```

The actual number of iterations is given by the pre-closure value of the right visitation number of the root SELECT right FROM Frammis WHERE left = 1 minus the number of nodes left in the tree SELECT COUNT(*) FROM Frammis.

This method keeps the code fairly simple at this level, but the VIEWs under it are pretty tricky and could take a lot of execution time. It would seem reasonable to use the gap size to speed up the closure process, but that can get tricky when more than one node has been dropped.

26.3.7 Summary Functions on Trees

There are tree queries that deal strictly with the nodes themselves and have nothing to do with the tree structure at all. For example, what is the name of the president of the company? How many people are in the company? Are there two people with the same name working here? These queries are handled with the usual SQL queries and there are no surprises.

Other types of queries do depend on the tree structure. For example, what is the total weight of a finished assembly (i.e., the total of all of its subassembly weights)? Do Harry and John report to the same boss? And so forth.

Let's consider a sample database that shows a parts explosion for a frammis again, but this time in visitation representation. The leaf nodes are the basic parts, the root node is the final assembly, and the nodes in between are subassemblies. Each part or assembly has a unique catalog number (in this case a single letter), a weight, and the quantity of this unit that is required to make the next unit above it. The declaration looks like this:

```
CREATE TABLE Frammis
(part CHAR (2) PRIMARY KEY,
 qty INTEGER NOT NULL CHECK (qty >= 0),
 wgt INTEGER NOT NULL CHECK (wgt >= 0),
 left INTEGER NOT NULL CHECK (left < right),
 right INTEGER NOT NULL);
```

We initially load it with this data:

Frammis

part	qty	wgt	left	right
A	1	0	1	28
B	1	0	2	5
C	2	0	6	19
D	2	5	20	27
E	2	12	3	4
F	5	0	7	16
G	2	6	17	18
H	3	0	21	26
I	4	8	8	9
J	1	0	10	15
K	5	3	22	23
L	1	4	24	25
M	2	7	11	12
N	3	2	13	14

Notice that the weights of the subassemblies are initially set to zero and only parts (leaf nodes) have weights.

```
UPDATE Frammis
   SET wgt = 0
 WHERE left < right - 1;
```

The weight of an assembly will be calculated as the total weight of all its subassemblies. The tree initially looks like this:

Fig. 26.7

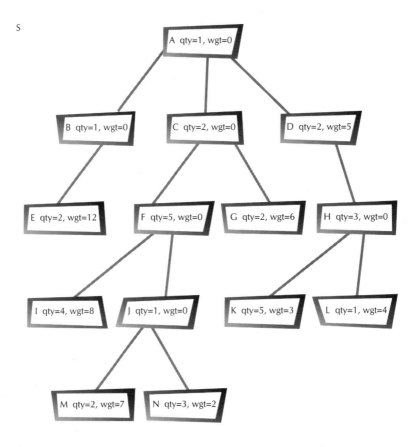

Look at the M and N leaf nodes. The table says that we need two M units weighing 7 kilograms each, plus three N units weighing 2 kilograms each, to make one J assembly. So that is $((2 * 7) + (3 * 2)) = 20$ kilograms per J assembly.

The UPDATE to set all of the weights to their correct values looks like this, and has to be repeated several times:

```
UPDATE Frammis
    SET wgt = (SELECT SUM (F2.qty * F2.wgt)
            FROM Frammis AS F2
        WHERE F2.left > left
            AND F2.right < right)
WHERE wgt = 0;
```

There are two tricks here. The first is to exclude the root node of each assembly subtree by using "greater than" and "less than" operators instead of a BETWEEN expression as we have before. The second trick is to use the WHERE wgt = 0 clause to prevent attempts to UPDATE nodes more than once as the statement is re-executed.

When I attempted this UPDATE in WATCOM SQL, it worked in one invocation, but only with a vendor extension that allows you to do an UPDATE with an ORDER BY clause. However, in other SQLs, the UPDATE could be done in a loop over a cursor. On each iteration, the UPDATE statement would progress from the leaf nodes to the root, and would be stopped when the weight at the root was no longer zero. Look at node F in the Frammis tree; M and N compute J, as we have shown, but node F will use I, J, M, and N as they stand at that time. The result is $((4*8) + (1*0) + (2*7) + (3*2)) = 52$ kilograms the first time because J is still has a zero weight, which is wrong.

The UPDATE has to be repeated until either the root node weight is the same twice in a row, or repeated for (the height of the tree minus 1) iterations.

If we find a way to reduce the weight of a part and therefore must correct the whole, this UPDATE will still work. Simply set the weight of all nonleaf nodes to zero first and redo the first UPDATE.

Once the proper weights and quantities are in place, it is fairly easy to find averages and other aggregate functions within a subtree.

26.3.8 Inserting and Updating Trees

Updates to the nodes are done by searching for the key of each node; there is nothing special about them. Rearranging the structure of the tree is best done by drawing a picture of the desired tree and figuring out the left and right visitation numbers for yourself. As a programming project, you might want to build a tool that takes a "boxes-and-arrows" graphic and converts it into a series of UPDATE and INSERT statements.

Inserting a subtree or a new node involves finding a place in the tree for the new nodes, spreading the other nodes apart by incrementing their visitation numbers, then renumbering the subtree to fit. This is basically the deletion procedure in reverse. First determine the parent for the node, then spread the visitation numbers out two positions to the right. For example, let's insert a new node, G1, under part G. We can insert one node at a time like this:

```
BEGIN
INSERT INTO Frammis (part, qty, wgt, left, right)
VALUES ('G1', 3, 4, 0, 0);
UPDATE Frammis            -- move right numbers over
    SET right = right + 2
WHERE right > (SELECT right
          FROM Frammis AS F1
       WHERE part = 'G');
UPDATE Frammis            -- move left numbers over
    SET left = left + 2
WHERE left > (SELECT left
          FROM Frammis AS F1
       WHERE part = 'G');
UPDATE Frammis            -- set new node numbers
    SET left = (SELECT left + 1
          FROM Frammis AS F1
       WHERE part = 'G')
    SET right = (SELECT right + 2
          FROM Frammis AS F1
       WHERE part = 'G');
-- notice new node is a leaf node
END;
```

This procedure will add the new node to the leftmost child position. The code could be modified to add the new node to the rightmost child position or between existing children, but it is more difficult.

26.4 Vendor Tree Extensions

As you can see from the examples above, you very quickly get into recursive or procedural code to handle trees. Since the single-table edge representation is popular, several vendors have added extensions to SQL to handle this approach. Here are descriptions of two such extensions.

26.4.1 Oracle Tree Extensions

Oracle has CONNECT BY PRIOR and START WITH clauses in the SELECT statement to provide partial support for reachability and path enumeration queries. The START WITH clause tells the engine which value the root of the tree has. The CONNECT BY PRIOR clause establishes the edges of the graph. The function LEVEL gives the distance from the root to the current node, starting at 1 for the root.

Let us use a list of parts and subcomponents as the example database table. The query "Show all subcomponents of part A1, including the substructure" can be handled by the following Oracle SQL statement:

```
SELECT LEVEL AS pathlength, assemblyno, subassemblyno
    FROM Blueprint
CONNECT BY PRIOR subassemblyno = assemblyno
    START WITH assemblyno = 'A1';
```

The query produces the following result:

Result1

pathlength	assemblyno	subassemblyno
1	A1	A2
2	A2	A5
2	A2	A6
3	A6	A8
3	A6	A9
1	A1	A3
2	A3	A6
3	A6	A8
3	A6	A9
2	A3	A7
1	A1	A4

The output is an adequate representation of the query result because it is possible to construct the path enumeration tree of Figure 27.1 from it. The CONNECT BY PRIOR clause provides traversal but not support for recursive functions. For example, it is not possible to sum the weights of all subcomponents of part A1 to find the weight of A1. The only recursive function supported by the CONNECT BY PRIOR clause is the LEVEL function. Another limitation of the CONNECT BY PRIOR clause is that it does not permit the use of JOINs.

The reason for disallowing JOINs is that the order in which the rows are returned in the result is important. The parent nodes appear before their children, so you know that if the pathlength increases, these are children; if it does not, they are new nodes at a higher level. This also means that an ORDER BY can destroy any meaning in the results. This means, moreover, that the CONNECT BY PRIOR result is not a true table, since a table by definition does not have an internal ordering. In addition, this means that it is not always possible to use the result of a CONNECT BY query in another query.

A trick for working around this limitation, which makes indirect use of the CONNECT BY PRIOR clause, is to hide it in a subquery that is used to make a JOIN at the higher level. For example, to attach a product category description, form another table to the parts explosion.

```
SELECT partno, categoryname
FROM Parts, ProductCategory
WHERE Parts.categoryid = ProductCategory.categoryid
    AND partno IN  (SELECT subassemblyno
               FROM Blueprint
            START WITH assemblyno = 'A1'
         CONNECT BY PRIOR subassemblyno = assemblyno);
```

The subquery has only one table in the FROM clause and complies with the restriction that there must be no JOINs in any query block that contains a CONNECT BY PRIOR. On the other hand, the main query involves a JOIN of two tables, which would not be possible with direct use of the CONNECT BY PRIOR clause.

Another query that cannot be processed by direct use of the CONNECT BY PRIOR clause is one that displays all parent-child relationships at all levels. A technique to process this query is illustrated by the following SQL:

```
SELECT DISTINCT PX.partno, PX.pname, PY.partno, PY.pname
    FROM Parts AS PX, Parts AS PY
WHERE PY.partno IN (SELECT Blueprint.subassemblyno
            FROM Blueprint
            START WITH assemblyno = PX.partno
        CONNECT BY PRIOR subassemblyno = assemblyno)
ORDER BY PX.partno, PY.partno;
```

Again, the outer query includes a JOIN, which is not allowed with the CONNECT BY PRIOR clause. Note that the correlated subquery references PX.partno.

26.4.2 XDB Tree Extension

XDB has a set of extensions similar to those in Oracle, but this product uses functions rather than clauses to hide the recursion. The PREVIOUS(<column>) function finds the parent node value of the <column>. The keyword LEVEL is a system constant for each row, which gives its path length from the root; the root is at LEVEL = 0. There is a special value for the pathlength of a leaf node, called BOTTOM. For example, to find all of the subcomponents of A1, you would write this query:

```
SELECT assemblyno
    FROM Blueprint
WHERE PREVIOUS(subassemblyno) = assemblyno
        AND assemblyno = 'A1'
        AND LEVEL <= BOTTOM;
```

Other vendors will do similar things, but they are all based on establishing a root and a relationship to JOIN the original table to a correlated copy of itself. Indexing can help, but such queries are still very expensive.

26.4.3 Date's EXPLODE Operator

In his book *Relational Database: Selected Writings* (Date 1986), Chris Date proposed an EXPLODE(<table name>) operator that would convert a table into another table with four columns: the level number, the current node, the subordinate node, and the sequence number. The sequence number was included to get around the problem of the ordering's having meaning in the hierarchy. The EXPLODE results are derived from simple tree-traversal rules.

26.4.4 Tillquist and Kuo's Proposals

John Tillquist and Feng-Yang Kuo proposed an extension wherein a tree is viewed as a special kind of GROUP BY clause (Tillquist and Kuo 1989). They would add a GROUP BY LEAVES (<major column>, <minor column>) that would find the set of all rows where the <minor column> value does not appear in the <major column>. This operator can be approximated with the query

```
SELECT *
    FROM TreeTable AS T1
WHERE NOT EXISTS (SELECT *
            FROM TreeTable AS T2
        WHERE T1.major = T2.minor)
GROUP BY boss;
```

The idea is that you get groups of leaf nodes, with their immediate parent as the single grouping column. Other extensions in Tillquist and Kuo's paper include a GROUP BY NODES (<major column>, <minor column>), which would use each node only once to prevent problems with cycles in the graph and would find all of the descendants of a given parent node. They then extend the aggregate functions with a COMPOUND function modifier (along the lines of DISTINCT) that carries the aggregation up the tree.

Graphs and Basic Terms

THE TERMINOLOGY IN graph theory pretty much explains itself; if it does not, you can read some of the books suggested in appendix B: Readings and Resources for graph theory. Graphs are important because they are a general way to represent many different types of data and their relationships. Here is a quick review of terms.

A *graph* is a data structure made up of *nodes* connected by *edges*. Edges can be directed (permit travel in only one direction) or undirected (permit travel in both directions). The number of edges entering a node is its *indegree*; likewise, the number of edges leaving a node is its *outdegree*. A set of edges that allow you to travel from one node to another is called a *path*. A *cycle* is a path that comes back to the node from which it started without crossing itself (this means that a big O is fine but a figure eight is not).

Recursively structured data relationships are either trees (hierarchies) or generalized directed graphs. A *tree* is a type of directed graph that is important enough to have its own terminology (see chapter 26 for trees in SQL). Its special properties and frequent use have made it important enough to be covered in a separate chapter. The following section will stress other useful kinds of generalized directed graphs.

Generalized directed graphs are classified into nonreconvergent and reconvergent graphs. In a reconvergent graph there are multiple paths between at least one pair of nodes. Reconvergent graphs are either cyclic or acyclic.

27.1 Two-Table Representation of a Graph

In the two-table representation of a graph, one table holds the nodes of the graph and the other table holds the edges. The edges are shown by their starting and ending nodes, which will be keys in the nodes table. The edge table might also contain other information about the relationships it represents. Let us begin with a two-table version of a parts explosion database, thus:

```
CREATE TABLE Parts -- this holds the nodes, which are parts
(assemblyno CHAR(2) PRIMARY KEY,
 pname CHAR(10) NOT NULL,
 wgt INTEGER NOT NULL CHECK(wgt >= 0),
 color CHAR(6) NOT NULL);


CREATE TABLE Blueprint -- the edges; how parts are assembled
(assemblyno CHAR(2) NOT NULL,
 subassemblyno CHAR(2) NOT NULL,
 quantity INTEGER CHECK(qty >= 0),
    PRIMARY KEY(assemblyno, subassemblyno),
    FOREIGN KEY assemblyno REFERENCES Parts(assemblyno),
    FOREIGN KEY subassemblyno REFERENCES Parts(assemblyno));
```

with the following data for constructing a frammis

Parts

assemblyno	pname	wgt	color
A1	frammis	5	Yellow
A2	gizmo	6	Green
A3	cam	7	Red
A4	clip	8	Red
A5	gear	9	Yellow

(cont.)	assemblyno	pname	wgt	color
	A6	jack	10	Red
	A7	nut	11	Yellow
	A8	pin	12	Red
	A9	plug	13	Green

Blueprint

assemblyno	subassemblyno	qty
A1	A2	2
A1	A3	2
A1	A4	2
A2	A5	3
A2	A6	2
A3	A6	1
A3	A7	3
A6	A8	2
A6	A9	1

Fig. 27.1

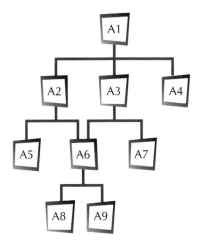

The relationships between the parts are shown in the Blueprint table, which simulates the traversal of a directed graph in which the Parts rows are the nodes and the Blueprint rows are the edges of the graph. We will assume that the normal direction of traversal is from assemblies to subassemblies. For example, the Blueprint row (A1, A2, 2) connects part A1 to part A2 and also carries the additional information that two units of A2 (i.e., two gizmos) go into making each A1 (frammis).

Please remember that a special assumption has been made here. We are assuming that each assembly is a part in its own right and not just the result of putting together all of its components. That is why a gizmo (A2) needs to have gears (A5) and jacks (A6) added to it. Think of each nonleaf node in the graph as a holder for the parts subordinate to it, like a circuit board that needs chips to become complete.

The data relationships are illustrated graphically in Figure 27.1. The graph is reconvergent because there are two paths connecting node A1 to any one of nodes A6, A8, and A9. For example, A1 and A6 are connected by a path that goes through A2 and another that goes through A3. The graph illustrates the hierarchical relationships between the various rows in the Parts table. For example, part A1 is made up of parts A2, A3, and A4. Part A2, in turn, is made up of parts A5 and A6. Part A3 is made up of parts A6 and A7. Notice that part A6 is a subcomponent of both part A2 and part A3. This is not a true tree structure, so it could not be represented by the single-table approaches used for trees in section 26.2.

27.2 Path Enumeration in a Graph

Reachability means finding all nodes that can be reached from one or more starting nodes. You have to assume that the graph can be traversed in only one direction, which in our case is from assemblies to subassemblies.

Reachability can be found by first building a path enumeration table. This table has the start and end nodes of all possible paths in the graph. This is a generalization of the edge table, extended to hold paths. A cycle will have a row with the same value for the start and end nodes, but the pathlength will be greater than zero. In fact, one of the problems with a cycle is deciding when to stop going around it when enumerating it. This is one reason that this section does not deal with cycles and that they are not often used.

At this point, you must decide whether you will include paths of length zero to represent the traversal from a node to itself. This can be handy for certain queries, since it means that the starting node will appear as a path of length zero when we are following paths that lead out of it. In other queries, however, you can find yourself with cycle problems.

The program to build the path enumeration table can be implemented using any procedural language that has SQL access capabilities. Ideally, the language should support recursion, because this is generally helpful in implementing graph traversal algorithms. Here is a pseudocode program using SQL inside a simple 4GL language and with no recursion:

```
PROCEDURE BuildPathEnum
BEGIN
DECLARE pathlength, oldsize, newsize INTEGER NOT NULL;

-- start with an empty table, no primary key
CREATE TABLE PathEnum
(assemblyno CHAR(2) NOT NULL,
 subassemblyno CHAR(2) NOT NULL,
 pathlength INTEGER CHECK(pathlength >= 0);

-- path of node to itself - this is optional
BEGIN
INSERT INTO PathEnum
SELECT DISTINCT subassemblyno, subassemblyno, 0 FROM Blueprint;

-- load paths of length = 1 into table
INSERT INTO PathEnum
SELECT assemblyno, subassemblyno, 1
FROM Blueprint;

-- insert rows only while table grows
oldsize := 0;
newsize := SELECT COUNT(*) FROM PathEnum;
WHILE (oldsize < newsize;)
```

```
DO BEGIN
    INSERT INTO PathEnum
    SELECT P1.assemblyno, B1.subassemblyno, (P1.pathlength + 1)
        FROM PathEnum AS P1, Blueprint AS B1
    -- advance existing paths by one level
    WHERE EXISTS (SELECT *
            FROM PathEnum AS P2
                WHERE B1.assemblyno = P2.subassemblyno
    -- insert only new rows into table
    AND NOT EXISTS (SELECT *
                    FROM PathEnum AS P3
                WHERE B1.assemblyno = P3.assemblyno
                    AND B1.subassemblyno = P3.subassemblyno);
    oldsize := newsize;
    newsize := SELECT COUNT(*) FROM PathEnum;
    END;
END;
END;
```

The result is

PathEnum

assemblyno	subassemblyno	pathlength
A1	A2	1
A1	A3	1
A1	A4	1
A1	A5	2
A1	A6	2
A1	A7	2
A1	A8	3
A1	A8	3
A1	A9	3
A1	A9	3
A2	A5	1
A2	A6	1
A2	A8	2
A2	A9	2

(cont.)	assemblyno	subassemblyno	pathlength
	A3	A6	1
	A3	A7	1
	A3	A8	2
	A3	A9	2
	A6	A8	1
	A6	A9	1

The reachability query "Where can I get to from here?" is now simply

```
SELECT DISTINCT assemblyno, subassemblyno
    FROM PathEnum
 WHERE assemblyno = :startnode;
```

The path enumeration table should be indexed for efficiency. Notice that in our example we could index on columns (assembly-no), (subassemblyno), (assemblyno, subassemblyno), or (subassemblyno, assemblyno); the choice would be determined by the most common direction of traversal and the sort of reports needed. In some applications it might be worth the effort to keep the information that the pathlength from a node to itself is zero in the table. That can then force the node to show up in queries that start with it.

Another approach is to develop a table of named paths that run from the root to the leaf nodes, using a slight modification of the procedural code. You have to capture the path identification number and the position of the step along the path. The procedural code for doing this will vary quite a bit from product to product and according to how well a given product supports cursors, an SQL topic that is not mentioned in this book at all. Attach the weight and quantity to it, since that information is useful for computing other functions. This will give us a table of simple paths that has the path identification number, the step within the path, and the start (assemblyno) and end (subassemblyno) of each step.

Using this table, we can build a complete path information table with a query like this:

```
CREATE TABLE Paths
(path INTEGER NOT NULL,   -- path id number
 step INTEGER NOT NULL,   -- step within the path
 assemblyno CHAR(2) NOT NULL,      -- assembly part number
 subassemblyno CHAR(2) NOT NULL,   -- subassembly part number
 wgt INTEGER NOT NULL,     -- weight of assembly
 subwgt INTEGER NOT NULL,  -- weight of subassembly
 qty INTEGER NOT NULL,    -- quantity of subassembly in assembly
 PRIMARY KEY (path, step)
);
```

The results should look like this:

Paths

path	step	assemblyno	subassemblyno	wgt	subwgt	qty
1	1	A1	A2	5	6	2
1	2	A2	A5	6	9	3
2	1	A1	A2	5	6	2
2	2	A2	A6	6	10	2
2	3	A6	A8	10	12	2
3	1	A1	A2	5	6	2
3	2	A2	A6	6	10	2
3	3	A6	A9	10	13	1
4	1	A1	A3	5	7	2
4	2	A3	A6	7	10	1
4	3	A6	A8	10	12	2
5	1	A1	A3	5	7	2
5	2	A3	A6	7	10	1
5	5	A6	A9	10	13	1
6	1	A1	A3	5	7	2
6	2	A3	A7	7	11	3
7	1	A1	A4	5	8	2

The reachability query is now more complex, but not bad. For node Y to be reachable from node X, they must be on the same path and Y must be "downhill" from X, which becomes the query

```
SELECT P2.subassemblyno
    FROM Paths AS P1, Paths AS P2
WHERE P1.assemblyno = :startnode
    AND P1.path = P2.path
    AND P1.step <= P2.step;
```

Though reachability became complex, finding all the paths that go through a given node regardless of their direction became very simple. (If the graph represented a transportation network instead of a parts explosion, this could be quite handy.) The query is

```
SELECT DISTINCT path
    FROM Paths
WHERE assemblyno = :startnode
      OR subassemblyno = :startnode;
```

Using both the assemblyno and the subassemblyno is important. This will take care of both root and leaf node situations. In the example of A6, we would get the result set of paths $(2 \rightarrow 3 \rightarrow 4 \rightarrow 5)$. To find the paths that do not go through a particular node, use this query:

```
SELECT *
    FROM Paths AS P1
WHERE NOT EXISTS (SELECT *
            FROM Paths AS P2
        WHERE (assemblyno = :startnode
              OR subassemblyno = :startnode)
            AND P1.path = P2.path);
```

These techniques have several obvious drawbacks. First, the path information tables require procedural code to construct. Second, the path information tables can be very large, depending on the sizes of the underlying base tables and the degree of reconvergence in the data relationships. Just compare the sizes of the sample tables to that of either the Parts or Blueprint table. Third, the tables represent a snapshot of the database at some particular point in time and have to be rebuilt procedurally whenever the underlying node and edge tables are changed, unlike a VIEW within the schema.

In practice, this is not really a big problem, because such data often tends to be relatively static; you do not redesign organizational charts or manufactured products on a regular basis. If it is a problem, you can store procedural code that automatically repopulates the graph tables.

27.3 Path Aggregation in a Graph

Path aggregation in a tree attempts to "flatten out" the tree structure of a path enumeration to come up with totals for each subtree in the graph. The most common example for a parts explosion problem is finding the total weight or cost of an assembly when you know the weight of each part and how many of them are used in each of its subassemblies.

The problem is that a subassembly may occur in several places in a reconvergent graph structure. This is particularly true for common parts, such as screws or connectors in mechanical assemblies. In our example, part A6 is a subassembly of both part A2 and part A3. So the total quantity of part A6 required to assemble part A1 must take into account the quantity of part A6 required to assemble both parts A2 and A3.

There is no straightforward way to handle a convergent graph in a table as there is in tree path enumeration. The best that can be done is to list the nodes reachable from a given start node, along with the aggregate function value associated with the node. The result of the query "What are the subparts of A1 and the total quantity of each in it?" is

Explosion

assemblyno	subassemblyno	qty	
A1	A2	2	
A1	A3	2	
A1	A4	2	
A1	A5	6	= (2 * 3)
A1	A6	4	= (2 * 2)
A1	A7	6	= (2 * 3)
A1	A8	12	= (2 * 2 * 2) + (2 * 1 * 2)
A1	A9	6	= (1 * 2 * 2) + (1 * 1 * 2)

What this table says is that an A1 part is made with two A2, two A3, and two A4 subassemblies. But in turn, each of the A2 assemblies uses three A5 subassemblies, which would give us a total of (2 * 3) or 6 A5s in the A1 unit. The problem becomes worse when we have to count the A8 and A9 parts, which are shared by more than one subassembly.

This can be done with procedural code that uses the path and step columns to guide itself through the graph. However, the best technique seems to be to use node splitting, which we will discuss in the next section.

27.4 Node Splitting

An example of a path enumeration query where a portion of the resulting tree must be pruned is the following: "Show all subparts of part A1, excluding part A3 and its subcomponents."

This query sounds as if we should prune the subtree rooted at node A3 with an SQL statement like this:

```
SELECT PE1.subassemblyno, SUM(qty)
    FROM PathEnum AS PE1, Blueprint AS B1
WHERE PE1.assemblyno ='A1'  -- the final assembly
    AND subassemblyno NOT IN
        (SELECT subassemblyno
            FROM PathEnum AS PE2
        WHERE PE2.assemblyno ='A3'   -- root of subtree
            OR PE2.subassemblyno ='A3')
    AND B1.subassemblyno = PE1.subassemblyno  -- join gets qty
GROUP BY PE1.assemblyno, PE1.subassemblyno;
```

However, this will work only for a tree and not for a convergent graph. Our query would first construct a subquery result table like this:

Subquery results

assemblyno	subassemblyno	pathlength
A3	A6	1
A3	A7	1
A3	A8	2
A3	A9	2
A1	A3	1

which would then reduce to

```
SELECT PE1.assemblyno, PE1.subassemblyno, SUM(qty)
    FROM PathEnum AS PE1
WHERE assemblyno = 'A1'  -- the final assembly
    AND subassemblyno NOT IN ('A3', 'A6', 'A7', 'A8', 'A9')
GROUP BY PE1.assemblyno, PE1.subassemblyno;
```

This in turn reduces, before joining and grouping, to

PE1 Result

assemblyno	subassemblyno	pathlength
A1	A2	1
A1	A4	1
A1	A5	2

The reconvergent nature of this graph means that our query also removed A6 from under A2 as well as from under A3. This would have worked fine with a tree, but it is not what we wanted. To support these kinds of queries in a graph, we must change the path enumeration table to differentiate among the paths that connect two nodes. That is why there are duplicate rows — (A1, A9), (A1, A8), and (A1, A6) — in the PathEnum table.

One trick is to duplicate (or split) the nodes to convert the convergent graph into a tree. The nodes that need splitting are those that have an indegree greater than 1; they can be found with this query:

```
SELECT subassemblyno, COUNT(*)
       FROM Blueprint
   GROUP BY subassemblyno
HAVING COUNT(*) > 1);
```

In the example graph, we will get A6, with a count of 2. Using a mix of SQL and procedural code, update the two rows with A6 as their subassembly with two new subassemblies; call them A6a and A6b, which are subordinate to A2 and A3, respectively. And they both link to A8 and to A9. Oops, that makes nodes A8 and A9 convergent, because they now have indegree 2, and the same process has to be done again until the graph is a tree. As you can see, the tree that is developed this way can get fairly big and have a lot of synonyms for common parts in it.

Blueprint with split node A6

subassemblyno	qty	left	right
A1	1	1	24
A2	2	2	11
A3	2	12	21
A4	2	22	23
A5	3	3	4
A6a	2	5	10
A6b	1	13	18
A7	3	19	20
A8a	2	6	7
A8b	2	14	15
A9a	1	8	9
A9b	1	16	17

Optimizing Queries

THERE IS NO set of rules for writing code that will take the best advantage of every query optimizer. The query optimizers are simply too different for universal rules; however, we can make some general statements. What would improve performance in one SQL implementation might not do anything at all in another — or could even make the performance worse.

There are two kinds of optimizers: cost-based and rule-based. A rule-based optimizer looks at the syntax of the query and plans how to execute without any consideration of the size of the tables or the statistical distribution of the data. A rule-based optimizer (such as Oracle before Version 7.0) will parse a query and execute it in the order in which it was written, perhaps doing some reorganization of the query into an equivalent form using some syntax rules.

A cost-based optimizer looks at both the query and the statistical data about the database itself and decides on the best way to execute the query. These decisions involve whether to use indexes, whether to use hashing, which tables to bring into main storage, what sorting technique to use, and so forth. Most of the time (but not all!), it will make better decisions than a human programmer would have simply because it has more information.

Ingres has one of the best optimizers, which extensively reorders a query before executing it. It is one of the few products that can find most semantically identical queries and reduce them to the same internal form. Rdb, from Oracle, uses a searching method (taken from an AI [artificial intelligence] game-playing program) to inspect the costs of several different approaches before making a decision. DB2 has a system table with a statistical profile of the base tables. In short, no two products use exactly the same optimization techniques.

The fact that each SQL engine uses a different internal storage scheme and access methods for its data makes some optimizations nonportable. Likewise, some optimizations depend on the hardware configuration and a technique that was excellent for one product on one hardware configuration could be a disaster in another product or on another hardware configuration.

28.1 Access Methods

For this discussion, let us assume that there are two basic methods of getting to data: table scans, or sequential reads of all the rows in the table, and access via some kind of index.

28.1.1 Sequential Access

The table scan is a sequential read of all the data in the order in which it appears in physical storage, grabbing one page of memory at a time. Most databases do not physically remove deleted rows, so a table can use a lot of physical space and yet hold little data. Depending on just how dynamic the database is, you may want to run a utility program to reclaim storage and compress the database. The performance can suddenly improve drastically after a database reorganization.

28.1.2 Indexed Access

Indexed access returns one row at a time. The index is probably going to be a B-tree of some sort, but it could be a hashed index, inverted file structures, or other format. Obviously, if you don't have an index on a table, then you cannot use indexed access on it.

An index can be clustered or unclustered. A clustered index is in the same order as the physical storage. Obviously, there can be only one clustered index on a table. Clustered indexes keep the table in sorted order, so a table scan will often produce results in that order. A clustered index will also tend to put duplicates of the indexed column values on the same page of physical memory, which may speed up access.

A hashed index divides the data into "buckets" that have the same hashing value. If the index is on a unique column, the ideal situation is what is called a *minimal perfect hashing function* — every value hashes to one physical storage address and there are no empty spaces. The next best situation for a unique column is what is called a *perfect hashing function* — every value hashes to one physical storage address, but there are some empty spaces in the physical storage.

A hashing function for a nonunique column should hash to a bucket small enough to fit into main storage.

28.2 Expressions and Unnested Queries

The optimizer is supposed to figure out when two queries are the same and will not be fooled by two queries with the same meaning and different syntax. For example, the SQL standard defines

```
SELECT *
    FROM Warehouse
WHERE quantity IN (SELECT quantity FROM Sales);
```

as identical to

```
SELECT *
    FROM Warehouse
WHERE quantity = ANY (SELECT quantity FROM Sales);
```

but you will find that some SQL engines prefer the first version to the second because they do not convert the expressions into a common internal form. Very often, things like the choice of operators and their order make a large performance difference.

28.2.1 Simple Expressions

A good rule of thumb is that given a chain of AND-ed predicates that test for constant values, put the most restrictive ones first. For example,

```
SELECT *
    FROM Students
WHERE sex = 'female';
        AND grade = 'A'
```

Will probably run slower than:

```
SELECT *
    FROM Students
WHERE grade = 'A'
        AND sex = 'female';
```

because there are fewer "A" students than number of female students. There are several ways that this query will be executed:

1. Assuming an index on grades, fetch a row from the Students table where grade = 'A'; if sex = 'female' then put it into the final results. The index on grades is called the driving index of the loop thorough the Students table.

2. Assuming an index on sex, fetch a row from the Students table where sex = 'female'; if grade = 'A' then put it into the final results. The index on sex is now the driving index of the loop through the Students table.

3. Assuming indexing on both, scan the index on sex and put pointers to the rows where sex = 'female' into results working file R1. Scan the index on grades and put pointers to the rows where grade = 'A' into results file R2. Sort and merge R1 and R2, keeping the pointers that appear twice. Use this result to fetch the rows into the final result. If the hardware can support parallel access, this can be quite fast.

Another application of the same principle is a trick with predicates that involve two columns to force the choice of the index that will be used. Place the table with the smallest number of rows last in the FROM clause and expression which uses that table first in the WHERE clause. For example, consider two tables, one for orders and one that translates a code number into English, each with an index on the join column:

```
SELECT *
    FROM Orders AS O1, Codes AS C1
WHERE C1.code = O1.code;
```

where the Codes table is noticeably smaller than the Orders table. This query will probably use a strategy of merging the index values. However, if you add a dummy expression, you can force a loop over the index on the smaller table. For example assume that all the order type codes are greater than or equal to '00' in our code translation example, so that the first predicate of this query is always TRUE:

```
SELECT *
    FROM Orders AS O1, Codes AS C1
WHERE O1.ordertype >= '00'
        AND C1.somecode = O1.ordertype;
```

The dummy predicate will force the SQL engine to use an index on Orders. This same trick can also be used to force the sorting in an ORDER BY clause to be done with an index.

Since SQL is not a computational language, implementations do not tend to do even simple algebra:

```
SELECT *
    FROM Sales
WHERE quantity = 500 + 1/2;
```

is the same thing as quantity = 500.50, but some dynamic SQLs will take a little extra time to compute and add a half as they check each row of the Sales table. The extra time adds up when the expression involves complex math and/or type conversions. However, this can have another effect that we will discuss in section 28.8 on expressions that contain indexed columns.

The <> comparison has some unique problems. Most optimizers assume that this comparison will return more rows than it rejects, so they will prefer a sequential scan and will not use an index on a column involved in such a comparison. This is not always true, however. For example, to find someone in Ireland who is not a Catholic, you would normally write:

```
SELECT *
    FROM Ireland
WHERE religion <> 'Catholic';
```

The way around this is to break up the inequality like this:

```
SELECT *
    FROM Ireland
WHERE religion < 'Catholic';
        OR religion > 'Catholic';
```

and force the use of an index. However, without an index on religion, the OR-ed version of the predicate could take longer to run.

Another trick is to avoid the x IS NOT NULL predicate and use x >= <minimal constant> instead. The NULLs are kept in different ways in different implementations, but almost never in the same physical storage area as their columns. As a result, the SQL engine has to do extra searching. For example, if we have a CHAR(3) column that holds a NULL or three letters, we could look for missing data with

```
SELECT *
    FROM Sales
WHERE alphacode IS NOT NULL
```

but it would be better written as

```
SELECT *
    FROM Sales
WHERE alphacode >= 'AAA';
```

because it avoids the extra reads.

Another trick that will often work is to use an index to get a
COUNT(), since the index itself may have the number of rows already
worked out. For example,

```
SELECT COUNT(*)
    FROM Sales;
```

might not be as fast as

```
SELECT COUNT(sale_id)
    FROM Sales;
```

where sale_id is the PRIMARY KEY (or any other unique non-NULL
column) of the Sales table. Being the PRIMARY KEY means that there is
a unique index on sale_id. A smart optimizer knows to look for
indexed columns automatically when it sees a COUNT(*), but it is
worth testing on your product.

28.2.2 String Expressions

Likewise, string expressions can be recalculated each time. A particular problem for strings is that the optimizer will often stop at the '%'
or '_' in the pattern of a LIKE predicate. This means that

```
SELECT *
    FROM Students
WHERE name LIKE 'Sm_th';
```

will not use an index on the name column; however,

```
SELECT *
    FROM Students
WHERE name BETWEEN 'Smath' AND 'Smzth';
```

can use an index on the name column.

28.3 Give Extra JOIN Information in Queries

Optimizers are not always able to draw conclusions that a human
being can draw. The more information contained in the query, the
better the chance that the optimizer will be able to find an improved

execution plan. For example, to JOIN three tables together on a common column, you might write

```
SELECT *
   FROM Table1, Table2, Table3
WHERE Table2.common = Table3.common
      AND Table3.common = Table1.common;
```

or, alternately, write

```
SELECT *
   FROM Table1, Table2, Table3
WHERE Table1.common = Table2.common
      AND Table1.common = Table3.common;
```

Some optimizers will JOIN pairs of tables based on the equi-join conditions in the WHERE clause in the order in which they appear. Let us assume that Table1 is a very small table and that Table2 and Table3 are large. In the first query, doing the Table2-Table3 JOIN first will return a large result set, which is then pruned by the Table1-Table3 JOIN. In the second query, doing the Table1-Table2 JOIN first will return a small result set, which is then matched to the small Table1-Table3 JOIN result set.

The best bet, however, is to provide all the information so that the optimizer can decide for itself when the table sizes change. This leads to redundancy in the WHERE clause,

```
SELECT *
   FROM Table1, Table2, Table3
WHERE Table1.common = Table2.common
      AND Table2.common = Table3.common
      AND Table3.common = Table1.common;
```

Do not confuse this redundancy with needless logical expressions that will be recalculated and can be expensive. For example,

```
SELECT *
   FROM Sales
WHERE alphacode BETWEEN 'AAA' AND 'ZZZ'
      AND alphacode LIKE 'A_C';
```

will redo the BETWEEN predicate for every row. It does not provide any information that can be used for a JOIN, and, very clearly, if the LIKE predicate is TRUE, then the BETWEEN predicate also has to be TRUE.

28.4 Index Tables Carefully

You should create indexes on the tables of your database to optimize query search time, but not create any more indexes than you absolutely need. Indexes have to be updated and possibly reorganized when you INSERT, UPDATE, or DELETE rows in a table. Too many indexes can result in extra time spent tending indexes that are seldom used. But even worse, the presence of an index can fool the optimizer into using it when it should not. For example, given the simple query

```
SELECT *
    FROM Warehouse
WHERE quantity = 500
       AND color = 'Purply Green';
```

with an index on color, but not on quantity, most optimizers will first search for rows with color = 'Purply Green' via the index, then apply the quantity = 500 test. However, if you were to add an index on quantity, the optimizer would likely take the tests in order, doing the quantity test first. I assume that very few items are 'Purply Green', so it would have been better to test for color first. A smart optimizer with detailed statistics would do this right, but to play it safe, order the predicates from the most restricting (i.e., the smallest number of qualifying rows in the final result) to the least.

Consider an actual example of indexes making trouble, in a database for a small club membership list that was indexed on the members' names as the PRIMARY KEY. There was a column in the table that had one of five status codes (paid member, free membership, expired, exchange newsletter, and miscellaneous). The report query on the number of people by status was

```
SELECT M1.status, C1.codetext, COUNT(*)
    FROM Members AS M1, Codes AS C1
WHERE M1.status = C1.status
GROUP BY M1.status, C1.codetext;
```

In a PC SQL database product, it ran an order of magnitude slower with an index on the status column than without one. The optimizer saw the index on the Members table and used it to search for each status code text. Without the index, the much smaller Codes table was brought into main storage and five buckets were set up for the COUNT(*); then the Members table was read once in sequence.

An index that is used to ensure uniqueness on a column or set of columns is called a primary index; those used to speed up queries on nonunique column(s) are called secondary. SQL implementations automatically create a primary index on a PRIMARY KEY or UNIQUE constraint. Implementations may or may not create indexes that link FOREIGN KEYs within the table to their targets in the referenced table. This link can be very important, since a lot of JOINs are done from FOREIGN KEY to PRIMARY KEY.

You also need to know something about the queries to run against the schema. Obviously, if all queries are asked on only one column, that is all you need to index. The query information is usually given as a statistical model of the expected inputs. For example, you might be told that 80% of the queries will use the PRIMARY KEY and 20% will use another column, picked at random. This is pretty much what you would know in a real-world situation, since most of the accesses will be done by production programs with embedded SQL in them and only a small percentage will be ad hoc queries.

Without giving you a computer science lecture, a computer problem is called NP-complete if it gets so big, so fast, that it is not practical to solve it for a reasonable-sized set of input values. Usually this means that you have to try all possible combinations to find the answer.

Finding the optimal indexing arrangement is known to be NP-complete (Comer 1978; Paitetsky-Shapiro 1983). This does not mean that you cannot optimize indexing for a particular database schema and set of input queries, but it does mean that you cannot write a program that will do it for all possible relational databases and query sets.

28.5 Watch the IN Predicate

The IN predicate is really shorthand for a series of OR-ed equality tests. There are two forms: Either an explicit list of values is given or a subquery is used to make such a list of values.

The database engine has no statistics about the relative frequency of the values in a list of constants, so it will assume that the list is in the order in which they are to be used. People like to order lists alphabetically or by magnitude, but it would be better to order the list from most frequently occurring values to least frequent. It is also pointless to have duplicate values in the constant list, since the predicate will return TRUE if it matches the first duplicate it finds and will never get to the second occurrence. Likewise, if the predicate is FALSE for that value, the program wastes computer time traversing a needlessly long list.

Many SQL engines perform an IN predicate with a subquery by building the result set of the subquery first as a temporary working table, then scanning that result table from left to right. This can be expensive in many cases; for example,

```
SELECT *
    FROM Personnel
WHERE firstname IN (SELECT firstname FROM BowlingTeam)
        AND lastname IN (SELECT lastname FROM BowlingTeam);
```

will not run as fast as

```
SELECT *
    FROM Personnel
WHERE firstname || lastname IN
        (SELECT firstname || lastname FROM BowlingTeam);
```

because the first version of the query may make two passes through the Bowling Team table to construct two separate result tables. The second version makes only one pass to construct the concatenation of the names in its result table.

28.6 Avoid UNIONs

UNIONs are often done by constructing the two result sets, then merge-sorting them together. The optimizer works only within a single SELECT statement or subquery. For example,

```
SELECT *
    FROM Personnel
WHERE work = 'New York'
UNION
SELECT *
    FROM Personnel
WHERE home = 'Chicago';
```

is the same as

```
SELECT DISTINCT *
    FROM Personnel
WHERE work = 'New York'
        OR home = 'Chicago';
```

which will run faster.

Another trick is to use the UNION ALL in place of the UNION whenever duplicates are not a problem. The UNION ALL is implemented as an append operation, without the need for a sort to aid duplicate removal.

28.7 Prefer JOINs over Nested Queries

A nested query is hard to optimize. Optimizers try to "flatten" nested queries so that they can be expressed as JOINs and the best order of execution can be determined. Consider the database

```
Authors (authorno, authorname);
Titles (title, bookno, advance);
TitleAuthors (authorno, royalty);
```

This query finds authors who are getting less than 50% royalties:

```
SELECT authorno
   FROM Authors
WHERE authorno IN
      (SELECT authorno
         FROM TitleAuthors
        WHERE royalty < 0.50)
```

which could also be expressed as

```
SELECT DISTINCT Author.authorno
   FROM Authors, TitleAuthors
WHERE (Authors.authorno = TitleAuthors.authorno)
   AND (royalty < 0.50);
```

The SELECT DISTINCT is important. Each author's name will occur only once in the Authors table. Therefore, the IN predicate query should return one occurrence of O'Leary. Assume that O'Leary wrote two books; with just a SELECT, the second query would return two O'Leary rows, one for each book.

28.8 Avoid Expressions on Indexed Columns

If a column appears in a mathematical or string expression, then its indexes cannot be used by the optimizer. For example, given a table of tasks and their start and finish dates, to find the tasks that took three days to complete in 1994, we could write

```
SELECT taskno
   FROM Tasks
WHERE (finish - start) = 3
      AND start >= '1994-01-01';
```

But since most of the reports deal with the finish dates, we have an index on that column. This means that the query will run faster if it is rewritten as

```
SELECT taskno
   FROM Tasks
WHERE finish = (start + 3)
      AND start >= '1994-01-01';
```

This same principle applies to columns in string functions and, very often, to LIKE predicates.

However, this can be a good thing for queries with small tables, since it will force those tables to be loaded into main storage instead of being searched by index.

28.9 Avoid Sorting

The SELECT DISTINCT, UNION, INTERSECT, and EXCEPT clauses can do sorts to remove duplicates; the exception is when an index exists that can be used to eliminate the duplicates without sorting. The GROUP BY often uses a sort to cluster groups together, does the aggregate functions and then reduces each group to a single row, based on duplicates in the grouping columns. Each sort will cost you ($n*\log2(n)$) operations, which is a lot of extra computer time that you can save if you do not need to use these clauses.

If a SELECT DISTINCT clause includes a set of key columns in it, then all the rows are already known to be unique. Since SQL-92 now has the ability to declare a set of columns to be a PRIMARY KEY in the table declaration, an optimizer can spot such a query and automatically change SELECT DISTINCT to just SELECT. However, SQL-89 implementations do not have this advantage and it is up to the programmer to do the optimization by hand.

You can often replace a SELECT DISTINCT clause with an EXISTS subquery, in violation of another rule of thumb that says to prefer unnested queries to nested queries. For example, a query to find the students who are majoring in the sciences would be

```
SELECT DISTINCT S1.name
     FROM Students AS S1, ScienceDepts AS D1
WHERE S1.dept = D1.dept;
```

This can be better replaced with

```
SELECT S1.name
     FROM Students AS S1
WHERE EXISTS (SELECT *
          FROM ScienceDepts AS D1
        WHERE S1.dept = D1.dept);
```

Another problem is that the DBA might not declare all candidate keys or might declare superkeys instead. Consider a table for a school schedule:

```
CREATE TABLE Schedule
(room INTEGER NOT NULL,
 course CHAR(7) NOT NULL,
 teacher CHAR(20) NOT NULL,
   period INTEGER NOT NULL,
 PRIMARY KEY (room, period));
```

This says that if I know the room and the period, I can find a unique teacher and course — "Third-period Freshman English in Room 101 is taught by Ms. Jones." However, I might have also added the constraint UNIQUE (teacher, period), since Ms. Jones can be in only one room and teach only one class during a given period. If the table was not declared with this extra constraint, the optimizer could not use it in parsing a query. Likewise, if the DBA decided to declare PRIMARY KEY (room, course, teacher, period), the optimizer could not break down this superkey into candidate keys and optimize SELECT DISTINCT teacher, period FROM Schedule; by removing DISTINCT.

Avoid using a HAVING or a GROUP BY clause if the SELECT or WHERE clause can do all the needed work. One way to avoid grouping is in situations where you know the group criterion in advance and make it a constant. This example is a bit extreme, but you can convert

```
SELECT project, AVG(cost)
      FROM Tasks
   GROUP BY project
HAVING project = 'bricklaying';
```

to the simpler and faster

```
SELECT 'bricklaying', AVG(cost)
     FROM Tasks
WHERE project = 'bricklaying';
```

Both queries have to scan the entire table to inspect values in the project column. The first query will simply throw each row into a bucket based on its project code, then look at the HAVING clause to throw away all but one of the buckets before computing the average. The second query rejects those unneeded rows and arrives at one sub-set of projects when it scans.

SQL-92 has ways of removing GROUP BY clauses that SQL-89 did not, because it can use a subquery in a SELECT statement. This is easier to show with an example in which you are now in charge of the Widget-Only Company inventory. You get requisitions that tell how many widgets people are putting into or taking out of the warehouse on a given date. Sometimes that quantity is positive (returns); some-times it is negative (withdrawals). The table of requisitions looks like this:

```
CREATE TABLE Requisitions
(reqdate DATE NOT NULL,
 qty INTEGER NOT NULL CHECK (qty <> 0)
);
```

Your job is to provide a running balance on the quantity on hand with a query. We want something like

RESULT

reqdate	qty	qty_on_hand
1994-07-01	100	100
1994-07-02	120	220
1994-07-03	−150	70
1994-07-04	50	120
1994-07-05	−35	85

The classic SQL-89 solution would be

```
SELECT R1.reqdate, R1.qty, SUM(R2.qty) AS qty_on_hand
    FROM Requisitions AS R1, Requisitions AS R2
WHERE R2.reqdate <= R1.reqdate
GROUP BY R1.reqdate, R1.qty;
```

SQL-92 can use a subquery in the SELECT list, even a correlated query. The rule is that the result must be a single value, hence the name *scalar subquery;* if the query results are an empty table, the result is a NULL.

In this problem, we need to do a summation of all the requisitions posted up to and including the date we are looking at. The query is a nested self-join, thus:

```
SELECT R1.reqdate, R1.qty, (SELECT SUM(R2.qty)
            FROM Requisitions AS R2
          WHERE R2.reqdate <= R1.reqdate)
        AS qty_on_hand
    FROM Requisitions AS R1
ORDER BY R1.reqdate, R1.qty;
```

Frankly, both solutions are going to run slowly compared to a procedural solution that could build the current quantity on hand from the previous quantity on hand from a sorted file of records. Both queries will have to build the subquery from the self-joined table based on dates. However, the first query will also probably sort rows for each group it has to build. The earliest date will have one row to sort, the second earliest date will have two rows, and so forth until the most recent date will sort all the rows. The second query has no grouping, so it just proceeds to the summation without the sorting.

28.10 Avoid CROSS JOINs

It is much easier to avoid unintentional CROSS JOINs in SQL-92 than in the older SQL-89 standard. Consider a three-table join in SQL-89

```
SELECT P1.color
    FROM Paints AS P1, Warehouse AS W1, Sales AS S1
WHERE W1.quantity + S1.quantity =
        P1.gallons/2.5;
```

Because all of the columns involved in the join are in a single expression, their indexes cannot be used. The SQL engine will construct the CROSS JOIN of all three tables first, then prune that teporary working table to get the final answer.

In SQL-92, you can first do a subquery with a `CROSS JOIN` to get one side of the equation:

```
(SELECT (W1.quantity + S1.quantity) AS stuff
   FROM Warehouse AS W1 CROSS JOIN Sales AS S1)
```

and push it into the `WHERE` clause, like this:

```
SELECT color
   FROM Paints AS P1
WHERE EXISTS ((SELECT (W1.quantity + S1.quantity)
         FROM Warehouse AS W1 CROSS JOIN Sales AS S1)
      = (P1.gallons/2.5));
```

The SQL engine, we hope, will do the two-table `CROSS JOIN` subquery and put the results into a temporary table. That temporary table will then be filtered using the Paints table, but without generating a three-table `CROSS JOIN` as the first form of the query did. With a little algebra, the original equation can be changed around and different versions of this query built with other combinations of tables.

A good rule of thumb is that the `FROM` clause should only have those tables that provide columns to its matching `SELECT` clause.

28.11 Recompile Static SQL After Schema Changes

In most implementations, static SQL is compiled in a host program with a fixed execution plan. If a database schema object is altered, execution plans based on that object have to be changed. In the old SQL-89 standard, if a schema object was dropped, the programmer had to recompile the queries that referred to it. The SQL engine was not required to do any checking and most implementations did not. Instead, you could get a runtime error. Even worse, you could have a scenario like this:

1. Create table A
2. Create view VA on table A
3. Use view VA
4. Drop table A
5. Create a new table A
6. Use view VA

What happens in step 6? That depended on your SQL product, but the results were not good. The worst result was that the entire schema could be hopelessly messed up. The best result was that the VIEW VA in step 3 was not the VIEW VA in step 6, but was still usable.

The SQL-92 standard has added the option of specifying the behavior of any of the DROP statements as either CASCADE or RESTRICT. The RESTRICT option is the default, and it will disallow the dropping of any schema object that is being used to define another object. For example, you cannot drop a base table that has VIEWs defined on it or is part of a referential integrity constraint if RESTRICT is used. The CASCADE option will drop any of the dependent objects from the schema when the original object is removed. Be careful with this!

Some products will automatically recompile static SQL when an index is dropped and some will not. However, few products automatically recompile static SQL when an index is added. Furthermore, few products automatically recompile static SQL when the statistical distribution within the data has changed. DEC's Rdb is an exception to this, since it investigates possible execution paths when each query is invoked.

The DBA usually has to update the statistical information explicitly and ask for a recompilation. What usually happens is that one person adds an index and then compiles his program. The new index could either hinder or help other queries when they are recompiled, so it is hard to say whether the new index is a good or a bad thing for the overall performance of the system.

However, a situation that is always bad is when two programmers build indexes that are identical in all but name and never tell each other. Most SQL implementations will not detect this. The duplication will waste both time and space. Whenever one index is updated, the other one will have to be updated also. This is one reason that only the DBA should be allowed to create schema objects.

28.12 Learn to Use Indexes Carefully

By way of review, most indexes are tree structures. They consist of a page or node that has values, from the columns of the table from which the index is built, and pointers. The pointers point to other nodes of the tree and eventually point to rows in the table that has been indexed. The idea is that searching the index is much faster than searching the table itself in a sequential fashion (called a table scan).

The index is also ordered on the columns used to construct it; the rows of the table may or may not be in that order. When the index and the table are sorted on the same columns, the index is called a clustered index. The best example of this in the physical world is a large dictionary with a thumb-notch index — the index and the words in the dictionary are both in alphabetical order.

For obvious physical reasons, you can use only one clustered index on a table. The decision as to which columns to use in the index can be important to performance. There is a "superstition" among older DBAs who have worked with ISAM files and network and hierarchical databases that the primary key must be done with a clustered index. This stems from the fact that in the older file systems, files had to be sorted or hashed on their keys. All searching and navigation was based on this.

This is not true in SQL systems. The primary key's uniqueness will probably be preserved by a unique index, but it does not have to be a clustered unique index. Consider a table of employees keyed by a unique employee identification number. Updates are done with the employee ID number, of course, but very few queries use it. Updating individual rows in a table will actually be about as fast with a clustered or a nonclustered index. Both tree structures will be the same, except for the final physical position to which they point.

However, it might be that the most important corporate unit for reporting purposes is the department, not the employee. A clustered index on the employee ID number would sort the table in employee-ID-number order. There is no inherent meaning in the ID-number ordering; in fact, I would be more likely to sort a list of employees by their last names than by their ID numbers. However, a clustered index on the (nonunique) department code would sort the table in department order and put employees in the same department on the same physical page of storage. The result would be that fewer pages would be read to answer queries.

28.13 Order Indexes Carefully

Consider the Employees table again. There may be a difference among these CREATE INDEX statements:

1. CREATE INDEX XDeptDiv
   ON Employees (dept, division);

2. CREATE INDEX XDivDept
   ON Employees (division, dept);

3. CREATE CLUSTERED INDEX XCDeptDiv
   ON Employees (dept, division);

4. CREATE CLUSTERED INDEX XCDivDept
   ON Employees (division, dept);

In cases 1 and 2, some products build an index only on the first column and ignore the second column. This is because their SQL engine is based on an older product that allows only single-column indexing, and the parser is throwing out the columns it cannot handle. Other products use the first column to build the index tree structure and the secondary columns in such a way that they are searched much more slowly. Both types of SQL engine are like an alphabetic accordion file. Each pocket of an accordion file locates a letter of the alphabet, but within each pocket you have to do a manual search for a particular paper.

If your implementation suffers from this problem, the best thing to do is to order the columns by their granularity; that is, put the column with the most values first and the column with the fewest values last. In our example, assume that we have a few divisions located in major cities, and within each division we have lots of departments. An indexed search that stops at the division will leave us with a scan over the many departments. An indexed search that stops at the department will leave us with a scan over the few divisions.

In some products, you may find that the order will not matter or that separate nonunique indexes will do as well as or better than a unique compound index. The reason is that they use hashing or bit-map indexes. Foxpro and Nucleus are two examples of products that use different bit-map schemes, but they have some basic features in common. Imagine an array with table row numbers or pointers on its columns and values for that column on its rows. If a table row has that value in that position, then the bit is set; if not, the bit is zeroed. A search is done by doing bitwise ANDs, ORs, and NOTs on the bit vectors.

This might be easier to explain with an example of the technique. Assume we have a table of Parts which has columns for the attributes color and weight.

Parts

pno	pname	color	weight	city	
p1	Nut	Red	12	London	*Physical row # 3*
p2	Bolt	Green	17	Paris	*Physical row # 4*
p3	Cam	Blue	12	Paris	*Physical row # 7*
p4	Screw	Red	14	London	*Physical row # 9*
p5	Cam	Blue	12	Paris	*Physical row # 11*
p6	Cog	Red	19	London	*Physical row # 10*

The bit indexes are built by using the physical row and the values of the attributes in an array, thus:

INDEX Parts(color)

Rows	1	2	3	4	5	6	7	8	9	10	11
Blue	0	0	0	0	0	0	1	0	0	0	1
Green	0	0	0	1	0	0	0	0	0	0	0
Red	0	0	1	0	0	0	0	0	0	1	1

INDEX Parts(weight)

Rows	1	2	3	4	5	6	7	8	9	10	11
12	0	0	1	0	0	0	1	0	0	0	1
17	0	0	0	1	0	0	0	0	0	0	0
14	0	0	0	0	0	0	0	0	1	0	0
19	0	0	0	0	0	0	0	0	0	1	0

To find a part that weighs 12 units and is red, you would perform a bitwise AND and get a new bit vector as the answer:

Red	0	0	1	0	0	0	0	0	0	1	1
AND											
12	0	0	1	0	0	0	1	0	0	0	1
answer	0	0	1	0	0	0	0	0	0	0	1

To find a part that weighs 12 units or is colored red, you would perform a bitwise OR and get a new bit vector as the answer:

Red	0	0	1	0	0	0	0	0	0	1	1
OR											
12	0	0	1	0	0	0	1	0	0	0	1
answer	0	0	1	0	0	0	1	0	0	1	1

Searches become a combination of bitwise operators on the indexes before any physical access to the table is done.

28.14 Temporary Tables Are Handy

Another trick is to use temporary tables to hold intermediate results to avoid CROSS JOINs and excessive recalculations. A materialized VIEW is also a form of temporary table, but you cannot index it.

In this problem, we want to find the total amount of the latest balances in all our accounts. Assume that the Payments table holds the details of each payment and that the payment numbers are increasing over time. The Accounts table shows the account identification number and the balance after each payment is made. The query might be done like this:

```
SELECT SUM(A1.balance)
    FROM Accounts AS A1, Payments AS P1
 WHERE P1.acct = A1.acct
       AND P1.payment_number = (SELECT MAX(payment_number)
             FROM Payments AS P2
          WHERE P2.acct = A1.acct);
```

Since this uses a correlated subquery with an aggregate function, it will take a little time to run for each row in the answer. It would be faster to create a temporary working table or VIEW like this:

```
BEGIN
CREATE TABLE LastPayments
(acct INTEGER NOT NULL,
 last_payment_number INTEGER NOT NULL,
 amount DECIMAL(8, 2) NOT NULL,
 payment_date DATE NOT NULL,
 ... );

CREATE INDEX LPX ON LastPayment(acct, payment_number);

INSERT INTO LastPayments
SELECT acct, payment_number, MAX(payment_number)
   FROM Payments
GROUP BY acct, payment_number;

SELECT SUM(A1.balance) -- final answer
   FROM Accounts AS A1, LastPayments AS LP1
WHERE LP1.acct = A1.acct
       AND LP1.payment_number = A1.payment_number;

DROP TABLE LastPayments;

END;
```

Consider this three-table query that creates a list of combinations of items and all the different packages for which the selling price (price and box cost) is 10% of the warranty plan cost. Assume that any item can fit into any box we have and that any item can be put on any warranty plan.

```
SELECT I1.item
   FROM Inventory AS I1, Packages AS P1, Warranty AS W1
WHERE I1.price + P1.box = W1.plancost * 10;
```

Since all the columns appear in an expression, the engine cannot use indexes, so the query will become a large CROSS JOIN in most SQL implementations. This query can be broken down into a temporary table that has an index on the calculations, thus:

```
BEGIN
CREATE TABLE SellingPrices
(sellprice DECIMAL (8, 2) NOT NULL);

-- optional index on the calculation
CREATE INDEX SPX ON SellingPrices(sellprice);

-- do algebra and get everything on one side of an equation
INSERT INTO SellingPrices
SELECT DISTINCT (P1.box + I1.price) * 0.1
    FROM Inventory AS I1, packages AS P1;

SELECT I1.item
    FROM SellingPrices AS SP1, Warranty AS W1
WHERE SP1.sellprice = W1.plancost;

END;
```

CHAPTER 29

Data Design

BEFORE YOU CAN put data into a database, you actually need to think about how it will be represented and manipulated. This is true not just of SQL but of any record-keeping system. If you don't believe that the representation is important, then try taking a square root in Roman numerals, in Mayan numerals, and in Hindu-Arabic numerals. The *numbers* are all the same, but the *numerals* are different, and it makes a world of difference in what you can do with the data.

This chapter deals with the representation of individual attributes of the entities we are trying to model in a database.

29.1 Scales and Measurements

Measure all that is measurable and attempt to make measurable that which is not yet so. — Galileo (1564–1642)

Databases often store units of measure, which are measured using a scale of some sort. This is a short introduction to measurement theory and scales, so that you will have a good theoretical foundation to do any practical work. Besides, this is interesting stuff. Trust me.

Measurement is not just assigning numbers to things or their attributes so much as it is assigning to things a structural property that can be expressed in numbers or other computable symbols.

This structure is the scale used to take the measurement; the numbers or symbols represent units of measure.

Scales are classified into types by the properties they do or do not have. The properties with which we are concerned are described below.

1. A natural origin point on the scale. This is sometimes called a zero, but it does not have to be literally a numeric zero. For example, if the measurement is the distance between objects, the natural zero is zero meters — you cannot get any closer than that. If the measurement is the temperature of objects, the natural zero is zero degrees Kelvin — nothing can get any colder than absolute zero. However, consider time; it goes from an eternal past into an eternal future, so you cannot find a natural origin for it.

2. Meaningful operations that can be performed on the units. It makes sense to add weights together to get a new weight. However, adding names or shoe sizes together is absurd.

3. A natural ordering of the units. It makes sense to speak about an event's occurring before or after another, or a thing's being heavier, longer, or hotter than another. But the alphabetical order imposed on a list of names is arbitrary, not natural — a foreign language, with different names for the same objects, would impose another ordering.

4. A natural metric function on the units. A metric function has nothing to do with the "metric system" of measurements, which is more properly called SI, for *Système international d'unités*. Metric functions have the following three properties:

    a. The metric between an object and itself is the natural origin of the scale. We can write this in a semimathematical notation as $M(a, a) = 0$.

    b. The order of the objects in the metric function does not matter. Again in the notation, $M(a, b) = M(b, a)$.

    c. There is a natural additive function that obeys the rule that $M(a, b) + M(b, c) >= M(a, c)$, which is also known as the triangular inequality.

This notation is meant to be more general than just arithmetic. The "zero" in the first property is the origin of the scale, not just a numeric zero. The third property, defined with a "plus" and a "greater than or equal" sign, is a symbolic way of expressing more general ordering relationships. The "greater than or equal" sign refers to a natural ordering on the attribute being measured. The "plus" sign refers to a meaningful operation in regard to that ordering, not just arithmetic addition.

The special case of the third property, where the "greater than or equal to" is always "greater than," is very desirable to people because it means that they can use numbers for units and do simple arithmetic with the scales. This is called a strong metric property. For example, human perceptions of sound and light intensity follow a cube root law — that is, if you double the intensity of light, the perception of the intensity increases by only 20% (Stevens 1957). The actual formula is "Physical intensity to the 0.3 power equals perceived intensity." Knowing this, designers of stereo equipment use controls that work on a logarithmic scale internally, but that show evenly spaced marks on the control panel of the amplifier.

It is possible to have a scale that has any combination of the metric properties. For example, instead of measuring the distance between two places in meters, measure it in units of effort. Does it have the property that $M(a, a) = 0$? Yes; it takes no effort to get to where you already are located. Does it have the property that $M(a, b) = M(b, a)$? No; it takes less effort to go downhill than to go uphill. Does it have the property that $M(a, b) + M(b, c) >= M(a, c)$? Yes; the amount of effort needed to go directly to a place will always be less than the effort of making another stop along the way.

29.1.1 Range and Granularity

Range and granularity are properties of the way the measurements are made. Since we have to store data in a database within certain limits, they are very important to a database designer.

Range

A scale also has other properties that are of interest to someone building a database. First, scales have a range — what are the highest and lowest values which can appear on the scale? It is possible to have a finite or an infinite limit on either the lower or the upper bound. Overflow and underflow errors are the result of range violations inside the database.

Database designers do not have infinite storage, so we have to pick a subrange to use in the database when we have no upper or lower bound. For example, very few computer calendar routines will handle geological time periods. But then very few companies have bills that have been outstanding for that long, either, so we do not mind.

Granularity and Precision

Look at a ruler and a micrometer. They both measure length, using the same scale, but there is a difference. A micrometer is more precise because it has a finer granularity of units. Granularity is a static property of the scale itself — how many notches there are on your ruler. In Europe, all industrial drawings are done in millimeters; the U.S. has been using ½ of an inch.

Precision is the degree of refinement in the calculations done with the units. Accuracy is a measure of how repeatable a measurement is.

Both depend on granularity, but they are not the same thing. Human nature says that a number impresses according to the square of the number of decimal places. Hence, some people will use a computer system to express things to as many decimal places as possible, even when it makes no sense. For example, civil engineering in the United States uses decimal feet for road design. Nobody can build a road any more precise than that, but you will see civil engineering students turning in work that is expressed in ten-thousandths of a foot. You don't use a micrometer on asphalt!

A database often does not give the user a choice of precision for many calculations. In fact, the SQL standards leave the number of decimal places in the results of many arithmetic operations to be implementer-defined.

The ideas are easier to explain with handgun targets, which are scales to measure the ability of the shooter to put bullets in the center of a target. A bigger target has a wider range compared to a smaller target. A target with more rings has a higher granularity.

Once you start shooting, a group of shots that are closer together is more precise because the shots were more repeatable. A shot group that is closer to the center is more accurate because the shots were closer to the goal. Notice that precision and accuracy are not the same thing! If I have a good gun whose sights are off, I can get a very tight cluster that is not near the bull's eye.

Fig. 29.1

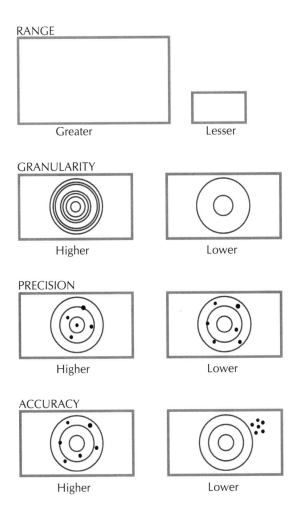

29.1.2 Types of Scales

The lack or presence of precision and accuracy determines the kind of scale you should choose. Scales are either quantitative or qualitative. The quantitative scales are what most people mean when they think of measurements, because these scales can be manipulated and are usually represented as numbers. Qualitative scales attempt to impose an order on an attribute, but they do not allow for computations — just comparisons.

Nominal Scales

The simplest scales are the nominal scales. They simply assign a unique symbol, usually a number or a name, to each member of the set that they attempt to measure. For example, a list of city names is a nominal scale.

Right away we are into philosophical differences, because many people do not consider listing to be measurement. Since there is no clear property being measured, that school of thought would tell us this cannot be a scale.

There is no natural origin point for a set, and likewise there is no ordering. We tend to use alphabetic ordering for names, but it makes just as much sense to use frequency of occurrence or increasing size or almost any other attribute that does have a natural ordering.

The only meaningful operation that can be done with such a list is a test for equality — "Is this city New York or not?" — which will test either TRUE, FALSE, or UNKNOWN.

Nominal scales are very common in databases because they are used for unique identifiers, such as names and descriptions.

Absolute Scales

An absolute scale is a count of the elements in a set. Its natural origin is zero, or the empty set. The count is the ordering (a set of five elements is bigger than a set of three elements, and so on). Addition and subtraction are metric functions. Each element is taken to be identical and interchangeable. For example, when you buy a dozen Grade A eggs, you assume that for your purposes any Grade A egg will do the same job as any other Grade A egg.

Again, absolute scales are very common in databases because they are used for quantities.

Ordinal Scales

Ordinal scales put things in order, but have no origin and no operations. For example, geologists use a scale to measure the hardness of minerals using Moh's Scale for Hardness (MSH for short). It is based on a set of standard minerals, which are ordered by relative hardness (talc = 1, gypsum = 2, calcite = 3, fluorite = 4, apatite = 5, feldspar = 6, quartz = 7, topaz = 8, sapphire = 9, diamond = 10). To measure an unknown mineral, you try to scratch the polished surface of one of the standard minerals with it; if it scratches the surface, the unknown is harder. Notice that I can get two different unknown minerals with the same measurement that are not equal to each other, and that I can get minerals that are softer than my lower bound or harder than my upper bound. There is no origin point and operations on the measurements make no sense (e.g., if I add 10 talc units I do not get a diamond).

Perhaps the most common use we see of ordinal scales today is to measure preferences or opinions. You are given a product or a situation and asked to decide how much you like or dislike it, how much you agree or disagree with a statement, and so forth. The scale is usually given a set of labels such as "strongly agree" through "strongly disagree," or the labels are ordered from 1 to 5.

Consider pairwise choices between ice cream flavors. Saying that vanilla is preferred over wet leather in our taste test might well be expressing a universal truth, but there is no objective unit of "likability" to apply. The lack of a unit means that such things as opinion polls that try to average such scales are meaningless; the best you can do is a bar graph of the number of respondents in each category.

Another problem is that an ordinal scale may not be transitive. Transitivity is the property of a relationship in which if $R(a, b)$ and $R(b, c)$ then $R(a, c)$. We like this property, and expect it in the real world where we have relationships like "heavier than," "older than," and so forth. This is the result of a strong metric property.

But an ice cream taster, who has just found out that the shop is out of vanilla, might prefer squid over wet leather, prefer wet leather over wood, and yet prefer wood over squid, so there is no metric function or linear ordering at all. Again, we are into philosophical differences, since many people do not consider a nontransitive relationship to be a scale.

If you are interested in the problems of nontransitive relationships, look at the book *Wheels, Life, and Other Mathematical Amusements* (Gardner 1983), which has a chapter on nontransitive relationships. Voting theory is a branch of political science that shows that there are still problems even when an individual's preferences are well ordered (Celko 1992b).

Rank Scales

Rank scales have an origin and an ordering, but no natural operations. The most common example of this would be military ranks. Nobody is lower than a private and that rank is a starting point in your military career, but it makes no sense to somehow combine three privates to get a sergeant.

Rank scales have to be transitive: a sergeant gives orders to a private, and since a major gives orders to a sergeant, he can also give orders to a private. You will see ordinal and rank scales grouped together in some of the literature if the author does not allow nontransitive ordinal scales. You will also see the same fallacies committed when people try to do statistical summaries of such scales.

Quantitative Scales and Sets

There are some subtle differences among different quantitative scales. To make the point, we will use four army buddies and try to measure them on different quantitative scales. Let us start with their military ranks:

    Tom = sergeant
    Dick = corporal
    Richard = corporal
    Harry = private

Clearly, Tom has the highest rank and Harry has the lowest. Dick and Richard have the same rank. If Tom or Harry were to get shot in combat, Dick and Richard would still have the rank of corporal. Likewise, the rank of corporal would still be on the scale even if there were no members at that level. A ranking can have zero or more elements in each unit of the scale.

The boys now get out of the Army and go to school. The grades on their first report card are

Tom = A
Dick = B
Richard = B
Harry = C

Clearly, Tom is the top student. But note that Harry is fourth in his class because there are three students with better grades than his. If Richard drops out of school, Harry moves up to third in the class. Class standing is not a ranking; it is a positioning. Each position must have one or more members, so there has to be a promotion rule when an element is taken from the dataset. The convention in schools has been to give both Dick and Richard the honor of being second in their class, with Harry as third. That is, we fill all the gaps from first to nth standing with one or more data items. See section 21.5.4 for a discussion of rankings and class standings in SQL queries.

Now the boys go to work for the same company as salesmen. Their boss has a sales contest, in which they perform like this:

Tom = $100,000
Dick = $90,000
Richard = $90,000
Harry = $80,000

Nobody beats Tom, and he is the Salesman of the Month. Harry is fourth because there are three other people who sold more than he did. Again, the promotion rule applies if one of the boys should get hit by a beer truck. But what is the contest standing for Dick and Richard? The convention here is to allow gaps and say that they are both third and nobody is second.

These last two situations, class standing and contest placement, are not scales. Their values depend on a rule that needs the rest of the set, whereas a scale is external to the dataset. If you try to put a standing or a placement in a database, then you have to recalculate it every time you change anything in the database. These last two situations are statistics and can be useful.

Interval Scales

Interval scales have a metric function, ordering, and meaningful operations among the units, but no natural origin. Calendars are the best example; some arbitrary historical event is the starting point for the scale and all measurements are related to it using identical units or intervals. Time, then, extends from a past eternity to a future eternity.

The metric function is the number of days between two dates. Looking at the three properties: (1) $M(a, a) = 0$: there are zero days between today and today. (2) $M(a, b) = M(b, a)$: there are just as many days from today to next Monday as there are from next Monday to today. (3) $M(a, b) + M(b, c) >= M(a, c)$: the number of days from today to next Monday plus the number of days from next Monday to Christmas is the same as the number of days from today until Christmas.

Ordering is very natural and strong: 1900-July-1 occurs before 1993-July-1.

Aggregations of the basic unit (days) into other units (weeks, months, and years) are also arbitrary. For a good discussion of the history of these aggregated units, see *The Seven Day Circle* (Zerubavel 1985).

Ratio Scales

Ratio scales are what people think of when they think about a measurement. Ratio scales have an origin (usually zero units), an ordering, and a set of operations that can be expressed in arithmetic. They are called ratio scales because all measurements are expressed as multiples or fractions of a certain unit or interval.

Length, mass, and volume are examples of this type of scale. The unit is what is arbitrary; mass is still mass whether it is measured in kilograms or in pounds. Another nice property is that the units are identical; a kilogram is still a kilogram whether it is measuring feathers or bricks.

Absolute and ratio scales are also called extensive scales because they deal with quantities, as opposed to the remaining scales, which are intensive because they measure qualities. Quantities can be added and manipulated together; qualities cannot.

Type of scale	Natural Ordering	Natural Origin	Natural Functions	Example
Nominal	No	No	No	City names
Absolute	Yes	Yes — 0	Yes — integer math	Egg cartons
Ordinal	Yes	No	No	Preferences
Rank	Yes	Yes	No	Contests
Interval	Yes	No	Yes — additive	Time
Ratio	Yes	Yes — 0	Yes — various	Length, weight

29.1.3 Scale Conversion

The important principle of measurement theory is that you can convert from one scale to another only if they are of the same type and measure the same attribute.

Absolute scales do not convert, which is why they are called absolute scales. Five apples are five apples, no matter how many times you count them or how you arrange them on the table.

Nominal scales are converted to other nominal scales by a mapping between the scales. That means you look things up in a table. For example, I can convert my English city names to Polish city names with a dictionary. The problem comes when there is not a one-to-one mapping between the two nominal scales. For example, English uses the word "cousin" to identify the offspring of your parents' siblings, and tradition treats them all pretty much alike. Chinese language and culture have separate words for the same relations based on the genders of your parents' siblings and the age relationships among them (e.g., the oldest son of your father's oldest brother is a particular type of cousin and you have different social obligations to him). Something is lost in translation.

Ordinal scales are converted to ordinal scales by a monotonic function. That means you preserve the ordering when you convert.

Looking at the MSH scale for geologists, I can pick another set of minerals, plastics, or metals to scratch, but rock samples that were definitely softer than others will still be softer. Again, there are problems when there is not a one-to-one mapping between the two scales. My new scale may be able to tell the difference between rocks where the MSH scale could not.

Rank scales are converted to rank scales by a monotonic function that preserves the ordering, like ordinal scales. Again, there are problems when there is not a one-to-one mapping between the two scales. For example, different military branches have slightly different ranks that don't quite correspond to each other.

In both the nominal and the ordinal scales, the problem was that things that looked equal on one scale were different on another. This has to do with range and granularity, which we discussed in section 29.1.1.

Interval scales are converted to interval scales by a linear function; that is, a function of the form $y = a*x + b$. This preserves the ordering, but shifts the origin point when you convert. For example, I can convert temperature from degrees Celsius to degrees Fahrenheit using the formula $F = (9/5 * C) + 32$.

Ratio scales are converted to ratio scales by a constant multiplier, since both scales have the same ordering and origin point. For example, I can convert from pounds to kilograms using the formula $p = 0.4536 * k$. This is why people like to use ratio scales.

29.1.4 Derived Units

Many of the scales that we use are not primary units, but derived units. These are measures that are constructed from primary units, such as miles per hour (time and distance), or square miles (distance and distance). You can use only ratio and interval scales to construct derived units.

If you use an absolute scale with a ratio or interval scale, you are dealing with statistics, not measurements. For example, using weight (ratio scale) and the number of people in New York (absolute scale), we can compute the average weight of a New Yorker, which is a statistic, not a unit of measurement.

The SI measurements use a basic set of seven units (meter for length, kilogram for mass, second for time, ampere for electrical current, degree Kelvin for temperature, mole for molecules, and candela for light) and construct derived units. ISO standard 2955 ("Information Processing — Representation of SI and other units for use in systems with limited character sets") for expressing derived units as formulas has a notation for expressing SI units in ASCII character strings. (For ISO standards, see appendix B: Readings and Resources.)

The notation uses parentheses, spaces, multiplication (shown by a period), division (shown by a solidus, or slash) and exponents (shown by numerals immediately after the unit abbreviation). There are also names for most of the standard derived units. For example, "100 kg.m/s2" converts to 10 newtons (the unit of force), written as "10 N."

29.1.5 Punctuation and Standard Units

A database stores measurements as numeric data represented in a binary format, but when the data is input or output, a human being wants readable characters and punctuation. Punctuation serves to identify the units being used, and can be used for prefix, postfix, or infix symbols. It can also be implicit or explicit.

If I write "$25.15," you know that the unit of measure is the dollar because of the explicit prefix dollar sign. If I write "160 lbs.," you know that the unit of measure is pounds because of the explicit postfix abbreviation for the unit. If I write "1989 MAR 12," you know that this is a date because of the implicit infix separation among month, day, and year, achieved by changing from numerals to letters, and the optional spaces. The ISO and SQL defaults represent the same date, using explicit infix punctuation, with 1989-03-12 instead. Likewise, a column header on a report that gives the units used is explicit punctuation.

Databases do not generally store punctuation. The sole exception might be the MONEY or CURRENCY datatype found in many SQL implementations as a vendor extension. Punctuation wastes storage space and the units can be represented in some internal format that can be used in calculations. Punctuation is only for display.

It is possible to put the units in a column next to a numeric column that holds their quantities. This is awkward and wastes storage space. If everything is expressed in the same unit, the units column is redundant. If things are expressed in different units, you have to convert them to a common unit to do any calculations. Why not store them in a common unit in the first place?

The DBA has to be sure that all data in a column of a table is expressed in the same units before it is stored. There are some horror stories about multinational companies sending the same input programs used in the United States to their European offices, where SI and English measurements were mixed into the same database without conversion.

Ideally, the DBA should be sure that data is kept in the same units in all the tables in the database. If different units are needed, they can be provided in a VIEW that hides the conversions (thus the office in the United States sees English measurements and the European offices see SI units and date formats; neither is aware of the conversions being done for it).

29.1.6 General Guidelines for Using Scales in a Database

The following are general guidelines for using measurements and scales in a database and not firm, hard rules. You will find exceptions to all of them.

1. Use CHECK() clauses on table declarations to make sure that only the allowed values appear in the database. If you have the CREATE DOMAIN feature of SQL-92, use it to build your scales. Nominal scales would have a list of possible values; other scales would have range-checking.

    Likewise, use the DEFAULT() clauses to be sure that each scale starts with its origin value, a NULL, or a default value that makes sense.

2. Declare at least one more decimal place than you think you will need for units that can be expressed as fractions. In most SQL implementations, rounding and truncation will improve with more decimal places.

The downside of SQL is that precision and the rules for truncation and rounding are implementation-dependent, so a query with calculations might not give the same results on another product. However, SQL is more merciful than older file systems, since the DBA can ALTER a numeric column so it will have more precision and a greater range without destroying existing data or queries. Host programs may have to be changed to display the extra characters in the results, however.

3. Try to store primary units rather than derived units. This is not always possible, since you might not be able to measure anything but the derived unit. Look at your new tire gauge; it is set for pascals (newtons per square meter) and will not tell you how many square meters you have on the surface of the tire or the force exerted by the air. And you simply cannot figure these things out from the pascals.

A set of primary units can be arranged in many different ways to construct any possible derived unit desired. Never store both the derived and the primary units in the same table. Not only is this redundant, but it opens the door to possible errors when a primary-unit column is changed and the derived units based on it are not updated. Also, most computers can recalculate the derived units much faster than they can read a value from a disk drive.

4. Use the same punctuation whenever a unit is displayed. For example, do not mix ISO and ANSI date formats, or express weight in pounds and kilograms on the same report. Ideally, everything should be displayed the same way in the entire application system.

29.2 Data Encoding Schemes

You do not put data directly into a database. You convert it into an encoding scheme first, then put the encoding into the rows of the tables. Words have to be written in an alphabet and belong to a language; measurements are expressed as numbers. We are so used to seeing words and numbers that we no longer think of them as encoding schemes. We also often fail to distinguish among the possible ways to identify (and therefore to encode) an entity or property. Do we encode the person receiving medical services or the policy that is paying for them? That might depend on whether the database is for the doctor or for the insurance company. Do we encode the first title of a song or the alternate title or both? Or should we include the music itself in a multimedia database? And should it be as an image of the sheet music or as an audio recording?

Nobody teaches people how to design these encoding schemes, so they are all too often done "on the fly." Where standardized encoding schemes exist, they are too often ignored in favor of some ad hoc scheme. Beginning programmers have the attitude that encoding schemes do not really matter because the computer will take care of it, so they don't have to spend time on the design of their encoding schemes. This attitude has probably gotten worse with SQL than it was before. The database designer thinks that an ALTER statement can fix any bad things he did at the start of the project.

Yes, the computer can take care of a lot of problems. But the data entry and validation programs become very complex and hard to maintain. Database queries that have to follow the same convoluted encodings will cost both computer time and money. And a human being still has to use the code at some point. Bad schemes give rise to errors in data entry and misreadings of outputs, and can lead to incorrect data models.

29.2.1 Bad Encoding Schemes

To use an actual example, the automobile tag system for a certain southern state started as a punch-card system written in Cobol. Many readers are too young to remember card-punching (keypunch) machines. A punch card is a piece of stiff paper in which a character is represented as one or more rectangular holes made into one of 80 vertical columns on the card. Contiguous groups of columns make up fixed-length fields of data. The keypunch machine has a typewriter-like keyboard; it automatically feeds cards into the punch as fast as a human being can type. The position, length, and alphabetic or numeric shift for each field on the card can be set by a control card in the keypunch machine to save the operator keystrokes. This is a very fixed format and a very fast input method, and making changes to a program once it is in place is very hard.

The auto tag system had a single card column for a single-position numeric code to indicate the type of tag: private car, chauffeured car, taxi, truck, public bus, and so forth. As time went on, more tag types were added for veterans of assorted wars, for university alumni, and for whatever other pressure group happened to have the political power to pass a bill allowing it a special auto tag.

Soon there were more than 10 types, so a single-digit could not represent them. There was room on the punch card to change the length of the field to two digits. But Cobol uses fixed-length fields, so changing the card layout would require changes in the programs and in the keypunch procedures.

The first new tag code was handled by letting the data-entry clerk press a punctuation-mark key instead of changing from numeric lock to manual shift mode. Once that decision was made, it was followed for each new code thereafter, until the scheme looked like everything on the upper row of keys on a typewriter.

Unfortunately, different makes and models of keypunch machines have different punctuation marks in the same keyboard position, so each deck of cards had to have a special program to convert its punches to the original model IBM 026 keypunch codes before the master file was updated. This practice continued even after all the original machines had been retired to used-equipment heaven.

The edit programs could not check for a simple numeric range to validate input, but had to use a small lookup routine with over 20 values in it. That does not sound like much until you realize that the system had to handle over three million records in the first quarter of the year. The error rate was quite high, and each batch needed to know which machine had punched the cards before it could use a lookup table.

If the encoding scheme had been designed with two digits (00 to 99) at the beginning, all of the problems would have been avoided. If I were to put this system into a database today, using video terminals for data entry, the tag type could be INTEGER and it could hold as many tag types as I would ever need. This is part of the legacy database problem.

The second example was reported in *Information Systems Week* (ISW 1987). The first sentence told the whole story: "The chaos and rampant error rates in New York City's new Welfare Management System appear to be due to a tremendous increase in the number of codes it requires in data entry and the subsequent difficulty for users in learning to use it."

The rest of the article explained how the new system attempted to merge several old existing systems. In the merger, the error rates increased from 2% to over 20% because the encoding schemes used could not be matched up and consolidated.

29.2.2 Characteristics of a Bad Encoding Scheme

How do you know a bad encoding scheme when you see one? One bad feature is the failure to allow for growth. Talk to anyone who had to reconfigure a fixed-length record system to allow for the change from the old ZIP codes to the current ZIP + 4 codes. SQL does not have this as a physical problem, but it can show up as a logical problem.

Another bad property is ambiguous encodings in the scheme. Perhaps the funniest example of this problem was the Italian telephone system's attempt at a "time of day" service. They used a special three-digit number, like the 411 information number in the United States. But the three digits they picked were also those of a telephone exchange in Milan, so nobody could call into that exchange without getting the time signal before they completed their call.

This happens more often than you would think, but the form that it usually takes is that of a "miscellaneous" code that is too general. Very different cases are then encoded as identical and the user is given incorrect or misleading information when he does a query.

A bad encoding scheme lacks codes for missing, unknown, not applicable, or miscellaneous values. The classic story is the man who bought a prestige auto tag reading "NONE" and got thousands of traffic tickets as a result. The police had no special provision for a missing tag on the tickets, so when a car had no tag, they wrote "none" in the field for the tag number. The database simply matched his name and address to every unpaid missing-tag ticket on file at the time.

Before you say that the NULL in SQL is a quick solution to this problem, think about how NULL is ignored in many SQL functions. The SQL query SELECT tagno, SUM(fine) FROM tickets GROUP BY tagno; will give the total fines on each car. But it also puts all the missing tags into one group (i.e., one car) although we want to see each one as a separate case, since it is very unlikely that there is only one untagged car in all of California. We will discuss this further in the section on GROUP BY clauses.

There are also differences among "missing," "unknown," "not applicable," and "miscellaneous" values. They are subtle but important. For example, the International Classification of Disease uses 999.999 for miscellaneous illness. It means that we have diagnosed the patient, know that he has an illness, and cannot classify it; a very scary condition for the patient, but not quite the same thing as a missing disease code (just admitted, might not be sick), an inapplicable disease code (pregnancy complications in a male), or an unknown disease code (sick and awaiting lab results).

29.2.3 Encoding Scheme Types

The following is my classification system for encoding schemes and suggestions for using each of them. You will find some of these same ideas in library science and other fields, but I have never seen anyone else attempt a classification system for data processing.

Enumeration Encoding

An enumeration encoding arranges the attribute values in some order and assigns a number or a letter to each value. Numbers are usually a better choice than letters, because they can be increased without limit as more values are added. Enumeration schemes are a good choice for a short list of values, but a bad choice for a long list. It is too hard to remember a long list of codes, and very soon any natural ordering principle is violated as new values are tacked on the end.

A good heuristic is to order the values in some natural manner, if one exists in the data, so that table lookup will be easier. Chronological order (1 occurs before 2) or procedural order (1 must be done before 2) is often a good choice. Another good heuristic to order the values from most common to least common. That way you will have shorter codes for the most common cases. Other orderings could be based on physical characteristics such as largest to smallest, rainbow-color order, and so on.

After arguing for a natural order in the list, I must admit that the most common scheme is alphabetical order, because it is simple to implement on a computer and makes it easy for a person to look up values in a table. ANSI standard X3.31, "Structure for the Identification of Counties of the United States for Information Interchange," encodes county names within a state by first alphabetizing the names, then numbering them from 1 to whatever is needed.

Scale Encoding

A scale encoding is given in some unit of measure, such as pounds, meters, volts, or liters. This can be done in one of two ways. The column contains an implied unit of measure and the numbers represent the quantity in that unit. But sometimes the column explicitly contains the unit. The most common example of the second case would be money fields where a dollar sign is used in the column; you know that the unit is dollars, not pounds or yen, by the sign.

Scales and measurement theory are a whole separate topic and are discussed in detail in section 29.1.

Abbreviation Encoding

Abbreviation codes shorten the attribute values to fit into less storage space, but they are easily understood by the reader on sight. The codes can be either of fixed length or of variable length, but computer people tend to prefer fixed length. The most common example is the two-letter postal state abbreviations ('CA' for California, 'AL' for Alabama), which replaced the old variable-length abbreviations ('Calif.' for California, 'Ala.' for Alabama).

A good abbreviation scheme is very handy, but as the set of values becomes larger, the possibility for misunderstanding increases. The three-letter codes for airport baggage are pretty obvious for major cities: 'LAX' for Los Angeles, 'SFO' for San Francisco, 'BOS' for Boston, 'ATL' for Atlanta. But nobody can figure out the abbreviations for the really small airports.

Rounding numbers before they are stored in the database is actually a special case of abbreviation. But people usually think of rounding as a range or granularity problem, not as an encoding choice.

Algorithmic Encoding

Algorithmic encoding takes the value to be encoded and puts it through an algorithm to obtain the encodings. The algorithm should be reversible, so that the original value can be recovered. Though it is not required, the encoding is usually shorter (or at least of known maximum size) and more uniform in some useful way compared to the original value.

Computer people are used to using Julianized dates, which convert a date into an integer. Usually it is a number between 1 and 365 or 366, which represents the ordinal position of the day within the year, but it can be the number of days (or microseconds) since a particular event.

Algorithms take up computer time in both data input and output, but the encoding is useful in itself because it allows searching or calculations to be done that would be hard using the original data. Julianized dates can be used for computations; Soundex names give a phonetic matching that would not be possible with the original text.

Another example is hashing functions, which convert numeric values into other numeric values for placing them in storage and retrieving them.

The difference between an abbreviation and an algorithm is not that clear. An abbreviation can be considered a special case of an algorithm, which tells you how to remove or replace letters. The tests to tell them apart are (1) when a human can read it without effort, it is an abbreviation, and (2) an algorithmic encoding can return the same code for more than one value, but an abbreviation is always one-to-one.

Hierarchical Encoding

A hierarchy partitions the set of values into disjoint categories, then partitions those categories into subcategories, and so forth until some final level is reached. Such schemes are shown either as nested sets or as tree charts. Each category has some meaning in itself and the subcategories refine meaning further.

The most common example is the ZIP code, which partitions the United States geographically. Each digit, as you read from left to right, further isolates the location of the address first by postal region, then by state, then by city, and finally by the post office that has to make the delivery. For example, given the ZIP code 30310, we know that the 30000-to-39999 range means the southeastern United States. Within in the southeastern codes, we know that the 30000 to 30399 range is Georgia and that 30300 to 30399 is metropolitan Atlanta. Finally, the whole code, 30310, identifies substation A in the West End section of the city. The ZIP code can be parsed by reading it from left to right, reading first one digit, then two, and then the last two digits.

Another example is the Dewey decimal system, used in public libraries in the United States. The 500 number series covers "Natural Sciences"; within that, the 510s cover "Mathematics"; finally, 512 deals with "Algebra" in particular. The scheme could be carried further, with decimal fractions for kinds of algebra.

Hierarchical encoding schemes are great for large data domains that have a natural hierarchy. They organize the data for searching and reporting along that natural hierarchy and make it very easy. But there can be problems in designing these schemes. First of all, the tree structure does not have to be neatly balanced, so some categories may need more codes than others and hence more breakdowns. Eastern and ancient religions are shortchanged in the Dewey decimal system, reflecting a prejudice toward Christian and Jewish writings. Asian religions were pushed into a very small set of codes. Today, the Library of Congress has more books on Buddhist thought than on any other religion on Earth.

Second, you might not have made the right choices as to where to place certain values in the tree. For example, in the Dewey decimal system, books on logic are encoded as 164, in the philosophy section, and not under the 510s, mathematics. In the nineteenth century, there was no mathematical logic. Today, nobody would think of looking for logic under philosophy. Dewey was simply following the conventions of his day. And like today's programmers, he found that the system specifications changed while he was working.

Vector Encoding

A vector is made up of a fixed number of components. These components can be ordered or unordered, but are almost always ordered; they can be of fixed or variable length. The components can be dependent on or independent of each other, but the code applies to a single entity. The components of the vector can be determined by punctuation, symbol-set changes, or position within the code.

The most common example is a date, whose components are year, month, and day. The parts have some meaning by themselves, but the real meaning is in the vector — the date — as a whole. The different date formats used in computer systems give examples of all the options. The three components can be written in year-month-day order, month-day-year order, or just about any other way you wish.

The limits on the values for the day are dependent on the year (is it leap year or not?) and the month (28, 29, 30, or 31 days?). The components can be separated by punctuation (12/1/1990, using slashes and American date format), symbol-set changes (1990 DEC 01, using digits-letters-digits) or position (19901201, using positions 1 to 4, 5 to 6, and 7 to 8 for year, month, and day, respectively).

Another example is the ISO code for tire sizes, which is made up of a wheel diameter (scaled in inches), a tire type (abbreviation code), and a width (scaled in centimeters). Thus, 15R155 means a 15-inch radial tire that is 155 centimeters wide, whereas 15SR155 is a steel-belted radial tire with the same dimensions. In spite of the mixed American and ISO units, this is a general physical description of a tire in a single code.

Vector schemes are very informative and allow you to pick the best scheme for each component. But they have to be disassembled to get to the components (many database products provide special functions to do this for dates, street addresses, and people's names). Sorting by components is hard unless you want them in the order given; try to sort the tire sizes by construction, width, and diameter instead of by diameter, construction, and width.

Another disadvantage is that a bad choice in one component can destroy the usefulness of the whole scheme. Another problem is extending the code. For example, if the standard tire number had to be expanded to include thickness in millimeters, where would that measurement go? Another number would have to be separated by a punctuation mark. It could not be inserted into a position inside the code without giving ambiguous codes. The code cannot be easily converted to a fixed-position vector encoding without changing many of the database routines.

Concatenation Encoding

A concatenation code is made up of a variable number of components that are concatenated together. As in a vector encoding, the components can be ordered or unordered, dependent on or independent of each other, and determined by punctuation, symbol-set changes, or position.

A concatenation code is often a hierarchy that is refined by additions to the right. These are also known as facet codes in Europe. Or the code can be a list of features, any of which can be present or missing. The order of the components may or may not be important.

Concatenation codes were popular in machine shops at the turn of the century: a paper tag was attached to a piece of work, and workers at different stations would sign off on their parts of the manufacturing process. Concatenation codes are still used in parts of the airplane industry, where longer codes represent subassemblies of the assembly in the head (also called the *root* or *parent*) of the code.

Another type of concatenation code is a quorum code, which is not ordered. These codes say that n out of k marks must be present for the code to have meaning. For example, three out of five inspectors must approve a part before it passes.

The most common use of concatenation codes is in keyword lists in the header records of documents in textbases. The author or librarian assigns each article in the system a list of keywords that describe the material covered by the article. The keywords are picked from a limited, specialized vocabulary that belongs to a particular discipline.

Concatenation codes fell out of general use because their variable length made them harder to store in older computer systems, which used fixed-length records (think of a punch card). The codes had to be ordered and stored as left-justified strings to sort correctly. These codes could also be ambiguous if they were poorly designed. For example, is the head of 1234 the 1 or the 12 substring?

When concatenation codes are used in databases, they usually become a set of "yes/no" check boxes, represented as adjacent columns in the file. This makes them Boolean vector codes, instead of true concatenation codes.

29.2.4 General Guidelines for Designing Encoding Schemes

These are general guidelines for designing encoding schemes in a database, not firm, hard rules. You will find exceptions to all of them.

Existing Encoding Standards

The use of existing standard encoding schemes is always recommended. You can get quite a lot of help from your local government printing office and even obtain schemes on magnetic media. Commonly used schemes are supposed to be registered with and available through the FIPS (Federal Information Processing Standards) program. The idea is that if everyone uses the same codes, data will be easy to transfer and collect in a uniform manner. Also, someone who sat down and did nothing else but work on this scheme probably did a better job than you could while trying to get a database up and running.

The U.S. government is a good source for such encoding schemes. The Bureau of Labor Statistics published the Dictionary of Occupational Titles (DOT), which encodes job descriptions, and the Standard Industrial Classification (SIC), which encodes businesses by type. The Bureau of the Census has lots of encoding schemes for demographic data. ZIP-code tapes can be had from the U.S. Postal Service.

Unfortunately, not all government agencies are that eager to help the public. In the 1970s, the Social Security Administration provided programs and files to validate social security numbers under the name "Project Clean Data," but later discontinued the practice.

The FBI administers the NCIC (National Crime Information Center), which logs stolen automobiles. The automobile codes are a good, complete system for describing a car and would be useful for dealers, companies, and other institutions that deal with a large number of automobiles. But the FBI no longer shares its encoding scheme, on the grounds that this is confidential information. The only other standard way to identify a vehicle is by the VIN (Vehicle Identification Number) on the engine block, which contains the manufacturer, make, model, and year, as well as a unique identifier for that vehicle. But it is a complicated task to get that information out of the VIN. The FBI has deliberately made reporting a stolen car take longer and be less accurate than it should be.

Industry groups often have standard encoding schemes. The insurance industry is a good source for medical and dental codes, which are used to process claims.

Allow for Expansion

Allow for expansion of the codes. The ALTER statement can create more storage when a single-character code becomes a two-character code, but it will not change the spacing on the printed reports and screens. Start with at least one more decimal place or position than you think you will need. Visual psychology makes "01" look like an encoding, whereas "1" looks like a quantity.

Avoid NULLs

Avoid the SQL general NULL as much as possible by putting special values in the encoding scheme instead. SQL handles NULLs differently from values and NULLs don't tell you what kind of missing value you are dealing with.

All-zeros are often used for missing values; all-nines, for miscellaneous values. For example, the ISO gender codes are 0 = Unknown, 1 = Male, 2 = Female, and 9 = Not Applicable. "Not Applicable" means a lawful person, such as a corporation, which has no gender.

This is another holdover from the days of punch cards. Versions of Fortran before the 1977 standard read blank (unpunched) columns as zeros, so if you did not know a value, you skipped those columns and punched them later, when you did know. Likewise, using encoding schemes with leading zeros was a security trick to prevent blanks in a punch card from being altered. The Fortran 77 standard fixed this problem.

The use of all nines or all Z's for miscellaneous values will make those values sort to the end of the screen or report. NULLs sort either always to the front or always to the rear, but which way they sort is implementation-defined.

Read chapter 6, on NULLs, then determine which meanings of NULL you wish to capture in your encoding scheme.

Translate Codes for the User

As much as possible, avoid displaying pure codes to the user, but try to provide a translation for him. For some things, this is not possible or reasonable. For example, most people do not need to see the two-letter state abbreviation written out in full or the parts of the ISO tire-size vector code explained. At the other extreme, however, nobody could read the billing codes used by several long distance telephone companies.

A part of translation is formatting the display so that it can be read. Punctuation marks, such as dashes, commas, currency signs, and so forth, are important. There is a discussion of them in section 29.1.5 on scales.

Keep the Codes in the Database

There should be a part of the database that has all of the codes stored in tables. These tables can be used to validate input, to translate codes in displays, and as part of the system documentation.

I was amazed to go to a major hospital in Los Angeles in mid-1993 and see the clerk still looking up codes in a dog-eared looseleaf notebook instead of bringing them up on her terminal screen. The hospital is still using a very old IBM mainframe system, which has "dumb" 3270 terminals, rather than a client/server system with workstations. There was not even a help screen available to the clerk.

The translation tables can be downloaded to the workstations in a client/server system to reduce network traffic. They can also be used to build picklists on interactive screens and thereby to reduce typographical errors. Changes to the codes are thereby propagated in the system without anyone's having to rewrite application code. If the codes change over time, the table for a code should have to include a pair of "date effective" fields. This will allow a data warehouse to correctly read and translate old data.

29.3 Check Digits

Charles Babbage, the father of the computer, observed in the mid-1800s that an inseparable part of the cost of obtaining data is the cost of verifying its accuracy (Babbage). He was concerned with errors because he conceived of his "difference engine" as a way to calculate accurate mathematical tables for the British navy. The manual calculations done by clerks were filled with errors; no chart or table then in use was regarded as accurate when it was issued. Dionysus Lardner, a well-known popular science writer, wrote in 1834 that a random selection of 40 books of mathematical tables had a total of 3,700 known errata, some of which had their own errors (Lardner 1834).

The best situation is to exclude bad data on entry so that it is never in the system. If the data itself can contain its own verification, then we do not have to rely on another program or database to check what we are putting into the system. That is the idea of a check digit.

Just consider the problem of entering data at a supermarket checkout. The scanner reads the UCC bar code (Universal Container Code; formerly called the UPC, for Universal Product Code) on the package, looks up the code in the database, displays the description on the cash register for the clerk, and prints the description and price on the receipt. But the scanner does not read the code correctly every time.

Statistics classifies errors as either Type I or Type II. A Type I error rejects truth and a Type II error accepts falsehood. If the bar code reader cannot scan the package, the clerk can read the code, printed in numerals under the bars, enter it manually, and verify the description shown on the cash register display against the actual package to avoid Type I errors — in this case, rejecting a valid purchase. But what about Type II errors?

The Type II errors are handled in the bar code itself. The UCC is 10 digits long, 5 for the manufacturer and 5 for the product, but the bar code also includes extra digits, which are not usually printed in numerals on the package. One of these digits is a check digit, as opposed to the 10 information digits that do the work. By applying a formula to the information digits, the scanner should get the check digit as a result. If it does, it assumes that it has read the code correctly; if it does not, it assumes it has made a read error and asks for a rescan.

Before you can design a formula, you have to know something about the keying errors that you can expect to have in the data. Banks, insurance companies, the U.S. Army, and other organizations that are interested in keeping statistics and reducing errors have already done that work for us. F. J. Damerau (Damerau 1964) reported that four common input errors cause 80% of the total spelling errors:

1. A single missing character
2. A single extra character
3. A single erroneous character
4. Pairwise-transposed characters

Verhoeff gave more details in his study, "Error-Detecting Decimal Codes"(Verhoeff 1969). The single erroneous, missing, or extra character explained 60% to 95% of all errors in his sample of 12,000 errors; pairwise transposes accounted for 10% to 20% of the total.

The first three categories can be expanded to more than a single character, but the single-character cases are by far the most common. In the last category, pairwise transposes ("ab" becomes "ba") are far more common than jump transposes (transposes of pairs with one or more characters between them, as when "abc" becomes "cba"). If a human is doing the data entry from verbal input, you might wish to include a special case for phonetic errors, which are language-dependent (e.g., *thirty* and *thirteen* sound alike in English, but the corresponding words in other languages do not).

29.3.1 Error Detection and Error Correction

The distinction between error-detecting and error-correcting codes is worth mentioning. The error-detecting code will find that an encoding is wrong, but gives no help in finding the error itself. An error-correcting code will try to repair the problem. Error-correcting schemes for binary numbers play an important part in highly reliable computers, but require several extra digits on each computer word to work. If you would like to do research on error-correction codes, some of the algorithms are

Hamming codes
Fire codes
Bose-Chandhuri-Hocquenghem (BCH) codes
Reed-Solomon (RS) codes
Goppa codes

On the other hand, error detection can be done with only one extra digit. This section is concerned only with error-detecting codes for decimal numbers. This is enough work, and is pretty important to people who use base-10 numbers to design codes for parts, accounts, employees, and other objects in a database.

29.3.2 MOD Functions and Casting Functions

Check-digit algorithms usually involve either modulo (MOD) functions or casting functions to reduce the calculations to a single digit. Both functions have a fixed base, or modulus, which is applied against the other argument to produce a result.

MOD Function

The MOD function, also called "remainder arithmetic" in elementary algebra books, is very common in programming languages. It returns the remainder of integer division of the argument by the modulus. For example, $4123 \text{ MOD } 23 = 6$ because $(179 * 23) + 6 = 4123$.

Different programming languages handle a negative argument or a negative modulus differently, but this is usually not a programming problem for check-digit work, since all the numbers are positive. Notice that a MOD function can always produce a zero result if the argument is a multiple of the modulus.

The arithmetic laws of the MOD function make it useful for quickly checking calculations. Here are some of the rules:

Addition:

$(\text{MOD}(a, m) = \text{MOD}(b, m))$ AND $(\text{MOD}(c, m) = \text{MOD}(d, m))$
implies that $(\text{MOD}(a + c, m) = \text{MOD}(b + d, m))$

Multiplication:

$$(MOD(a, m) = MOD(b, m)) \text{ AND } (MOD(c, m) = MOD(d, m))$$
$$\text{implies that } (MOD(a*c, m) = MOD(b*d, m))$$

Exponentiation:

$$(MOD(a, m) = MOD(b, m))$$
$$\text{implies that } (MOD(a^n, m) = MOD(b^n, m))$$

As an example of how this can be useful, let $m = 10$, so that the result of $MOD(x, 10)$ is the last digit of the number. Let $a = 7$ and $b = 117$. Is the last digit of $(117^5) = 21{,}924{,}480{,}357$ correct or not? It has to be the same as the last digit of $(7^5) = 16{,}807$, so we know that at least the last digit is right.

Casting Functions

Casting functions were first used as a way of checking arithmetic results. The most popular system was *casting nines,* and was taught in the U.S. public schools until the early 1960s. Though other bases are possible, *casting* usually means *casting nines* unless otherwise stated. The easiest way to define casting nines is to think of it as repeatedly summing the digits of a number until you are left with a single-digit answer. Using the previous example, `CAST(4123)` = $(4 + 1 + 2 + 3)$ = 10, and then `CAST(10)` = $(1 + 0) = 1$.

The `CAST` function has an arithmetic property of being invariant over addition, subtraction, multiplication, and division, which is why it could be used to check results. For example, to check 785 * 456 = 357,860, we would do the following:

```
CAST(CAST(785) * CAST(456)) = CAST(357,860)
CAST(CAST(20) * CAST(15)) = CAST(29)
CAST(2 * 6) = CAST(11)
CAST(12) = 2
       3 = 2  (Error!)
```

Sure enough, the correct answer was 357,960. The reason this was a popular method before computers and calculators is that it can be done manually by scanning a digit at a time across the number and remembering the final result.

The casting function can also be done with a simple program using MOD and integer division (DIV) operators; however, the multiplication and division operations hidden in those operators are expensive in terms of computer time, and faster algorithms exist. Given single digits x and y and digit strings a and b, we know that

1) CAST $(x) = x$;
2) CAST $(xy) = ((x + y)$ DIV $10) + ((x + y)$ MOD $10)$;
3) CAST $(ab) =$ CAST$($CAST$(a) +$ CAST$(b))$;

The only way that a casting function can produce a zero result is with a zero input. Casting is considered weak because any permutation of the same digits will cast to the same result, so this method cannot find any transposes.

This is also a method for obtaining check digits. The ability to test arithmetic operations can be a bonus in some situations. The problem is that this is one of the worst methods for finding input errors. It will not detect transposes, extra zeros, missing zeros, or a host of other errors.

The SKU (stock control unit) code used in the garment industry is always seven digits. The rightmost digit is the check digit; it is calculated by a cast function with base 9.

A slightly better version of the same idea is called *casting elevens*: you alternate adding and subtracting the digits in the number from right to left. This is a weighted sum, with the weights alternating from 1 to −1 and 11 as the divisor. Although this fixes the problem with pairwise transposes, it still suffers from the other weaknesses of any simple modulus scheme. The problem above, done by casting elevens, looks like this:

```
CAST11(CAST11(785) * CAST11(456)) = CAST11(357,960)
CAST11((+ 7 − 8 + 5) * (+ 4 − 5 + 6)) = (− 3 + 5 − 7 + 9 − 6 + 0)
CAST11(4 * 5) = −2
CAST11(20) = −2
CAST11(−2 + 0) = −2
−2 = −2
```

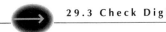

29.3.3 Classes of Algorithms

The most common check-digit procedures come in a few broad classes. One class takes the individual digits, multiplies them by a constant value (called a weight) for each position, sums the results, divides the sum by another constant, and uses the remainder as the check digit. These are called weighted-sum algorithms.

Another approach is to use functions based on group theory, a branch of abstract algebra; these are called algebraic algorithms. A discussion of group theory is a little too complex to take up here, so I will do a little hand-waving when I get to the mathematics.

Finally, you can use lookup tables for check-digit functions that cannot be easily calculated. The lookup tables can be almost anything, including functions that are tuned for the data in a particular application.

Weighted-Sum Algorithms

Weighted-sum algorithms are probably the most common class of check digit. They have the advantages of being easy to compute by hand, since they require no tables or complex arithmetic, so they were first used in manual systems. Casting elevens, which we discussed in section 29.3.2, is an example of these algorithms.

A better method using modulus 11 is the International Standard Book Number (ISBN) check digit. If you have a book, look on the back of it or on the back of the title page. You will see the ISBN. It consists of 10 digits, broken into four groupings by dashes. The first grouping is the language of the book (zero is English), the second is the publisher (the bigger the publisher, the smaller the group), the third group is the title code, and the last digit is the check digit. There are always 10 digits.

Starting at the left side, multiply each digit by its position. Sum the products and divide the result by 11. The remainder is the check digit. For example, given the ISBN 0-201-14460-3, you would check it by this calculation:

$$1 * 0 = 0$$
$$2 * 2 = 4$$
$$3 * 0 = 0$$
$$4 * 1 = 4$$
$$5 * 1 = 5$$
$$6 * 4 = 24$$
$$7 * 4 = 28$$
$$8 * 6 = 48$$
$$9 * 0 = 0$$

total 113
113 MOD 11 = 3

To use this scheme with a number longer than 10 positions, weight the positions as 1 through 10 repeatedly. That is, each weight is the position MOD 11; a position with a weight of 11 is useless because of the division by 11.

This is one of the most popular check-digit procedures, because it will detect most of the four types of errors we discussed earlier for single characters and pairwise transposes. However, it is not perfect. The first thing you will see is that you could have a remainder of 10, which would require two positions, not one. The ISBN uses an *X* for 10, like the Roman numeral; other implementations use a zero for both zero and 10. This second method will lose many of the advantages of the algorithm in exchange for an all-decimal encoding.

It is also possible for a pairwise transpose to be accepted if the digits 5 and 6 appear in positions five and six, as in the case of ISBN 0-201-56235-9 and ISBN 0-201-65235-9. One way around this problem is to disallow the use of certain digits in certain positions by checking for them.

Another common weighted sum that uses MOD 10 is the *Bank Check Digit*, whose weights are 3, 7, and 1, repeated as needed. This is used in the United States on personal checks, where the bank processing numbers have eight information digits. Look at the lower-left-hand corner of your checkbook in the MICR (Magnetic Ink Character Recognition) numbers for your bank's code. The formula uses the check digit itself in the formula, so that the result should be a constant zero for correct numbers. Otherwise, you could use "10 − (total

MOD 10) = check digit" for your formula. This scheme fails when the digits of a pairwise transpose differ by 5. Here is an example of that scheme:

$1 * 3 = 3$
$2 * 7 = 14$
$2 * 1 = 2$
$0 * 3 = 0$
$0 * 7 = 0$
$0 * 1 = 0$
$6 * 3 = 18$
$6 * 7 = 42$
$1 * 1 = 1$
total 80
80 MOD 10 = 0

A better scheme is the *IBM Check,* whose weights alternate between 1 and $f(x)$, where $f(x)$ is defined by the lookup table given below or by the formula $f(x) = (x + x)$ MOD 9.

$f(0) = 0$
$f(1) = 2$
$f(2) = 4$
$f(3) = 6$
$f(4) = 8$
$f(5) = 1$
$f(6) = 3$
$f(7) = 5$
$f(8) = 7$
$f(9) = 9$

The reason for mentioning the lookup table as well as the formula is that a lookup table is usually faster than doing the arithmetic and the tables for these schemes are usually not too big.

Power-Sum Check Digits

The weights can be defined as variable powers of a fixed base, with a prime number as the modulus. The most common schemes use a base of 2 or 3 with a modulus of 7, 10, or 11. The combination of 2 and 11 with a separate symbol for a remainder of 10 is one of these types of check digit.

For example, using base 2 and modulus 11, we could check the code 2354 with these calculations:

$$((2^2) + (2^3) + (2^5)) = 44$$
$$44 \text{ MOD } 11 = 4$$

Bull Check Digits

Another popular version of the weighted-sum check digit is the *Bull codes,* which use the sum of two alternating sums, each with a modulus less than 10. The modulus pair has to be relatively prime. The most popular pairs, in order of increasing error detection ability, are (4, 5), (4, 7), (3, 7), (3, 5), (5, 6) and (3, 8).

For example, using the pair (4, 5) and modulus 7, we could check the code 2345-1 with these calculations:

$$((2*4) + (3*5) + (4*4) + (5*5)) = 64$$
$$64 \text{ MOD } 7 = 1$$

Verhoeff's Dihedral Five Check Digits

A very good, but somewhat complicated, scheme was proposed by J. Verhoeff in a tract from the Mathematical Centre in Amsterdam, Netherlands (Verhoeff 1969). It is based on the properties of multiplication in an algebraic structure known as the *dihedral five group.*

Though some of the calculations could be done with arithmetic formulas, the easiest and fastest way is to build lookup tables into the functions. The lookup tables involved are a multiplication lookup table, an inverse lookup table, and a permutation table. This makes the programs look larger, but the superior ability of this scheme to detect errors more than makes up for the very slight increase in size.

APPENDIX A

Check-Digit Programs

T HE FOLLOWING PASCAL functions will compute the different check digits given
in chapter 29. They assume that the program has the following
global declarations.

```
CONST
    N = 10; { size of information digits string }
TYPE
    InfoDigits = ARRAY [1..N] OF INTEGER;
```

N is replaced by a literal value in all of the programs for a particular application, so these are more templates than programs. The
InfoDigits datatype assumes that the number to be given a check
digit is stored in an array of integers, with the leftmost digit in
position 1.

Verhoeff's Dihedral Five Check Digits

```
FUNCTION MakeCheck(a : InfoDigits; n : INTEGER) : INTEGER;
{ This will generate Verhoeff's Dihedral Five check digit }
CONST
```

```
MultTable : ARRAY [0..9, 0..9] OF INTEGER =
    (( 0, 1, 2, 3, 4, 5, 6, 7, 8, 9),
     ( 1, 2, 3, 4, 0, 6, 7, 8, 9, 5),
     ( 2, 3, 4, 0, 1, 7, 8, 9, 5, 6),
     ( 3, 4, 0, 1, 2, 8, 9, 5, 6, 7),
     ( 4, 0, 1, 2, 3, 9, 5, 6, 7, 8),
     ( 5, 9, 8, 7, 6, 0, 4, 3, 2, 1),
     ( 6, 5, 9, 8, 7, 1, 0, 4, 3, 2),
     ( 7, 6, 5, 9, 8, 2, 1, 0, 4, 3),
     ( 8, 7, 6, 5, 9, 3, 2, 1, 0, 4),
     ( 9, 8, 7, 6, 5, 4, 3, 2, 1, 0));

PermTable : ARRAY [0..9, 0..9] OF INTEGER =
    (( 0, 1, 2, 3, 4, 5, 6, 7, 8, 9),
     ( 1, 5, 7, 6, 2, 8, 3, 0, 9, 4),
     ( 5, 8, 0, 3, 7, 9, 6, 1, 4, 2),
     ( 8, 9, 1, 6, 0, 4, 3, 5, 2, 7),
     ( 9, 4, 5, 3, 1, 2, 6, 8, 7, 0),
     ( 4, 2, 8, 6, 5, 7, 3, 9, 0, 1),
     ( 2, 7, 9, 3, 8, 0, 6, 4, 1, 5),
     ( 7, 0, 4, 6, 9, 1, 3, 2, 5, 8),
     ( 8, 1, 2, 3, 4, 5, 6, 7, 8, 9),
     ( 9, 5, 7, 6, 2, 8, 3, 0, 9, 4));

InverseTable : ARRAY [0..9] OF INTEGER =
    ( 0, 4, 3, 2, 1, 5, 6, 7, 8, 9);
VAR
    Check, i : INTEGER;
BEGIN
Check := 0;
FOR i := 1 TO n
DO Check := MultTable[Check, PermTable[(i MOD 8), a[i]]];
MakeCheck := InverseTable[Check];

END;
```

```
FUNCTION VerifyCheck(a : InfoDigits; n : INTEGER) : BOOLEAN;
{ This will verify Verhoeff's Dihedral Five check digit. Note that
it is different from the generator. }
CONST
MultTable : ARRAY [0..9, 0..9] OF INTEGER =
    (( 0, 1, 2, 3, 4, 5, 6, 7, 8, 9),
     ( 1, 2, 3, 4, 0, 6, 7, 8, 9, 5),
     ( 2, 3, 4, 0, 1, 7, 8, 9, 5, 6),
     ( 3, 4, 0, 1, 2, 8, 9, 5, 6, 7),
     ( 4, 0, 1, 2, 3, 9, 5, 6, 7, 8),
     ( 5, 9, 8, 7, 6, 0, 4, 3, 2, 1),
     ( 6, 5, 9, 8, 7, 1, 0, 4, 3, 2),
     ( 7, 6, 5, 9, 8, 2, 1, 0, 4, 3),
     ( 8, 7, 6, 5, 9, 3, 2, 1, 0, 4),
     ( 9, 8, 7, 6, 5, 4, 3, 2, 1, 0));

PermTable : ARRAY [0..9, 0..9] OF INTEGER =
    (( 0, 1, 2, 3, 4, 5, 6, 7, 8, 9),
     ( 1, 5, 7, 6, 2, 8, 3, 0, 9, 4),
     ( 5, 8, 0, 3, 7, 9, 6, 1, 4, 2),
     ( 8, 9, 1, 6, 0, 4, 3, 5, 2, 7),
     ( 9, 4, 5, 3, 1, 2, 6, 8, 7, 0),
     ( 4, 2, 8, 6, 5, 7, 3, 9, 0, 1),
     ( 2, 7, 9, 3, 8, 0, 6, 4, 1, 5),
     ( 7, 0, 4, 6, 9, 1, 3, 2, 5, 8),
     ( 8, 1, 2, 3, 4, 5, 6, 7, 8, 9),
     ( 9, 5, 7, 6, 2, 8, 3, 0, 9, 4));
VAR
    Check, i : INTEGER;
BEGIN
Check := 0;
FOR i := 1 TO n
DO Check := MultTable[Check, PermTable[(i MOD 8), a[i]]];
VerifyCheck := (Check = 0);
END;
```

Bull Function

```
FUNCTION BullCheck(a : InfoDigits; n, x, y : INTEGER) : INTEGER;
{ The most popular pairs (x, y), in order of  increasing error
detection ability, are (4, 5), (4, 7), (3, 7), (3, 5), (5, 6), and
(3, 8). }
VAR
    CheckX, CheckY, i : INTEGER;
BEGIN
CheckX := 0;
CheckY := 0;
FOR i := 1 TO n
DO IF (Odd(i))
        THEN CheckX := CheckX + a[i]
        ELSE CheckY := CheckY + a[i];
BullCheck := (CheckX MOD X)+ (CheckY MOD Y)
END;
```

Power Function

```
FUNCTION PowerCheck(a : InfoDigits; base, x : INTEGER) : INTEGER;
{ base is usually 2 or 3.  x is usually 7, 10, or 11.  }
VAR
    Check, i, Term : INTEGER;
BEGIN
Check := 0;
Term := 1;
FOR i := 1 TO n
DO BEGIN
        Check := Check + (Term * a[i]);
        Term := Term * base;
        END;
PowerCheck := (Check MOD x)
END;
```

ISBN Function

This check-digit function is used for other purposes besides the International Standard Book Number, but since that is the most common place where people will see it, I have given it that name.

```
FUNCTION ISBNCheck(a : InfoDigits) : INTEGER;
VAR
    Check, i : INTEGER;
BEGIN
Check := 0;
FOR i := 1 TO n
DO Check := Check + (i * a[i]);
ISBNCheck := (Check MOD 11)
{ Let calling program handle a value of 10 as X as it wishes.  }
END;
```

Casting Nines

The iterative algorithm is based on the idea that you keep repeating the casting operation as a scan from right to left, over and over, until the result is less than 10. This means two nested loops, an inner one to do the summing and an outer one to control it.

```
FUNCTION IterativeCast9 (inputnumber : INTEGER) : INTEGER;
{ loops from right to left, totaling as it goes.
    Keeps looping until the total is less than 10 }
VAR
    total : INTEGER;
BEGIN
WHILE (inputnumber >= 10)
DO BEGIN
    total := 0;
    WHILE (inputnumber > 0)
    DO BEGIN
        { cut off the rightmost digit }
        total := total + (inputnumber MOD 10);
        inputnumber := inputnumber DIV 10;
```

```
        END;
    inputnumber := total;
    END;
IterativeCast9 := inputnumber;
END;
```

This is not the fastest algorithm. The table lookup algorithm requires a constant table stored as an array of 100 integers. This one scans from right to left, but uses the table to find the running total and cast the answer "on the fly." By inspection, n digits require n iterations. You can generalize this approach by cutting off the rightmost n-tuple of digits, and use a huge table (10^n by 10^n elements) and tricky logic. This is a good choice for speed at the expense of space.

```
FUNCTION LookupCast9 (inputnumber : INTEGER) : INTEGER;
{ scans from right to left, keeping inputnumber running.  Casting
is  done  via the lookup table during the scan }
VAR check : INTEGER;
CONST
CastTable : ARRAY [0..9, 0..9] OF INTEGER =
    (( 0, 1, 2, 3, 4, 5, 6, 7, 8, 9),
     ( 1, 2, 3, 4, 5, 6, 7, 8, 9, 1),
     ( 2, 3, 4, 5, 6, 7, 8, 9, 1, 2),
     ( 3, 4, 5, 6, 7, 8, 9, 1, 2, 3),
     ( 4, 5, 6, 7, 8, 9, 1, 2, 3, 4),
     ( 5, 6, 7, 8, 9, 1, 2, 3, 4, 5),
     ( 6, 7, 8, 9, 1, 2, 3, 4, 5, 6),
     ( 7, 8, 9, 1, 2, 3, 4, 5, 6, 7),
     ( 8, 9, 1, 2, 3, 4, 5, 6, 7, 8),
     ( 9, 1, 2, 3, 4, 5, 6, 7, 8, 9));
BEGIN check := 0;
WHILE (inputnumber > 0)
DO BEGIN
    { cut off the rightmost digit and use for table look up }
    check := CastTable [check, (inputnumber MOD 10)];
    inputnumber := inputnumber DIV 10;
    END;
LookupCast9 := check;
END;
```

The following routine was submitted by J. R. Yozallinas of Chicago, IL (Yozallinas 1991). He claims better performance than the array lookup method because the simple arithmetic involved uses only increment and decrement operations, which are usually built into the computer hardware.

```
FUNCTION CastNine(a : InNumber) : INTEGER;
VAR
    total : INTEGER;
BEGIN
IF (InNumber > 9)
THEN BEGIN
    total := 0;
    WHILE (InNumber > 0)
    DO BEGIN
        total := total + (InNumber MOD 10);
        IF (total > 9) THEN total := total - 9;
        InNumber := InNumber DIV 10;
        END;
    END
ELSE total := InNumber;
CastNine := total
END;
```

SKU Code Algorithm

The SKU code is a weighted-sum code used in the garment industry and in other retail industries. Though not as sophisticated as other check-digit schemes, it is very easy to implement in simple cash register hardware.

```
FUNCTION GarmentChk (a : INTEGER) : BOOLEAN;
{ returns TRUE if the item code is valid }
VAR
    total, i, workdigit : INTEGER;
BEGIN
total := 0;
FOR i := 1 TO 7
```

```
DO BEGIN
        workdigit := a MOD 10;
{ double even digits }
        IF NOT (Odd(i))
        THEN workdigit := workdigit + workdigit;
{ cast nines }
        total := total + ((workdigit MOD 10) + (workdigit DIV 10));
{ get next digit from rightmost side }
        a := a DIV 10;
{ return a Boolean result }
GarmentChk := ((total MOD 10) = 0)
END;
```

APPENDIX

B

Readings and Resources

Missing Values

Codd, E. F. "Understanding Relations." *FDT* 7 (1975):3–4.

Grahne, G. "Horn Tables — An Efficient Tool for Handling Incomplete Information in Databases." *ACM SIGACT/SIGMOD/SIGART Symposium on Principles of Database Systems* (1989):75–82.

Grant, J. "Null Values in a Relational Database." *Information Processing Letters* 6, 5 (October 1977):156–7.

———. "Partial Values in a Tabular Database Model." *Information Processing Letters* 9, 2 (August 1979):97–9.

Honeyman. "Functional Dependencies and the Universal Instance Property in the Relational Model of Database Systems." (Ph.D diss., Princeton University, 1980).

Lien. "Multivalued Dependencies with Null Values in Relational Databases." *Proceedings of the Fifth International Conference on Very Large Databases.* New York: ACM; Piscataway, NJ: IEEE, 1979.

Lipski, W. "On Databases with Incomplete Information." *Journal of the ACM* 28, 1 (1981):41–70.

————. "On Semantic Issues Connected with Incomplete Information." *ACM Transactions on Database Systems* (September 1981):262–96.

Rozenshtein, D. "Implementing Null Values in Relations." (unpublished, May 1981).

SPARC Study Group on Database Management Systems. "Interim Report 75-02-08 to the ANSI X3." *FDT-Bulletin ACM SIGMOD* 7, 2. (1975).

Vassiliou, Y. "Functional Dependencies and Incomplete Information." *Proceedings of the Sixth International Conference on Very Large Databases*. New York: ACM; Piscataway, NJ: IEEE, 1980.

————. "Null Values in Database Management — A Denotational Semantics Approach." *ACM SIGMOD Conference Proceedings* (1979):162–9.

Walker. "A Universal Table Relational Database Model with Blank Entries." (unpublished, 1979).

Zaniolo, C. "Database Relations with Null Values." *Journal of Computer and System Sciences* 28, 1 (1984):142–66.

Updatable Views

Codd, E. F. "RV-6 VIEW Updating." *The Relational Model for Database Management: Version 2*. Reading, MA: Addison-Wesley, 1990.

Date, C. J. "Updating VIEWs." *Relational Database: Selected Writings*. Reading, MA: Addison-Wesley, 1986.

Date, C. J., and Hugh Darwen. *Relational Database: Writings, 1989–1991*. "Role of Functional Dependencies in Query Decomposition." Reading, MA: Addison-Wesley, 1992.

Goodman, Nathan. "VIEW Update is Practical." *InfoDB* 5, 2 (summer 1990).

Umeshar, Dayal, and P. A. Bernstein. "On the Correct Translation of Update Operations on Relational VIEWs." *ACM Transactions on Database Systems* 7, 3 (September 1982).

Datetime Datatypes

Zerubavel, Eviatar. *The Seven Day Circle*. New York: The Free Press, 1985.

Optimizing Queries

Gulutzan, Peter, and Trudy Pelzer. *Optimizing SQL: Embedded SQL in C*. Lawrence KS: R&D Publications, 1994.

Shasha, Dennis E. *Database Tuning: a Principled Approach*. Englewood Cliffs, NJ: Prentice-Hall, 1992.

Normalization and Theory

Dutka, Alan, and Howard Hanson. *Fundamentals of Data Normalization*. Reading, MA: Addison-Wesley, 1989.

Fleming, Candace C., and Barbara von Halle. *Handbook for Relational Database Design*. Reading, MA: Addison-Wesley, 1989.

Maier, David. *The Theory of Relational Databases*. New York: Computer Science Press, 1983.

Teorey, Toby J. *Database Modeling and Design: The Fundamental Principles*, 2d ed. San Francisco: Morgan Kaufmann, 1994.

Graph Theory

Eve, Shimon. *Graph Algorithms*. New York: Computer Science Press, 1979.

Fulkerson, D. R., ed. *Studies in Graph Theory*, 2 vols. Providence, RI: American Mathematical Association, 1975.

Harary, Frank. *Graph Theory*. Reading, MA: Addison-Wesley, 1972.

McHugh, James A. *Algorithmic Graph Theory*. Englewood Cliffs, NJ: Prentice-Hall, 1990.

Ore, Oystein (revised by Robin J. Wilson). *Graphs and Their Uses*. Providence, RI: American Mathematical Association, 1990.

Books on SQL-92

Cannan, Stephen, and Gerard Otten. *SQL: The Standard Handbook.* New York: McGraw-Hill, 1992.

Date, C. J., and Hugh Darwen. *A Guide to the SQL Standard.* Reading, MA: Addison-Wesley, 1993.

Gruber, Martin. *SQL Instant Reference.* Alameda, CA: Sybex, 1994.

Gruber, Martin. *Understanding SQL.* Alameda, CA: Sybex, 1990.

Melton, Jim, and Alan Simon. *Understanding the New SQL: A Complete Guide.* San Francisco: Morgan Kaufmann, 1993.

Introductory SQL Books

Atzeni, Paolo, and Valeria De Antonellis. *Relational Database Theory.* Redwood City, CA: Benjamin-Cummings, 1993.

Codd, E. F. *The Relational Model for Database Management: Version 2.* Reading, MA: Addison-Wesley, 1990.

Date, C. J. *An Introduction to Database Systems.* 6th ed. Reading, MA: Addison-Wesley, 1995.

Date, C. J. *Database, a Primer.* Reading, MA: Addison-Wesley, 1983.

Date, C. J. *Relational Database: Selected Writings.* Reading, MA: Addison-Wesley, 1986.

Date, C. J. *Relational Database Writings, 1985-1989.* Reading, MA: Addison-Wesley, 1990.

Date, C. J. *Relational Database: Writings, 1989-1991.* Reading, MA: Addison-Wesley, 1992.

Date, C. J. *Relational Database Writings, 1991-1994.* Reading, MA: Addison-Wesley, 1995.

Groff, James R., and Paul N. Weinberg. *LAN Times Guide to SQL.* New York: McGraw-Hill, 1994.

Gruber, Martin. *Understanding SQL.* Alameda, CA: Sybex, 1990.

Lorie, Raymond A., and Jean-Jacques Daudenarde. *SQL and Its Applications*. Englewood Cliffs, NJ: Prentice-Hall, 1991.

Lusardi, Frank. *The Database Expert's Guide to SQL*. New York: McGraw-Hill, 1988.

Pascal, Fabian. *SQL and Relational Basics*. New York: M&T Books, 1989.

Pascal, Fabian. *Understanding Relational Databases*. New York: M&T Books, 1993.

Shasha, Dennis E. *Database Tuning: A Principled Approach*. Englewood Cliffs, NJ: Prentice-Hall, 1992.

Stonebraker, Michael. *Readings in Database Systems*, 2d ed. San Francisco: Morgan Kaufmann, 1993.

Trimble, Harvey, and David Chappel. *A Visual Introduction to SQL*. New York: John Wiley, 1989.

van der Lans, Rick F. *The SQL Standard, A Complete Reference*. Englewood Cliffs, NJ: Prentice-Hall International; Schoonhaven: Academic Service, 1989.

Wellesley Software Group. *Learning Advanced SQL*. Englewood Cliffs, NJ: Prentice-Hall, 1992.

Wellesley Software Group. *Learning SQL*. Englewood Cliffs, NJ: Prentice-Hall, 1991.

Standards and Related Groups

For ANSI and ISO standards

Director of Publications
American National Standards Institute
11 West 42nd Street
New York, NY 10036
phone: (212) 642-4900

For ANSI X3H2 documents

> X3 Secretariat, ITI
> 1250 Eye Street, NW, Suite 200
> Washington, DC 20005-3922
> phone: (202) 737-8888

Copies of the SQL-92 document and other ANSI documents can be purchased from

> Global Engineering Documents Inc.
> 18201 McDurmott West, Suite B
> Irvine, CA 92714
> phone: (800) 854-7179

Other consortiums are

> NIST (National Institute for Standards and Technology)
> Technology A-266
> Gaithersberg, MD 20899
> Attn: FIPS-127 test suites
> phone: (301) 975-2000

> Object Management Group
> 492 Old Connecticut Path
> Framingham, MA 01701
> phone: (508) 820-4300

> TPC Council
> c/o Shanley Public Relations
> 777 North First Street #600
> San Jose, CA 95112-6113
> phone: (408) 295-8894

> X/Open
> 1010 El Camino Real #380
> Menlo Park, CA 94025
> phone : (415) 323-7992

REFERENCES

Adams, Douglas. 1979. *Hitchhiker's Guide to the Galaxy*. New York: Harmony Books.

Association for Computing Machinery (ACM). 1980. "Algorithm 199." *Collected Algorithms from the ACM*. New York: Association for Computing Machinery.

Babbage, Charles. For information on Charles Babbage, contact the Charles Babbage Institute, University of Minnesota.

Bernstein, P. A. 1976. "Synthesizing Third Normal Form Relations from Functional Dependencies." *ACM Transactions on Database Systems*. 1, 4 (December):277–98.

Boole, George. 1854, 1951. *An Investigation of the Laws of Thought, on Which are Founded the Mathematical Theories of Logic and Probabilities*. New York: Macmillan and Co., 1854; New York: Dover, 1951.

Celko, Joe. 1981. "Father Time Software Secrets Allows Updating of Dates." *Information Systems News*. (February).

———. 1992a. "Implementing T-Joins in SQL Queries." *DBMS*. (March).

———. 1992b. "SQL Explorer: Voting Systems." *DBMS*. (November).

———. 1993. "Views: More than Meets the Eye." *Database Programming & Design*. (September). Citing Nelson Mattos, from an ANSI X3H2 paper. See appendix B: Readings and Resources for information on obtaining ANSI X3H2 papers.

Celko, Joe, and C. J. Date. 1993. "Access Path: Lauds and Lectures, Kudos and Critiques." (letter to the editor). *Database Programming & Design*. (September):9.

CFO. 1991. CFO. (July).

Codd, E. F. 1970. "A Relational Model of Data for Large Shared Data Banks." *Communications of the ACM.* 13, 6:377-87. New York: Association for Computing Machinery.

————. 1990. *The Relational Model for Database Management: Version 2.* Reading, MA: Addison-Wesley.

Comer, D. 1978. "The Difficulty of Optimum Index Selection." *ACM Transaction on Database Systems.* 3, 4:440–5.

Damerau, F. J. 1964. "A Technique for Computer Detection of Correction of Spelling Errors." *Communications of the ACM.* 7, 3 (March).

Date, C. J. 1983. *Database, a Primer.* Reading, MA: Addison-Wesley.

————. 1986. *Relational Database: Selected Writings.* Reading, MA: Addison-Wesley.

————. 1990. *Relational Database Writings, 1985-1989.* Reading, MA: Addison-Wesley. 227.

————. 1992a. "According to Date: Shedding Some Light." *Database Programming & Design.* (February):15–7.

————. 1992b. *Relational Database: Writings, 1989-1991.* Reading, MA: Addison-Wesley.

————. 1995a. *An Introduction to Database Systems.* 6th ed. Reading, MA: Addison-Wesley. Originally published 1975.

————. 1995b. *Relational Database Writings, 1991-1994.* Reading, MA: Addison-Wesley.

Gardner, Martin. 1983. *Wheels, Life, and Other Mathematical Amusements.* New York: W.H. Freeman.

Goodman, Nathan. 1990. "VIEW Update is Practical." *InfoDB.* 5, 2 (summer).

Gulutzan, Peter, and Trudy Pelzer. 1994. *Optimizing SQL: Embedded SQL in C.* Lawrence, KS: R & D Publications.

Hitchens, Randall L. 1991. "Viewpoint." *Computerworld.* (January).

Huff, Darrell. 1954. *How to Lie with Statistics.* New York: Norton.

Information Systems Week (ISW). 1987. "Code Overload Plagues NYC Welfare System." *Information Systems Week.* (December).

Lardner, Dionysus. 1834. *A Treatise on Arithmetic, Practical and Theoretical.* London: Longman, Rees, Orme, Brown, Green, & Longman.

Limeback, Rudy. "SQL Workshop Challenge." *Explain.* (18). Undated publication; no.18 issued 1991-1993.

Lorie, Raymond A., and Jean-Jacques Daudenarde. 1991. *SQL and Its Applications.* Englewood Cliffs, NJ: Prentice-Hall.

Martinis, Miljenko. 1992. Letters column. *DBMS.* (May).

McGoveran, David. 1993. "Nothing from Nothing Part I (or, What's Logic Got to Do With It?). *Database Programming & Design.* 6, 13 (December):32.

———. 1994a. "Nothing from Nothing Part II: Classical Logic: Nothing Compares 2 U." *Database Programming & Design.* 7, 1 (January):54.

———. 1994b. "Nothing from Nothing Part III: Can't Lose What You Never Had." *Database Programming & Design.* 7, 2 (February):42.

———. 1994c. "Nothing from Nothing Part IV: It's in the Way that You Use It." *Database Programming & Design.* 7, 3 (March):54.

Melton, Jim, and Alan R. Simon. 1993. *Understanding the New SQL: A Complete Guide.* San Francisco: Morgan Kaufmann.

Murchison, Rory. "SQL Workshop Challenge." *Explain.* (16). Undated publication; no.16 issued 1991-1993.

Paitetsky-Shapiro, G. 1983. "The Optimal Selection of Secondary Indexes in NP-Complete." *SIGMOD Record.* 13, 2:72–5.

Philips, Lawrence. 1990. "Hanging on the Metaphone. (A Phonetic Text-Retrieval Algorithm Better than Soundex)." *Computer Language.* 7, 12 (December):38.

Rozenshtein, D., Anatoly Abramovich, and Eugene Birger. 1993. "Loop-Free SQL Solutions for Finding Continuous Regions." *SQL Forum.* 2, 6 (November-December).

Smithwick, Terry. 1991. Pascal version of Lawrence Philips' Metaphone. CompuServe. CLMFORUM. Originally published by Lawrence Philips. 1990. "Hanging on the Metaphone. (A Phonetic Text-Retrieval Algorithm Better than Soundex)." *Computer Language.* 7, 12 (December):38.

SPARC Study Group on Database Management Systems. 1975. "Interim Report 75-02-08 to the ANSI X3." *FDT-Bulletin ACM SIGMOD.* 7, 2.

SQL Forum. 1993, 1994. *SQL Forum.* See articles by Anatoly Abramovich, Yelena Alexandrova, and Eugene Birger (July/August 1993, March/April 1994).

Stevens, S. S. 1957. "On the Psychophysical Law." *Psychological Review*. 64:153–81.

Tillquist, John, and Feng-Yang Kuo. 1989. "An Approach to the Recursive Retrieval Problem in the Relational Database." *Communications of the ACM*. 32, 2 (February):239.

van der Lans, Rick. 1991. "SQL Portability" *The Relational Journal*. 2, 6 (December 1990/January 1991).

Verhoeff, J. 1969. "Error Detecting Decimal Codes." *Mathematical Centre Tract #29*. Amsterdam: The Mathematical Centre.

Vicik, Rick. 1993. "Advanced Transact SQL" *SQL Forum*. (July/August).

Wankowski, Jim. "SQL Workshop Solutions." *Explain*. (17). Undated publication; no.17 issued 1991-1993.

Yozallinas, J. R. 1981. Letters column. *Tech Specialist*. (May).

Zerubavel, Eviatar. 1985. *The Seven Day Circle*. New York: The Free Press.

INDEX

NOTES